HISTORIANS AT WORK

Other Books by Peter Gay:

Style in History (1974)

The Bridge of Criticism: Dialogues on the Enlightenment (1970)

The Enlightenment: An Interpretation

Volume II, The Science of Freedom (1969)

Weimar Culture: The Outsider as Insider (1968)

A Loss of Mastery: Puritan Historians in Colonial America (1966)

The Enlightenment: An Interpretation

Volume I, The Rise of Modern Paganism (1966)

The Party of Humanity: Essays in the French Enlightenment (1964)

Voltaire's Politics: The Poet as Realist (1959)

The Dilemma of Democratic Socialism: Eduard Bernstein's Challenge to Marx (1952)

Translations with Introductions:

Voltaire: Candide (1963)

Voltaire: Philosophical Dictionary, 2 vols. (1962)

Ernst Cassirer: The Question of Jean Jacques Rousseau (1954)

Anthologies:

Deism: An Anthology (1968)

John Locke on Education (1964)

NEW YORK, EVANSTON, SAN FRANCISCO, LONDON

Historians at Work

VOLUME III

Edited by Peter Gay

and Victor G. Wexler

Harper & Row, Publishers

1817

 For information address Harper & Row, Publishers, Inc., 10 East 53rd Street, New York, N.Y. 10022. Published simultaneously in Canada by Fitzhenry & Whiteside Limited, Toronto.

FIRST EDITION

Designed by Sidney Feinberg

Library of Congress Cataloging in Publication Data (Revised)

Gay, Peter, 1923– comp.
Historians at work.
Vol. edited by P. Gay and V. G. Wexler.
Includes bibliographical references.
1. History—Addresses, essays, lectures.
I. Cavanaugh, Gerald J., joint comp. II. Wexler,
Victor G., joint comp. III. Title.
D6.G35 908 75–123930
ISBN 0–06–011473–8 (v. 1)
ISBN 0–06–011472–X (v. 2)
ISBN 0–06011474–6 (v. 3)
ISBN 0–06–011476–2 (v. 4)

---

75 76 77 78 79 10 9 8 7 6 5 4 3 2 1

Contents

Preface to Volume III

The nineteenth century is the century in which the craft of history became a thoroughly modern profession. It is the age of great historians —of Ranke and Mommsen, Burckhardt and Fustel de Coulanges, Macaulay and Maitland—and of that great subverter of accepted pieties, Karl Marx. These historians, and others, wrote imperishable masterpieces defining new fields and bringing new methods and new perspectives to familiar subject matter. Their books are imperishable, in part because their authors were all stylists whom we continue to read for pleasure, even if our profit has somewhat diminished; the nineteenth-century servants of Clio did not desert her long-time associate, literature. That desertion would come later.

But while nineteenth-century historians did not turn their back on beauty, their passion for truth came first. Their predecessors in the eighteenth century had rendered history immense services, far greater than nineteenth-century historians were inclined to acknowledge. The historian-philosophes—Hume, Voltaire, Robertson, and Gibbon—had liberated history from the shackles of theology, widened historical vistas beyond Western civilization, and made pioneering forays into the fascinating regions of social and cultural history. But, while the philosophes had ambitiously aspired to make history into a science, they had been relatively indifferent to the refinements of historical techniques; they were voracious consumers, but only rarely contributors to scholarship. In addition, their overriding philosophical animus against religion in general and Christianity in particular had given their historical perception a certain two-dimensional quality. They found it hard to believe that medieval monks were anything but fools or knaves, and their highest praise for an ancient philosopher was that he was in some measure like them. Now, nineteenth-century historians, the unwitting and unappreciative heirs of the eighteenth century, fastened on the defects of

Enlightenment historiography and overlooked its contributions to inner freedom and professional competence, contributions from which they greatly profited. But this ingratitude—hardly surprising to anyone familiar with the conflict of generations—had its positive results. Seeing the bias of Voltaire and Gibbon against large stretches of the past, nineteenth-century historians undertook to treat all of the past evenhandedly. In the writings of Ranke and of the historicist school that derived from him, impartiality became a shibboleth that acquired an almost religious status. And seeing the contempt of Voltaire and Hume for "pedantry," nineteenth-century historians decided to take up the pursuit of technique where leading seventeenth-century scholars like Jean Mabillon had left it. What makes the best of nineteenth-century history so magisterial, and what requires at least generous excerpts, is an unprecedented combination of qualities, or at least ambitions: scholarly imagination, principled fairness, literary energy.

As in earlier centuries, the great nineteenth-century historians worked securely in a cultural context which they reflected and to some degree shaped. The profusion of historical masterpieces came naturally to an age increasingly committed to a historical view of things, a view that invaded the study of cultures, inquiries into religion, and, most subversively, geology and biology. The age of Ranke was also the age of Lyell and of Darwin. In many hands this historicizing attitude degenerated into a complacent evolutionary perspective in which all earlier cultures and ages served as mere imperfect prefigurations of the high culture that Western civilization had now happily achieved. But for the most acute and self-aware, the historical attitude was an opportunity of placing oneself and one's time into a vast stream of universal change. Like most human ambitions, the nineteenth-century historians' program for complete empathy and complete impartiality was not wholly realized. As Karl Marx and a few other cultural gadflies pointed out, though for many years in vain, scientific history concealed troublesome biases, all the more troublesome for being concealed. But with the professionalization of criticism, a judicious mixture of private self-criticism and public mutual criticism, the road to historical objectivity lay open, at least in principle.

Here too, in its growing professionalization, history formed part of a wider cultural movement. Unshapely, almost boundless fields of inquiry like natural history were now subdivided ever more minutely, into biology, anthropology, zoology, and others. This increased specialization of knowledge brought a narrowing of focus, but what was lost in breadth was gained in depth. It is not an accident that most of the historians in this volume were professors; the old ideal of the amateur was rapidly vanishing. So was the related Renaissance ideal of the universal man;

not without resistance, it was being replaced by a new ideal, the well-informed specialist. Nineteenth-century historians were on both sides of this historic fence; they were still versatile—the aged Ranke climaxed his long career by beginning, though not completing, a world history—but they were concentrated more and more, in their published work if not in their lectures, on one country or one epoch. It is significant that it was in this period that historians began to form themselves into professional associations and to issue professional journals: the German *Historische Zeitschrift* first came out in 1859; the French *Revue historique* came next, in 1876, to be followed by the *English Historical Review* in 1886 and the *American Historical Review* in 1895. Three years before, in 1892, Harvard established the first chair of economic history, the first sign that that specialty, history, could be further subdivided. While the twentieth century, especially the years after the end of World War I, would see some far-reaching changes in the contours of the historical craft, by the nineteenth century its modern character was firmly established.

Barthold Georg Niebuhr

1776—1831

1

Barthold Georg Niebuhr was an accomplished statesman as well as one of the most influential historians of his time. Before coming to Prussia during the Napoleonic wars, he served his native Denmark as a member of the Commission for Economics and Commerce, where he demonstrated a particular interest that later stimulated his study of ancient Rome. He entered the service of the Prussian state at the request of the reform minister, Baron Vom Stein. Fearful that the Napoleonic hegemony would extinguish the independent life of the German state, Niebuhr despaired at the humiliating defeat at Jena in 1806 and the onerous Peace of Tilsit of the following year. His greatest contribution to Prussia and to all of Europe resulted from his appointment as a lecturer at the newly founded University of Berlin in 1810. Here he presented his brilliant series of lectures on Roman history and here he attracted students such as Ranke.

The University of Berlin rapidly became the center of Prussia's intellectual life. After the defeat at Jena, the Prussian Minister of Education wrote to the king that the state must replace by intellectual force what it had lost in physical power, and the king used these very words in his proclamation which called the University into being. Within a generation, not only Niebuhr but Ranke, Fichte, and Hegel also had joined the faculty. Karl von Savigny, a distinguished student of Niebuhr, spoke for all these giants when he wrote that Niebuhr's work stimulated more research than any other historian of his time.

Niebuhr may have inspired many students, but he was himself an autodidact. In fact, much of his criticism of historical studies concerning ancient Rome was based on the contention that historians too often relied on each other's works instead of examining the original sources, thus perpetuating error upon error. In constructing his *History of Rome,* which first appeared in 1811, he scrupulously avoided secondary works and relied on original evidence, no matter how fragmentary. According to Niebuhr, the misjudgments of ancient historians like Livy were merely repeated by moderns like Machiavelli, and even by seventeenth- and eighteenth-century philologists, whom he disparaged even though they had advanced historical thinking in their own time. Niebuhr's passion for discrediting the work of his predecessors prompted Goethe to remark that his history should have been entitled "a critique of the authors of Roman history."

Skeptical as he was of the authority of ancient authors, Niebuhr struggled to glean all that was reliable from the fragments he could use, to render the history of the Roman republic vivid as well as accurate. As he wrote in the "Introduction" to the second volume of his *History,* our first selection, he wished to make "the study of Rome during the period following the league with the Latins no less authentic and substantial than that of much later periods, where we are in a like manner left without contemporary records." Because Livy had written "in the same spirit in which the marvelous legends of the heroic ages were commonly drawn down into history," Niebuhr had to be all the more critical of what he could draw into his own work.

Our second selection, from Niebuhr's chapter, "Of the Public Land and its Occupation," exemplifies the application of his method to a specific question of great interest to him—the agrarian laws of the Roman republic. Relying on the Justinian Code and on all the extant technical treatises on land surveying he could find, Niebuhr determined that Rome, unlike much of the rest of the ancient world, regarded land tenure as an inviolable right of its citizens. He came to the conclusion that the Roman constitution gradually developed into a coherent institution capable of incorporating new laws in response to changing economic and social conditions. Niebuhr the historian thus became as partisan a supporter of the ancient republic as he was of the reform movement in contemporary Prussia.

In 1815 Niebuhr assumed his responsibilities as the Prussian Ambassador to Rome and proceeded to use his office as much for his historical projects as for diplomacy. In the Vatican library he found fragments from the writings of Cicero and Seneca and quickly became embroiled in philological disputes concerning their authenticity. After returning to Germany in 1823, he revised his *History of Rome,* lectured once more at the University of Berlin, and became the editor of several highly specialized historical journals, as well as the editor of the first collection of epigraphic sources of the Byzantine period. When Ranke hailed Niebuhr as the founder of a new school of ancient historiography, he gave proper acknowledgment to his mentor and colleague.

Not all historians have been as generous as Ranke in their assessment of Niebuhr. Later in the century, Theodor Mommsen gave Roman studies a new direction, and he was quite willing to admit that his work had replaced that of Niebuhr. The contribution of a scholar as outstanding as Niebuhr is never wholly replaced or outdated, but it is true that Niebuhr is seldom read today, much less so than Mommsen; however, this is more the fault of Niebuhr's art than of his science. Macaulay was right, in his inimitable and unkind way, when he wrote that Niebuhr was "a man who would have been the first writer of his time if his talent for communicating truths had borne any proportion to his talent for investigating them." Perhaps it is best, when we think of historians at work in the nineteenth century, to recall Niebuhr's role in the professionalization of history rather than the tortured text of his own *History.*

Selected Bibliography

Hajo Holborn's "History and the Study of the Classics," *Journal of the History of Ideas* XIV (January, 1953), 33–50, is a lucid and learned account of the type of philology that inspired historians like Niebuhr. On Niebuhr himself there is little that can be recommended. Renate Bridenthal's "Barthold Georg Niebuhr, Historian of Rome: A Study in Methodology" (unpublished Ph.D. dissertation, Columbia University, 1970) is a thorough and comprehensive examination of Niebuhr's achievement. Bridenthal has a condensed version of some of her conclusions in "Was There a Roman Homer? Niebuhr's Thesis and Its Critics," *History and Theory* XI:2 (1972), 193–213. Antoine Guillard, in *Modern Germany and Her Historians* (1915), offers some interesting but superficial comments on Niebuhr's career as a statesman. G. P. Gooch, in *History and Historians in the Nineteenth Century* (1913), has a full chapter on Niebuhr, which may be used as a guide to some of the older works about this historian.

THE HISTORY OF ROME

INTRODUCTION

It was one of the most important objects of the first volume to prove that the story of Rome under the kings was altogether without historical foundation. I have sifted the legends which have taken the place of history: such fragments of the same sort as lay scattered about, I have collected, with the view of restoring the manifold forms they once bore; though with no thought that this could bring us nearer to historical knowledge. For, while the grandeur of the monarchy, the seat of which was on the seven hills, is attested by the monuments it left behind, the recollections of its history have been purposely destroyed: and to fill up the void, the events of a narrow sphere, such as the pontiffs after the Gallic irruption were familiar with, have been substituted for the forgotten transactions of an incomparably wider empire. Even Fabius beyond doubt knew nothing more than the story that has come down to us: and it would hardly have been possible for him to find any authentic records, unless in the writings of forein nations; which he could never have reconciled with his own story, or made any use of. On the other hand his age was in possession of a real history, though in many parts tinged with fable, since the insurrection of the commonalty: and though this has only reacht us in a very defective state, disfigured by arbitrary transformations, yet from this time forward it becomes my cheering task to undertake the restoration of a genuine, connected, substantially perfect history.

This would be absurd, if the story of the city before its destruction by the Gauls had been left almost exclusively to oral tradition, and if the scanty records then existing of an age little given to writing had perisht. Were such the case, we could only replace it, like that of the kings, by an illusion. Livy however assuredly did not go so far as to assume this. Nor will anybody who has a feeling for the truth think it possible, with regard to much the greater part of the occurrences related out of the century before the coming of the Gauls, that they should be fabrications: stories are often invented, not so a multitude of insulated facts. What led Livy to speak thus positively, was probably that the Annals of the pontiffs began from that event; as Claudius Quadrigarius, perhaps influenced by this very circumstance, commenced his at the same point. This writer was one of the annalists whom Livy had before him: and perhaps Livy's words merely repeat what he alleged to justify his deviating from the common practice of like chroniclers. It is pretty clear too that he must be the Clodius, whom Plutarch quotes as asserting, what he probably said on the same occasion, that the pedigrees, so far as they went back beyond that date, were fabrications. Where an errour has gained general sway, the first expressions of a mind that feels called to assert its freedom are almost always exaggerated: and such was the case with Claudius in his disgust at finding such a mass of imposture. He overlookt that there was no external reason to warrant his rejecting the genealogies of those patricians whose ancestors had their Lares on the Capitoline hill, like the Manlii and Quinctii, as spurious during the earlier ages: and how could he examine them in detail? Had he, or had Livy attended to constitutional law, they must have perceived that its excellent historians had drawn information from the books of the pontiffs, the authenticity of which was quite as indisputable as that of the twelve tables, of the compacts between the estates, and of other laws and treaties belonging to that period. Equally well establisht is that of the returns of the censuses, were it only because their statements must in later times have sounded utterly incredible and inconceivable. It is true, the copies of most of the censorian families must have flowed originally from transcripts of a few, preserved in the Capitol, or in neighbouring towns: but it was enough for their coming down in a genuine form to posterity, if a single one remained and was multiplied.

It cannot be doubted that, as these rolls were preserved for memorials in the censorian families, so those who had the image of a consul among their ancestors, kept consular fasti, wherein memorable events, at least of the year they were interested in, were noted down: and many others must have been in possession of similar documents. These were original annals, which arose independently of those of the pontiffs, and were drawn up by various persons; not always contemporaneously, but in their earliest parts from the recollections, sometimes no doubt erroneous ones, of the writer himself, or of his neighbours, touching past events. Hence the dates are often contradictory: the Auruncian war for instance is placed in the years 251, 252, or 258; the battle of Regillus in 255, or 258; discrepancies only to be accounted for from there having been sundry annals of different origin. It is impossible to pronounce whether any contemporary ones were preserved or not, which began any number of years before the insurrection of the commonalty. That none of them can have gone back so far as the origin of the consulate, is clear from the confusion in the Fasti for the first years of the republic, and from the disappearance of every trace of a genuine history during this period. To preserve the recollection of events, and to give the memory a hold, they were noted in the Fasti under a year of the Capitoline era, and of the consuls; in the same way as the calendars recorded, under a certain day, that on that same day the dictator Tubertus had gained a victory, as well as what days had become inauspicious by the defeats on the Allia, at Trasimene, and at Cannae. Neither these accounts, nor the former gave any detail of occurrences, but merely mentioned them. Of the notices so recorded some few have come down to us, manifestly handed from very ancient times, with scarcely an alteration even in the wording. I will not however by any means deny that some sort of narrative may have been mixt up with them very early: in which case they must have resembled the chronicle of Marcellinus and the like.

But the appropriate place for narrative was in the funeral orations peculiar to Rome, the use of which was derived from time immemorial: for women were admitted to a share in this honour even before the Gallic war, or immediately after. These writings, in which assuredly it was no less vain to look for an accurate representation of facts, than for eloquence, Livy, if they crost his thoughts, would hardly have deemed a historical source; since in another passage he concurs with Cicero in reprehending their want of truth. Yet they cannot have been liable to this charge from the first. Only in course of time, when it became customary to enumerate the ancestors of a house up to its origin, along with their honours and their exploits, could vanity indulge in inventions concerning them. One may easily satisfy oneself that, in the history prior to the taking by the Gauls, many stories, for instance about the Valerii, the Claudii, the Fabii, the Quinctii, and the Servilii, have flowed from this source. Several among them, such as those concerning the Servilii, are worthy of full faith: those too more in detail about the Fabii contain matter of undeniable authenticity. With others the case is very different. I am sorry to say that those of the Valerii are less deserving of credit than any others; just as their pedigree betrays singular carelessness. These documents, as well as the former, were deposited in the hall of the house; and they were probably lost and then restored together. Those living traditions however, by means of which the times of their ancestors became the common property of the Romans, were preserved by those who escaped the sword of the Gauls: and if Livy was speaking of these, he was unquestionably right in saying that the record of events was trusted to memory.

The same thing has happened among every people whose annals were a mere dry catalogue of events: and not only does the imagination in such cases mould a subject taken from history with the same freedom and plastic power as one created by poetry; but the characters have incidents, which elsewhere are told of others, transferred, and often purely arbitrary fictions ascribed to them; which gain credit, like Charlemagne's pretended expedition to the Holy Land. Such legends, whether concerning the personages of history, or those of poetry, were equally termed *fabulae.* That at Rome as elsewhere they shaped themselves in verse—that the virtue of Coriolanus, and the victories of Camillus, were sung in the same manner as the first Punic war—does not to my feelings admit of a doubt. If the bards are nameless, so are those of the Nibelungen and the Cid. But the rhythmical form is a secondary matter. The main point is, that we should recognize how the very stories which speak to the feelings, are those which tradition treats freely and creatively; how it does not give back the chain of incidents one by one, as it receives them; and how, in proportion as a story is listened to with general interest, it is the more liable to be transformed without any limit, until it becomes fixt in some book: while on the other hand such facts as excite no emotion come down just as they were recorded, to the historian who likes to employ himself in putting some life into them. This is not disputed by scholars, whose concurrence I should be loth to forgo, yet who think it hazardous to build on the assumption that the Romans had a body of popular poems now lost: and so I will not disturb the consciousness of our being substantially agreed, by labouring to make them adopt the whole of my own conviction. Besides I am far from asserting that all those traditions were originally circulated in song: nor do I doubt that some, which began in verse, were turned into prose-tales, when writing became more and more an employment; just as the popular storybook of Siegfried arose out of the Nibelungen. Among the legends of the class I have been describing, those of Coriolanus, of Cincinnatus, of the fall of the Decemvirs, of Camillus, are not to be mistaken. Of the same kind, with some excursions into the region of the marvellous, are those of Curtius and Cipus.

Long before there is any such thing as a national literature, many a man will write down an account of what has befallen him, for the use of his family. In the progress of things almost every one will aim at surpassing his predecessors, will go more into detail, take in more objects, and make approaches to a complete narrative of contemporary events: and as every chronicle must begin from the beginning, a new one subjoining itself as a continuation to a repetition of some older annals already extant, attempts are made to render these too less meagre, by incorporating popular traditions. At Rome the funeral orations likewise were drawn upon; though there was a difficulty in making such insertions, owing to the form of the Annals, which required that everything should be set down under a particular year. In this way a variety of popular books must have grown up, which, before a different taste and standard became prevalent, were great favorites, and which in the fifth and sixth century of the city must have spread the more widely, in proportion as the old legends lost the freshness of their original colouring: in aftertimes however they were neglected by literary history, for this among other reasons, that their authors were unknown. The oldest remaining Florentine annals are themselves pieced together out of some no less dry and meagre than the original Roman ones, along with fables and traditions. In the history ascribed to Malispini they are enlarged, and prolonged by a series of continuations. This work, by which they were superseded, and which itself has been thrown into oblivion by Villani, is of the same kind as those fuller Roman chronicles I have been speaking of: the existence of which however was totally forgotten by the classical writers of Rome, as the sayings of Appius the Blind would have been, unless Panaetius had spoken of them. In such books Coruncanius and the Marcii read the story of their fathers; and later writers added little of importance, any more than Villani could do to what Dante had read in Malispini.

The Fabian house, as they were eminent for their skill in the arts, and their familiarity with Greek literature, would probably be especially careful in keeping such a chronicle: the account of the campaign of the great Q. Rullus in the year 451 is evidently taken from contemporary sources. Out of this house came the historian whom Polybius censures for his partiality to his countrymen; a partiality occasioned by the hostile feelings of the Greeks, for whom, and not for his fellow-citizens, he wrote in Greek, like Cincius and Acilius, in order that they might think more worthily of Roman story. Though this might be sufficient for foreiners, it did not satisfy the Italians, who were already desirous of becoming Roman citizens, and were acquainted with the Latin language: which may have been one of the causes that at length in the seventh century Roman authors wrote the history of their country for readers in their mother tongue. That the Romans had a general knowledge of their ancient history, is proved by the fact that Cincius treated of chronology, of constitutional law, and of sundry antiquarian questions, which imply such a knowledge; and yet did not think it necessary to write his history in Latin. For the same reason Cato only handled the Roman history as part of that of Italy. After the time of Cassius Hemina however the historians of Rome were numerous. The perpetual discrepancies in them show that there was a great variety of old chronicles: and their all thinking it their business to tell the whole of the ancient history anew is a sign that every one of them, on finding any chronicles previously neglected, incorporated fresh matter from them. For assuredly no notion of distinguishing himself by any peculiar merits in his views or style was ever entertained either by Fabius Servilianus or by Vennonius; or by writers who lived considerably later, indeed after the time of Sylla, Cn. Gellius and Q. Quadrigarius. To the same class belongs Q. Valerius Antias; who however obtained a scandalous notoriety by his falsehoods, and by fabricating circumstantial narratives and definite numbers.

L. Piso had a peculiar object in view. He fancied that the ancient legends, however contradictory and incredible, were only history run wild, and that he was the person destined to restore them to their genuine form. Men's minds however in his days had still so much of poetry in them, that his ungenial efforts produced no effect. Notwithstanding the old censor's great personal respectability, his annals were not more successful than any others in attaining to the reputation enjoyed among the Greeks by the work of Ephorus; which was recognized to be the basis of their national history, and as such was continued by one writer after another. Even after the time of Piso the early history was the subject of fresh investigations: for men had learnt to make use of ancient documents; and as Philochorus corrected the history of Athens by their means, the same service was rendered to that of Rome by C. Licinius Macer, a contemporary of Cicero, with whom the list of the annalists properly so called closes. Macer's influence on the history that has come down to us is very important. We cannot suppose that Dionysius and Livy did anything for the speeches they insert, except work them up as pieces of oratory. Those speeches however are frequently something more, and contain allusions to circumstances of which their narratives shew no knowledge, but which cannot possibly have been brought in at random. Where such is the case, they must have found something of the kind in some annalist whose imperfect work they were remoulding. Now it is not likely that those who wrote in the simple old times would have employed so much art: whereas of Macer we are told by Cicero that he was immoderately fond of speeches. He may not have been successful in them: but we can easily conceive that the only one among all the annalists after Piso who had taken part in public life, wherein he had displayed a very honorable character, would like to dwell on those points where he was in his own element. Of him too we may believe that he would trace the changes in the constitution with intelligence and interest. The oldest Roman books, of which the names have been handed down, were collections of statutes: and I have already mentioned the writings of Cincius on constitutional law. Eighty years after his time, C. Junius, who from his friendship with the younger Gracchus was surnamed Gracchanus, wrote a history of the constitution and the great offices of state, which went back to the time of the kings; and which from the establishment of the consulate enumerated, under the years of the Capitoline era, what new magistracies had been instituted, and what changes made in the duties of the old ones. Copious remains of this invaluable work, which must have been entirely compiled from the writings of the pontiffs, and the other most authentic sources, have come down to us, owing to the circumstance that Gaius prefixt a history of the Roman magistracies to his books on the twelve tables; of which history much has been preserved in the honest extracts of Lydus, and in what Pomponius has appropriated. Had Livy and Dionysius, some statements in whose works can only have come originally from Gracchanus, themselves made use of him, there are a number of other things that they would not have left out. But they might easily pass them over, if Macer, who assuredly was not similarly negligent, was the source whence they drew these solitary passages, not considering the information of this sort as of higher value than the other matter derived from the Annals, a great deal of which they omitted. And if, as would appear from hence, they did not directly make use of that admirable teacher of constitutional law, unquestionably the nameless chronicles were to them a mere dead letter. A proof how rapidly Latin books disappeared after the rise of a classical literature, for the sake of which that of the primitive ages was utterly despised, is that in the beginning of the eighth century the memoirs of Scaurus and the elder Q. Catulus were as completely forgotten as those of J. J. Moser are nowadays in Germany. The only works used by the two ingenious authors who wrote histories of Rome contemporaneously under Augustus, were those of Fabius and the later annalists; the contents of which they moulded into a uniform body, without any regard to their origin. As Poggius and Leonardus were cast into the shade by Machiavel, in like manner the annalists of the seventh century were so eclipst by the excellence of Livy, that they were never brought forward again till after the time of Hadrian, when the partisans of antiquity affected to be fond of them. Nor did this last long: for no fashion can be durable, which runs counter to the real inclinations of mankind. Thenceforward the history of Rome was received and related exclusively under the shape those two writers had given to it: although Dion Cassius emancipated himself from this state of dependence, and returned to the most genuine form of the old tradition in Fabius. Nor can he have neglected Gracchanus, who at that time was known to every jurist: for the history of the constitution was his main and constant object.

It is also mine: and the highest aim of my researches is to approach to the notion which Fabius and Gracchanus had of the constitution and its changes. Beyond a doubt their views concerning it were unqualifiedly right. Surely however we may hold that our age can distinguish fable from reality more successfully than theirs. Nor is it an audacious undertaking to try to make out in the narratives of the historians, what part is due to their misunderstandings, prejudices, or arbitrary insertions,—what part rests on authentic documents,—and, to distinguish, among the materials which they found in the annalists, how much comes from each of the before-mentioned sources,—and moreover, with regard to the time before the destruction of the city, whether the statements were borrowed from earlier sources, or fabricated. Yet even if we had the books of the seventh century, on which no art had been exercised in softening the most glaring inconsistencies, this analysis could not be so successful as to extract an unbroken history from them in the simple style of a chronicle. For though that which really happened has often been recorded in the Annals along with the legend, and though the latter, having been engrafted on the record, may be separated from it easily and perfectly, the legend still oftener, and probably very early, entirely occupied the place of the brief statement of the truth, and has so completely supplanted it that no trace of it remains, and no ingenuity can effect its palingenesy. It is easy to shew that the taking of Veii by a mine is a sheer fable: but we cannot divine the real state of the case, as in some other instances we may without difficulty or uncertainty.

It is in the history of the constitution that we may feel the greatest confidence in restoring many of the steps that are wanting. Those which precede and follow enable us to determine them, like the data in a problem. On the other hand we here meet with a peculiar difficulty, from the circumstance that not a few of the most important statements, among those too which are derived from the very highest authorities, sound utterly unmeaning, because the persons who have handed them down to us were quite unable to understand them. Dionysius excogitated the most erroneous representations, which pervert whatever they exhibit; because he never suspected that he wanted the fundamental idea of the constitution, and did not resolve to abandon all attempts at making out the enigma. Lydus stammers words without thoughts. If we discover the delusive medium however, by which objects were distorted before the eyes of the acute historian, and can guess what the simple compiler must have heard of, these enigmas turn into valid evidence, and so form grounds for further results.

I cannot disguise from myself that these inquiries touching the changes of the constitution, and still more those about other insulated occurrences, can hardly produce the same kind of general conviction as the investigation of what the constitution originally was. The forms of the latter may be traced through centuries in their operation, and even in the modifications they underwent: and what we do not find recorded in one people, we learn from the analogy of a kindred one. The former are events that stand alone, depending on accident and caprice, or at least on the will of individuals: and the true account, it must be owned, is not always the most probable. But when an inquirer, after gazing for years with ever renewed undeviating stedfastness, sees the history of mistaken, misrepresented, and forgotten events rise out of mists and darkness, and assume substance and shape, as the scarcely visible aerial form of the nymph in the Sclavonic tale takes the body of an earthly maiden beneath the yearning gaze of love,—when by unwearied and conscientious examination he is continually gaining a clearer insight into the connexion of all its parts, and discerns that immediate expression of reality which emanates from life,—he has a right to demand that others, who merely throw their looks by the way on the region where he lives and has taken up his home, should not deny the correctness of his views, because they perceive nothing of the kind. The learned naturalist, who has never left his native town, will not recognize the animal's track, by which the hunter is guided: and if any one, on going into Benvenuto's prison, when his eyes had for months been accustomed to see the objects around him, had asserted that Benvenuto like himself could not distinguish anything in the darkness, he would surely have been somewhat presumptuous.

The portion of history comprised in this volume has been given up and cast aside, ever since the multitude of impossibilities and contradictions in the current narrative were noticed. Indeed a sensible man could not hesitate how to choose, were there no other alternative, except to defend what has been made of it, or to get rid of it altogether. The best things in the world degenerate in course of time, and often in no long one; and worthless appendages attach themselves thereto: and then, if a foolish zealot would force us to do homage to them, as before they were degraded and corrupted, he repells reason from them, which might otherwise restore their character, and thereby revive the feelings they formerly excited: for reason can forgo knowledge, but cannot put up with absurdities. Historical criticism, by merely lopping off what is worthless, replacing tradition on its proper footing, demonstrating its real dignity, and thus securing it from ridicule and censure, will render the story of Rome during the period following the league with the Latins no less authentic and substantial than that of many much later periods, where we are in like manner left without contemporary records.

OF THE PUBLIC LAND AND ITS OCCUPATION

It is not exactly true that the agrarian law of Cassius was the earliest so called. Every law by which the commonwealth disposed of its public land, bore that name; as for instance that by which the domain of the kings was parceled out among the commonalty, and those by which colonies were planted. Even in the narrower sense, of a law whereby the state exercised its ownership in removing the old possessors from a part of its domain, and making over its right of property therein, such a law existed among those of Servius Tullius.

In the room of these significations, very general currency has been given to the term, *an agrarian law,* in the sense of an enactment relating to the landed property of all the citizens, setting a limit to it, and assigning all beyond that limit to the destitute. The regulation of Cleomenes, the equal partition of land demanded by the frantic levelers in the French revolution, are termed agrarian laws: while in cases to which the word might suitably be applied, where a strict right of property has been unfeelingly enforced against tenants at will, cultivating a piece of ground transmitted to them from their forefathers, the word is never thought of: and the rapacious landlord, who turns a village into a solitude, regarding its fields as property he may dispose of in whatever way he can make the most of it, if he has ever heard the name of the Gracchi, will condemn their agrarian law as an atrocity.

This misconception is as old as the revival of philology. Neither Sigonius nor Manutius doubted that the tribunes had limited landed property to 500 jugers, and had assigned the excess to the poorer citizens: nor had Beaufort any other notion, nor Hooke; though they all had the statement before their eyes, that the measure referred to the conquered lands, which the Greek historians insist on as so essential a point. They only mention this by way of explaining how such vast estates could have arisen. That there was a kind of landed property to which no limit had been set, they had no conception. Yet every one of them must have been aware that there was a riddle to be solved here: but they tacitly gave it up. Ferguson on the other hand never perceived that there was one: nor did Machiavel, or Montesquieu; the value of whose reflexions on Roman history is no way affected by their mistakes as to the historical facts. I should not even mention the mistakes of these two great men here, were it not instructive to observe that they are far from condemning the agrarian laws, even when taken in the common sense. I would not myself share their boldness in looking with approbation on the sacrifice of all private rights to the hope of good for the community. Yet in them this boldness was excusable: because the one lived in a republic that had been agitated for centuries by incessant convulsions, and accustomed to every kind of violation of legal rights; and the other at a time when men had grown weary of repose, and, not having known a revolution for many generations, longed for one to season the insipidity of life. The greatest mind is still akin to its age.

Machiavel believed simply that the agrarian laws establisht a limit for landed property, and assigned the rich man's surplus to the needy. He adds, that the interests of every republic demand that the state should be rich, and the citizens poor; and that at Rome the laws requisite for this end seem either to have been wholly wanting in earlier times, or to have been framed imperfectly, or to have been insensibly relaxt. Moreover, though he conceives the agrarian laws to have led to the ruin of the republic, he yet considers the contest about them as the main cause of its having lasted so long. Montesquieu assumes it as a historical fact, that Romulus distributed the territory of Rome among the first setlers in small equal parcels. Prepossest with the notion of the immense population of ancient Rome, he deems this equality the ground of her strength: and in his opinion the tribunician commotions, like the revolution effected at Sparta by the last Heraclids, were so many attempts to bring back the constitution to its original principles.

On the breaking out of a revolution, which nobody would have thought compatible with the tameness of modern times, the agrarian laws and the Gracchi were much talkt of. This led Heyne to do history a service, by pointing out that the laws of the tribunes related simply and solely to the public domain: and guided by this remark accounts of the Gracchic troubles were written, before the revolutionary frenzy had quite spent itself, acquitting the Gracchi of the charge of having shaken property. It is to Heyne's essay that I myself owe my conviction of this truth, which I have firmly retained ever since I began my researches on Roman history. At the same time this merely negative certainty threw my mind into as painful a state of perplexity as was ever experienced. This torment, of being utterly unable to conceive a proposition, the reverse of which I saw it was absolutely necessary to reject—a feeling nearly akin to the despair excited by vain efforts to fathom the mysteries of theology,—grew as I advanced to manhood, and engaged in public business, still, in intervals of leisure, turning my eyes toward my beloved field of antiquity; while with the ripening of experience I felt a more pressing desire to comprehend the ancient world no less distinctly than the present, more especially in those relations of civil life with which my profession rendered me conversant.

Appian's statement, that a fixt portion of the produce of the domain lands was paid for the use of them, stood in direct contradiction to Plutarch's, that they were farmed to the highest bidder: and the more closely Plutarch's account was examined, the more impossibilities it shewed in all its parts. The rich, he says, engrost the farms by outbidding others. But a rich man can never afford to pay so high a rent for a small piece of ground, as the peasant who tills it with his own hands. And how was it possible for the immense domains of the Roman state to be let out in small parcels? Supposing however that they had been so let, the limit prescribed to them might easily have been restored by a single upright censor who examined the register without respect of persons. Leases were made for a lustre; but in the case of the public land we hear of a possession transmitted by inheritance or purchase for centuries. *Possession* and *possessors* are the terms always employed, when the use of the public lands is spoken of: but a farmer could not be said to possess a piece of ground in the Roman sense: possessing a thing, and renting it, are contradictory notions.

Thus a conception, which, though erroneous, was clear, intelligible, and productive of consequences, though of false ones, had given way to one from which for many years I despaired of extracting a meaning. Perhaps I never should have done so, had not the footing on which the possession of land and the landtax stand in India, supplied me with an existing image of the Roman possession, the Roman *vectigal,* and the mode of leasing it. In India the soverain is the sole proprietor of the soil: he may at pleasure confiscate the land cultivated by the Ryot. Nevertheless the latter may transmit it to his heir, and may alienate it: he renders a larger or smaller definite portion of the produce in kind: this the state leases or sells to the Zemindars; unless it has granted the revenue of a district or of a piece of ground to some temple or pious foundation for ever, or to some of its vassals and officers for life.

Leopold von Ranke 1795—1885

2

Wie es eigentlich gewesen. If there exists a single phrase in German that graduate students (and many of their teachers) in the Western World attempt to articulate with authority, it is this classic formulation first uttered by Leopold von Ranke in the "Preface" to his *Histories of the Latin and Germanic Nations from 1494–1514.* The phrase takes on its full meaning when rendered as part of the thought from which it is taken: "History has been assigned the office of judging the past, of instructing our time for the benefit of future years. This essay does not aspire to such high offices; it wants only to show how it had really been—*wie es eigentlich gewesen."* This notion makes such perfect sense that it might easily be construed as commonplace, but it is not. Ranke's contention that the historiography of the Enlightenment was not history at all but rather some unhistorical form of philosophy or propaganda, his own staggering achievement in applying his principle of scientific history to the enormous range of his own works, and a later generation's veneration of his doctrine as historicism make this phrase a virtual declaration of war; and historians have reacted to it with the alternations of enthusiasm and criticism that such declarations typically encounter in the political arena.

Ranke's influence on his contemporaries and later generations of historians makes that of Niebuhr seem slight by comparison. His long life; his sixty volumes on modern European history; his fifty-year association with the University of Berlin, where his seminar became world famous, and where he trained many of the best German historians in the nineteenth century; his political involvement and publications; and his close alliance with the Prussian state and with Metternich—all made him an awesome figure in his own lifetime. On the occasion of his ninetieth birthday Ranke was made an honorary member of the newly founded American Historical Association and was told by George Bancroft in no uncertain terms that he was "the greatest living historian." In later years, some highly qualified members of that association, such as Charles Beard, cringed at the thought, but it was true. Whatever the shortcomings of objective or scientific history and of historicism, no matter how many hidden biases one may find in his works, it must be recognized that no modern historian has equaled him in his learning or in his productivity.

Romanticism enjoyed great popularity in Ranke's native Saxony when he was a young man; and he seems to have been attracted by much of what this literary, philosophical, and historical movement symbolized. Motivated by the desire to heal the wounds of rebellion and violence that attended the French Revolution and the Napoleonic wars, the Romantics stressed continuity between modern and medieval Europe. As a result, medieval studies regained some of the importance they had lost during the Enlightenment, and along with the interest in the age of belief went a revival of interest in religion itself. Ranke, a firm and lifelong believer, was caught up by the passion of this movement for the past, but he objected to the Romantics' distortion of the events and people who made it. After reading some of the modish novels of Walter Scott, Ranke recalled later in life that he "was sufficiently attracted by them, but hurt by the way in which Charles the Bold and Louis XI were treated in his *Quentin Durward,* in full contradiction to the historical sources. . . . Thereafter, I turned away from romantic fiction, and decided to avoid everything fictitious and fanciful and to cling strictly to the facts."

In his first major work, the *Histories of the Latin and Germanic Nations,* published in the summer of 1824, Ranke demonstrated both the Romantic's fascination for the persistence of the past in the present and the historian's conviction of the importance of factual accuracy based on contemporary records. The theme of the book—the historical unity and the common origin of the two nations—as well as its scholarship and style brought him the official recognition of the Prussian government, which transferred him from the Gymnasium in Frankfurt an der Oder, where he had been teaching, to the University of Berlin. The proximity of state machinery reinforced Ranke's attachment to the well-being of the establishment.

Devoted to the strict narration of facts as they fitted into a nationalistic and religious interpretation of modern European history, Ranke was a conservative whose work endeared him to the leaders of Restoration Europe. He soon left Berlin in search of the *Relazioni* of the Venetian ambassadors, a hitherto neglected storehouse of letters and dispatches that illuminated the diplomatic history of early modern Europe. The friendship and sponsorship of Prince Metternich—the political mastermind of the Restoration—gained him access to the archives throughout Italy, with the exception of those of the Vatican. Upon his return from Italy in 1831, Ranke undertook the editorship of the *Historische-Politische Zeitschrift,* a government-sponsored journal where the opinions of the editor not very coincidentally stressed the importance of the preservation of the state and the monarchy. As a historian Ranke pointed out the unfortunate results of the French republican experiment; as a political commentator he warned against disrespect for legitimate princes. Neither the journal nor its editor was very successful in converting the advocates of other political views. In 1836, Ranke ended his career as a political publicist and retired to his study. Three years later appeared his first historical masterpiece.

The *History of the Popes* was a great achievement. It artfully combined the reports of the Venetian ambassadors with thousands of other documents to produce a minutely detailed account of the inner workings of papal diplomacy. Although it is clear enough to present-day readers that Ranke was interested in telling the story of "Protestant deliverance" from the designs of universal Catholic monarchy, many of his contemporaries thought that he was too neutral, too much captivated by his concern for objectivity, to be a good German Protestant. In his *History of the Reformation in Germany,* published in 1840, he rebutted that charge all too well. Based on at least ninety-six volumes of reports of the Frankfurt deputies to the Imperial Diet in the fifteenth and sixteenth centuries, and on countless other documents he uncovered in the archives of Berlin, Weimar, Dresden, and Brussels, this is nevertheless a partisan recounting of Luther's struggle and triumph.

Our selection from this work reveals Ranke's assessment of the Reformation as a moral victory for Germany and for Luther, who appears as an ardent but conservative reformer. In later sections of this *History,* Ranke contrasts Luther's commendable conservatism with the rash policies and attitudes of the Swiss reformer Zwingli. In his subsequent works on Prussian history, Ranke found little to blame, and much to praise, in some of the more powerful and more despotic of the Hohenzollerns. When it came to the history of his own country, the historian fell far short of his goal of complete impartiality.

Ranke followed up his works on Prussian history with national histories of France and England in which he concentrated on the periods of religious civil war. At the age of seventy he retired from teaching but continued to work indefatigably, adhering to a schedule that required the assistance of at least two younger historians every day. At the age of eighty-three he began his last historical project, a universal history, which he had brought down to the end of the fifteenth century by the time he died in Berlin at the age of ninety-one. That he should undertake such a project at the end of his prodigious life surprised no one. Despite his emphasis on the individual event, the uniqueness of each historical epoch, the incomparable quality of each human experience, Ranke sought to synthesize all that was diverse in the history of man, to show the orderliness of God's creation.

In our century the works of Friedrich Meinecke have done much to deify the reputation of Ranke, at least among the admirers of Meinecke, who have decided that Ranke was the creator and single most significant practitioner of historicism, that is, of a brand of history that stresses the ineffable, inimitable, and impartial in the recounting of human events. No matter what one thinks about historicism, it is not necessary to agree with Meinecke that Ranke's works "mark one of the summits in a specific line of great products of the human mind," to realize that Ranke's contribution to history was as vast as it was profound.

Selected Bibliography

Theodore H. von Laue's *Leopold Ranke: The Formative Years* (1950) is a carefully reasoned assessment of Ranke's historical achievement before the *History of the Popes* and an objective account of his political activities until that time. Hajo

Holborn's "The Science of History," in *The Interpretation of History* (1943), Joseph R. Strayer, ed., is brief but sound and well informed. For an evaluation of Ranke as a German historian consult G. P. Gooch, "Ranke's Interpretation of German History," in *Studies in German History* (1948), as well as Lord Acton's "German Schools of History," in his *Historical Essays and Studies* (1907). For a devastating attack on Ranke—his methods, his purposes, and his life—Charles A. Beard's presidential address before the American Historical Association, "That Noble Dream," *American Historical Review* XIV (October, 1935), 74–87, cannot be matched. A complete and useful history of Ranke and his time is Eugen Guglia, *Rankes Leben und Werke* (1893), which is in part brought up to date by H. F. Helmolt in *Rankes Leben und Wirkung* (1921).

HISTORY OF THE REFORMATION IN GERMANY

EARLY HISTORY OF LUTHER AND OF CHARLES V, 1517–1521

Chapter 1. Origin of the Religious Opposition

Whatever hopes we may entertain of the final accomplishment of the prophecies of an universal faith in one God and Father of all which have come down to us in the Hebrew and Christian Scriptures, it is certain that after the lapse of more than ten centuries that faith had by no means overspread the earth. The world was filled with manifold and widely differing modes and objects of worship.

Even in Europe, the attempts to root out paganism had been but partially successful; in Lithuania, for example, the ancient worship of the serpent endured through the whole of the 15th and 16th centuries, and was even invested with a political significance; and if this was the case in Europe, how much more so in other portions of the globe. In every clime men continued to symbolise the powers of nature, and to endeavour to subdue them by enchantments or to propitiate them by sacrifices: throughout vast regions the memory of the dead was the terror of the living, and the rites of religion were especially designed to avert their destructive interference in human things; to worship only the sun and moon supposed a certain elevation of soul, and a considerable degree of civilisation.

Refined by philosophy, letters, and arts, represented by vast and powerful hierarchies, stood the mightiest antagonists of Christianity—the Indian religion and Islam; and it is remarkable how great an internal agitation prevailed within them at the epoch of which we are treating.

Although the Brahminical faith was, perhaps, originally founded on monotheistic ideas, it had clothed these in a multiform idolatry. But at the end of the 15th and beginning of the 16th century, we trace the progress of a reformer in Hindostan. Nanck, a native of Lahore, endeavoured to restore the primitive ideas of religion, and to show the advantages of a pure morality over a merely ceremonial worship: he projected the abolition of castes, nay, even a union of Hindoos and Moslem; he presents one of the most extraordinary examples of peaceful unfanatical piety the world ever beheld. Unfortunately, his efforts were unsuccessful. The notions he combated were much too deeply rooted; even those who called themselves his disciples—the Sikhs—paid idolatrous honours to the man who laboured to destroy idolatry.

A new and very important development of the other branch of the religions of India—Buddhism—also took place in the fifteenth century. The first regenerated Lama appeared in the monastery of Brepung, and was universally acknowledged throughout Thibet; the second incarnation of the same (from 1462 to 1542) had similiar success in the most remote Buddhist countries; from that time hundreds of millions revere in the Dalailama at Lhassa the living Buddha of the present,—the unity of the divine trinity,—and throng thither to receive his blessing. It cannot be denied that this religion had a beneficial influence on the manners of rude nations; but, on the other hand, what fetters does such a fantastic deification of human nature impose on the mind! Those nations possess the materials for forming a popular literature, a wide diffusion of the knowledge of the elements of science, and the art of printing; but the literature itself—the independent exercise and free utterance of the mind, can never exist; nor are such controversies as those between the married and unmarried priests, or the yellow and the red professions which attach themselves to different chiefs, at all calculated to give birth to it. The rival Lamas make pilgrimages to each other, and reciprocally recognise each other's divine character.

The same antagonism which prevailed between Brama and Buddha, subsisted in the bosom of Islam, from its very foundation, between the three elder Chalifs and Ali; in the beginning of the sixteenth century the contest between the two sects, which had been dormant for awhile, broke out with redoubled violence. The sultan of the Osmans regarded himself (in his character of successor to Abubekr and the first Chalifs) as the religious head of all Sunnites, whether in his own or foreign countries, from Morocco to Bokhara. On the other hand, a race of mystic Sheiks of Erdebil, who traced their origin from Ali, gave birth to a successful warrior, Ismail Sophi, who founded the modern Persian monarchy, and secured once more to the Shiites a powerful representation and an illustrious place in history. Unfortunately, neither of these parties felt the duty or expediency of fostering the germ of civilisation which had lain in the soil since the better times of the early Chalifat. They only developed the tendency to despotic autocracy which Islam so peculiarly favours, and worked up political hostility to an incredible pitch of fury by the stimulants of fanaticism. The Turkish historians relate that the enemy who had fallen into Ismail's hands were roasted and eaten. The Osman, Sultan Selim, on the other hand, opened the war against his rival by causing all the Shiites in his land, from the age of seven to seventy, to be hunted out and put to death in one day; "forty thousand heads," says Seadeddin, "with base souls." The antagonists were, as we perceive, worthy of each other.

In Christendom, too, a division existed between the Græco-Oriental and the Latin Church, which, though it did not lead to acts of such savage violence, could not be healed. Even the near approach of the resistless torrent of Turkish power which threatened instant destruction, could not move the Greeks to accede to the condition under which the assistance of the West was offered them—the adoption of the distinguishing formulæ of confession—except for the moment, and ostensibly. The union which was brought about at Florence, in the year 1439, with so much labour, met with little sympathy from some, and the most violent opposition from others: the patriarchs of Alexandria, Antioch, and Jerusalem, loudly protested against the departure from canonical and synodal tradition, which such an union implied; they threatened the Greek emperor with a schism on their own part, on account of the indulgence he showed to the Latin heterodoxy.

If we inquire which of these several religions had the greater external and political strength, we are led to the conclusion that Islam had unquestionably the advantage. By the conquests of the Osmans in the 15th century, it had extended to regions where it had been hitherto unknown, almost on the borders of Europe; combined too with political institutions which must inevitably lead to the unceasing progress of conversion. It reconquered that sovereignty over the Mediterranean which it had lost since the eleventh century. Its triumphs in India soon equalled those in the West. Sultan Baber was not content with overthrowing the Islamite princes who had hitherto held that land. Finding, as he expressed it, "that the banners of the heathen waved in two hundred cities of the faithful—that mosques were destroyed and the women and children of the Moslem carried into slavery," he proclaimed a holy war against the Hindoos, as the Osmans had done against the Christians. On the eve of a battle he resolved to abjure the use of wine; he repealed taxes which were inconsistent with the Koran, and enkindled the ardour of his troops by a vow sworn upon this their sacred book; his reports of his victories are conceived in the same spirit of religious enthusiasm, and he thus earned the title of Gazi. The rise of so mighty a power, actuated by such ideas, necessarily gave a vast impulse to the propagation of Islam throughout the East.

But if, on the other hand, we endeavour to ascertain which of these different systems possessed the greatest internal force,—which was pregnant with the most important consequences to the destiny of the human race,—we can as little fail to arrive at the conviction (whatever be our religious faith), that the superiority was on the side of Latin Christendom.

Its most important peculiarity lay in this—that a slow but sure and unbroken progress of intellectual culture had been going on within its bosom for a series of ages. While the East had been convulsed to its very centre by torrents of invasion like that of the Mongols, the West had indeed always been agitated by wars, in which the various powers of society were brought into motion and exercise; but neither had foreign tribes overrun the land, nor had there been any of those intestine convulsions which shake the foundations of a society in an early and progressive stage of civilisation. Hence all the vital and productive elements of human culture were here united and mingled: the development of society had gone on naturally and gradually; the innate passion and genius for science and for art constantly received fresh food and fresh inspiration, and were in their fullest bloom and vigour; civil liberty was established upon firm foundations; solid and symmetrical political structures arose in beneficent rivalry, and the necessities of civil life led to the combination and improvement of physical resources; the laws which eternal Providence has impressed on human affairs were left to their free and tranquil operation; what had decayed crumbled away and disappeared, while the germs of fresh life continually shot up and flourished: in Europe were found united the most intelligent, the bravest, and the most civilised nations, still in the freshness of youth.

Such was the world which now sought, like its eastern rival, to extend its limits and its influence. Four centuries had elapsed since, prompted by religious motives, it had made attempts at conquest in the East; but after a momentary success these had failed—only a few fragments of these acquisitions remained in its possession. But at the end of the fifteenth century, a new theatre for boundless activity was opened to the West. It was the time of the discovery of both Indies. All elements of European culture—the study of the half-effaced recollections of antiquity, technical improvements, the spirit of commercial and political enterprise, religious zeal—all conspired to render the newly-discovered countries tempting and profitable. All the existing relations of nations, however, necessarily underwent a change; the people of the West acquired a new superiority, or at least became capable of acquiring it.

Above all, the relative situation of religions was altered. Christianity, especially in the forms it had assumed in the Latin Church, gained a fresh and unexpected ascendancy in the remotest regions. It was therefore doubly important to mankind, what might be the present or the future form and character of the Latin Church. The Pope instantly put forth a claim, which no one contested, to divide the countries that had been, or that yet might be found, between the two States by which they were discovered.

Position of the Papacy with Regard to Religion

The question, at what periods and under what circumstances the distinguishing doctrines and practices of the Romish Church were settled, and acquired an ascendancy, merits a minute and elaborate dissertation.

It is sufficient here to recall to the mind of the reader, that this took place at a comparatively later period, and precisely in the century of the great hierarchical struggles.

It is well known that the institution of the Seven Sacraments, whose circle embraces all the important events of the life of man, and brings them into contact with the church, is ascribed to Peter Lombard, who lived in the twelfth century. It appears upon inquiry that the notions regarding the most important of them, the Sacrament of the Altar, were by no means very distinct in the church itself, in the time of that great theologian. It is true that one of those synods which, under Gregory VII., had contributed so much to the establishment of the hierarchy, had added great weight to the doctrine of the real presence by the condemnation of Berengar: but Peter Lombard as yet did not venture to decide in its favour: the word transubstantiation first became current in his time; nor was it until the beginning of the thirteenth century, that the idea and the word received the sanction of the church: this, as is well known, was first given by the Lateran confession of faith in the year 1215; and it was not till later that the objections which till then had been constantly suggested by a deeper view of religion, gradually disappeared.

It is obvious, however, of what infinite importance this doctrine became to the service of the church, which has crystallized (if I may use the expression) around the mystery it involves. The ideas of the mystical and sensible presence of Christ in the church were thus embodied in a living image; the adoration of the Host was introduced; festivals in honour of this greatest of all miracles, incessantly repeated, were solemnized. Intimately connected with this is the great importance attached to the worship of the Virgin Mary, the mother of Christ, in the latter part of the middle ages.

The prerogatives of the priesthood are also essentially connected with this article of faith. The theory and doctrine of the priestly character were developed; that is, of the power communicated to the priest by ordination, "to make the body of Christ" (as they did not scruple to say); "to act in the person of Christ." It is a product of the thirteenth century, and is to be traced principally to Alexander of Hales and Thomas Aquinas. This doctrine first gave to the separation of the priesthood from the laity, which had indeed other and deeper causes, its full significancy. People began to see in the priest the mediator between God and man.

This separation, regarded as a positive institution, is also, as is well known, an offspring of the same epoch. In the thirteenth century, in spite of all opposition, the celibacy of the priesthood became an inviolable law. At the same time the cup began to be withheld from the laity. It was not denied that the efficacy of the Eucharist in both kinds was more complete; but it was said that the more worthy should be reserved for the more worthy—for those by whose instrumentality alone it was produced. "It is not in the participation of the faithful," says St. Thomas, "that the perfection of the sacrament lies, but solely in the consecration of the elements." And in fact the church appeared far less designed for instruction or for the preaching of the Gospel, than for the showing forth of the great mystery; and the priesthood is, through the sacrament, the sole depository of the power to do this; it is through the priest that sanctification is imparted to the multitude.

This very separation of the priesthood from the laity gave its members boundless influence over all other classes of the community.

It is a necessary part of the theory of the sacerdotal character above alluded to, that the priest has the exclusive power of removing the obstacles which stand in the way of a participation in the mysterious grace of God: in this not even a saint had power to supersede him. But the absolution which he is authorized to grant is charged with certain conditions, the most imperative of which is confession. In the beginning of the thirteenth century it was peremptorily enjoined on every believer as a duty, to confess all his sins, at least once in a year, to some particular priest.

It requires no elaborate argument to prove what an all-pervading influence auricular confession, and the official supervision and guidance of consciences, must give to the clergy. With this was connected a complete, organized system of penances.

Above all, a character and position almost divine was thus conferred on the high-priest, the pope of Rome; of whom it was assumed that he occupied the place of Christ in the mystical body of the church, which embraced heaven and earth, the dead and the living. This conception of the functions and attributes of the pope was first filled out and perfected in the beginning of the thirteenth century; then, too, was the doctrine of the treasures of the church, on which the system of indulgences rests, first promulgated. Innocent III. did not scruple to declare, that what he did, God did, through him. Glossators added, that the pope possessed the uncontrolled will of God; that his sentence superseded all reasons: with perverse and extravagant dialectic, they propounded the question, whether it were possible to appeal from the pope to God, and answered it in the negative; seeing that God had the same tribunal as the pope, and that it was impossible to appeal from any being to himself.

It is clear that the papacy must have already gained the victory over the empire,—that it could no longer have any thing to fear either from master or rival,—before opinions and doctrines of this kind could be entertained or avowed. In the age of struggles and conquests, the theory of the hierarchy gained ground step by step with the fact of material power. Never were theory and practice more intimately connected.

Nor was it to be believed that any interruption or pause in this course of things took place in the fifteenth century. The denial of the right of the clergy to withhold the cup was first declared to be heresy at the council of Constance: Eugenius IV. first formally accepted the doctrine of the Seven Sacraments; the extraordinary school interpretation of the miraculous conception was first approved by the councils, favoured by the popes, and accepted by the universities, in this age.

It might appear that the worldly dispositions of the popes of those times, whose main object it was to enjoy life, to promote their dependents and to enlarge their secular dominions, would have prejudiced their spiritual pretensions. But, on the contrary, these were as vast and as arrogant as ever. The only effect of the respect inspired by the councils was, that the popes forbade any one to appeal to a council under pain of damnation. With what ardour do the curalist writers labour to demonstrate the infallibility of the pope! John of Torquemada is unwearied in heaping together analogies from Scripture, maxims of the fathers and passages out of the false decretals, for this end; he goes so far as to maintain that, were there not a head of the church who could decide all controversies and remove all doubts, it might be possible to doubt of the Holy Scriptures themselves, which derived their authority only from the church; which, again, could not be conceived as existing without the pope. In the beginning of the sixteenth century, the well-known Dominican, Thomas of Gaeta, did not hesitate to declare the church a born slave, who could have no other remedy against a bad pope, than to pray for him without ceasing.

Nor were any of the resources of physical force neglected or abandoned. The Dominicans, who taught the strictest doctrines in the universities and proclaimed them to the people from the pulpit, had the right to enforce them by means of fire and sword. Many victims to orthodoxy were offered up after John Huss and Jerome of Prague. The contrast between the worldly-mindedness and sensuality of Alexander VI. and Leo X., and the additional stringency and rigour they gave to the powers of the Inquisition, is most glaring. Under the authority of similarly disposed predecessors, this institution had recently acquired in Spain a more fearful character and aspect than it had ever yet presented to the world; and the example of Germany shows that similar tendencies were at work in other countries. The strange distortion of the fancy which gave birth to the notion of a personal intercourse with Satan, served as the pretext for bloody executions; the "Hexenhammer" (Hammer for Witches) was the work of two German Dominicans. The Spanish Inquisition had originated in a persecution of the Jews: in Germany, also, the Jews were universally persecuted in the beginning of the sixteenth century, and the Dominicans of Cologne proposed to the emperor to establish an Inquisition against them. They had even the ingenuity to invent a legal authority for such a measure. They declared that it was necessary to examine how far the Jews had deviated from the Old Testament, which the emperor was fully entitled to do, since their nation had formally acknowledged before the judgment-seat of Pilate the authority of the imperial majesty of Rome. If they had succeeded, they would certainly not have stopped at the Jews.

Meanwhile the whole intellectual energy of the age flowed in the channels marked out by the church. Germany is a striking example to what an extent the popular mind of a nation of the West received its direction from ecclesiastical principles.

The great workshops of literature, the German universities, were all more or less colonies or branches of that of Paris—either directly sprung from it, like the earlier; or indirectly, like the later. Their statutes sometimes begin with a eulogy on the Alma Mater of Paris. From that most ancient seat of learning, too, had the whole system of schoolmen, the controversy between Nominalism and Realism, the preponderancy of the theological faculty,—"that brilliant star from which every thing received light and life,"—passed over to them. In the theological faculty the Professor of Sentences had the precedency, and the Baccalaureus who read the Bible was obliged to allow him to determine the hour of his lecture. In some universities, none but a clerk who had received at least inferior ordination, could be chosen Rector. The whole of education, from the first elements to the highest dignities of learning, was conducted in one and the same spirit. Dialectical distinctions intruded themselves into the very rudiments of grammar; and the elementary books of the eleventh and twelfth centuries were constantly retained as the groundwork of learning: here, too, the same road was steadily pursued which had been marked out at the time of the foundation of the hierarchical power.

Art was subject to the same influences. The minsters and cathedrals, in which the doctrines and ideas of the church are so curiously symbolised, rose on every side. In the year 1482, the towers of the church of St. Sebaldus at Nürnberg were raised to their present height; in 1494, a new and exquisitely wrought gate was added to Strasburg minster; in 1500, the king of the Romans laid the first stone of the choir of the Reichsgotteshaus (Church of the Empire) St. Ulrich, in Augsburg, with silver trowel, rule, and hod; he caused a magnificent block of stone to be brought from the mountains, out of which a monument was to be erected "to the well-beloved lord St. Ulrich, our kinsman of the house of Kyburg": upon it was to stand a king of the Romans, sword in hand. In 1513, the choir of the cathedral of Freiburg, in 1517, that of Bern, was finished; the porch on the northern transept of the church of St. Lawrence in Nürnberg dates from 1520. The brotherhoods of the masons, and the secrets which arose in the workshops of German builders, spread wider and wider. It was not till a later period that the redundancy of foliage, the vegetable character, which so remarkably distinguishes the so-called gothic architecture became general. At the time we are speaking of, the interior of churches was principally adorned with countless figures, either exquisitely carved in wood, or cast in precious metals, or painted and enclosed in gold frames, which covered the altars or adorned the aisles and porches. It is not the province of the arts to produce ideas, but to give them a sensible form; all the creative powers of the nation were now devoted to the task of representing the traditional conceptions of the church. Those wondrous representations of the Mother of God, so full of sweet and innocent grace, which have immortalized Baldung, Schaffner, and especially Martin Schön, are not mere visions of an artist's fancy; they are profoundly connected with that worship of the Virgin which was then peculiarly general and fervent. I venture to add that they cannot be understood without the rosary, which is designed to recall the several joys of the Holy Mary;—the angelic salutation, the journey across the mountains, the child-bearing without pain, the finding of Jesus in the temple, and the ascension; as the prayer-books of that time more fully set forth.

These prayer-books are altogether singular monuments of a simple and credulous devotion. There are prayers to which an indulgence for 146 days, others to which one for 7000 or 8000 years are attached: one morning benediction of peculiar efficacy was sent by a pope to a king of Cyprus; whosoever repeats the prayer of the venerable Bede the requisite number of times, the Virgin Mary will be at hand to help him for thirty days before his death, and will not suffer him to depart unabsolved. The most extravagant expressions were uttered in praise of the Virgin: "The eternal Daughter of the eternal Father, the heart of the indivisible Trinity": it was said, "Glory be to the Virgin, to the Father, and to the Son." Thus, too, were the saints invoked as meritorious servants of God, who, by their merits, could win our salvation, and could extend peculiar protection to those who believed in them; as, for example, St. Sebaldus, "the most venerable and holy captain, helper and defender of the imperial city of Nürnberg."

Relics were collected with great zeal. Elector Frederick of Saxony gathered together in the church he endowed at Wittenberg, 5005 particles, all preserved in entire standing figures, or in exquisitely wrought reliquaries, which were shown to the devout people every year on the Monday after Misericordia. In the presence of the princes assembled at the diet, the high altar of the cathedral of Treves was opened, and "the seamless coat of our dear Lord Jesus Christ," found in it; the little pamphlets in which this miracle was represented in wood-cuts, and announced to all the world, are to be found in the midst of the acts of the diet. Miraculous images of Our Lady were discovered;—one, for example, in Eischel in the diocese of Constance; at the Iphof boundary, by the road-side, a sitting figure of the Virgin, whose miracles gave great offence to the monks of Birklingen, who possessed a similar one; and in Regensburg, the beautiful image, for which a magnificent church was built by the contributions of the faithful, out of the ruins of a synagogue belonging to the expelled Jews. Miracles were worked without ceasing at the tomb of Bishop Benno in Meissen; madmen were restored to reason, the deformed became straight, those infected with the plague were healed; nay, a fire at Merseburg was extinguished by Bishop Bose merely uttering the name of Benno; while those who doubted his power and sanctity were assailed by misfortunes. When Trithemius recommended this miracle-worker to the pope for canonization, he did not forget to remark that he had been a rigid and energetic supporter of the church party, and had resisted the tyrant Henry IV. So intimately were all these ideas connected. A confraternity formed for the purpose of the frequent repetition of the rosary (which is, in fact, nothing more than the devout and affectionate recollection of the joys of the Holy Virgin) was founded by Jacob Sprenger, the violent and fanatical restorer of the Inquisition in Germany,—the author of the "Hexenhammer."

For it was one single and wondrous structure which had grown up out of the germs planted by former ages, wherein spiritual and temporal power, wild fancy and dry school-learning, the tenderest devotion and the rudest force, religion and superstition, were mingled and confounded, and were bound together by some mysterious quality common to them all;—and, amidst all the attacks it sustained, and all the conquests it achieved—amidst those incessant conflicts, the decisions of which constantly assumed the character of laws,—not only asserted its claim to universal fitness for all ages and nations—for this world and the next—but to the regulation of the minutest particulars of human life.

I know not whether any man of sound understanding—any man, not led astray by some phantasm, can seriously wish that this state of things had remained unshaken and unchanged in Europe; whether any man persuades himself that the will and the power to look the genuine, entire and unveiled truth steadily in the face—the manly piety acquainted with the grounds of its faith—could ever have been matured under such influences. Nor do I understand how any one could really regard the diffusion of this most singular condition of the human mind (which had been produced by circumstances wholly peculiar to the West) over the entire globe, as conducive to the welfare and happiness of the human race. It is well known that one main ground of the disinclination of the Greeks to a union with the Roman church, lay in the multitude of rules which were introduced among the Latins, and in the oppressive autocracy which the See of Rome had arrogated to itself. Nay, was not the Gospel itself kept concealed by the Roman church? In the ages in which the scholastic dogmas were fixed, the Bible was forbidden to the laity altogether, and even to the priesthood, in the mother tongue. It is impossible to deny that, without any serious reference to the source from which the whole system of faith had proceeded, men went on to construct doctrines and to enjoin practices, shaped upon the principle which had become the dominant one. We must not confound the tendencies of the period now before us with those evinced in the doctrines and practices established at the Council of Trent; at that time even the party which adhered to Catholicism had felt the influences of the epoch of the Reformation, and had begun to reform itself: the current was already arrested. And this was absolutely necessary. It was necessary to clear the germ of religion from the thousand folds of accidental forms under which it lay concealed, and to place it unencumbered in the light of day. Before the Gospel could be preached to all nations, it must appear again in its own lucid, unadulterated purity.

It is one of the greatest coincidences presented by the history of the world, that at the moment in which the prospect of exercising dominion over the other hemisphere opened on the Romano-Germanic nations of the Latin church, a religious movement began, the object of which was to restore the purity of revelation.

Whilst other nations were busied in the conquest of distant lands, Germany, which had little share in those enterprises, undertook this mighty task. Various events concurred to give that direction to the mind of the country, and to incite it to a strenuous opposition to the See of Rome.

Opposition Raised by the Secular Powers

The efforts to obtain a regular and well compacted constitution, which for some years had occupied the German nation, were very much at variance with the interests of the papacy, hitherto exercising so great an influence over the government of the empire. The pope would very soon have been made sensible of the change, if that national government which was the object of such zealous and ardent endeavours had been organised.

The very earliest projects of such a constitution, in the year 1487, were accompanied with a warning to the pope to abolish a tithe which he had arbitrarily imposed on Germany, and which in some places he had actually levied. In 1495, when it became necessary to form a council of the empire, the intention was expressed to authorize the president to take into consideration the complaints of the nation against the church of Rome. Scarcely had the States met the king in 1498, when they resolved to require the pope to relinquish the Annates which he drew to so large an amount from Germany, in order to provide for a Turkish war. In like manner, as soon as the Council of Regency was formed, an embassy was sent to the pope to press this request earnestly upon him, and to make representations concerning various unlawful encroachments on the gift and employment of German benefices. A papal legate, who shortly after arrived for the purpose of causing the jubilee to be preached, was admonished by no means to do anything without the advice and knowledge of the imperial government; care was taken to prevent him from granting indulgences to breakers of the Public Peace: on the contrary, he was charged expressly to uphold it; imperial commissioners were appointed to accompany him, without whose presence and permission he could not receive the money when collected.

We find the Emperor Maximilian occasionally following the same course. In the year 1510 he caused a more detailed and distinct statement of the grievances of the German nation to be drawn up, than had hitherto existed; he even entertained the idea of introducing into Germany the Pragmatic Sanction, which had proved so beneficial to France. In the year 1511 he took a lively interest in the convocation of a council at Pisa: we have an edict of his, dated in the January of that year, wherein he declares that, as the court of Rome delays, he will not delay; as emperor, steward and protector of the Church, he convokes the council of which she is so greatly in need. In a brief dated June, he promises to those assembled his protection and favour till the close of their sittings, "by which they will, as he hopes, secure to themselves the approbation of God and the praise of men." And, in fact, the long-cherished hope that a reform in the church would be the result of this council, was again ardently indulged. The articles were pointed out in which reforms were first anticipated. For example, the cumulation of benefices in the hands of the cardinals was to be prevented; a law was demanded, in virtue of which a pope whose life was stained with notorious vice, might be summarily deposed. But neither had the council authority enough to act upon ideas of this sort, nor was Maximilian the man to follow them out. He was of too weak a nature; and the same Wimpheling who drew up the statement of grievances, remarked to him how many former emperors had been deposed by an incensed pope leagued with the princes of the empire —certainly no motive to resolute perseverance in the course he had begun. Independent of this, every new turn in politics gave a fresh direction to his views on ecclesiastical affairs. After his reconciliation with Pope Julius II. in 1513, he demanded succours from the empire in order to take measures against the schism which was to be feared. Had there really been reason to fear it, he himself would have been mainly to blame for the encouragement he had given to the Council of Pisa.

It is sufficiently clear that this opposition to Rome had no real practical force. The want of a body in the state, armed with independent powers, crippled every attempt, every movement, at its very commencement. But, in the public mind, that opposition still remained in full force; loud complaints were incessantly heard.

Hemmerlin, whose books were in those times extensively circulated and eagerly read, exhausted the vocabulary for expressions to paint the cheating and plunder of which the court of Rome was guilty.

In the beginning of the sixteenth century there were the bitterest complaints of the ruinous nature of the Annates. It was probably in itself the most oppressive tax in the empire: occasionally a prelate in order to save his subjects from it, tried to mortgage some lordship of his see. Diether of Isenburg was deposed chiefly because he was unable to fulfil the engagements he had entered into concerning his Pallium. The more frequent the vacancies, the more intolerable was the exaction. In Passau, for example, these followed in 1482, 1486, 1490, 1500: the last-appointed bishop repaired to Rome in the hope of obtaining some alleviation of the burthens on his see; but he accomplished nothing, and his long residence at the papal court only increased his pecuniary difficulties. The cost of a pallium for Mainz amounted to 20,000 gulden; the sum was assessed on the several parts of the see: the Rheingau, for example, had to contribute 1000 gulden each time. In the beginning of the sixteenth century vacancies occurred three times in quick succession—1505, 1508, 1513; Jacob von Liebenstein said that his chief sorrow in dying was that his country would so soon again be forced to pay the dues; but all appeal to the papal court was fruitless; before the old tax was gathered in, the order for a new one was issued.

We may imagine what was the impression made by the comparison of the laborious negotiations usually necessary to extract even trifling grants from the diet, and the great difficulty with which they were collected, with the sums which flowed without toil or trouble to Rome. They were calculated at 300,000 gulden yearly, exclusive of the costs of law proceedings, or the revenues of benefices which lapsed to the court of Rome. And for what purpose, men asked themselves, was all this? Christendom had, nevertheless, lost two empires, fourteen kingdoms, and three hundred towns within a short space of time: it was continually losing to the Turks; if the German nation were to keep these sums in its own hands and expend them itself, it would meet its hereditary foe on other terms, under the banners of its valiant commanders.

The financial relations to Rome, generally, excited the greatest attention. It was calculated that the barefooted monks, who were not permitted by their rule to touch money, collected a yearly income of 200,000 gulden; the whole body of mendicant friars, a million.

Another evil was the recurrence of collisions between the temporal and spiritual jurisdictions, which gradually became the more frequent and obvious, the more the territorial sovereignties tended towards separation and political independence. In this respect Saxony was pre-eminent. In the different possessions of the two lines, not only the three Saxon bishops, but the archbishops of Mainz and Prag, the bishops of Würzburg and Bamberg, Halberstadt, Havelberg, Brandenburg and Lebus, had spiritual jurisdiction. The confusion which must, at all events, have arisen from this, was now enormously increased by the fact that all disputes between laity and clergy could only be decided before spiritual tribunals, so that high and low were continually vexed with excommunication. In the year 1454, we find Duke William complaining that the evil did not arise from his good lords and friends the bishops, but from the judges, officials, and procurators, who sought therein only their own profit. In concurrence with the counts, lords, and knights of his land, he issued certain ordinances to prevent this abuse, in support of which, privileges granted by the popes were alleged; but in 1490 the old complaints were revived, the administration of justice in the temporal courts was greatly obstructed and thwarted by the spiritual, and the people were impoverished by the consequent delays and expenses. In the year 1518, the princes of both lines, George and Frederick, combined to urge that the spiritual jurisdiction should be restricted to spiritual causes, and the temporal to temporal; the diet to decide what was temporal and what was spiritual. Duke George was still more zealous in the matter than his cousin. But the grievances and complaints which fill the proceedings of the later diets were universal, and confined to no class or portion of the empire.

The cities felt the exemptions enjoyed by the clergy peculiarly burthensome. It was impossible to devise any thing more annoying to a well-ordered civic community, than to have within their walls a corporate body which neither acknowledged the jurisdiction of the city, nor contributed to bear its burthens, nor deemed itself generally subject to its regulations. The churches were asylums for criminals, the monasteries the resort of dissolute youth; we find examples of monks who made use of their exemption from tolls, to import goods for sale, or to open a tavern for the sale of beer. If any attempt was made to assail their privileges, they defended themselves with excommunication and interdict. We find the municipal councils incessantly occupied in putting some check to this evil. In urgent cases they arrest offenders even in sanctuary, and then take measures to be delivered from the inevitable interdict by the interposition of some powerful protector; they are well inclined to pass over the bishops and to address themselves directly to the pope; they try to effect reforms in their monasteries. They thought it a very questionable arrangement that the parish priest should take part in the collection of the Common Penny; the utmost that they would concede was that he should be present, but without taking any active share. The cities always vehemently opposed the emperor's intention of appointing a bishop to be judge in the Imperial Chamber.

The general disapprobation excited by the church on such weighty points, naturally led to a discussion of its other abuses. Hemmerlin zealously contends against the incessant augmentation of ecclesiastical property, through which villages disappeared and districts became waste; against the exorbitant number of holidays, which even the council of Basle had endeavoured to reduce; against the celibacy of the clergy, to which the rules of the Eastern Church were much to be preferred; against the reckless manner in which ordination was granted, as, for example, that two hundred priests were yearly ordained in Constance: he asks to what all this is to lead.

Things had gone so far that the constitution of the clergy was offensive to public morals: a multitude of ceremonies and rules were attributed to the mere desire of making money; the situation of priests living in a state of concubinage and burthened with illegitimate children, and often, in spite of all purchased absolutions, tormented in conscience and oppressed with the fear that in performing the sacrifice of the mass they committed a deadly sin, excited mingled pity and contempt: most of those who embraced the monastic profession had no other idea than that of leading a life of self-indulgence without labour. People saw that the clergy took from every class and station only what was agreeable, and avoided what was laborious or painful. From the knightly order, the prelate borrowed his brilliant company, his numerous retinue, the splendidly caparisoned horse, and the hawk upon his fist: with women, he shared the love of gorgeous chambers and trim gardens; but the weight of the mailed coat, the troubles of the household, he had the dexterity to avoid. If a man wishes to enjoy himself for once, says an old proverb, let him kill a fat fowl; if for a year, let him take a wife; but if he would live joyously all the days of his life, then let him turn priest.

Innumerable expressions of the same sentiment were current; the pamphlets of that time are full of them.

Character and Tendencies of the Popular Literature

This state of the public mind acquired vast importance from its coincidence with the first drawings of a popular literature which thus, at its very commencement, became deeply and thoroughly imbued with the prevalent sentiment of disapprobation and disgust towards the clergy.

It will be conceded on all sides that in naming Rosenblüt and Sebastian Brant, the Eulenspiegel (Owlglass) and the edition of Reineke Fuchs (Reynard the Fox) of the year 1498, we cite the most remarkable productions of the literature of that time. And if we inquire what characteristic they have in common, we find it to be that of hostility to the Church of Rome. The Fastnachtspiele (Carnival Sports) of Hans Rosenblüt have fully and distinctly this character and intention; he introduces the Emperor of Turkey, in order through his mouth to say the truth to all classes of the nation. The vast success of the Eulenspiegel was not to be attributed so much to its clownish coarseness and practical jokes, as to the irony which was poured over all classes; the wit of the boor, "who scratches himself with a rogue's nails," put that of all others to shame. It was under this point of view alone that the German writer recast the fable of the fox; he saw in it the symbolic representation of the defects and vices of human society, and he quickly defected its application to the several classes of men, and laboured to develop the lesson which the poet reads to each. The same purpose is obvious to the first glance in Brant's Ship of Fools. The ridicule is not directed against individual follies: on the one side is vice, nay crime, on the other, lofty aspirations and pursuits which rise far above vulgar ends (as, for example, where the devotion of the whole mind to the task of describing cities and countries, the attempt to discover how broad is the earth, and how wide the sea) are treated as folly. Glory and beauty are despised as transient; "nothing is abiding but learning."

In this general opposition to the prevailing state of things, the defects in the ecclesiastical body are continually adverted to. The Schnepperer declaims violently against the priests, "who ride high horses, but will not do battle with the heathen." The most frequent subject of derision in the Eulenspiegel is the common priests, with their pretty ale-wives, well-groomed nags, and full larders; they are represented as stupid and greedy. In Reineke too the Papemeierschen—priests' households, peopled with little children—play a part. The commentator is evidently quite in earnest; he declares that the sins of the priests will be rated more highly than those of the laity on account of the evil example they set. Doctor Brant expresses his indignation at the premature admission into the convent, before the age of reason; so that religious duties are performed without the least sentiment of devotion: he leads us into the domestic life of the uncalled priests, who are at last in want of the means of subsistence, while their soul is heavy laden with sins; "for God regardeth not the sacrifice which is offered in sin by sinful hands."

This, however, is not the exclusive, nor, indeed, the principal matter of these books; their significance is far more extensive and general.

While the poets of Italy were employed in moulding the romantic materials furnished by the middle ages into grand and brilliant works, these excited little interest in Germany: Titurel and Parcival, for example, were printed, but merely as antiquarian curiosities, and in a language even then unintelligible.

While, in Italy, the opposition which the institutions of the middle ages encountered in the advancing development of the public mind, took the form of satire, became an element of composition, and as it were the inseparable but mocking companion of the poetical Ideal; in Germany that opposition took up independent ground, and directed its attacks immediately against the realities of life, not against their reproduction in fiction.

In the German literature of that period the whole existence and conduct of the several classes, ages and sexes were brought to the standard of the sober good sense, the homely morality, the simple rule of ordinary life; which, however, asserted its claim to be that "whereby kings hold their crowns, princes their lands, and all powers and authorities their due value."

The universal confusion and ferment which is visible in the public affairs of that period, proves by inevitable contrast, that the sound common sense of mankind is awakened and busy in the mass of the nation; and prosaic, homely, vulgar, but thoroughly true, as it is, constitutes itself judge of all the phenomena of the world around it.

We are filled with admiration at the spectacle afforded by Italy, where men of genius, reminded by the remains of antiquity around them of the significance of beautiful forms, strove to emulate their predecessors, and produced works which are the eternal delight of cultivated minds; but their beauty does not blind us to the fact that the movement of the national mind of Germany was not less great, and that it was still more important to the progress of mankind. After centuries of secret growth it now became aware of its own existence, broke loose from tradition, and examined the affairs and the institutions of the world by the light of its own truth.

Nor did Germany entirely disregard the demands of form. In Reinecke Fuchs, it is curious to observe how the author rejects every thing appropriate to the style of romantic poetry; how he seeks lighter transitions, works out scenes of common life to more complete and picturesque reality, and constantly strives to be more plain and vernacular (for example, uses all the familiar German names): his main object evidently is to popularise his matter,—to bring it as much as possible home to the nation; and his work has thus acquired the form in which it has attracted readers for more than three centuries. Sebastian Brant possesses an incomparable talent for turning apophthegms and proverbs; he finds the most appropriate expression for simple thoughts; his rhymes come unsought, and are singularly happy and harmonious. "Here," says Geiler von Keisersperg, "the agreeable and the useful are united; his verses are goblets of the purest wine; here we are presented with royal meats in finely wrought vessels." But in these, as well as in many other works of that time, the matter is the chief thing;—the expression of the opposition of the ordinary morality and working-day sense of mankind to the abuses in public life and the corruptions of the times.

At the same period another branch of literature,—the learned, took an analogous direction; perhaps with even greater force and decision.

Condition and Character of Learned Literature

Upon this department of letters Italy exercised the strongest influence.

In that country neither the metaphysics of the schools, nor romantic poetry, nor Gothic architecture, had obtained complete dominion: recollections of antiquity survived, and at length in the fifteenth century, expanded into that splendid revival which took captive all minds and imparted a new life to literature.

This reflorescence of Italy in time reacted on Germany, though at first only in regard to the mere external form of the Latin tongue.

In consequence of the uninterrupted intercourse with Italy occasioned by ecclesiastical relations, the Germans soon discovered the superiority of the Italians; they saw themselves despised by the disciples of the grammarians and rhetoricians of that country, and began to be ashamed of the rudeness of their spoken, and the poverty of their written language. It was not surprising, therefore, that young aspiring spirits at length determined to learn their Latin in Italy. At first they were only a few opulent nobles—a Dalberg, a Langen, a Spiegelberg, who not only acquired knowledge themselves, but had the merit of bringing back books, such as grammatical treatises and better editions of the classics, which they communicated to their friends. A man endowed with the peculiar talent necessary for appropriating to himself the classical learning of the age then arose—Rudolf Huesmann of Gröningen, called Agricola. His scholarship excited universal admiration; he was applauded in the schools as a Roman, a second Virgil. He had, indeed, no other object but his own advancement in learning; the weary pedantries of the schools were disgusting to him, nor could he accommodate himself to the contracted sphere assigned to a learned man in Germany. Other careers which he entered upon did not satisfy his aspirations, so that he fell into a rapid decline and died prematurely. He had, however, friends who found it less difficult to adapt themselves to the necessities of German life, and to whom he was ever ready to afford counsel and help. A noble and intimate friendship was formed in Deventer, between Agricola and Hegius, who attached himself to him with all the humility and thirst for knowledge of a disciple; he applied to him for instruction, and received not only assistance but cordial sympathy. Another of his friends, Dringenberg, followed him to Schletstadt. The reform which took place in the Low German schools of Münster, Hervord, Dortmund, and Hamm, emanated from Deventer, which also furnished them with competent teachers. In Nürnberg, Ulm, Augsburg, Frankfurt, Memmingen, Hagenau, Pforzheim, &c., we find schools of poetry of more or less note. Schletstadt at one time numbered as many as nine hundred students. It will not be imagined that these literati, who had to rule, and to instruct in the rudiments of learning, a rude undisciplined youth compelled to live mainly on alms, possessing no books, and wandering from town to town in strangely organized bands, called Bachantes and Schützen, were very eminent scholars themselves, or made such; nor was that the object: their merit, and a sufficient one, was that they not only kept the public mind steady to the important direction it had taken, but carried it onwards to the best of their ability, and founded the existence of an active literary public. The school-books hitherto in use gradually fell into neglect, and classical authors issued from the German press. As early as the end of the fifteenth century, Geiler of Keisersberg, who was not himself devoted to these pursuits, reproached the learned theologians with their Latin, which, he said, was rude, feeble, and barbarous—neither German nor Latin, but both and neither.

For since the school learning of the universities, which had hitherto entirely given the tone to elementary instruction, adhered to its wonted forms of expression, a collision between the new and humanistic method, now rapidly gaining ground, and the old modes, was inevitable. Nor could their collision fail to extend from the universal element of language into other regions.

It was this crisis in the history of letters that produced an author whose whole life was devoted to the task of attacking the scholastic forms prevailing in universities and monasteries; the first great author of the modern opposition, the champion of the modern views,—a low German, Erasmus of Rotterdam.

On a review of the first thirty years of the life of Erasmus, we find that he had grown up in ceaseless contradiction with the spirit and the systems which presided over the conventual life and directed the studies of that time;—indeed that this had made him what he was. We might say that he was begotten and born in this contradiction, for his parents had not been able to marry, because his father was destined to the cloister. He had not been admitted to a university, as he wished, but had been kept at a very imperfect conventual school, from which he soon ceased to derive any profit or satisfaction; and, at a later period, every art was practised to induce him to take the vows, and with success. It was not till he had actually taken them, that he felt all the burthen they imposed: he regarded it as a deliverance when he obtained a situation in a college at Paris: but here, too, he was not happy; he was compelled to attend Scotist lectures and disputations; and he complains that the unwholesome food and bad wine on which he was forced to live, had entirely destroyed his health. But in the meanwhile he had come to a consciousness of his own powers. While yet a boy, he had lighted upon the first trace of a new method of study, and he now followed it up with slender aid from without, but with the infallible instinct of genuine talent; he had constructed for himself a light, flowing style, formed on the model of the ancients, not by a servile imitation of particular expressions, but in native correctness and elegance far surpassing anything which Paris had to offer. He now emancipated himself from the fetters which bound him to the convent and the schools, and boldly trusted to the art of which he was master, for the means of subsistence. He taught, and in that way formed connections which not only led to present success, but to security for the future; he published some essays which, as they were not less remarkable for discreet choice of matter than for scholarly execution, gained him admirers and patrons; he gradually discovered the wants and the tastes of the public, and devoted himself entirely to literature. He composed schoolbooks treating of method and form of instruction; translated from the Greek, which he learned in the process; edited the classics of antiquity, and imitated them, especially Lucian and Terence. His works abound with marks of that acute and nice observation which at once instructs and delights; but great as these merits were, the grand secret of his popularity lay in the spirit which pervades all he wrote. The bitter hostility to the forms of the devotion and the theology of that time, which had been rendered his habitual frame of mind by the course and events of his life, found vent in his writings; not that this was the premeditated aim or purpose of them, but it broke forth sometimes in the very middle of a learned disquisition—in indirect and unexpected sallies of the most felicitous and exhaustless humour. In one of his works, he adopts the idea, rendered so popular by the fables of Brant and Geiler, of the element of folly which mingles in all human affairs. He introduces Folly herself as interlocutor. Moria, the daughter of Plutus, born in the Happy Islands, nursed by Drunkenness and Rudeness, is mistress of a powerful kingdom, which she describes and to which all classes of men belong. She passes them all in review, but dwells longer and more earnestly on none than on the clergy, who, though they refuse to acknowledge her benefits, are under the greatest obligations to her. She turns into ridicule the labyrinth of dialectic in which theologians have lost themselves,—the syllogisms with which they labour to sustain the church as Atlas does the heavens,—the intolerant zeal with which they persecute every difference of opinion. She then comes to the ignorance, the dirt, the strange and ludicrous pursuits of the monks, their barbarous and objurgatory style of preaching; she attacks the bishops, who are more solicitous for gold than for the safety of souls; who think they do enough if they dress themselves in theatrical costume, and under the name of the most reverend, most holy, and most blessed fathers in God, pronounce a blessing or a curse; and lastly, she boldly assails the court of Rome and the pope himself, who, she says, takes only the pleasures of his station, and leaves its duties to St. Peter and St. Paul. Amongst the curious woodcuts, after the marginal drawings of Hans Holbein, with which the book was adorned, the pope appears with his triple crown.

This little work brought together, with singular talent and brevity, matter which had for some time been current and popular in the world, gave it a form which satisfied all the demands of taste and criticism, and fell in with the most decided tendency of the age. It produced an indescribable effect: twenty-seven editions appeared even during the lifetime of Erasmus; it was translated into all languages, and greatly contributed to confirm the age in its anticlerical dispositions.

But Erasmus coupled with this popular warfare a more serious attack on the state of learning. The study of Greek had arisen in Italy in the fifteenth century; it had found its way by the side of that of Latin into Germany and France, and now opened a new and splendid vista, beyond the narrow horizon of the ecclesiastical learning of the West. Erasmus adopted the idea of the Italians,—that the sciences were to be learned from the ancients; geography from Strabo, natural history from Pliny, mythology from Ovid, medicine from Hippocrates, philosophy from Plato; and not out of the barbarous and imperfect school-books then in use: but he went a step further—he required that divinity should be learned not out of Scotus and Thomas Aquinas, but out of the Greek fathers, and, above all, the New Testament. Following in the track of Laurentius Valla, whose example had great influence generally on his mind, he showed that it was not safe to adhere to the Vulgate, wherein he pointed out a multitude of errors; and he then himself set about the great work,—the publication of the Greek text; which was as yet imperfectly and superficially known to the West. Thus he thought, as he expresses it, to bring back that cold word-contender, Theology, to her primal sources; he showed the simplicity of the origin whence that wondrous and complicated pile had sprung, and to which it must return. In all this he had the sympathy and assent of the public for which he wrote. The prudence wherewith he concealed from view an abyss in the distance, from which that public would have shrunk with alarm, doubtless contributed to his success. While pointing out abuses, he spoke only of reforms and improvements, which he represented as easy; and was cautious not to offend against certain opinions or principles to which the faith of the pious clung. But the main thing was his incomparable literary talent. He worked incessantly in various branches, and completed his works with great rapidity; he had not the patience to revise and polish them, and accordingly most of them were printed exactly as he threw them out; but this very circumstance rendered them universally acceptable; their great charm was that they communicated the trains of thought which passed through a rich, acute, witty, intrepid, and cultivated mind, just as they arose, and without any reservations. Who remarked the many errors which escaped him? His manner of narrating, which still rivets the attention, then carried every one away. He gradually became the most celebrated man in Europe; public opinion, whose pioneer he had been, adorned him with her fairest wreaths; presents rained upon his house at Basle; visitors flocked thither, and invitations poured in from all parts. His person was small, with light hair, blue, half-closed eyes, full of acute observation, and humour playing about the delicate mouth—his air was so timorous that he looked as if a breath would overthrow him, and he trembled at the very name of death.

If this single example sufficed to show how much the exclusive theology of the universities had to fear from the new tendency letters had acquired, it was evident that the danger would become measureless if the spirit of innovation should attempt to force its way into these fortresses of the established corporations of learning. The universities, therefore, defended themselves as well as they could. George Zingel, pro-chancellor of Ingolstadt, who had been dean of the theological faculty thirty times in three-and-thirty years, would hear nothing of the introduction of the study of heathen poets. Of the ancients, he would admit only Prudentius; of the moderns, the Carmelite Baptista of Mantua: these he thought were enough. Cologne, which had from the very beginning opposed the introduction of new elementary books, would not allow the adherents of the new opinions to settle in their town: Rhagius was banished for ten years by public proclamation; Murmellius, a pupil of Hegius, was compelled to give way and to become teacher in a school; Conrad Celtes of Leipzig was driven away almost by force; Hermann von dem Busch could not maintain his ground either in Leipzig or Rostock; his new edition of Donatus was regarded almost as a heresy. This was not, however, universal. According to the constitution of the universities, every man had, at least after taking his degree as Master of Arts, a right to teach, and it was not every one who afforded a reason or a pretext for getting rid of him. In some places, too, the princes had reserved to themselves the right of appointing teachers. In one way or another, teachers of grammar and of classical literature did, as we find, establish themselves; in Tübingen, Heinrich Bebel, who formed a numerous school; in Ingolstadt, Locher, who, after much molestation, succeeded in keeping his ground, and left a brilliant catalogue of princes, prelates, counts, and barons, who had been his pupils; Conrad Celtes in Vienna, where he actually succeeded in establishing a faculty of poetry in the year 1501; and in Prague, Hieronymo Balbi, an Italian, who gave instructions to the young princes, and took some share in public affairs. In Freiburg the new studies were connected with the Roman law; Ulrich Zasius united the two professorships in his own person with the most brilliant success; Pietro Tommai of Ravenna, and his son Vincenzo, were invited to Greifswald, and afterwards to Wittenberg in the same double capacity: it was hoped that the combined study of antiquity and law would raise that university. Erfurt felt the influence of Conrad Muth, who enjoyed his canonry at Gotha "in blessed tranquillity" *("in glückseliger Ruhe")* as the inscription on his house says: he was the Gleim of that age—the hospitable patron of young men of poetical temperament and pursuits. Thus, from the time the new spirit and method found their way into the lower schools, societies of grammarians and poets were gradually formed in most of the universities, completely opposed to the spirit of those establishments as handed down from their fountain-head, Paris. They read the ancients, and perhaps allowed something of the petulance of Martial, or the voluptuousness of Ovid, to find its way into their lives; they made Latin verses, which, stiff and barbarous as they generally were, called forth an interchange of admiration; they corresponded in Latin, and took care to interlard it with a few sentences of Greek; they Latinised and Græcised their names. Genuine talent or accomplished scholarship were very rare; but the life and power of a generation does not manifest itself in mere tastes and acquirements: for a few individuals these may be enough, but, for the many the tendency is the important thing. The character of the universities soon altered. The scholars were no longer to be seen with their books under their arms, walking decorously after their Magister; the scholarships were broken up, degrees were no longer sought after—that of bachelor especially (which was unfrequent in Italy) was despised. On some occasions the champions of classical studies appeared as the promoters of the disorders of the students; and ridicule of the dialectic theologians, nominalists as well as realists, was hailed with delight by the young men.

The world, and especially the learned world, must be other than it is for such a change to be effected without a violent struggle.

The manner, however, in which this broke out is remarkable. It was not the necessity of warding off a dangerous attack or a declared enemy that furnished the occasion: this was reserved for the most peaceful of the converts to the new system, who had already fulfilled the active task of life, and at that moment devoted himself to more abstruse studies,—John Reuchlin.

Reuchlin, probably the son of a messenger at Pforzheim, was indebted to his personal gifts for the success which attended him in his career. A fine voice procured him admittance to the court of Baden; his beautiful handwriting maintained him during his residence in France; the pure pronunciation of Latin which he had acquired by intercourse with foreigners, caused him to be appointed member of an embassy to Rome, and this led to an important post and considerable influence at the court of Würtemberg, and with the Swabian league generally. His qualities, both external and internal, were very unlike those of Erasmus. He was tall and well made, and dignified in all his deportment and actions, while the mildness and serenity of his appearance and manner won instant confidence towards his intellectual superiority. As an author, he could never have gained the applause of the large public of Latin scholars; his style is not above mediocrity, nor does he evince any nice sense of elegance and form. On the other hand, he was inspired by a thirst for learning, and a zeal for communicating, which were without a parallel. He describes how he picked up his knowledge bit by bit,—crumbs that fell from the lord's table—at Paris and in the Vatican, at Florence, Milan, Basle, and at the Imperial Court; how, like the bird of Apollonius, he left the corn for the other birds to eat. He facilitated the study of Latin by a dictionary, which in great measure supplanted the old scholastic ones, and of Greek, by a small grammar; he spared neither labour nor money to get copies of the classics brought across the Alps, either in manuscript, or as they issued from the Italian press. What no prince, no wealthy city or community thought of doing, was done by the son of a poor errand man; it was under his roof that the most wondrous production of distant ages—the Homeric poems—first came in contact with the mind of Germany, which was destined in later times to render them more intelligible to the world. His Hebrew learning was still more highly esteemed by his contemporaries than all his other acquirements, and he himself regarded his labours in that field as his most peculiar claim to distinction. "There has been none before me," exclaims he with well-grounded self-gratulation, to one of his adversaries, "who has been able to collect the rules of the Hebrew language into a book, though his heart should burst with envy, still I am the first. Exegi monumentum ære perennius." In this work he was chiefly indebted to the Jewish Rabbis whom he sought out in all directions, not suffering one to pass by without learning something from him: by them he was led to study not only the Old Testament, but other Hebrew books, and especially the Cabbala. Reuchlin's mind was not one of those to which the labours of a mere grammarian or lexicographer are sufficient for their own sake. After the fashion of his Jewish teachers, he applied himself to the study of the mystical value of words. In the name of the Deity as written in the Holy Scriptures, in its elementary composition, he discovers the deepest mystery of his being. For, he says, "God, who delights in intercourse with a holy soul, will transform it into himself, and will dwell in it: God is Spirit; the Word is a breath; Man breathes; God is the Word. The names which He has given to Himself are an echo of eternity; in them is the deep abyss of his mysterious working expressed; the God-Man called himself the Word." Thus, at its very outset, the study of language in Germany was directed towards its final end and aim—the knowledge of the mysterious connection of language with the Divine—of its identity with the spirit. Reuchlin is like his contemporaries, the discoverers of the New World, who sailed some north, some south, some right on to the west, found portions of coast which they described, and while at the beginning, often thought they had reached the end. Reuchlin was persuaded that he should find in the road he had taken, not only the Aristotelic and Platonic philosophies, which had already been brought to light, but that he should add to them the Pythagorean,—an offspring of Hebraism. He believed that by treading in the footsteps of the Cabbala, he should ascend from symbol to symbol, from form to form, till he should reach that last and purest form which rules the empire of mind, and in which human mutability approaches to the Immutable and Divine.

But while living in this world of ideas and abstractions, it was his lot to be singled out by the enmity of the scholastic party: he unexpectedly found himself involved in the heat of a violent controversy.

We have already alluded to the inquisitorial attempts of the Dominicans of Cologne, and their hostility to the Jews. In the year 1508, a book was published by an old Rabbi, who at the age of fifty had abandoned his wife and child, and become a Christian priest. In this he accused his former co-religionists of the grossest errors; for example, adoration of the sun and moon; but, above all, of the most horrible blasphemies against the Christian faith, which he endeavoured to prove from the Talmud. It was mainly on this ground that the theologians of Cologne urged the emperor to order the publication of the Talmud, and gave him, at his request, the opinion in which they affirmed his right to proceed against the Jews as heretics. The Imperial Council, however, deemed it expedient to consult another master of Hebrew literature. They referred the matter to the reviver of the cabbalistic philosophy—Reuchlin.

Reuchlin gave his opinion, as might be expected, in favour of the

Judaical books. His report is a beautiful monument of pure dispassionate judgment and consummate sagacity. But these qualities were just those fitted to draw down the whole storm of fanatical rage upon himself.

The Cologne theologians, irritated to fury by the rejection of their proposition, which they ascribed, not without reason, to the adverse opinion of Reuchlin, incited one of their satellites to attack him; he answered; they condemned his answer; he rejoined, upon which they appointed a court of inquisition to try him.

This was the first serious encounter of the two parties. The Dominicans hoped to establish their tottering credit by a great stroke of authority, and to intimidate the adversaries who threatened to become dangerous to them, by the terrors which were at their disposal. The innovators—the teachers and disciples of the schools of poetry whom we have mentioned—were fully sensible that Reuchlin's peril was their own; but their efforts and aspirations were checked by the consciousness of opposition to existing authority, and of the dubious position which they occupied.

In October, 1513, a court of inquisition was formed at Mainz, composed of the doctors of the university and the officers of the archbishopric, under the presidency of the inquisitor of heretical wickedness—Jacob Hogstraten; and it remained to be seen whether such a sentence as that pronounced some years before against John of Wesalia, would now be given.

But times were totally altered. That intensely Catholic spirit which had rendered it so easy for the Inquisition to take root in Spain, was very far from reigning in Germany. The Imperial Council must have been, from the outset, indisposed towards the demands of the Cologne divines, or they would not have appealed to such a man as Reuchlin for advice. The infection of the prevalent spirit of literature had already spread too widely, and had created a sort of public opinion. We have a whole list of members of the higher clergy who are cited as friends of the literary innovation—Gross and Wrisberg, canons of Augsburg, Nuenar of Cologne, Adelmann of Eichstadt, Andreas Fuchs, dean of Bamberg, Lorenzo Truchsess of Mainz, Wolfgang Tanberg of Passau, Jacob de Bannissis of Trent. Cardinal Lang, the most influential of the emperor's councillors, shared these opinions. The superior clergy were not more disposed than the people to allow the Inquisition to regain its power.

Elector Diether had consented to the trial of Wesalia, against his will, and only because he feared the puissant Dominicans might a second time effect his deposition; now, however, the heads of the church were no longer so timorous, and after the tribunal had already taken its seat to pronounce judgment, Dean Lorenz Truchsess persuaded the Elector to command it to suspend its proceedings, and to forbid his own officers to take part in them.

Nay, another tribunal, favourable to Reuchlin, was appointed to hold its sittings under the Bishop of Spires, in virtue of a commission obtained from Rome; the sentence pronounced by this court on the 24th April, 1514, was, that the accusers of Reuchlin, having falsely calumniated him, were condemned to eternal silence and to the payment of the costs.

So widely diffused and so powerful was the antipathy which the Dominicans had excited. So lively was the sympathy which the higher and educated classes testified in the efforts of the new school of literature. So powerful already was the opinion of men of learning. It was their first victory.

Persecuting orthodoxy found no favour either with the emperor or with the higher clergy of Germany. But its advocates did not give up the contest. At Cologne, Reuchlin's books were condemned to be burnt: unanimous sentences to the same effect were obtained from the faculties of Erfurt, Mainz, Louvain, and Paris; thus fortified, they applied to the supreme tribunal at Rome; the representatives of orthodox theology presented themselves before the pope, and urged him to give his infallible decision in aid of the ancient champions of the Holy See against innovators.

But even Rome was perplexed. Should she offend public opinion represented by men so influential from their talents and learning? Should she act in opposition to her own opinions? On the other hand, would it be safe to set at nought the judgment of powerful universities? to break with the order which had so zealously contended for the prerogatives of the Roman see, and had preached the doctrine and furthered the sale of indulgences all over the world?

In the commission appointed by the pope at Rome, the majority was for Reuchlin, but a considerable minority was against him, and the pope held it expedient to defer his decision. He issued a *mandatum de supersedendo.*

Reuchlin, conscious of a just cause, was not perfectly satisfied with this result, especially after all that had gone before: he expected a formal and complete acquittal; nevertheless, even this was to be regarded as little less than a victory. The fact that the party which assumed to represent religion and to have exclusive possession of the true doctrines, had failed to carry through their inquisitorial designs, and even, as secret reports said, had only escaped a sentence of condemnation by means of gold and favour was enough to encourage all their adversaries. Hitherto the latter had only stood on the defensive; they now assumed an attitude of open, direct offence. Reuchlin's correspondence, which was published expressly to show the respect and admiration he enjoyed, shows how numerously and zealously they rallied round him. We find the spiritual lords we have mentioned; patricians of the most important cities, such as Pirkheimer of Nürnberg, who delighted in being considered as the leader of a numerous band of Reuchlinists; Peutinger of Augsburg, Stuss of Cologne; preachers like Capito and Œcolampadius; the Austrian historians, Lazius and Cuspinian; doctors of medicine—all, in short, who had any tincture of letters; but chiefly those poets and orators in the schools and universities who beheld their own cause in that of Reuchlin, and now rushed in throngs to the newly-opened arena; at their head Busch, Jäger, Hess, Hutten, and a long list of eminent names.

The remarkable production in which the whole character and drift of their labours is summed up, is, the Epistolæ Obscurorum Virorum. That popular satire, already so rife in Germany, but hitherto confined to generals, here found a particular subject exactly suited to it. We must not look for the delicate apprehension and tact which can only be formed in a highly polished state of society, nor for the indignation of insulted morality expressed by the ancients: it is altogether caricature,—not of finished individual portraits, but of a single type;—a clownish, sensual German priest, his intellect narrowed by stupid wonder and fanatical hatred, who relates with silly *naïveté* and gossiping confidence the various absurd and scandalous situations into which he falls. These letters are not the work of a high poetical genius, but they have truth, coarse strong features of resemblance, and vivid colouring. As they originated in a widely-diffused and powerful tendency of the public mind, they produced an immense effect: the See of Rome deemed it necessary to prohibit them.

It may be affirmed generally that the genius of the literary opposition was triumphant. In the year 1518, Erasmus looked joyfully around him; his disciples and adherents had risen to eminence in every university—even in Leipsig, which had so long resisted: they were all teachers of ancient literature.

Was it indeed possible that the great men of antiquity should have lived in vain? That their works, produced in the youth-time of the human race, —works with whose beauty and profound wisdom nothing that has since arisen is to be compared, should not be restored to later ages in their primitive form and perfection? It is an event of the greatest historical importance, that after so many convulsions by which nations were overthrown and others constituted out of their ruins,—by which the old world had been obliterated and all its elements replaced by other matter,—the relics of its spirit, which could now exercise no other influence than that of form, were sought with an avidity hitherto unknown, and widely diffused, studied, and imitated.

The study of antiquity was implanted in Germany as early as the first introduction of Christianity; in the 10th and 11th centuries it had risen to a considerable height, but at a later period it was stifled by the despotism of the hierarchy and the schools. The latter now returned to their original vocation. It was not to be expected, that great works of literary art could as yet be produced; for that, circumstances were not ripe. The first effect of the new studies showed itself in the nature and modes of instruction—the more natural and rational training of the youthful mind which has continued to be the basis of German erudition. The hierarchical system of opinions which, though it had been wrought up to a high point of brilliancy and refinement, could not possibly endure, was thus completely broken up. A new life stirred in every department of human intelligence. "What an age!" exclaims Hutten, "learning flourishes, the minds of men awake; it is a joy to be alive." This was peculiarly conspicuous in the domain of theology. The highest ecclesiastic of the nation, Archbishop Albert of Mainz, saluted Erasmus as the restorer of theology.

But an intellectual movement of a totally different kind was now about to take place.

Early Career of Luther

The authorities, or the opinions which rule the world, rarely encounter their most dangerous enemies from without; the hostilities by which they are overthrown are usually generated and nurtured within their own sphere.

In the bosom of theological philosophy itself, discords arose from which a new era in the history of life and thought may be dated.

We must not omit to notice the fact, that the doctrines of Wickliffe, which had spread from Oxford over the whole of Latin Christendom, and broke out with such menacing demonstrations in Bohemia, had not, in spite of all the barbarities of the Hussite wars, been extirpated in Germany. At a much later period we find traces of them in Bavaria, where the Böklerbund drew upon itself the suspicions of Hussite opinions; in Swabia and Franconia, where the council of Bamberg at one time thought it necessary to compel all the men in that city to abjure the Hussites; and even in Prussia, where the adherents of Wickliffite and Hussite doctrines at length submitted, though only in appearance. It was the more remarkable that after such measures, the society of the Bohemian brethren arose out of the fierce tempest of Hussite opinions and parties, and once more exhibited to the world a Christian community in all the purity and simplicity of the primitive church. Their religion derived a new and singular character from the fundamental principle of their secession—that Christ himself was the rock on which the church was founded, and not Peter and his successors. Their settlements were in those districts where the Germanic and Slavonic elements are intermingled, and their emissaries went forth and traversed unnoticed the wide domain of either language, seeking those already allied to them in opinion, or endeavouring to gain over new proselytes. Nicholas Kuss of Rostock, whom they visited several times, began at this time to preach openly against the pope (A.D. 1511.).

The opposition to the despotism of the Dominican system still subsisted in the universities themselves. Nominalism, connected at the very moment of its revival with the adversaries of the papacy, had found great acceptance in Germany, and was still by no means suppressed. The most celebrated nominalist of that time, Gabriel Biel, the collector, is mainly an epitomizer of Occam. This party was in the minority, and often exposed to the persecutions of its enemies who wielded the powers of the Inquisition; but it only struck deeper and firmer root. Luther and Melanchthon are the offspring of nominalism.

And perhaps a still more important circumstance was, that in the 15th century the stricter Augustinian doctrines were revived in the persons of some theologians.

Johann de Wesalia taught election by grace; he speaks of the Book in which the names of the elect are written from the beginning. The tendency of his opinions is shown by the definition of the Sacrament which he opposes to that given by Peter Lombard: the former is that of St. Augustine in its original purity, while the latter is an extension of it; the general aim of his works is, the removal of the additions made in later times to the primitive doctrines of the church. He denies the binding force of priestly rules, and the efficacy of indulgences; he is filled with the idea of the invisible church. He was a man of great intellectual powers, capable of playing a distinguished part at a university like that of Erfurt: he arrived at these convictions by degrees, and when convinced did not conceal them even in the pulpit; nor did he shrink from a connexion with Bohemian emissaries. At length, however, when advanced in age, he was dragged, leaning on his staff, before the Inquisition, and thrown into prison, where he died.

Johann Pupper of Goch, who founded a convent of nuns of the rule of St. Augustine at Mechlin about the year 1460–70, made himself remarkable by accusing the dominant party in the church of a leaning to Pelagianism. He calls Thomas Aquinas the prince of error. He attacked the devotion to ceremonies, and the Pharisaism of vows, upon Augustinian principles.

How often have the antagonists of the church of Rome made this the ground of their opposition!—from Claudius of Turin in the beginning of the ninth, to Bishop Janse in the seventeenth century, and his followers in the 18th and 19th. The deeper minds within her pale have always felt compelled to point back to those fundamental doctrines on which she was originally based.

The principles of the opposition now assumed the form of a scientific structure. In the works of Johann Wessel, of Gröningen, we see a manly mind devoted to truth, working itself free from the bonds of the mighty tradition which could no longer satisfy a religious conscience. Wessel lays down the maxim that prelates and doctors are to be believed only so far as their doctrines are in conformity with the Scriptures, the sole rule of faith, which is far above pope or church; he writes almost in the spirit of a theologian of later times. It was perfectly intelligible that he was not permitted to set foot in the university of Heidelberg.

Nor were these efforts completely isolated.

At the time of the council of Basle, the German provincial society of the Augustin Eremites had formed themselves into a separate congregation, and had from that moment made it their chief endeavour to uphold the more rigorous doctrines of the patron of their order. This was peculiarly the aim of the resolute and undaunted Andreas Proles, who for nearly half a century administered the Vicariate of that province. Another and a congenial tendency came in aid of this in the beginning of the 16th century. The despotism of the schools had been constantly opposed by all those who were inclined to mystical contemplation: the sermons of Tauler, which had several times issued from the press, became extremely popular from their mild earnestness, their depth of thought and reason, and the tone of sincerity so satisfactory to the German mind and heart. The Book of German Theology, which appeared at that time, may be regarded as an offspring of Tauler's teaching. It chiefly insisted on the inability of the creature, of himself to comprehend the Infinite and the Perfect, to attain to inward peace, or to give himself up to that Eternal Good, which descends upon him of its own free motion. Johann Staupitz, the successor of Proles, adopted these ideas, and laboured to develop and to diffuse them. If we examine his views of the subject,—as for example, the manner in which he treats of the love "which a man can neither learn of himself nor from others, nor even from the Holy Scriptures,—which he can only possess through the indwelling of the Holy Spirit,"—we are struck with their perfect connexion and accordance with the stricter ideas of grace, faith, and free-will; a connexion, indeed, without which these doctrines would not have been intelligible to the age. We must not assume that all Augustine convents, or even all the members of the one in question, were converted to these opinions; but it is certain that they first struck root among this order, whence they spread abroad and tended to foster the resistance to the prevailing doctrines of the schools.

It is manifest that all these agitations of opinion, from whatever source they proceeded, were allies of the literary opposition to the tyranny of the Dominican system. The fact that these various but converging tendencies at length found representatives within the circle of one university, must be regarded as in itself an important event for the whole nation.

In the year 1502, Elector Frederick of Saxony founded a new university at Wittenberg. He accomplished this object chiefly by obtaining the pope's consent to incorporate a number of parishes with the richly endowed church attached to the palace, and transforming the whole into a foundation, the revenues of which he then allotted to the new professors. The same course had been pursued in Treves and in Tübingen; the clerical dignities of the institution were connected with the offices in the university. The provost, dean, scholaster, and syndic formed the faculty of law; the archdeacon, cantor, and warden, that of theology; the lectures on philosophy and the exercises of the candidates for the degree of master of arts were attached to five canonries. The eminent Augustine convent in the town was to take part in the work.

We must recollect that the universities were then regarded not only as establishments for education, but as supreme tribunals for the decision of scientific questions. In the charter of Wittenberg, Frederick declares that he, as well as all the neighbouring states, would repair thither as to an oracle; "so that," says he, "when we have come full of doubt, we may, after receiving the sentence, depart in certainty."

Two men, both unquestionably belonging to the party hostile to the reigning theologico-philosophical system, had the greatest influence on the foundation and first organisation of this university. The one was Dr. Martin Pollich of Melrichstadt, physician to the elector, whose name stands at the head of the list of the rectors of the Leipzig university, where he was previously established. We know that he had contended against the fantastic exaggerations of scholastic learning, and the strange assertions to which they gave birth; such as that the light created on the first day was theology; that discursive theology was inherent in the angels. We know that he had already perceived the necessity of grounding that science on a study of letters generally.

The other was Johann Staupitz, the mystical cast of whose opinions, borrowed from St. Augustine, we have just mentioned; he was the first dean of the theological faculty, the first act of which was, the promotion of Martin Pollich to be doctor of theology: as director of the Augustine convent, he likewise enjoyed peculiar influence. It was not an insignificant circumstance that the university had just then declared St. Augustine its patron. Notwithstanding his strong tendency to speculation, Staupitz was obviously an excellent man of business; he conducted himself with address at court, and a homely vein of wit which he possessed, enabled him to make his part good with the prince; he undertook an embassy, and conducted the negotiation with success; but the deeper spring of all his conduct and actions is clearly a genuine feeling of true and heartfelt religion, and an expansive benevolence.

It is easy to imagine in what spirit these men laboured at the university. But a new star soon arose upon it. In the year 1508, Staupitz conducted thither the young Luther.

We must pause a moment to consider the early years of this remarkable man.

"I am a peasant's son," says he; "my father, grandfather, and ancestors were genuine peasants; afterwards, my father removed to Mansfeld, and became a miner; that is my native place." Luther's family was from Möhra, a village on the very summit of the Thuringian forest, not far from the spot celebrated for the first preaching of Christianity by Boniface; it is probable that Luther's forefathers had for centuries been settled on their hide of land *(Hufe)* as was the custom with those Thuringian peasants, one brother among whom always inherited the estate, while the others sought a subsistence in other ways. Condemned by such a destiny to seek a home and hearth for himself, Hans Luther was led to the mines at Mansfeld, where he earned his bread by the sweat of his brow, while his wife, Margaret, often fetched wood from the forest on her back. Such were the parents of Martin Luther. He was born at Eisleben, whither his sturdy mother had walked to the yearly fair; he grew up in the mountain air of Mansfeld.

The habits and manners of that time were generally harsh and rude, and so was his education. Luther relates that his mother once scourged him till the blood came, on account of one miserable nut; that his father had punished him so severely that it was with great difficulty that he could get over the child's terror and alienation; at school he was flogged fifteen times in one forenoon. He had to earn his bread by singing hymns before the doors of houses, and new year's carols in the villages. Strange —that people should continually exalt and envy the happiness of childhood, in which the only certain foretaste of coming years is the feeling of the stern necessities of life; in which existence is dependent on foreign help, and the will of another disposes of every day and hour with iron sway. In Luther's case, this period of life was full of terrors.

From his fifteenth year his condition was somewhat better. In Eisenach, where he was sent to the high school, he found a home in the house of some relations of his mother; thence he went to the university of Erfurt, where his father, whose industry, frugality and success had placed him in easier circumstances, made him a liberal allowance: his hope was, that his son would be a lawyer, marry well and do him honour.

But in this weary life the restraints of childhood are soon succeeded by troubles and perplexities. The spirit feels itself freed from the bonds of the school and is not yet distracted by the wants and cares of daily life; it boldly turns to the highest problems, such as the relation of man to God, and of God to the world, and while eagerly rushing on to the solution of them, it falls into the most distressing state of doubt. We might be almost tempted to think that the Eternal Source of all life appeared to the youthful Luther only in the light of the inexorable judge and avenger, who punishes sin (of which Luther had from nature an awful and vivid feeling) with the torments of hell, and can only be propitiated by penance, mortification and painful service. As he was returning from his father's house in Mansfeld to Erfurt, in the month of July, 1505, he was overtaken in a field near Stotternheim by one of those fearful tempests which slowly gather on the mountains and at length suddenly burst over the whole horizon. Luther was already depressed by the unexpected death of an intimate friend. There are moments in which the agitated desponding heart is completely crushed by one overwhelming incident, even of the natural world. Luther, traversing his solitary path, saw in the tempest the God of wrath and vengeance; the lightning struck some object near him; in his terror he made a vow to St. Anne, that if he escaped, he would enter a convent. He passed one more evening with his friends, enjoying the pleasures of wine, music, and song; it was the last in which he indulged himself; he hastened to fulfil his vow, and entered the Augustine Convent at Erfurt.

But he was little likely to find serenity there; imprisoned, in all the buoyant energy of youth, within the narrow gates and in the low and gloomy cell, with no prospect but a few feet of garden within the cloisters, and condemned to perform the lowest offices. At first he devoted himself to the duties of a novice with all the ardour of a determined will. "If ever a monk got to heaven by monkish life and practices [*durch Möncherei*], I resolved that I would enter there," were his words. But though he conformed to the hard duty of obedience, he was soon a prey to the most painful disquiet. Sometimes he studied day and night, to the neglect of his canonical hours, which he then passed his nights in retrieving with penitent zeal. Sometimes he went out into some neighbouring village, carrying with him his mid-day repast, preached to the shepherds and ploughmen, and then refreshed himself with their rustic music; after which he went home, and shutting himself up for days in his cell, would see no one. All his former doubts and secret perplexities returned from time to time with redoubled force.

In the course of his study of the Scriptures, he fell upon texts which struck terror into his soul; one of these was, "Save me in thy righteousness and thy truth." "I thought," said he, "that righteousness was the fierce wrath of God, wherewith he punishes sinners." Certain passages in the Epistles of St. Paul haunted him for days. The doctrine of grace was not indeed unknown to him, but the dogma that sin was at once taken away by it, produced upon him, who was but too conscious of his sins, rather a sense of rejection—a feeling of deep depression, than of hope. He says it made his heart bleed—it made him despair of God. "Oh, my sins, my sins, my sins!" he writes to Staupitz, who was not a little astonished when he received the confession of so sorrowful a penitent, and found that he had no sinful acts to acknowledge. His anguish was the longing of the creature after the purity of the Creator, to whom it feels itself profoundly and intimately allied, yet from whom it is severed by an immeasurable gulph: a feeling which Luther nourished by incessant solitary brooding, and which had taken the more painful and complete possession of him because no penance had power to appease it; no doctrine truly touched it, no confessor would hear of it. There were moments when this anxious melancholy arose with fearful might from the mysterious abysses of his soul, waved its dusky pinions over his head, and felled him to the earth. On one occasion when he had been invisible for several days, some friends broke into his cell and found him lying senseless on the ground. They knew their friend; with tender precaution they struck some chords on a stringed instrument they had brought with them; the inward strife of the perplexed spirit was allayed by the well-known remedy; it was restored to harmony and awakened to healthful consciousness.

But the eternal laws of the universe seem to require that so deep and earnest a longing of the soul after God should at length be appeased with the fulness of conviction.

The first who, if he could not administer comfort to Luther in his desperate condition, at least, let fall a ray of light upon his thick darkness, was an old Augustine friar who with fatherly admonitions pointed his attention to the first and simplest truth of Christianity,—the forgiveness of sins through faith in the Redeemer; and to the assertion of St. Paul (Rom. iii.), that man is justified without works, by faith alone: doctrines which he might indeed have heard before, but obscured as they were by school subtleties, and a ceremonial worship, he had never rightly understood. They now first made a full and profound impression on him. He meditated especially on the saying "The just shall live by faith." He read St. Augustine's commentary on this passage. "Then was I glad," says he, "for I learned and saw that God's righteousness is his mercy, by which he accounts and holds us justified; thus I reconciled justice with justification, and felt assured that I was in the true faith." This was exactly the conviction of which his mind stood in need: it was manifest to him that the same eternal grace whence the whole race of man is sprung, mercifully brings back erring souls to itself and enlightens them with the fulness of its own light; that an example and irrefragable assurance of this is given us in the person of Christ: he gradually emerged from the gloomy idea of a divine justice only to be propitiated by the rigours of penance. He was like a man who after long wanderings has at length found the right path, and feeling more certain of it at every step, walks boldly and hopefully onward.

Such was Luther's state when he was removed to Wittenberg by his provincial (A.D. 1508). The philosophical lectures which he was obliged to deliver, sharpened his desire to penetrate the mysteries of theology, "the kernel of the nut," as he calls it, "the heart of the wheat." The books, which he studied were St. Paul's Epistles, St. Augustine against the Pelagians, and, lastly, Tauler's sermons: he troubled himself little with literature foreign to this subject; he cared only to strengthen and work out the convictions he had gained.

A few years later we find him in the most extraordinary frame of mind, during a journey which he took for the affairs of his order to Rome. As soon as he descried the towers of the city from a distance, he threw himself on the ground, raised his hands and exclaimed, "Hail to thee, O holy Rome!" On his arrival, there was no exercise in use among the most pious pilgrims which he did not perform with earnest and deliberate devotion, undeterred by the levity of other priests; he said he was almost tempted to wish that his parents were dead, that so he might have been able certainly to deliver them from the fire of purgatory by these privileged observances. Yet, at the same time, he felt how little such practices were in accordance with the consolatory doctrine which he had found in the Epistle to the Romans and in St. Augustine. While climbing the Scala Santa on his knees in order to obtain the plenary indulgence attached to that painful and laborious work of piety, he heard a reproving voice continually crying within him, "The just shall live by faith."

After his return in 1512, he became Doctor of the Holy Scripture, and from year to year enlarged his sphere of activity. He lectured at the university on both the Old and New Testament; he preached at the Augustine church, and performed the duties of the priest of the parochial church of the town during his illness; in 1516, Staupitz appointed him administrator of the order during his absence on a journey and we trace him visiting all the monasteries in the province, appointing or displacing priors, receiving or removing monks. While labouring to introduce a profounder spirit of piety, he did not overlook the smallest economical details; and besides all this, he had to manage his own crowded and extremely poor convent. Some things, written in the years 1515 and 1516, enable us to understand the state and workings of his mind during that period. Mystical and scholastic ideas had still great influence over him. In the first words of his on religious subjects in the German language which we possess,—a sketch of a sermon dated November, 1515,—he applies, in somewhat coarse terms, the symbolical language of the Song of Songs to the operations of the Holy Ghost, which acts on the spirit through the flesh; and also to the inward harmony of the Holy Scriptures. In another, dated December of the same year, he endeavours to explain the mystery of the Trinity by the Aristotelic theory of being, motion, and rest. Meanwhile his thoughts were already turned to a grand and general reform of the church. In a speech which appears to have been intended to be uttered by the provost of Lietzkau at the Lateran council, he sets forth that the corruption of the world was to be ascribed to the priests, who delivered to the people too many maxims and fables of human invention, and not the pure word of God. For, he said, the word of life alone is able to work out the regeneration of man. It is well worthy of remark, that, even then, Luther looked for the salvation of the world far less to an amendment of life, which was only secondary in his eyes, than to a revival of the true doctrines: and there was none with the importance of which he was so penetrated and filled as with that of justification by faith. He continually insists on the absolute necessity of a man denying himself, and fleeing for refuge under the wings of Christ; he seizes every opportunity of repeating the saying of St. Augustine, that faith obtains what the law enjoins. We see that Luther was not yet completely at one with himself; that he still cherished opinions fundamentally at variance with each other; but all his writings breathe a powerful mind, a youthful courage, still restrained within the bounds of modesty and reverence for authority, though ready to overleap them; a genius intent on essentials, tearing asunder the bonds of system, and pressing forward in the new path it has discovered. In the year 1516, we find Luther busily occupied in defending and establishing his doctrine of justification. He was greatly encouraged by the discovery of the spuriousness of a book attributed to Augustine, on which the schoolmen had founded many doctrines extremely offensive to him, and which was quoted almost entire in Lombard's book, "De vera et falsa Penitentia"; and he now took heart to attack the doctrine of the Scotists on love, and that of the Magister Sententiarum on hope; he was already convinced that there was no such thing as a work in and for itself pleasing to God—such as prayer, fasts and vigils; for as their whole efficacy depended on their being done in the fear of God, it followed that every other act or occupation was just as good in itself.

In opposition to some expressions of German theologians which appeared to him of a Pelagian tendency, he embraced with uncompromising firmness even the severer views of Augustine: one of his disciples held a solemn disputation in defence of the doctrine of the subjection of the will, and of the inability of man to fit himself for grace, much more to obtain it, by his own powers.

If it be asked wherein he discovered the mediating power between divine perfection and human sinfulness, we find that it was solely in the mystery of the redemption, and the revealed word; mercy on the one side, and faith on the other. These opinions led him to doubt of many of the main dogmas of the church. He did not yet deny the efficacy of absolution; but no later than the year 1516, he was perplexed by the doubt how man could obtain grace by such means: the desire of the soul was not appeased by it, nor was love infused; those effects could only be produced by the enlightenment of the mind, and the kindling of the will by the immediate operation of the Eternal Spirit; for, he added, he could conceive of religion only as residing in the inmost depth of the heart. He doubted whether all those outward succours for which it was usual to invoke the saints, ought to be ascribed to them.

Such were the doctrines, such the great general direction of mind immediately connected with the opinions implanted by Pollich and Staupitz, which Luther disseminated among the Augustine friars of his convent and his province, and, above all, among the members of the university. For a time Jodocus Trutvetter of Eisenach sustained the established opinions; but after his death in the year 1513, Luther was the master spirit that ruled the schools. His colleagues, Peter Lupinus and Andreas Carlstadt, who for a time withstood his influence, at length declared themselves overcome and convinced by the arguments of Augustine and the doctrines of the Holy Scripture which had made so deep an impression on him; they were almost more zealous than Luther himself. A totally different direction was thus given to the university of Wittenberg from that in which the other seats of learning continued to move. Theology itself, mainly indeed in consequence of its own internal development, made similar claims to those asserted by general literature. In Wittenberg arose the opposition to the theologians of the old and the new way, the nominalists and the realists, and more especially to the reigning thomistical doctrines of the Dominicans; men turned to the scriptures and the fathers of the church, as Erasmus (though rather as a conscientious critic than an enthusiastic religionist) had recommended. In a short time there were no hearers for the lectures given in the old spirit.

Such was the state of things in Wittenberg when the preachers of papal indulgences appeared in the country about the Elbe, armed with powers such as had never been heard of before, but which Pope Leo X. did not scruple, under the circumstances in which he found himself, to grant.

For no fear whatever was now entertained at Rome of any important division in the church.

In the place of the council of Pisa, one had been convoked at the Lateran, in which devotion to the see of Rome, and the doctrine of its omnipotence, reigned unalloyed and undisputed.

At an earlier period, the college of Cardinals had often made an attempt to limit the powers of the papacy, and to adopt measures with regard to it like those employed by the German chapters towards their bishoprics; they had elected Leo because they thought he would submit to these restraints. But the event proved how utterly they had miscalculated. The men who had chiefly promoted Leo's election were precisely those who now most severely felt his power. Their rage knew no bounds.

Cardinal Alfonso Petrucci several times went to the college with a dagger concealed beneath the purple; he would have assassinated the pope had he not been withheld by the consideration of the effect which the murder of a pope by a cardinal would produce on the world. He therefore held it to be more expedient to take another and less violent way to the same end—to get rid of the pope by poison. But this course required friends and allies among the cardinals and assistants in the palace, and thus it happened that he was betrayed.

What stormy consistories followed this discovery! The persons standing without, says the Master of the Ceremonies, heard loud clamours,—the pope against some of the cardinals, the cardinals against each other, and against the pope. Whatever passed there, Leo did not allow such an opportunity of establishing his power for ever, to escape him. Not only did he get rid of his formidable adversary, but he proceeded to create at one stroke thirty-one cardinals, thus insuring to himself a majority in all contingencies, and a complete supremacy.

The state, too, was convulsed by a violent storm. Francesco Maria, Duke of Urbino, who had been driven out of his territory, had returned, and had set on foot a war, the result of which long kept the pope in a state of mingled exasperation and shame: gradually, however, he mastered this opposition also, the war swallowed up streams of gold, but means were found to raise it.

The position which the pope, now absolute lord of Florence and master of Siena, occupied, the powerful alliances he had contracted with the other powers of Europe, and the views which his family entertained on the rest of Italy, rendered it absolutely indispensable for him, in spite of the prodigality of a government that knew no restraint, to be well supplied with money. He seized every occasion of extracting extraordinary revenues from the church.

The Lateran council was induced, immediately before its dissolution (15th of March, 1517), to grant the pope a tenth of all church property throughout Christendom. Three different commissions for the sale of indulgences traversed Germany and the northern states at the same moment.

These expedients were, it is true, resorted to under various pretexts. The tenths were, it was said, to be expended in a Turkish war, which was soon to be declared; the produce of indulgences was for the building of St. Peter's Church, where the bones of the martyrs lay exposed to the inclemency of the elements. But people had ceased to believe in these pretences.

Devoted as the Lateran council was to the pope, the proposition was only carried by two or three votes: an extremely large minority objected to the tenths, that it was impossible to think of a Turkish war at present.

Who could be a more zealous catholic than Cardinal Ximenes, who then governed Spain? Yet even in the year 1513, he had opposed the attempt to introduce the sale of indulgences into that country; he made vehement professions of devotion to the pope, but he added, as to the tenths, it must first be seen how they were to be applied.

For there was not a doubt on the mind of any reasonable man, that all these demands were mere financial speculations. There is no positive proof that the assertion then so generally made—that the proceeds of the sale of indulgences in Germany was destined in part for the pope's sister Maddelena—was true. But the main fact is indisputable, that the ecclesiastical aids were applied to the uses of the pope's family. We have a receipt now lying before us, given by the pope's nephew Lorenzo to the king of France, for 100,000 livres which that monarch paid him for his services. Herein it is expressly said that the king was to receive this sum from the tenths which the council had granted to the pope for the Turkish war. This was, therefore, precisely the same thing as if the pope had given the money to his nephew; or, perhaps even worse, for he gave it him before it was raised.

The only means of resistance to these impositions were therefore to be sought in the powers of the state, which were just now gradually acquiring stability, as we see by the example of Ximenes in Spain; or in England, where the decision of the Lateran council could not have reached the government, at the time when it forced the papal collectors to take an oath that they would send neither money nor bills of exchange to Rome. But who was there capable of protecting the interests of Germany? The Council of Regency no longer existed; the emperor was compelled by his uncertain political relations (especially to France) to keep up a good understanding with the pope. One of the most considerable princes of the empire, the Archchancellor of Germany, Elector Albert of Mainz, born Markgrave of Brandenburg, had the same interests as the pope,—a part of the proceeds were to go into his own exchequer.

Of the three commissions into which Germany was divided, the one which was administered by Arimbold, a member of the Roman prelature, embraced the greater part of the dioceses of Upper and Lower Germany; another, which included only Switzerland and Austria, fell to the charge of Cristofero Numai of Forli, general of the Franciscans; and the Elector of Mainz himself had undertaken the third in his own vast archiepiscopal provinces, Mainz and Magdeburg: and for the following reasons.

We remember what heavy charges had been brought upon the archbishopric of Mainz by the frequent recurrence of vacancies. In the year 1514 the chapter elected Markgrave Albert for no other reason than that he promised not to press heavily on the diocese for the expenses of the pallium. But neither was he able to defray them from his own resources. The expedient devised was, that he should borrow 30,000 gulden of the house of Fugger of Augsburg, and detain one half of the money raised by indulgences to repay it. This financial operation was perfectly open and undisguised. Agents of the house of Fugger travelled about with the preachers of indulgences. Albert had authorized them to take half of all the money received on the spot, "in payment of the sum due to them." The tax for the plenary indulgence reminds us of the measures taken for the collection of the Common Penny. We possess diaries in which the disbursements for spiritual benefits are entered and calculated together with secular purchases.

And it is important to examine what were the advantages which were thus obtained.

The plenary indulgence for all, the alleged object of which was to contribute to the completion of the Vatican Basilica, restored the possessor to the grace of God, and completely exempted him from the punishment of purgatory. But there were three other favours to be obtained by further contributions: the right of choosing a father confessor who could grant absolution in reserved cases, and commute vows which had been taken into other good works; participation in all prayers, fasts, pilgrimages, and whatever good works were performed in the church militant; lastly, the release of the souls of the departed out of purgatory. In order to obtain plenary indulgence, it was necessary not only to confess, but to feel contrition; the three others could be obtained without contrition or confession, by money alone. It is in this point of view that Columbus extols the worth of money: "he who possesses it," says he seriously, "has the power of transporting souls into Paradise."

Never indeed were the union of secular objects with spiritual omnipotence more strikingly displayed than in the epoch we are now considering. There is a fantastic sublimity and grandeur in this conception of the church, as a community comprehending heaven and earth, the living and the dead; in which all the penalties incurred by individuals were removed by the merit and the grace of the collective body. What a conception of the power and dignity of a human being is implied in the belief that the pope could employ this accumulated treasure of merits in behalf of one or another at his pleasure! The doctrine that the power of the pope extended to that intermediate state between heaven and earth, called purgatory, was the growth of modern times. The pope appears in the character of the great dispenser of all punishment and all mercy. And this most poetical, sublime idea he now dragged in the dust for a miserable sum of money, which he applied to the political or domestic wants of the moment. Mountebank itinerant commissioners, who were very fond of reckoning how much they had already raised for the papal court, while they retained a considerable portion of it for themselves, and lived a life of ease and luxury, outstripped their powers with blasphemous eloquence. They thought themselves armed against every attack, so long as they could menace their opponents with the tremendous punishments of the church.

But a man was now found who dared to confront them.

While Luther's whole soul was more and more profoundly embued with the doctrine of salvation by faith, which he zealously diffused not only in the cloister and the university, but in his character of parish priest of Wittenberg, there appeared in his neighborhood an announcement of a totally opposite character, grounded on the merest external compromise with conscience, and resting on those ecclesiastical theories which he, with his colleagues, disciples and friends, so strenuously combated. In the neighbouring town of Jüterbock, the multitude flocked together around the Dominican friar, John Tetzel, a man distinguished above all the other pope's commissioners for shamelessness of tongue. Memorials of the traffic in which he was engaged are preserved (as was fitting) in the ancient church of the town. Among the buyers of indulgences were also some people from Wittenberg; Luther saw himself directly attacked in his cure of souls.

It was impossible that contradictions so absolute should approach so near without coming into open conflict.

On the vigil of All Saints, on which the parochial church was accustomed to distribute the treasure of indulgences attached to its relics,—on the 31st October, 1517,—Luther nailed on its gates ninety-five propositions;—"a disputation for the purpose of explaining the power of indulgences."

We must recollect that the doctrine of the treasure of the church, on which that of indulgences rested, was from the very first regarded as at complete variance with the sacrament of the power of the keys. The dispensation of indulgences rested on the overflowing merits of the church: all that was required on the one side was sufficient authority: on the other a mark or token of connection with the church,—any act done for her honour or advantage. The sacrament of the keys, on the contrary, was exclusively derived from the merits of Christ: for that, sacerdotal ordination was necessary on the one side, and, on the other, contrition and penance. In the former case the measure of grace was at the pleasure of the dispenser; in the latter, it must be determined by the relation between the sin and the penitence. In this controversy, Thomas Aquinas had declared himself for the doctrine of the treasure of the church and the validity of the indulgences which she dispensed: he expressly teaches that no priest is necessary, a mere legate can dispense them; even in return for temporal services, so far as these were subservient to a spiritual purpose. In this opinion he was followed by his school.

The same controversy was revived, after the lapse of ages, by Luther; but he espoused the contrary side. Not that he altogether denied the treasures of the church; but he declared that this doctrine was not sufficiently clear, and, above all, he contested the right of the pope to dispense them. For he ascribed only an inward efficacy to this mysterious community of the church. He maintained that all her members had a share in her good works, even without a pope's brief; that his power extended over purgatory only in so far as the intercessions of the church were in his hand; but the question must first be determined whether God would hear these intercessions: he held that the granting of indulgences of any kind whatsoever without repentance, was directly contrary to the Christian doctrine. He denied, article by article, the authority given to the dealers in indulgences in their instructions. On the other hand, he traced the doctrine of absolution to that of the authority of the keys. In this authority, which Christ delegated to St. Peter, lay the power of the pope to remit sin. It also extended to all penances and cases of conscience; but of course to no punishments but those imposed for the purpose of satisfaction; and even then, their whole efficacy depended on whether the sinner felt contrition, which he himself was not able to determine much less another for him. If he had true contrition, complete forgiveness was granted him; if he had it not, no brief of indulgence could avail him: for the pope's absolution had no value in and for itself, but only in so far as it was a mark of Divine favour.

It is evident that this attack did not originate in a scheme of faith new to the church, but in the very centre of the scholastic notions; according to which the fundamental idea of the papacy—viz. that the priesthood, and more especially the successors of St. Peter, were representatives and vice-gerents of Christ,—was still firmly adhered to, though the doctrine of the union of all the powers of the church in the person of the pope was just as decidedly controverted. It is impossible to read these propositions without seeing by what a daring, magnanimous, and constant spirit Luther was actuated. The thoughts fly out from his mind like sparks from the iron under the stroke of the hammer.

Let us not forget to remark, however, that as the abuse complained of had a double character, religious and political, or financial, so also political events came in aid of the opposition emanating from religious ideas.

Frederick of Saxony had been present when the Council of Regency prescribed to Cardinal Raimund very strict conditions for the indulgence then proclaimed (A.D. 1501); he had kept the money accruing from it in his own dominions in his possession, with the determination not to part with it, till an expedition against the infidels, which was then contemplated, should be actually undertaken; the pope and, on the pope's concession, the emperor had demanded it of him in vain: he held it for what it really was—a tax levied on his subjects; and after all the projects of a war against the Turks had come to nothing, he had at length applied the money to his university. Nor was he now inclined to consent to a similar scheme of taxation. His neighbour, Elector Joachim of Brandenburg, readily submitted to it: he commanded his States to throw no obstacles in the way of Tetzel or his sub-commissioners; but his compliance was clearly only the result of the consideration that one half of the amount would go to his brother. For this very reason, however, Elector Frederick made the stronger resistance: he was already irritated against the Elector of Mainz in consequence of the affairs of Erfurt, and he declared that Albert should not pay for his pallium out of the pockets of the Saxons. The sale of indulgences at Jüterbock and the resort of his subjects thither, was not less offensive to him on financial grounds than to Luther on spiritual.

Not that the latter were in any degree excited by the former; this it would be impossible to maintain after a careful examination of the facts; on the contrary, the spiritual motives were more original, powerful, and independent than the temporal, though these were important, as having their proper source in the general condition of Germany. The point whence the great events arose which were soon to agitate the world, was the coincidence of the two.

There was, as we have already observed, no one who represented the interests of Germany in the matter. There were innumerable persons who saw through the abuse of religion, but no one who dared to call it by its right name and openly to denounce and resist it. But the alliance between the monk of Wittenberg and the sovereign of Saxony was formed; no treaty was negotiated; they had never seen each other; yet they were bound together by an instinctive mutual understanding. The intrepid monk attacked the enemy; the prince did not promise him his aid—he did not even encourage him; he let things take their course.

Yet he must have felt very distinctly what was the tendency and the importance of these events, if we are to believe the story of the dream which he dreamt at his castle of Schweinitz, where he was then staying, on the night of All Saints, just after the theses were stuck up on the church door at Wittenberg. He thought he saw the monk writing certain propositions on the chapel of the castle at Wittenberg, in so large a hand that it could be read in Schweinitz; the pen grew longer and longer, till at last it reached to Rome, touched the pope's triple crown and made it totter; he was stretching out his arm to catch it, when he woke.

Luther's daring assault was the shock which awakened Germany from her slumber. That a man should arise who had the courage to undertake the perilous struggle, was a source of universal satisfaction, and as it were tranquillised the public conscience. The most powerful interests were involved in it;—that of sincere and profound piety, against the most purely external means of obtaining pardon of sins; that of literature, against fanatical persecutors, of whom Tetzel was one; the renovated theology against the dogmatic learning of the schools, which lent itself to all these abuses; the temporal power against the spiritual, whose usurpations it sought to curb; lastly, the nation against the rapacity of Rome.

But since each of these interests had its antagonist, the resistance could not be much less vehement than the support. A numerous body of natural adversaries arose.

The university of Frankfurt on the Oder, like that of Wittenberg, was an off-shoot of Leipzig, only founded at a later date, and belonging to the opposite party. Determined opponents to all innovation had found appointments there. Conrad Koch, surnamed Wimpina, an old enemy of Pollich, who had often had a literary skirmish with him, had acquired a similar influence there to that possessed by Pollich at Wittenberg. Johann Tetzel now addressed himself to Wimpina, and with his assistance (for he was ambitious of being a doctor as well as his Augustine adversary) published two theses, on one of which he intended to hold a disputation for the degree of licentiate, on the other, for that of doctor: both were directed against Luther. In the first he attempted to defend the doctrine of indulgences by means of a new distinction between expiatory and saving punishment. The pope, he said, could remit the former, though not the latter. In the second thesis he extols most highly the power of the pope, who had the exclusive right of settling the interpretation of Scripture, and deciding on articles of faith; he denounces Luther, not indeed by name, but with sufficient distinctness, as a heretic, nay a stiff-necked heretic. This now resounded from pulpit and chair. Hogstraten thundered out invectives, and clearly intimated that such a heretic was worthy of death; while a manuscript confutation by an apparent friend, Johann Eck of Ingolstadt, was circulated, containing insinuations concerning the Bohemian poison. Luther left none of these attacks unanswered: and in every one of his polemical writings he gained ground. Other questions soon found their way into the controversy; *e.g.* that concerning the legend of St. Anne, the authenticity of which was disputed by a friend of Luther's at Zwickau, but obstinately maintained by the Leipzig theologians. The Wittenberg views concerning the Aristotelian philosophy and the merit of works spread abroad: Luther himself defended them at a meeting of his order at Heidelberg; and if he experienced opposition from the elder doctors, a number of the younger members of the university became his adherents. The whole theological world of Germany was thrown into the most violent agitation.

But already a voice from Rome was heard through the loud disputes of excited Germany. Silvester Mazolini of Prierio, master of the sacred palace, a Dominican, who had given out a very equivocal and cautious opinion concerning the necessity of repentance and the sinfulness of lying, but had defended the system of teaching practised by his order with inflexible zeal;—who, in Reuchlin's controversy, had been the only member of the commission that had prevented it from coming to a decision favourable to that eminent scholar, now deemed himself called upon to take up arms against this new and far more formidable assailant. He rose, as he said, from the commentary in "Primam Secundæ" of St. Thomas, in the composition of which he was absorbed, and devoted a few days to throw himself like a buckler between the Augustine monk and the Roman See, against which he had dared to rear his head; he thought Luther sufficiently confuted by the mere citation of the opinions of his master, St. Thomas. An attack emanating from Rome made some impression even upon Luther: feeble and easy to confute as Silvester's writing appeared to him, he now paused; he did not wish to have the Curia his open and direct foe. On the 30th May he sent an explanation of his propositions to the pope himself, and seized this occasion of endeavouring to render his opinions and conduct generally intelligible to the Holy Father. He did not as yet go so far as to appeal purely and exclusively to the Scriptures; on the contrary, he declared that he submitted to the authority of the fathers who were recognised by the church, and even to that of the papal decrees. But he could not consider himself bound to accept the opinions of Thomas Aquinas as articles of faith, since his works were not yet sanctioned by the church. "I may err," he exclaims, "but a heretic I will not be, let my enemies rage and rail as they will."

Affairs, however, already began to wear the most threatening aspect at Rome.

The papal fiscal, Mario Perusco, the same who had rendered himself celebrated by the investigation of the conspiracy of cardinals, commenced criminal proceedings against Luther; in the tribunal which was appointed the same Silvester who had thrown down the gauntlet to the accused on the literary ground was the only theologian. There was not much mercy to be expected.

There is no question that German influences were also at work here. Elector Albert, who instantly felt that the attack from Wittenberg was directed in part against himself, had referred Tetzel to Wimpina; the consequence of this was, that Frederick was attacked in Tetzel's theses (indirectly indeed, but with the utmost bitterness), as a prince who had the power to check the heretical wickedness, and did not—who shielded heretics from their rightful judge. Tetzel at least affirms, that the Elector had had an influence in the trial. Personal differences, and the jealousies of neighbouring states, had influenced, from the very beginning, the course of these events.

Such was the state of the spiritual power in Germany. As yet, a secession or revolt from the pope was not thought of; as yet, his power was universally acknowledged, but indignation and resistance rose up against him from all the depths of the national feeling and the national will. Already had his sworn defenders sustained a defeat;—already some of the foundations of the edifice of dogma, on which his power rested, tottered; the intense desire of the nation to consolidate itself into a certain unity, took a direction hostile to the authority of the Court of Rome. An opposition had arisen which still appeared insignificant, but which found vigorous support in the temper of the nation and in the favour of a powerful prince of the empire.

Jules Michelet

1798—1874

3

It is difficult to imagine careers and philosophies of history as divergent as those of Leopold von Ranke and Jules Michelet. The religious Ranke—conservative and monarchical in politics, protected by the state, recognized and often honored by the establishment, well-disciplined in his style and in his personal life, devoted to a genre of history that relied almost exclusively on the documents left by diplomats and political leaders—is in every aspect the opposite of France's first great nationalist historian. Not long before Napoleon began to govern France, Michelet was born in a Parisian church that had been desecrated during the French Revolution. The son of a poor printer who was persecuted by Napoleon, Michelet was never baptized and was not very much interested in religion, except in later years when he launched a biting campaign against the Jesuits, the Church, and Christianity itself. He liked to think of himself as a child of the Revolution and of the people, that is, of the masses who had made that Revolution. As an old man, disillusioned by the reactionary course of history in the country whose republican aspirations he loved so well, he wrote movingly of his origins: "I felt in my sombre cave what the Jew dreamt of when he built the pyramids; what the man in the Middle Ages dreamt when he drew his furrow under the shade of the feudal tower." Nostalgia for plebeian Paris and the people who lived there influenced Michelet's entire life and his life's work as well.

Michelet's conviction that it was the people who made history was kindled while he was a young man teaching secondary school by his discovery of the eighteenth-century Neapolitan scholar Vico. In his *Scienza Nuova,* Vico maintained that history should include all of the sciences in an organic whole. For this type of history, folklore and legends, as evidenced by ballads, songs, poetry, architecture, and a variety of other sources, were all necessary. Vico and his disciple Michelet believed that the key to understanding the past lay not in biographies of great men but in the world of society as a whole. Michelet did not follow Vico in all things—Vico, for example, was a fervent Catholic—but Michelet's abridgment and translation of Vico's work brought him a post at the prestigious École Normale Supérieure, an extraordinary feat for a scholar at the age of twenty-nine.

In addition to his responsibilities at the École Normale, Michelet also lectured at the Sorbonne and at the Collège de France, where he was appointed to a chair in 1838. His love for teaching did not prevent his accepting the directorship of the historical section of the National Archives, where he began his life's work: the history of his native France, or more precisely, the history of the French people. His goal was what he termed a *résurrection intégrale* of medieval French society. He desired to conjure up the spirit of the Middle Ages, to re-create the life of the ordinary peasant, and to present his readers with a picture of France as a peasant would have seen it in the tenth century.

The first six volumes of the *History of France,* published from 1833 to 1844, are Michelet's most enduring historical achievement. He described the method he employed in writing these volumes very well himself: "I shut the books, and placed myself among the people to the best of my power, the lonely writer plunged amongst the crowd, listened to their noise, noted their words." Thus it is that a picture, a medallion, a coin, a fragment of an old building, a rustic proverb, or a bit of an old song are all fused together to allow us to glimpse a distant and romantic past. Our selection, from the famous "Picture of France," contained in Michelet's third volume, is a survey of the French countryside as it appeared in the Middle Ages. It is an effusive description, too lurid perhaps for present-day taste; it is also a very personal tribute of the historian to his country.

The France that Michelet loved deteriorated in the late 1840's; so did the historian's career and the quality of his writing. The popular revolution that Michelet had called for in his book *The People* (1846) failed dramatically in 1848. The Church began to retaliate against Michelet, whose work *The Jesuits* (1843) was a virulent diatribe denouncing clerical hypocrisy. By the winter of 1851, Michelet's course at the Collège de France had been suspended; within a year he was deprived both of his professorship and of his official position at the Archives. The coup d'état of Louis Napoleon meant a life in exile for Michelet, who would never swear allegiance to the Second Empire. In the meantime, a series of personal tragedies, including the death of his first wife as well as of his intimate friend Mme. Dumesnil, embittered the historian and colored his work.

The History of the French Revolution is the initial product of Michelet's overt anticlerical phase. Completed in 1853, it is the first history to offer a republican interpretation of the Revolution. More than any of his predecessors, Michelet wrote the history of the Revolution from its official records, supplemented by memoirs and eyewitness accounts; but Michelet became so obviously engrossed in the struggle against monarchy and Christianity that his work takes on an evangelical character, and his faith in the wisdom of the masses is so unquestioning that his history simply cannot be considered a satisfactory account of a great event. Michelet insisted that in writing this history he became one of the revolutionaries, "an intimate in that strange world." This intimacy makes his work vivid; it also destroys all historical perspective.

The last volumes of the *History of France* were completed in 1867. In principle, they are meant to recount French history from the Renaissance to the Revolution; in fact, they are largely horrific visions of what Michelet termed "perverted gods and rotten kings." He hoped that these volumes would make Rabelais and Voltaire laugh in their graves. It is more likely that these master satirists would have pitied the disappointed and defeated republican.

The composition of Michelet's last works was noticeably influenced by his marriage to Athénais Mialaret in 1849. In the 1850's and 1860's, he wrote a series of pamphlets on nature, which were pleasant enough, as well as some essays on women and love, which were mildly erotic and altogether crude. It is hard to know exactly how much Mme. Michelet added to these books, since she tampered with her husband's journals after his death. Michelet's final historical project was a history of the nineteenth century. The teacher and scholar who had suffered at the hand of France's second emperor was intent on blackening every aspect of the rule of its first. Again, Michelet is powerful, deeply involved in his subject; again, his history degenerates into pages of hallucination.

The outbreak of the Franco-Prussian war in 1870 and the burning of his house in Paris by the Communards were perhaps the most painful blows Michelet had to sustain during his long and tumultuous life. Throughout his life and his writings he never lost faith in the people. He once wrote, "Before I made books, I composed them; I arranged letters before I grouped ideas; and I worked with letters before I grouped ideas; and I am not ignorant of the sadness of the workshop, and the weariness of long hours." We may hope that his affinity for his subject was of some comfort to him during a lifetime of polemics in behalf of his ideals.

Selected Bibliography

The most important and most helpful study of Michelet's life and work is Gabriel Monod's *La vie et la pensée de Jules Michelet* (1923). An earlier version of this work, which contains some curious fragments from Michelet's journals, is reviewed both in *The Nation* LXXII (March, 1906), 244–246, and in the *Edinburgh Review* XXI (1906), 395-396. A partisan but penetrating view of Michelet appears in the *Quarterly Review* CXCLLL (1910), 130–150. Oscar A. Haac in *Les principles inspirateurs de Michelet* (1951) offers a careful analysis of Michelet's major works. The popularity and significance of the Annales school in recent years has enhanced Michelet's standing among practitioners of the new social history. One of the greatest of these historians, Lucien Febvre, the co-founder with Marc Bloch of the *Annales,* has paid fitting tribute to a nineteenth-century predecessor in *Michelet* (1946).

HISTORY OF FRANCE

BOOK THE THIRD

Picture of France

The history of France begins with the French language. Language is the distinguishing mark of nationality. The earliest monument of our language is the oath dictated by Charles the Bald to his brother, at the treaty of 843. In the half century following, the different countries of France, up to that time confounded in a vague and obscure unity, assume distinctive characters from the feudal dynasties established in them. Their population, so long floating and unsettled, is fixed and seated. We know where are the respective people of each: and at the same time that they all begin to exist and act apart, they gradually acquire a voice: each has its history, which each relates for itself.

Through the infinite variety of the feudal world, and the multiplicity of objects with which it at first distracts the eye and the attention, France nevertheless stands manifest. For the first time she displays herself under her geographic form. When the wind dissipates the vain and fantastic fog with which the German empire had covered and obscured every thing, the country comes out into full light, with all its local differences defined by its mountains and its rivers. The political correspond with the physical divisions. Far from there having been, as is commonly stated, confusion and chaos, all was order—inevitable and fated regularity. Strange! our eighty-six departments correspond, or very nearly so, with the eighty-six districts of the Capitularies, whence sprang most of the feudal sovereignties; and the revolution which gave the death-blow to feudalism was fain to imitate it.

The true starting-point of our history is a political division of France, founded on its natural and physical division. At first, history is altogether geography. It is impossible to describe the feudal or the *provincial* period (the latter epithet is equally characteristic) without first tracing the peculiarities of the provinces. Nor is it sufficient to define the geographical form of these different countries. They are to be thoroughly illustrated by their fruits alone—I mean by the men and the events of their history. From the point of view where we are about to place ourselves, we shall predict what each of them will do and produce; we shall indicate to them their destiny, and dower them in the cradle.

And first, let us view France in its whole, that we may see how it will divide of itself.

Let us ascend one of the highest summits of the Vosges, or, if you choose, let us seat ourselves on the Jura—our back to the Alps. Could our sight take in an horizon of three hundred leagues, we should distinguish an undulating line, extending from the wood-crowned hills of Luxembourg and of Ardennes to the balloon-shaped hills of the Vosges, and thence along the viny slopes of Burgundy to the volcanic crags of the Cevennes, and to the vast wall of the Pyrenees. This line marks the great water-shed. On its western side descend to the ocean the Seine, the Loire, and the Garonne; on the other, the Meuse flows to the north, the Saône and Rhône to the south. In the distance are two continental islands, as it were—Brittany, low and rugged, of quartz and granite only, a huge shoal placed at the angle of France to sustain the shock of the current of the strait; and Auvergne, green and rude, a vast extinct fire, with its forty volcanoes.

The basins of the Rhône and of the Garonne, notwithstanding their importance, are only secondary. In the north alone life exists in the fulness of strength; and in it was wrought the great movement of the nations. In ancient times there set a current of races from Germany into France; the grand political struggle of modern times has lain between France and England. These two nations are placed facing each other, as if to invite to contest. On their most important sides the two countries slope towards each other, or you may say that they form but one valley, of which the Straits of Dover are the bottom. On this side are the Seine and Paris; on that, London and the Thames. But England presents to France that portion of her which is German—keeping behind her the Celts of Wales, Scotland, and Ireland. France, on the contrary, backed by her Germanic provinces (Lorraine and Alsace) opposes her Celtic front to England. Each country views the other on its most hostile side.

Germany is not opposed to France, but rather lies parallel with her. Like the Meuse and the Scheldt, the Rhine, Elbe, and Oder run into the northern seas. Besides, German France sympathizes with Germany, her parent. As for Roman and Iberian France, notwithstanding the splendor of Marseilles and of Bordeaux, she only faces the old world of Africa and of Italy, or else the vague abyss of ocean. From Spain we are severed by the Pyrenees even more completely than she is by the sea from Africa. Rising above the region of rain and of the lower clouds to the *por* of Venasque, and prolonging our view over Spain, we see that there Europe ends. A new world opens; before us is the blazing sun of Africa; behind, a fog undulating with a constant wind.

Looking at France in its latitude, its zones are at once discriminated by their products. In the north are the low and rich plains of Belgium and of Flanders, with their fields of flax, hops, and of colewort, and the bitter northern vine. From Reims to the Moselle begins the region of the true vine and of wine; all spirit in Champagne, and good and warm in Burgundy, it grows heavier and duller in Languedoc, to awaken again at Bordeaux. The mulberry and the olive appear at Montauban; but these delicate children of the south are ever exposed to risk in the unequal climate of France. Longitudinally, the zones are not less distinct. We shall presently see the intimate relations which connect, as in one long belt, the frontier provinces of Ardennes, of Lorraine, of Franche-Compté, and of Dauphiny. The oceanic zone, formed on the one hand by Flanders, Picardy, and Normandy, and, on the other, by Poitou and Guienne, would float at its immense length, were it not bound tightly round the middle by the hard knot of Brittany.

It has been said, *Paris, Rouen, and Havre are one city, of which the Seine is the high street.* Betake yourself to the south of this magnificent street, where castles join castles, villages join villages. Pass from the lower Seine to Calvados, and from Calvados to the Channel—whatever be the richness and fertility of the country, the towns become fewer, arable decreases, pasture increases. The aspect of the country is serious; it soon becomes wild and gloomy. To the lofty castles of Normandy succeed the humble manor-houses of the Bretons. The costume seems to follow the change of architecture. The triumphal bonnet of the women of Caux, which bespeaks so fitly the daughters of the conquerors of England, widens out towards Caen, grows flat at Ville-Dieu, divides and figures in the wind at St. Malo; sometimes like the sails of a mill, at others like those of a ship. On another side, dresses of skins begin at Laval. The increasing density of the forests, the solitude of La Trappe—where the monks lead together a savage life—the expressive names of the towns Fougères and Rennes (both signifying heath or fern), the gray waters of the Mayenne and the Villaine—all announce the wildness of the country.

It is here, however, that we wish to begin our study of France. The Celtic province, the eldest born of the monarchy, claims our first glance. Hence we will pass on to the old rivals of the Celts, the Basques and the Iberians, not less obstinate in their mountains than the Celt in his heaths and marshes. Then we may proceed to the countries blended and confounded by the Roman and German conquests. We shall thus have studied geography in chronological order, and have travelled at once in space and in time.

Brittany, poor and hard, the resistant clement of France, extends her fields of quartz and of schistus from the slate-quarries of Châteaulin, near Brest, to the slate-quarries of Angers. This is her extent, geologically speaking. However, from Angers to Rennes, the country is a *debateable* land, a *border* like that between England and Scotland, which early escaped from Brittany. The Breton tongue does not even begin at Rennes, but about Elven, Pontivy, Loudéac, and Châtelaudren. Thence, as far as Cape Finisterre, it is true Brittany—*Breton* Brittany (Bretagne bretonnante), a country which has become altogether foreign from ours, exactly because it has remained too faithful to our primitive condition, the more unlike the French that it is like the Gaul, and which would have slipped from us more than once, had we not held it grasped, as if in a vise, between four French cities of rough and decisive character, Nantes and St. Malo, Rennes and Brest.

And yet this poor old province has saved us more than once. Often when our country has been held at bay and been at the point of despair, Breton heads and breasts have been found harder than the stranger's sword. When the Northmen were ravaging with impunity our coasts and rivers, the Breton, Nomenoé, was the first to resist. The English were repulsed in the fourteenth century by Duguesclin; in the fifteenth, by Richemont; and, in the seventeenth, were chased through every sea by Duguay-Trouin. The wars of religious and those of political liberty present no more purely and innocently glorious names than Lanoue's, and that of Latour d'Auvergne, the first grenadier of the republic. The story runs, that it was a native of Nantes who uttered the last exclamation heard at Waterloo—*"The guard dies, but does not surrender!"*

The Breton character is that of untameable resistance, and of blind, obstinate, intrepid opposition—for instance, Moreau, the opponent of Bonaparte. In the history of philosophy and literature, this character is still more plainly evidenced. The Breton, Pelagius, who infused stoicism into Christianity, and was the first churchman who uplifted his voice in behalf of human liberty, was succeeded by the Breton Abelard, and the Breton Descartes. Each of these three gave the impetus to the philosophy of his own age. However, Descartes' disdain of facts, and contempt for history and languages, clearly show that this independent genius, who founded psychology, and doubled the sphere of mathematics, was rather vigorous than comprehensive.

This spirit of opposition, which is natural to Brittany, manifested itself in the last century and in ours, by two apparently contradictory facts. The same part of Brittany (St. Malo, Dinan, and St. Brieuc) which, in Louis the Fifteenth's day, produced the unbelievers Duclos, Maupertuis, and Lamétrie, has given birth in our own time to the poet and to the orator of Catholicism, to Chateaubriand and to La Mennais.

Now, to take a rapid survey of the country.

At its two gates, Bretagne has two forests—the Norman Bocage, and the Vendean Bocage; and two cities—St. Malo and Nantes, the one the city of privateers, the other of Guineamen. St. Malo is of singularly ugly and sinister appearance; and there is in it, besides, something fantastical, observable throughout the whole peninsula as well, whether in costume, in pictures, or in monuments. It is a small, wealthy, sombre, and melancholy spot—the home of vultures and of ospreys; by turns, as the tide ebbs and flows, a peninsula and an island, and bordered with foul and fetid shoals where the seaweed rots at will. In the distance, is a coast of white, angular rocks, cut sheer as if with a razor. War is the harvest of St. Malo—they know no more delightful holiday. To feel this, one should have seen them on their black walls with their telescopes, which already brooded over the ocean, when, no long time since, they were filled with hopes of running down the vessels of the Hollander.

At its other extremity lies Brest, our great military port—planned by Richelieu, created by Louis XIV.; fort, arsenal, and bagnio, cannon and ships, armies and millions, the strength of France amassed at one end of France—and all this in a contracted harbor, where one is pent up and stifled between two mountains, covered with immense buildings. The entrance into the port is like passing into a small boat between two lofty vessels—the heavy masses seem about to close upon and crush you. Your general impression is grand, but painful. You see a prodigious effort of strength, at once a defiance to England and to nature. You everywhere are conscious of the effort, and so are you of the air of the Bagnio, and of the galley-slave's chain. It is precisely at the point on which the sea, escaping from the Straits of Dover, dashes with its utmost fury, that we have pitched our great naval arsenal. Certes, it is well guarded. I saw a thousand cannon there. All entrance is barred; but, at the same time, the port is not to be left at pleasure. More than one vessel has been lost in Brest channel. The whole coast is a grave-yard. Sixty vessels are wrecked on it every winter. The sea is English at heart. She loves not France, but dashes our ships to pieces, and blocks up our harbors with sand.

Nothing can be more sinister and formidable than the coast of Brest; it is the extreme limit, the point, the prow of the old world. Here the two enemies, land and sea, man and nature, are face to face. When the sea madly lashes herself into fury, you should see what monstrous waves she hurls on point St. Matthew, fifty, sixty, eighty feet high. The spray is flung as far as the church, where mothers and sisters are at prayers. And even in those moments of truce, when the sea is silent, who has passed along this funereal coast without exclaiming or feeling—*Tristis usque ad mortem!* (the shadow of death is here!).

'Tis that there is here what is worse than shoal or tempest. Nature is fierce, man is fierce; and they seem to understand each other. As soon as the sea casts a hapless vessel on the coast, man, woman, and child hurry to the shore, to fall on their quarry. Hope not to stay these wolves. They plunder at their ease under the fire of the coast-guard. It would be something if they always waited for shipwreck, but it is asserted that they often cause it. Often, it is said, a cow, led about with a lighted lantern at its horns, has lured vessels on the rocks. God alone knows the night-scenes that then take place! A man has been known to gnaw off a finger with his teeth, in order to get at a ring on the finger of a drowned woman.

On this coast, man is hard. The accursed son of creation, a true Cain, wherefore should he spare Abel? Nature spares not him. Does the wave spare him, when in the fearful nights of winter he roams the shoals to gather the floating seaweed which is to fertilize his sterile field—when the billow which bears the plant so often carries off the man? Does it spare him when he tremblingly glides beneath Cape Raz, by the red rocks, where the *hell of Plogoff* yearns for its prey; or along *Deadman's Bay,* whose currents have for so many centuries swept corpses with them? The Breton proverb says, "None pass the Raz without hurt or a fright"; another, "Help me, great God, at Cape Raz—my ship is so small, and the sea is so great!"

Here nature expires; humanity becomes mournful and cold. There is no poetry, little religion, and Christianity dates but from yesterday. Michel Noblet was the apostle of Batz in 1648. In the islands of Sein, Batz, and Ushant, the wedding festival itself is sad and severe. The very senses seem dead; and there is nor love, nor shame, nor jealousy. The girls unblushingly make the marriage proposals. Woman labors there harder than man, and in the Ushant isles she is taller and stronger. She tills the land, while the man remains seated in his boat, rocked and cradled by the sea, his rough nurse. The animals also degenerate, and seem to change their nature. Horses and rabbits are wonderfully diminutive in these islands.

Let us seat ourselves on this formidable Cape Raz, upon this overhanging rock, three hundred feet above the sea, and whence we descry seven leagues of coast-line. This is, in some sort, the sanctuary of the Celtic world. The dot you discern beyond *Deadman's Bay* is the island of Sein, a desolate, treeless, and all but unsheltered sand-bank, the abode of some poor and compassionate families, who yearly save the shipwrecked mariners. This island was the abode of the sacred virgins who gave the Celts fine weather or shipwreck. There they celebrated their gloomy and murderous orgies; and the seamen heard with terror, far off at sea, the clash of barbaric cymbals. This island is the traditionary birth-place of Myrddyn, the Merlin of the middle age. His tomb is on the other side of Brittany, in the forest of Broceliande, under the fatal stone where his Vyvyan has enchanted him. All these rocks around us are towns which have been swallowed up—this is Douarnenez, that is, the Breton Sodom; those two ravens you see, ever flying heavily on the shore, are the souls of king

Grallo and his daughter; and those shrill whistlings, which one would take for the voice of the tempest, are the *crierien,* the ghosts of the shipwrecked clamoring for burial.

At Lanvau, near Brest, there rises, as if to mark the limit of the continent, a large unhewn stone. From this spot as far as Lorient, and from Lorient again as far as Quiberon and Carnac, you cannot walk along the southern coast of Brittany without meeting at every step one of those shapeless monuments which are called druidical. You often descry them from the road on *landes* covered with briers and thistles. They consist of huge low stones, placed upright, and often a little rounded at top; or else of a stone laid flat on three or four standing stones. Whether we see in them altars, tombs, or mere memorials of events, these monuments are exceedingly imposing. Yet is the impression they make a saddening one, there being something singularly repulsive and rude in their effect. They seem to be the first essays in art of a hand already intelligent, but as hard and as little human as the rock which it has fashioned. Neither inscription nor sign is visible on them, if we except some marks under those stones of Loc Maria Ker that have been thrown down, so indistinct as to induce a belief that they are merely accidental. Question the people of the country, and they will briefly reply that they are the houses of the *Torrigans,* the *Courils,* wanton dwarfs, who at night bar your road, and force you to dance with them until you die of fatigue. In other parts they are fairies, who, descending from the mountains, spinning, have brought away these rocks in their aprons. Those scattered rocks are a whole wedding party petrified. One solitary stone, near Morlaix, bears witness to the miserable fate of a peasant, who was swallowed up by the moon for blasphemy.

Never shall I forget the day on which I set out, early in the morning, from Auray, the sacred city of the Chouans, to visit the great druidical monuments of Loc Maria Ker, and of Carnac, which are some leagues distant. The first of these villages lies at the mouth of the filthy and fetid river of the Auray, *with its islands of Morbihan, outnumbering the days of the year,* and looks across a small bay to the fatal shore of Quiberon. There was a fog, such as envelops these coasts one-half of the year. Sorry bridges lead across the marshes; at one point you meet with the low and sombre manor-house, with its long avenue of oaks—a feature religiously preserved in Brittany; at another, you encounter a peasant, who passes without looking at you, but he has scanned you askance with his night-bird eye,—a look which explains their famous war-cry, and the name of *Chouans* (owls) given them by the *blues.* There are no houses on the road-side; the peasants return nightly to their villages. On every side are vast *landes,* sadly set off by purple heath and gorse; the cultivated fields are white with buckwheat. The eye is rather distressed than refreshed by this summer-snow, and those dull and faded-looking colors—resembling *Ophelia's* coronet of straw and flowers. As you proceed to Carnac, the country saddens. The plains are all rock, with a few black sheep browsing on the flint. In the midst of this multitude of stones, many of which stand upright of themselves, the lines of Carnac inspire no astonishment; although there are several hundred stones still standing, the highest of which is fourteen feet.

Morbihan is sombre to look at, sombre in its traditions—a country of old feuds, of pilgrimages, and of civil war—a land of flint and a race of granite. There, all is lasting; even time passes more slowly than elsewhere. The priests there wield great power. Yet it is a mistake to suppose the people of the West, the Bretons and Vendeans, to be deeply religious. In several cantons, the saint who turns a deaf ear to prayers runs the risk of a severe scourging. In Brittany, as in Ireland, the Catholic religion is dear to men as the symbol of their nationality, and the influence of religion is in a large degree an affair of politics. An Irish priest who should favor the English party would soon be expelled his country. No church, in the middle ages, continued longer independent of Rome than those of Ireland and of Brittany. For a long time the latter endeavored to withdraw itself from the primacy of Tours—opposing to it that of Dôle.

The nobles, as well as the priests, are dear to Brittany and La Vendée, as defenders of old ideas and customs. No wide gulf separated the innumerable and poor nobility of Brittany from the laboring class. Some of the feelings of clanship prevailed there too. Numerous peasant families considered themselves noble; some traced their descent to Arthur and the fairy Morgana, and are said to have stuck their swords in the ground to mark the limits of their fields. They would sit down covered before their lord, to mark their independence. In several parts of the province serfhood was unknown. The domaniers and quevaisiers, however hard their condition might be, were personally free, though the land was in bondage. They would stand up in presence of the haughtiest Rohan, and say, in their solemn manner—*Me zo deuzar armorig*—I, too, am a Breton. A profound reflection has recently been made with regard to Vendée, and it is applicable to Brittany as well—*"The people are at heart republicans."* Social, not political republicanism, is here meant.

We need not be surprised that the Celtic race, the most obstinate of the ancient world, made some efforts in later times to prolong its nationality, just as it defended it in the middle ages. It required the Plantagenets to become, by two marriages, kings of England, and dukes of Normandy and of Aquitaine, before they could subject Brittany to Anjou, an event which did not take place till the twelfth century, when Brittany, to escape them, threw herself into the arms of France, but only after the French and English parties, the Blois and the Montforts, had carried on the war for a century longer. After the marriage of Anne of Brittany with Louis VII. had united the province to the kingdom, and Anne had written on the castle of Nantes the old device on the castle of the Bourbons—*Qui qu'en grogne, tel est mon plaisir* (Let who will grumble, such is my will)—there began the legal struggle of the states, of the parliament of Rennes, its defence of the common law of the country against the Roman, and the war between provincial rights and monarchical centralization. Sternly coerced by Louis XIV., the struggle recommenced in his successor's reign; and La Chalotais, in his dungeon in Brest, wrote with a toothpick his courageous plea against the Jesuits.

Resistance is now dying away, and Brittany is being gradually absorbed into France. Its language, undermined by the constant infiltration of the French tongue, recedes step by step. Even the talent for poetic improvisation, which has endured so long among the Celts of Ireland and of Scotland, and which is not altogether lost among the Bretons, is become rare and unusual. Formerly, when a girl was sought in marriage, the bazvalan would sing stanzas of his own composition, to which she would respond; but this has now degenerated into a set form, learned by rote. The attempts, rather bold than successful, which have been made by some of the natives to revive, by instruction, the nationality of their country, have only been received with laughter. I have myself seen at T * * * *, Le Brigant's learned friend, the aged M. D. (known here only by the name of M. Système). The poor solitary old man, sunk in an old armchair, with five or six thousand volumes scattered round, childless, and without a relative to care for him, was dying of fever, with an Irish grammar on one side, and a Hebrew one on the other. He rallied so as to repeat to me some stanzas in the Breton tongue, of emphatic and monotonous rhythm, which, however, was not without its charm. It touched me to the heart to see this representative of Celtic nationality—this dying champion of a dying language and dying poetry.

We may trace the Celtic world along the Loire, as far as the geological limits of Brittany to the slate-quarries of Angers; or else, to the great druidical monument at Saumur, the most important, perhaps, of all that still exist; or else, to Tours, the ecclesiastical metropolis of Brittany in the middle ages.

Nantes is a semi-Bordeaux, less showy and more staid—a mixture of colonial opulence and Breton sobriety—standing civilized in the midst of two scenes of savage atrocity, carrying on commerce in the midst of two civil wars, and thrown where it stands as if to break off all communication. The great Loire runs through it, sweeping with its eddies between Brittany and La Vendée—the river of the *Noyades. "What a torrent,"* wrote Carrier, drunk with the poetry of his crime; *"what a revolutionary torrent is this Loire!"*

It was at St. Florent, at the very spot marked by the column in honor of the Vendean, Bonchamps, that in the ninth century the Breton Nomenoé, the conqueror of the Northmen, had reared his own statue; which faced Anjou, faced France, that he looked upon as his prey. But the day was Anjou's. Its more disciplinable population was under the sway of the great feudal barons; while Brittany, with its innumerable petty nobility, could carry on no great war, nor effect any great conquest. The *black* city of Angers bears, not alone on its vast castle, and its Devil's Tower, but on its very cathedral, this feudal impress. The church of St. Maurice is crowded, not with saints, but with knights armed cap-à-pie—and in its halting spires, the one charged with sculpture, the other plain, is typified the unfulfilled destiny of Anjou. Despite its fine situation on the triple stream of the Maine, and close to the Loire—where one can distinguish by their color the waters flowing from four provinces, Angers is now asleep. It is enough for it to have united for a while, under its Plantagenets, England, Normandy, Brittany, and Aquitaine, and, at a later period, under the good René and his sons, to have possessed, contended for, or, at the least, claimed the thrones of Naples, of Arragon, of Jerusalem, and of Provence, while his daughter Margaret supported the red against the white rose, and Lancaster against York. And here slumber, likewise, to the murmurings of the Loire, the cities of Saumur and of Tours—the one, the capital of Protestantism—the other, that of Catholicism in France—Saumur, the little kingdom of the Calvinist preachers and of the aged Duplessis Mornay, in opposition to whom their good friend, Henri IV., built La Flèche for the Jesuits. The castle of Mornay and its vast *dolmen* will always render Saumur of historical import. And important historically, though in a different way, is the good city of Tours, with its tomb of St. Martin—the ancient asylum, the ancient oracle, the Delphi of France, where the Merovingians came to consult the lost—the great and lucrative resort of pilgrims, for the possession of which the counts of Blois and of Anjou splintered so many lances. Mans, Angers, and the whole of Brittany were included in the see of the archbishopric of Tours. The Capets, and the dukes of Burgundy and of Brittany, and the count of Flanders, and the patriarch of Jerusalem, and the archbishops of Mentz, of Cologne, and of Compostella were its canons. Money was coined here, as well as at Paris; and here were early manufactured the silks, the precious tissues, and, if it must be owned, the sweetmeats and *rillettes,* for which Tours and Reims—cities of priests and of sensuality—have been equally famous. But the trade of Tours has been injured by Paris, Lyons, and Nantes. Something may be ascribed, too, to the influence of the mild sun and softening Loire: labor seems unnatural in the idle climate of Tours, of Blois, and of Chinon, in the country of Rabelais, and near the tomb of Agnes Sorel. Chenonceaux, Chambord, Montbazon,

Langeai, and Loches—all favored by our kings or their mistresses, have their several castles seated on the Loire. It is the country of *laughter,* and of the *far niente.* The verdure is fresh in August as in May—fruits succeed fruits, trees succeed trees. Look into the river from the bank—the opposite bank seems hung in air, so faithfully is the sky reflected by the water. The sand glistens at the bottom; then comes the willow, bending down to drink of the stream; next you see the poplar, the aspen, and the walnut, and then islands floating in the midst of islands, and beyond, tufted trees, gently waving to and fro, and saluting each other. A soft and sensual country! the very spot to give birth to the idea of making woman queen of the monasteries, and of living under her in a voluptuous obedience, a compound of love and of holiness. And never was abbey so splendid as that of Fontevrault. Five of its churches still remain. More than one king desired to be buried there. Even the fierce Richard Cœur-de-Lion willed the nuns his heart, thinking, that murderous and parricidal as it was, it would win repose in woman's gentle hand, and sheltered by the prayers of virgins.

To find on this Loire something less soft and more severe, you must proceed up it to the angle by which it sweeps round towards the Seine, as far as the serious Orleans—in the middle ages, the city of legists, afterwards Calvinistical, then Jansenist, and now a manufacturing town. But I defer for the present speaking of the centre of France, in order to hurry to the South. I have spoken of the Celts of Brittany, and would now proceed to the Iberians, to the Pyrenees.

Poitou, which we meet with on the other side of the Loire, facing Brittany and Anjou, is a country composed of very different but still distinct elements. Three distinct races occupy three distinct belts of land, stretching from north to south; and hence the apparent contradictions presented by the history of this province. In the sixteenth century, Poitou is the centre of Calvinism, recruits the armies of Coligni, and attempts to found a protestant republic. In our own time, Poitou originated the Catholic and royalist opposition of la Vendée. The natives of the coast figure in the former attempt; those of the Vendean Bocage in the latter. Both, however, may be referred to the same principle, of which republican Calvinism and royalist Catholicism have been but the form—an indomitable feeling of opposition to the central government.

Poitou is the battle-field of the South and of the North. It was near Poitiers that Clovis defeated the Goths, that Charles-Martel repulsed the Saracens, and that the Anglo-Gascon army of the Black Prince took king John prisoner. Blending the Roman with the common law, giving her legists to the North and her troubadours to the South, Poitou is like its own Melusina, a compound of different natures, half-woman, half-serpent. The myth could have originated only in a mixed country—in a country of mules and of vipers.

This mixed and contradictory character has hindered Poitou from ever bringing any thing to a conclusion; but it began every thing. The old Roman city of Poitiers, now so deserted, was, with Arles and Lyons, the first Christian school of Gaul. St. Hilary shared the battles of St. Athanasius, in defence of the divinity of Jesus Christ. In some respects, Poitiers was the cradle of our monarchy as well as of Christianity. From her cathedral shone during the night the column of fire which guided Clovis against the Goths. The king of France was abbot of St. Hilary of Poitiers, as well as of St. Martin of Tours. The latter church, however, less literary, but better situated, more popular, and more fertile in miracles, prevailed over her elder sister. The last light of Latin poetry had shone at Poitiers in the person of Fortunatus, and the aurora of modern literature dawned there in the twelfth century—William VII. is the first troubadour. This William, excommunicated for having run away with the viscountess of Châtelleraut, led, it is said, a hundred thousand men to the holy land, but he likewise took with him a crowd of his mistresses. It is of him that an old author says, *"He was a good troubadour, a good knight, and he travelled a long time over the world, deceiving the ladies."* Poitou would seem to have been at this period a country of witty libertines and of freethinkers. Gilbert de la Porée, born at Poitiers, and afterwards its bishop, who was Abelard's colleague in the school of Chartres, taught with the same boldness, was, like him, attacked by St. Bernard, like him, retracted, but did not persist in his relapses like the Breton logician. Poitevin philosophy is born and dies with Gilbert.

The political power of Poitou had no better fate. It began in the ninth century with the struggle maintained against Charles the Bald by Aymon, father of Renaud, count of Gascony, and brother of Turpin, count of Angoulême. This family claimed its descent from the two famous heroes of romance, St. William of Toulouse, and Gerard of Roussillon, count of Burgundy. It was, indeed, great and powerful; and for some time found itself at the head of the south. They took the title of dukes of Aquitaine, but had too difficult a game to play with the people of Brittany and of Anjou, who pressed them on the north. The Angevins took from them part of Touraine, Saumur, Loudun, and turned them by seizing on Saintes. However, the counts of Poitou exhausted themselves in strenuous efforts to establish in the south, and especially over Auvergne and Toulouse, their great title of dukes of Aquitaine. They spent their substance in distant expeditions to Spain and Jerusalem. Showy and lavish, these knightly troubadours were often embroiled with the Church; their light and violent manners giving rise to adulteries and domestic tragedies, which have been a world's talk. It was not the first time that a countess of Poitiers had assassinated her rival, when the jealous Elinor of Guyenne forced fair Rosamond to swallow poison in the labyrinth where her husband had concealed her.

Elinor's sons, Henry, Richard Cœur-de-Lion, and John, never knew whether they were Poitevins or English, Angevins or Normans. This internal strife of two contradictory natures is figured in their fluctuating and stormy career. Henry III., John's son, was governed by Poitevin favorites. The civil wars to which this gave rise in England are well known. Once united with the monarchy, Poitou, both of the *marsh* and of the plain, followed the general movement of France. Fontenai supplied her with great legists, with the Tiraqueaus, the Beslys, the Brissons; and many a skilful courtier (Thouars, Mortemar, Meilleraie, Mauléon, &c.) issued from the nobility of Poitou. The greatest politician and the most popular writer of France belong to eastern Poitou—Richelieu and Voltaire. The last, who was born at Paris, sprang from a family belonging to Parthenai.

But we have not seen the whole of the province. From the plateau of the Deux Sèvres descend the two rivers so named, the one running towards Nantes, the other towards Niort and Rochelle. The two eccentric districts which they traverse, stand aloof from France. The lower, a petty Holland, spreading itself out in marshes and canals, faces only the ocean and Rochelle. Originally, the *white city,* like the black city—Rochelle, like St. Malo—was an asylum opened by the Church, for the Jews, the serfs, the *coliberts* of Poitou. The pope equally protected both against the barons, and, freed as they were from tithe and tribute, they rapidly increased. A swarm of adventurers, issuing from their nameless populace, opened up the seas as merchants or as pirates: others opened up the court, and placed at the service of their monarchs their democratic genius and hatred of the barons. Without going so far back as to the serf Leudastes, of the island of Rhé, whose curious story has been preserved to us by Gregory of Tours, we may cite the famous cardinal de Sion, who got the Swiss to take up arms for Julius II., and the chancellors Olivier, Balue, and Doriole—the first, under Charles IX., the two last under Louis XI., who loved to make use of these intriguers—saving that he would lodge them afterwards in an iron cage.

For a moment, Rochelle thought to become an Amsterdam, of which Coligni would have been the William of Orange. All know the two famous sieges it supported against Charles IX. and Richelieu, its numberless heroic efforts, its endurance, and the poniard which the mayor laid on the table of the Hôtel-de-Ville for his heart who should speak of surrender. Yet were its brave inhabitants constrained to yield, when England, betraying the Protestant cause and her own interest, suffered Richelieu to block up their port. The remains of the immense dike constructed for this purpose, are still distinguishable at low tide. Shut out from the sea, the amphibious city drooped and languished; and, to muzzle her the better, Louis XIV. founded Rochefort, a stone's throw from

Rochelle—the port of the monarch, by the side of the port of the people.

There was, however, a part of Poitou which had scarcely figured in history, which was but little known, and knew not itself. It was revealed by the Vendean war. The principal and the earliest scene of this fearful war, which kindled a conflagration throughout the whole west, was the basin of the Sèvre, Nantaise, the sombre hills with which it is surrounded, and the entire Vendean Bocage. This said Vendée, which has fourteen rivers, and not one navigable one—a country lost in its woods and hedges—despite all that has been said, was neither more religious nor more loyal than many other frontier provinces; but it clung to its habits. These had been but little disturbed by the ancient monarchy, with its imperfect centralization; but the revolution sought to uproot them, and to bring over the province at once to national unity. Precipitate, and violent, and startling by the sudden and hostile light it threw upon everything, it scared these children of the night. The peasants stood up, heroes. It is a fact, that Cathelineau, the carrier *(voiturier),* was kneading his bread when he heard the republican proclamation read. He just washed his hands, and shouldered his gun. Each did the same, and marched straight against the *blues:* and the struggle was not man to man, in woods and in darkness, as with the Chouans in Brittany—but in masses, and in the open plain. Nearly a hundred thousand men were present at the siege of Nantes. The war of Brittany is as a warlike ballad of the Scottish border; that of La Vendée, an Iliad.

Proceeding towards the south, we shall pass the sombre city of Saintes, with its beautiful plains—the battle-fields of Taillebourg and Jarnac—the grottoes of the Charente, and its vines in the salt-marshes. We must rapidly traverse the Limousin—that lofty, cold, rainy country, where so many rivers take their rise. Its beautiful granite hills, like semi-globes, and its vast chestnut forests, maintain an honest, but heavy race, timid, and awkward through their indecision; as if bearing the stamp of the sufferings inflicted on their country by the long struggle for its possession between England and France. Quite different with Lower Limousin—the lively and quick-witted character of the Southerns is already very striking there; and the names of the Segurs, St. Aulaires, Noailles, Ventadours, Pompadours, and especially of the Turennes, will serve to characterize the genius of the men here—to indicate their attachment to the central power, and the profit to which they put it. That extraordinary personage, cardinal Dubois, came from Brives-la-Gaillarde.

The mountains of Upper Limousin ramify with those of Auvergne, which, in their turn, join the Cevennes. Auvergne is formed by the valley of the Allier, over which towers, on the west, the mass of the Mont-Dor, which rises between the Pic or the Puy-de-Dôme and the group of the Cantal. It is a vast extinct fire—the ashes now almost everywhere covered by a rude and strong vegetation. The walnut strikes root in the basaltic rock, and the corn sprouts out of the pumice. Nor are the internal fires so far extinguished, but that smoke still rises in one of the valleys; and the *étouffis* of Mont-Dor remind one of Solfaterra and the Grotto del Cane. Built of lava, the towns (Clermont, St. Flour, &c.) have a black, heavy look; but the country is beautiful, whether you traverse the vast and solitary meadows of the Cantal and the Mont-Dor, to the monotonous sound of the waterfalls, or gaze upon the fertile Limagne and on the Puy-de-Dôme, that pretty *thimble* seven hundred toises high, and which is alternately veiled and unveiled by the clouds which love it, and can neither fly it nor remain with it. In fact, Auvergne is buffeted by a constant but shifting wind, whose currents whirl and chafe with the ever-changing direction of its mountain valleys. With a southern sky, the country is cold; you freeze on lava; and the inhabitants of the mountain district bury themselves all the winter in their stables, and surround themselves with a warm and thick atmosphere. Laden, like the Limousins, with Heaven knows how many thick and heavy garments, they may be considered a southern race, shivering in the bleak north wind, and pinched and stiffened by a foreign clime. Their wine is rough, their cheese bitter—like the rude herbage from which it is produced. They sell, too, their lava, their pumice-stones, the pebbles of the district, and the common fruits of the country, which are taken down the Allier in boats. Red—eminently the barbarian color—is that which they prefer: they like rough red wine, red cattle. Rather laborious than industrious, they still often till the deep and strong soils of their plains with the small plough of the south, which scarcely scratches the surface. Their yearly emigration from the mountains is thrown away; they bring back some money, but few ideas.

And yet there is real strength in the men of this race—a rough sap, sour perhaps, but full of life as the herbage of the Cantal. Age has no effect upon it. See the green old age of their old men, of the Dulaures, and the De Pradts—and the octogenarian Montlosier, who directs and superintends his workmen and all around him, who plants and who builds, and who, on the spur of the moment, could write a new book against the clergy *(parti-prêtre)* or in favor of feudalism—at once the friend and the enemy of the middle-ages.

This inconsequent and contradictory character, observable in other provinces of our middle zone, reaches its apogée in Auvergne. There sprang up those great legists, the logicians of the Gallican party, who never knew whether they were for or against the pope—the chancellor de l'Hôpital, a doubtful Catholic; the Arnauds; the severe Domat, that Jansenist Papinian, who endeavored to bound the law by Christianity, and his friend Pascal, the only man of the seventeenth century who felt the religious crisis going on between Montaigne's day and that of Voltaire, and in the struggles of whose conscience the battle of doubt and faith is so singularly depicted.

We might enter the great valley of the south by Rouergue, a province signalized by a rude hap; and which, indeed, under its sombre chestnut trees, is but one enormous heap of coal, iron, copper, and lead. Its coal mines have been for ages on fire for several leagues; a fire, however, unconnected with any thing volcanic. Exposed to every vicissitude of cold and heat by the variety of its aspects and of its climates, splintered by precipices, and cut up by two torrents, the Tarn and the Aveyron, the wild Cevennes need not envy it. But I prefer entering by Cahors. Here, nature is clad in vines. You meet with the mulberry before you reach Montauban. "The prospect before you, which contains a semicircle of a hundred miles diameter, has an oceanic vastness, in which the eye loses itself; an almost boundless scene of cultivation; an animated but confused mass of infinitely varied parts—melting gradually into the distant obscure, from which emerges the amazing frame of the Pyrenees, rearing their silvered heads far above the clouds." The ox, yoked by his horns, ploughs the fertile valley—the vine throws her tendrils round the elm. If you draw to the left, towards the mountains, you descry there the goat hanging on the arid hillside, and the mule, laden with oil, following the midway track. Southward there bursts a storm, and the country becomes a lake: in an hour, the whole has dried up before the thirsty sun. In the evening you reach some large and melancholy city; Toulouse, if you like. The sonorous accent which strikes your ear would lead you to fancy yourself in Italy; but the houses, built partly of wood, partly of brick, and the abrupt accost and bold and lively demeanor of the people, soon remind you that you are in France. The upper classes, at least, are French: the lower present quite a different physiognomy, and are, perhaps, Spanish or Moorish. You are in the ancient city of Toulouse, so great under its counts, which, through its parliament, became the monarch and tyrant of the south, whose hot and heady legists bore to Boniface VIII. the buffet of Philip the Fair, for which they made but too frequent atonement at the cost of the heretics—burning four hundred in less than a century, and who, at a later period, becoming the instruments of Richelieu's revenge, condemned Montmorency, and beheaded him in their beautiful hall, stained with red. The Toulousans made it their boast that they had the capitol of Rome, and the grotto dei morti of Naples—in which corpses remain for centuries without undergoing putrefaction. The city archives were kept in the capitol, in an iron chest, like those of the Roman flamens; and the motto on the walls of the Gascon senate-house was, *Videant consules ne quid respublica detrimenti capiat.*

Toulouse is the central point of the great southern basin. Here or near it meet the waters of the Pyrenees, and of the Cevennes, the Tarn, and the Garonne, to fall with their united streams into the ocean—the Garonne receiving the whole. The sinuous and quivering rivers of Limousin and of Auvergne, flow northward past Perigueux and Bergerac; while the Lot, the Viaur, the Aveyron, and the Tarn, after making several more or less abrupt turns, run from the east and the Cevennes, by Rodez and Alby. The north supplies rivers; the south torrents. The Arriège descends from the Pyrenees; and the Garonne, already swollen by the Gers and the Baize, makes a beautiful curve to the northwest, which the Adour imitates on a smaller scale towards the south. Toulouse separates, or nearly so, Languedoc from Guyenne; provinces which, lying in the same latitude, are yet widely different. The Garonne passes through the antique Toulouse, through the old Roman and Gothic Languedoc, and constantly increasing its flood, opens to the sea, like a sea, beyond Bordeaux. This last-named town, long the capital of English France, and long English at heart, turns, on account of its commercial interests, towards England, the ocean, and America. Here the Garonne, which we may now call the Gironde, is twice the width of the Thames at London.

Rich and beautiful as is this vale of the Garonne, we cannot linger there; the distant summits of the Pyrenees are too powerful an attraction. But the road is a serious obstacle. Whether you pass through Nérac, the sombre seigniory of the Albrets, or proceed along the coast, you have before you a sea of *landes,* only varied by cork-tree woods, vast *pinadas* —a lonely and a cheerless route, with no other signs of life than the flocks of black sheep that annually migrate from the Pyrenees to the *landes,* leaving the mountains for the plain under the charge of shepherds of the *landes,* and going northward in search of the warmth. The wandering life of the shepherds is one of the picturesque characteristics of the south. You meet them scaling the Cevennes and the Pyrenees from the plains of Languedoc, and ascending the mountains of Gap and Barcelonetta, from Crau in Provence. This nomad race, carrying their all with them, with the stars as the sole companions of their eternal solitude, half astronomers, half astrologers, bring the life of Asia, the life of Lot and of Abraham, into the heart of our western world. But, in France, the husbandmen fear their passage, and confine them to narrow routes. It is in the Apennines, in the plains of Apulia, and in the Campagna of Rome, that they roam with all the freedom of the ancient world; while in Spain they are kings and lay waste the whole country with impunity. Protected by the all-powerful company of the *Mesta,* which employs from forty to sixty thousand shepherds, the triumphant merinos devour the country from Estramadura to Navarre and Arragon. The Spanish shepherd, wilder than ours, wrapped up in his sheepskin, and with his *abarca* of rough cowhide fastened on his feet and legs with string, resembles one of his own shaggy flock.

At last we see the formidable barrier of Spain in all its grandeur. It is not, like the Alps, a complicated system of peaks and valleys, but one immense wall, lowered at either end. Every other passage is inaccessible to carriages, and even to mules and man himself, for six or eight months of the year. Two distinct people who, in reality, are neither Spanish nor French—the Basques on the west, and on the east the Catalans and people of Roussillon—are the porters of the two worlds. The portals are theirs, to open and to shut. Irritable and capricious, and tired of the constant passage of the nations, they open to Abder-Rahman, and shut to Roland. Many are the graves between Roncesvalles and the Seu of Urgel.

Thomas Babington Macaulay

1800—1859

4

No worse a fate could befall an English man of letters in the late 1820's and 1830's than to incur the wrath of Thomas Babington Macaulay. In addition to being a successful and influential politician and administrator, Macaulay, the most popular historian ever to write in the English language, was also a devastating literary and historical critic. During these years, Macaulay was a frequent contributor to the *Edinburgh Review,* the widely read organ of the Whig party, and he occasionally used this platform not only to shape the literary and historical taste of contemporary England but to take vengeance on his political enemies as well. Quite aware of being one of the cultural arbiters of his time, he deliberately set out to decimate a Tory foe, John W. Croker, with whom he had had various parliamentary encounters, "black and blue," when Croker's edition of Boswell was published. Macaulay's review was not a review at all but a vicious attack on Croker. Some years later, when Macaulay's own *History of England* came up for consideration in the *Quarterly Review,* Croker attempted to repay him in kind, but he could not match Macaulay's invective. It is not, however, Macaulay's ability to destroy his rivals that attracts our attention. It is his power to create great historical narrative that made his own *History* an extraordinary best seller and allowed his interpretation of English history to influence, if not govern, the historical consciousness of most of his countrymen.

Macaulay's was one of those legendary childhoods. According to his nephew and biographer, Sir George Otto Trevelyan, Macaulay initiated a lifetime of voracious reading before the age of five, and was already writing essays and poems when most children were first beginning to read. In 1818, he went up to Trinity College, Cambridge, which he later regarded as a second home, and where his monument in the chapel today is testimony to the high esteem in which he is still held there. In 1824, he won a college prize for an essay on the character of William III, a monarch who Macaulay believed was the incarnation of personal virtue and political wisdom. Two years later he was called to the bar, but he spent most of his time in London in the gallery of the House of Commons, whetting his appetite for a political career. His literary debut, an essay on Milton in the *Edinburgh Review* in 1825, was an immediate success. The editor of the magazine welcomed the essay and wrote to its author, "The more I think, the less I can conceive where you picked up that style." Macaulay eventually became the mainstay of the review. The irresistible style of the mature Macaulay is present in this essay; so is his personal interpretation of English history, which he later refined. It remains the most articulate expression of the famous Whig interpretation of English history.

A concise statement of that interpretation appears in Macaulay's 1835 essay on Sir James Mackintosh's *History of the Glorious Revolution of 1688.* Here Macaulay wrote, without a flinch, that "the history of England is emphatically the history of progress. It is the history of a constant movement of a great society. We see that society, at the beginning of the twelfth century, in a state more miserable than the state in which the most degraded nations of the East now are." Macaulay continues in this vein, emphasizing the despotism of the Stuart dynasty and the wisdom of the Whig party in the seventeenth century, which culminated in the "great blessing" of the Revolution of 1688. With complete confidence in his absolute judgments of men and events, Macaulay told a nation, deprived of a good history since Hume's, what it wanted to hear: that it was the most enlightened people living in the most enlightened country of all time. In the first chapter of his *History of England,* published in 1849, he was certain that "the history of our country during the last hundred and sixty years is eminently the history of physical, of moral, and of intellectual improvement."

Beginning in 1830, Macaulay was kept from pursuing his historical interests by an active career in the House of Commons. After his speech in favor of the Reform Bill in March, 1831, the Speaker told him that he had never seen the Commons in such a state of excitement. After the passage of the Reform Bill, Macaulay continued his fight for the Whig party and was rewarded with a seat on the Supreme Council of India, a position he held from 1834 to 1838. His accomplishments in India were noteworthy. He vindicated the liberty of the press, campaigned for equality of Indians and Europeans before the law, and helped draft a rational penal code. Upon his return to England, he again sat in Parliament and, in 1839, became a member of the Cabinet as the Secretary of War. Macaulay was happier out of office than in, since as a political outsider he could devote more time to his historical career. In 1839, he formally began the *History of England;* and from that time on he resisted as much as possible the temptations of politics and even of the notoriety fostered by the *Edinburgh Review.* The *History* was to be his greatest achievement. He even refused a chair at Cambridge in order to devote his energy to it.

When the first two volumes of the *History of England* appeared, Macaulay, with typical Whiggish confidence, announced that he had the year 2000 in mind as a terminal date for his story. This projection was fanciful, but he did promise to carry the narrative to the end of the reign of George III. It was more than his relatively short life that prevented him from reaching even this goal. When he died in 1859, he had not yet finished the reign of his hero, William III. The great effort made in collecting and shaping the material for his masterpiece more than compensated for the fact that he spent twenty years writing the history of the same period of time. The vitality of the *History* is the result not only of precise sentences and sparkling paragraphs but also of the firsthand knowledge Macaulay had gained in traveling to the localities he described. The siege of Londonderry and the massacre of Glencoe, dramatic events in the story of William's victory, come alive for the reader as do no other scenes in other works of history or even of historical fiction.

In an early essay entitled "History," printed in the *Edinburgh Review,* Macaulay wrote that "facts are the mere dross of history. It is from the abstract truth which interprets them, and lies latent among them like gold in the ore, that the mass derives its whole value." Macaulay's *History* does not lack in interpretation. As far as he was concerned, "the highest eulogy" of the Glorious Revolution "is that it was our last revolution. For the authority of law, for the security of property, for the peace in our streets, for the happiness of our homes, our gratitude is due, under Him who raises and pulls down nations, to the Long Parliament, to the Convention, and to William of Orange." Macaulay intended, and he achieved, a paean to the Revolution; it was for him, along with the Reform Bill of 1832, among the greatest events in the history of mankind.

Macaulay's supremely effective style—more than his knowledge or opinions—made his Whiggish view of history immensely popular. Lytton Strachey called Macaulay's style "that of a debater. The hard points are driven home like nails with unfailing dexterity; it is useless to hope for subtlety or refinement; one cannot hammer with delicacy. The repetitions, the antitheses, resemble revolving cogwheels; and indeed the total result produces an effect which suggests the operations of a machine more than anything else." Perhaps it was jealousy that prevented Strachey from remarking just how successful a debater and storyteller Macaulay was. The fact is that Macaulay, in his effort to write so that any literate person could understand him, lifted the narrative art to a new and unparalleled height in the English language. The sale of the *History* outdistanced that of the popular novels of Scott during Macaulay's lifetime. It was soon translated into every Western language, and its printings in English are now second only to those of the Bible. Our selection, which begins with James II's reaction to the news of William's invasion and concludes with the king's flight from London, shows Macaulay at his dramatic best. Although there are many brilliant sections in this work, such as the minutely detailed panorama of England in 1685 (the famous third chapter), Macaulay is seldom more forceful or Whiggish than when he recounts the flight of a villainous bigot and the arrival of a noble deliverer.

To life's more obvious pleasures, Macaulay seems to have been indifferent, but he was devoted to his family and, in later life, was a very generous friend. The marriage of his sister, Hannah, in 1834, to Sir Charles Trevelyan was the beginning of a family conglomerate of prominent Whigs, one which, to a large extent, shaped a pervasive attitude toward history and politics for several generations. That attitude has offended many. Matthew Arnold dubbed Macaulay "an ill-disguised Philistine," and Lord Melbourne spoke for many a reader when he remarked that he wished he "were as cocksure of anything as Macaulay is of everything." To be sure, there is much that is offensive in Macaulay's works. His portraits are outrageously partial and very often superficial. He appears to have had no interest in, or understanding of, the deeper motives of human behavior. His comments on the historical process would be considered jejune reflections by most historians today. His sledgehammer brutality in literary controversy is repellent. Yet with all this, he is the undisputed master of the art of historical narration, and his *History of England* continues to win new admirers.

Selected Bibliography

The most comprehensive work on Macaulay is the two-volume biography by his grateful nephew, Sir George Otto Trevelyan, *Life and Letters of Lord Macaulay* (1909). The sketch of Macaulay's life by Leslie Stephen in the *Dictionary of National Biography* (XII), 410–418, may be recommended, especially when accompanied by Sir Charles Firth's judicious examination of Macaulay's conception of history in *A Commentary on Macaulay's History of England* (1938). David Knowles reflected upon Macaulay's career and history at the centenary of Cambridge's most celebrated historian in a brief essay, "Lord Macaulay" (1960). Herbert Butterfield, in his *The Whig Interpretation of History* (1931), exposes some of the superficialities and fallacies of Whig historians. John Clive, in his recent and widely acclaimed *Macaulay: The Shaping of the Historian* (1973), admirably traces the forces, both political and personal, that influenced Macaulay's intellectual development.

HISTORY OF ENGLAND

On the sixth of November James, still uncertain on what part of the coast the invaders had landed, summoned the primate and three other bishops, Compton of London, White of Peterborough, and Sprat of Rochester, to a conference in the closet. The king listened graciously while the prelates made warm professions of loyalty, and assured them that he did not suspect them. "But where," said he, "is the paper that you were to bring me?" "Sir," answered Sancroft, "we have brought no paper. We are not solicitous to clear our fame to the world. It is no new thing to us to be reviled and falsely accused. Our consciences acquit us: your majesty acquits us: and we are satisfied." "Yes," said the king; "but a declaration from you is necessary to my service." He then produced a copy of the prince's manifesto. "See," he said, "how you are mentioned here." "Sir," answered one of the bishops, "not one person in five hundred believes this manifesto to be genuine." "No!" cried the king fiercely; "then those five hundred would bring the Prince of Orange to cut my throat." "God forbid," exclaimed the prelates in concert. But the king's understanding, never very clear, was now quite bewildered. One of his peculiarities was that, whenever his opinion was not adopted, he fancied that his veracity was questioned. "This paper not genuine!" he exclaimed, turning over the leaves with his hands, "Am I not worthy to be believed? Is my word not to be taken?" "At all events, sir," said one of the bishops, "this is not an ecclesiastical matter. It lies within the sphere of the civil power. God has entrusted your majesty with the sword: and it is not for us to invade your functions." Then the archbishop, with that gentle and temperate malice which inflicts the deepest wounds, said that he must be excused from setting his hand to any political document. "I and my brethren, sir," he said, "have already smarted severely for meddling with affairs of state; and we shall be very cautious how we do so again. We once subscribed a petition of the most harmless kind: we presented it in the most respectful manner; and we found that we had committed a high offence. We were saved from ruin only by the merciful protection of God. And, sir, the ground then taken by your majesty's attorney and solicitor was that, out of parliament, we were private men, and that it was criminal presumption in private men to meddle with politics. They attacked us so fiercely that for my part I gave myself over for lost." "I thank you for that, my Lord of Canterbury," said the king; "I should have hoped that you would not have thought yourself lost by falling into my hands." Such a speech might have become the mouth of a merciful sovereign, but it came with a bad grace from a prince who had gazed with pleasure on the contortions of wretches fainting in the boots, from a prince who had burned a woman alive for harbouring one of his flying enemies, from a prince round whose knees his own nephew had clung in vain agonies of supplication. The archbishop was not to be so silenced. He resumed his story, and recounted the insults which the creatures of the court had offered to the Church of England, among which some ridicule thrown on his own style occupied a conspicuous place. The king had nothing to say but that there was no use in repeating old grievances, and that he had hoped that these things had been quite forgotten. He who never forgot the smallest injury that he had suffered could not understand how others should remember for a few weeks the most deadly injuries that he had inflicted.

At length the conversation came back to the point from which it had wandered. The king insisted on having from the bishops a paper declaring their abhorrence of the prince's enterprise. They, with many professions of the most submissive loyalty, pertinaciously refused. The prince, they said, asserted that he had been invited by temporal as well as by spiritual peers. The imputation was common. Why should not the purgation be common also? "I see how it is," said the king. "Some of the temporal peers have been with you, and have persuaded you to cross me in this matter." The bishops solemnly averred that it was not so. But it would, they said, seem strange that, on a question involving grave political and military considerations, the temporal peers should be entirely passed over, and the prelates alone should be required to take a prominent part. "But this," said James, "is my method. I am your king. It is for me to judge what is best. I will go my own way; and I call on you to assist me." The bishops assured him that they would assist him in their proper department, as Christian ministers with their prayers, and as peers of the realm with their advice in his parliament. James, who wanted neither the prayers of heretics nor the advice of parliaments, was bitterly disappointed. After a long altercation, "I have done," he said, "I will urge you no further. Since you will not help me, I must trust to myself and to my own arms."

The bishops had hardly left the royal presence, when a courier arrived with the news that on the preceding day the Prince of Orange had landed in Devonshire. During the following week London was violently agitated. On Sunday, the eleventh of November, a rumour was circulated that knives, gridirons, and caldrons, intended for the torturing of heretics, were concealed in the monastery which had been established under the king's protection at Clerkenwell. Great multitudes assembled round the building, and were about to demolish it, when a military force arrived. The crowd was dispersed and several of the rioters were slain. An inquest sate on the bodies, and came to a decision which strongly indicated the temper of the public mind. The jury found that certain loyal and well-disposed persons, who had gone to put down the meetings of traitors and public enemies at a mass house, had been wilfully murdered by the soldiers; and this strange verdict was signed by all the jurors. The ecclesiastics at Clerkenwell, naturally alarmed by these symptoms of popular feeling, were desirous to place their property in safety. They succeeded in removing most of their furniture before any report of their intentions got abroad. But at length the suspicions of the rabble were excited. The two last carts were stopped in Holborn, and all that they contained was publicly burned in the middle of the street. So great was the alarm among the Catholics that all their places of worship were closed, except those which belonged to the royal family and to foreign ambassadors.

On the whole, however, things as yet looked not unfavourably for James. The invaders had been more than a week on English ground. Yet no man of note had joined them. No rebellion had broken out in the north or the east. No servant of the crown appeared to have betrayed his trust. The royal army was assembling fast at Salisbury, and, though inferior in discipline to that of William, was superior in numbers.

The prince was undoubtedly surprised and mortified by the slackness of those who had invited him to England. By the common people of Devonshire, indeed, he had been received with every sign of good will: but no nobleman, no gentleman of high consideration, had yet repaired to his quarters. The explanation of this singular fact is probably to be found in the circumstance that he had landed in a part of the island where he had not been expected. His friends in the north had made their arrangements for a rising, on the supposition that he would be among them with an army. His friends in the west had made no arrangements at all, and were naturally disconcerted at finding themselves suddenly called upon to take the lead in a movement so important and perilous. They had also fresh in their recollection, and indeed full in their sight, the disastrous consequences of rebellion, gibbets, heads, mangled quarters, families still in deep mourning for brave sufferers who had loved their country well but not wisely. After a warning so terrible and so recent, some hesitation was natural. It was equally natural, however, that William, who, trusting to promises from England, had put to hazard, not only his own fame and fortunes, but also the prosperity and independence of his native land, should feel deeply mortified. He was, indeed, so indignant, that he talked of falling back to Torbay, reembarking his troops, returning to Holland, and leaving those who had betrayed him to the fate which they deserved. At length, on Monday, the twelfth of November, a gentleman named Burrington, who resided in the neighbourhood of Crediton, joined the prince's standard, and his example was followed by several of his neighbours.

Men of higher consequence had already set out from different parts of the country for Exeter. The first of these was John Lord Lovelace, distinguished by his taste, by his magnificence, and by the audacious and intemperate vehemence of his Whiggism. He had been five or six times arrested for political offences. The last crime laid to his charge was, that he had contemptuously denied the validity of a warrant, signed by a Roman Catholic justice of the peace. He had been brought before the privy council and strictly examined, but to little purpose. He resolutely refused to criminate himself; and the evidence against him was insufficient. He was dismissed; but before he retired, James exclaimed in great heat, "My lord, this is not the first trick that you have played me." "Sir," answered Lovelace, with undaunted spirit, "I never played any trick to your majesty, or to any other person. Whoever has accused me to your majesty of playing tricks is a liar." Lovelace had subsequently been admitted into the confidence of those who planned the Revolution. His mansion, built by his ancestors out of the spoils of Spanish galleons from the Indies, rose on the ruins of a house of Our Lady in that beautiful valley through which the Thames, not yet defiled by the precincts of a great capital, nor rising and falling with the flow and ebb of the sea, rolls under woods of beech round the gentle hills of Berkshire. Beneath the stately saloon, adorned by Italian pencils, was a subterraneous vault, in which the bones of ancient monks had sometimes been found. In this dark chamber some zealous and daring opponents of the government had held many midnight conferences during that anxious time when England was impatiently expecting the Protestant wind. The season for action had now arrived. Lovelace, with seventy followers, well armed and mounted, quitted his dwelling, and directed his course westward. He reached Gloucestershire without difficulty. But Beaufort, who governed that county, was exerting all his great authority and influence in support of the crown. The militia had been called out. A strong party had been posted at Cirencester. When Lovelace arrived there he was informed that he could not be suffered to pass. It was necessary for him either to relinquish his undertaking or to fight his way through. He resolved to force a passage; and his friends and tenants stood gallantly by him. A sharp conflict took place. The militia lost an officer and six or seven men; but at length the followers of Lovelace were overpowered: he was made a prisoner, and sent to Gloucester Castle.

Others were more fortunate. On the day on which the skirmish took place at Cirencester, Richard Savage, Lord Colchester, son and heir of the Earl Rivers, and father, by a lawless amour, of that unhappy poet whose misdeeds and misfortunes form one of the darkest portions of literary history, came with between sixty and seventy horse to Exeter. With him arrived the bold and turbulent Thomas Wharton. A few hours later came Edward Russell, son of the Earl of Bedford, and brother of the virtuous nobleman whose blood had been shed on the scaffold. Another arrival still more important was speedily announced. Colchester, Wharton, and Russell belonged to that party which had been constantly opposed to the court. James Bertie, Earl of Abingdon, had, on the contrary, been regarded as a supporter of arbitrary government. He had been true to James in the days of the Exclusion Bill. He had, as Lord Lieutenant of Oxfordshire, acted with vigour and severity against the adherents of Monmouth, and had lighted bonfires to celebrate the defeat of Argyle. But dread of Popery had driven him into opposition and rebellion. He was the first peer of the realm who made his appearance at the quarters of the Prince of Orange.

But the king had less to fear from those who openly arrayed themselves against his authority, than from the dark conspiracy which had spread its ramifications through his army and his family. Of that conspiracy Churchill, unrivalled in sagacity and address, endowed by nature with a certain cool intrepidity which never failed him either in fighting or lying, high in military rank, and high in the favour of the Princess Anne, must be regarded as the soul. It was not yet time for him to strike the decisive blow. But ever thus early he inflicted, by the instrumentality of a subordinate agent, a wound, serious if not deadly, on the royal cause.

Edward, Viscount Cornbury, eldest son of the Earl of Clarendon, was a young man of slender abilities, loose principles, and violent temper. He had been early taught to consider his relationship to the Princess Anne as the groundwork of his fortunes, and had been exhorted to pay her assiduous court. It had never occurred to his father that the hereditary loyalty of the Hydes could run any risk of contamination in the household of the king's favourite daughter: but in that household the Churchills held absolute sway; and Cornbury became their tool. He commanded one of the regiments of dragoons which had been sent westward. Such dispositions had been made that, on the fourteenth of November, he was, during a few hours, the senior officer at Salisbury, and all the troops assembled there were subject to his authority. It seems extraordinary that, at such a crisis, the army on which every thing depended should have been left, even for a moment, under the command of a young colonel who had neither abilities nor experience. There can be little doubt that so strange an arrangement was the result of deep design, and as little doubt to what head and to what heart the design is to be imputed.

Suddenly three of the regiments of cavalry which had assembled at Salisbury were ordered to march westward. Cornbury put himself at their head, and conducted them first to Blandford and thence to Dorchester. From Dorchester, after a halt of an hour or two, they set out for Axminster. Some of the officers began to be uneasy, and demanded an explanation of these strange movements. Cornbury replied that he had instructions to make a night attack on some troops whom the Prince of Orange had posted at Honiton. But suspicion was awake. Searching questions were put, and were evasively answered. At last Cornbury was pressed to produce his orders. He perceived, not only that it would be impossible for him to carry over all the three regiments, as he had hoped, but that he was himself in a situation of considerable peril. He accordingly stole away with a few followers to the Dutch quarters. Most of his troops returned to Salisbury: but some who had been detached from the main body, and who had no suspicion of the designs of their commander, proceeded to Honiton. There they found themselves in the midst of a large force which was fully prepared to receive them. Resistance was impossible. Their leader pressed them to take service under William. A gratuity of a month's pay was offered to them, and was by most of them accepted.

The news of these events reached London on the fifteenth. James had been on the morning of that day in high good humour. Bishop Lamplugh had just presented himself at court on his arrival from Exeter, and had been most graciously received. "My lord," said the king, "you are a genuine old cavalier." The archbishopric of York which had now been vacant more than two years and a half, was immediately bestowed on Lamplugh as the reward of loyalty. That afternoon, just as the king was sitting down to dinner, arrived an express with the tidings of Cornbury's defection. James turned away from his intended meal, swallowed a crust of bread and a glass of wine, and retired to his closet. He afterwards learned that, as he was rising from table, several of the lords in whom he reposed the greatest confidence were shaking hands and congratulating each other in the adjoining gallery. When the news was carried to the queen's apartments she and her ladies broke out into tears and loud cries of sorrow. The blow was indeed a heavy one. It was true that the direct loss to the crown and the direct gain to the invaders hardly amounted to two hundred men and as many horses. But where could the king henceforth expect to find those sentiments in which consists the strength of states and of armies? Cornbury was the heir of a house conspicuous for its attachment to monarchy. His father Clarendon, his uncle Rochester, were men whose loyalty was supposed to be proof to all temptation. What must be the strength of that feeling against which the most deeply rooted hereditary prejudices were of no avail, of that feeling which could reconcile a young officer of high birth to desertion, aggravated by breach of trust and by gross falsehood? That Cornbury was not a man of brilliant parts or enterprising temper made the event more alarming. It was impossible to doubt that he had in some quarter a powerful and artful prompter. Who that prompter was soon became evident. In the meantime no man in the royal camp could feel assured that he was not surrounded by traitors. Political rank, military rank, the honor of a lord, the honor of a soldier, the strongest professions, the purest Cavalier blood, could no longer afford security. Every man might reasonably doubt whether every order which he received from his superior, was not meant to serve the purposes of the enemy. That prompt obedience without which an army is merely a rabble was necessarily at an end. What discipline could there be among soldiers who had just been saved from a snare by refusing to follow their commanding officer on a secret expedition, and by insisting on a sight of his orders?

Cornbury was soon kept in countenance by a crowd of deserters superior to him in rank and capacity: but during a few days he stood alone in his shame, and was bitterly reviled by many who afterwards imitated his example and envied his dishonourable precedence. Among these was his own father. The first outbreak of Clarendon's rage and sorrow was highly pathetic. "Oh God!" he ejaculated, "that a son of mine should be a rebel!" A fortnight later he made up his mind to be a rebel himself. Yet it would be unjust to pronounce him a mere hypocrite. In revolutions men live fast: the experience of years is crowded into hours: old habits of thought and action are violently broken; novelties, which at first sight inspire dread and disgust become in a few days familiar, endurable, attractive. Many men of far purer virtue and higher spirit than Clarendon were prepared, before that memorable year ended, to do what they would have pronounced wicked and infamous when it began.

The unhappy father composed himself as well as he could, and sent to ask a private audience of the king. It was granted. James said, with more than his usual graciousness, that he from his heart pitied Cornbury's relations, and should not hold them at all accountable for the crime of their unworthy kinsman. Clarendon went home, scarcely daring to look his friends in the face. Soon, however, he learned with surprise that the act which had, as he at first thought, for ever dishonored his family was applauded by some persons of high station. His niece, the Princess of Denmark, asked him why he shut himself up. He answered that he had been overwhelmed with confusion by his son's villany. Anne seemed not at all to understand this feeling. "People," she said, "are very uneasy about Popery. I believe that many of the army will do the same."

And now the king, greatly disturbed, called together the principal officers who were still in London. Churchill, who was about this time promoted to the rank of lieutenant-general, made his appearance with that bland serenity which neither peril nor infamy could ever disturb. The meeting was attended by Henry Fitzroy, Duke of Grafton, whose audacity and activity made him conspicuous among the natural children of Charles the Second. Grafton was colonel of the first regiment of Foot Guards. He seems to have been at this time completely under Churchill's influence, and was prepared to desert the royal standard as soon as the favourable moment should arrive. Two other traitors were in the circle, Kirke and Trelawney, who commanded those two fierce and lawless bands then known as the Tangier regiments. Both of them had, like the other Protestant officers of the army, long seen with extreme displeasure the partiality which the king had shown to members of his own Church; and Trelawney remembered with bitter resentment the persecution of his brother the Bishop of Bristol. James addressed the assembly in terms worthy of a better man and of a better cause. It might be, he said, that some of the officers had conscientious scruples about fighting for him. If so he was willing to receive back their commissions. But he adjured them as gentlemen and soldiers not to imitate the shameful example of Cornbury. All seemed moved; and none more than Churchill. He was the first to vow with well feigned enthusiasm that he would shed the last drop of his blood in the service of his gracious master. Grafton was loud and forward in similar protestations; and the example was followed by Kirke and Trelawney.

Deceived by these professions, the king prepared to set out for Salisbury. Before his departure he was informed that a considerable number of peers, temporal and spiritual, desired to be admitted to an audience. They came, with Sancroft at their head, to present a petition, praying that a free and legal parliament might be called, and that a negotiation might be opened with the Prince of Orange.

The history of this petition is curious. The thought seems to have occurred at once to two great chiefs of parties who had long been rivals and enemies, Rochester and Halifax. They both, independently of one another, consulted the bishops. The bishops warmly approved of the suggestion. It was then proposed that a general meeting of peers should be called to deliberate on the form of an address to the king. It was term time; and in term time men of rank and fashion then lounged every day in Westminster Hall as they now lounge in the clubs of Pall Mall and Saint James's Street. Nothing could be easier than for the lords who assembled there to step aside into some adjoining room and to hold a consultation. But unexpected difficulties arose. Halifax became first cold and then adverse. It was his nature to discover objections to everything; and on this occasion his sagacity was quickened by rivalry. The scheme, which he had approved while he regarded it as his own, began to displease him as soon as he found that it was also the scheme of Rochester, by whom he had been long thwarted and at length supplanted, and whom he disliked as much as it was in his easy nature to dislike anybody. Nottingham was at that time much under the influence of Halifax. They both declared that they would not join in the address if Rochester signed it. Clarendon expostulated in vain. "I mean no disrespect," said Halifax, "to my Lord Rochester: but he has been a member of the Ecclesiastical Commission: the proceedings of that court must soon be the subject of a very serious inquiry; and it is not fit that one who has sate there should take any part in our proceedings." Nottingham, with strong expressions of personal esteem for Rochester, avowed the same opinion. The authority of the two dissentient lords prevented several other noblemen from subscribing the address; but the Hydes and the bishops persisted. Nineteen signatures were procured; and the petitioners waited in a body on the king.

He received their address ungraciously. He assured them, indeed, that he passionately desired the meeting of a free parliament; and he promised them, on the faith of a king, that he would call one as soon as the Prince of Orange should have left the island. "But how," said he, "can a parliament be free when an enemy is in the kingdom, and can return near a hundred votes?" To the prelates he spoke with peculiar acrimony. "I could not," he said, "prevail on you the other day to declare against this invasion: but you are ready enough to declare against me. Then you would not meddle with politics. You have no scruple about meddling now. You would be better employed in teaching your flocks how to obey than in teaching me how to govern. You have excited this rebellious temper among them; and now you foment it." He was much incensed against his nephew Grafton, whose signature stood next to that of Sancroft, and said to the young man, with great asperity, "You know nothing about religion; you care nothing about it; and yet, forsooth, you must pretend to have a conscience." "It is true, sir," answered Grafton, with impudent frankness, "that I have very little conscience: but I belong to a party which has a great deal."

Bitter as was the king's language to the petitioners, it was far less bitter than that which he held after they had withdrawn. He had done, he said, far too much already in the hope of satisfying an undutiful and ungrateful people. He had always hated the thought of concession: but he had suffered himself to be talked over; and now he, like his father before him, had found that concession only made subjects more encroaching. He would yield nothing more, not an atom, and, after his fashion, he vehemently repeated many times, "Not an atom." Not only would he make no overtures to the invaders, but he would receive none. If the Dutch sent flags of truce, the first messenger should be dismissed without an answer;

the second should be hanged. In such a mood James set out for Salisbury. His last act before his departure was to appoint a council of five lords to represent him in London during his absence. Of the five, two were Papists, and by law incapable of office. Joined with them was Jeffreys, a Protestant indeed, but more detested by the nation than any Papist. To the other two members of this board, Preston and Godolphin, no serious objection could be made. On the day on which the king left London the Prince of Wales was sent to Portsmouth. That fortress was strongly garrisoned, and was under the government of Berwick. The fleet commanded by Dartmouth lay close at hand; and it was supposed that, if things went ill, the royal infant would, without difficulty, be conveyed from Portsmouth to France.

On the nineteenth James reached Salisbury, and took up his quarters in the episcopal palace. Evil news was now fast pouring in upon him from all sides. The western counties had at length risen. As soon as the news of Cornbury's desertion was known, many great landowners took heart and hastened to Exeter. Among them was Sir William Portman of Bryanstone, one of the greatest men in Dorsetshire, and Sir Francis Warre of Hestercombe, whose interest was great in Somersetshire. But the most important of the new comers was Seymour, who had recently inherited a baronetcy which added little to his dignity, and who, in birth, in political influence, and in parliamentary abilities, was beyond comparison the foremost among the Tory gentlemen of England. At his first audience he is said to have exhibited his characteristic pride in a way which surprised and amused the prince. "I think, Sir Edward," said William, meaning to be very civil, "that you are of the family of the Duke of Somerset." "Pardon me, sir," said Sir Edward, who never forgot that he was the head of the elder branch of the Seymours, "the Duke of Somerset is of my family."

The quarters of William now began to present the appearance of a court. More than sixty men of rank and fortune were lodged at Exeter; and the daily display of rich liveries, and of coaches drawn by six horses in the Cathedral Close, gave to that quiet precinct something of the splendour and gaiety of Whitehall. The common people were eager to take arms; and it would have been easy to form many battalions of infantry. But Schomberg, who thought little of soldiers fresh from the plough, maintained that, if the expedition could not succeed without such help, it would not succeed at all: and William, who had as much professional feeling as Schomberg, concurred in this opinion. Commissions therefore for raising new regiments were very sparingly given; and none but picked recruits were enlisted.

It was now thought desirable that the prince should give a public reception to the whole body of noblemen and gentlemen who had assembled at Exeter. He addressed them in a short but dignified and well considered speech. He was not, he said, acquainted with the faces of all whom he saw. But he had a list of their names, and knew how high they stood in the estimation of their country. He gently chid their tardiness, but expressed a confident hope that it was not yet too late to save the kingdom. "Therefore," he said, "gentlemen, friends, and fellow Protestants, we bid you and all your followers most heartily welcome to our court and camp."

Seymour, a keen politician, long accustomed to the tactics of faction, saw in a moment that the party which had begun to rally round the prince stood in need of organization. It was as yet, he said, a mere rope of sand: no common object had been publicly and formally avowed: nobody was pledged to anything. As soon as the assembly at the Deanery broke up, he sent for Burnet, and suggested that an association should be formed, and that all the English adherents of the prince should put their hands to an instrument binding them to be true to their leader and to each other. Burnet carried the suggestion to the prince and to Shrewsbury, by both of whom it was approved. A meeting was held in the cathedral. A short paper drawn up by Burnet was produced, approved, and eagerly signed. The subscribers engaged to pursue in concert the objects set forth in the prince's declaration; to stand by him and by each other; to take signal vengeance on all who should make any attempt on his person; and, even if such an attempt should unhappily succeed, to persist in their undertaking till the liberties and the religion of the nation should be effectually secured.

About the same time a messenger arrived at Exeter from the Earl of Bath, who commanded at Plymouth. Bath declared that he placed himself, his troops, and the fortress which he governed at the prince's disposal. The invaders therefore had now not a single enemy in their rear.

While the West was thus rising to confront the king, the North was all in a flame behind him. On the sixteenth Delamere took arms in Cheshire. He convoked his tenants, called upon them to stand by him, promised that if they fell in the cause, their leases should be renewed to their children, and exhorted every one who had a good horse either to take the field, or to provide a substitute. He appeared at Manchester with fifty men armed and mounted, and his force had trebled before he reached Boaden Downs.

The neighbouring counties were violently agitated. It had been arranged that Danby should seize York, and that Devonshire should appear at Nottingham. At Nottingham no resistance was anticipated. But at York there was a small garrison under the command of Sir John Reresby. Danby acted with rare dexterity. A meeting of the gentry and freeholders of Yorkshire had been summoned for the twenty-second of November to address the king on the state of affairs. All the deputy lieutenants of the three ridings, several noblemen, and a multitude of opulent esquires and substantial yeomen had been attracted to the provincial capital. Four troops of militia had been drawn out under arms to preserve the public peace. The common hall was crowded with freeholders, and the discussion had begun, when a cry was suddenly raised that the Papists were up, and were slaying the Protestants. The papists of York were much more likely to be employed in seeking for hiding places than in attacking enemies who outnumbered them in the proportion of a hundred to one. But at that time no story of Popish atrocity could be so wild and marvellous as not to find ready belief. The meeting separated in dismay. The whole city was in confusion. At this moment Danby at the head of about a hundred horsemen rode up to the militia, and raised the cry "No Popery! A free parliament! The Protestant religion!" The militia echoed the shout. The garrison was instantly surprised and disarmed. The governor was placed under arrest. The gates were closed. Sentinels were placed everywhere. The populace was suffered to pull down a Roman Catholic chapel; but no other harm appears to have been done. On the following morning the Guildhall was crowded with the first gentlemen of the shire, and with the principal magistrates of the city. The lord mayor was placed in the chair. Danby proposed a declaration setting forth the reasons which had induced the friends of the constitution and of the Protestant religion to rise in arms. This declaration was eagerly adopted, and received in a few hours the signatures of six peers, of five baronets, of six knights, and of many gentlemen of high consideration.

Devonshire meantime, at the head of a great body of friends and dependents, quitted the palace which he was rearing at Chatsworth, and appeared in arms at Derby. There he formally delivered to the mayor a paper stating the reasons which had moved him to this enterprise. He then proceeded to Nottingham, which soon became the head quarters of the northern insurrection. Here a proclamation was put forth couched in bold and severe terms. The name of rebellion, it was said, was a bugbear which could frighten no reasonable man. Was it rebellion to defend those laws and that religion which every king of England bound himself by oath to maintain? How that oath had lately been observed was a question on which, it was to be hoped, a free parliament would soon pronounce. In the meantime, the insurgents declared that they held it to be not rebellion, but legitimate self defence, to resist a tyrant who knew no law but his own will. The northern rising became every day more formidable. Four powerful and wealthy earls, Manchester, Stamford, Rutland, and Chesterfield, repaired to Nottingham, and were joined there by Lord Cholmondley and by Lord Grey de Ruthyn.

All this time the hostile armies in the south were approaching each other. The Prince of Orange, when he learned that the king had arrived at Salisbury, thought it time to leave Exeter. He placed that city and the surrounding country under the government of Sir Edward Seymour, and set out on Wednesday the twenty-first of November, escorted by many of the most considerable gentlemen of the western counties, for Axminster, where he remained several days.

The king was eager to fight; and it was obviously his interest to do so. Every hour took away something from his own strength, and added something to the strength of his enemies. It was most important, too, that his troops should be blooded. A great battle, however it might terminate, could not but injure the prince's popularity. All this William perfectly understood, and determined to avoid an action as long as possible. It is said that, when Schomberg was told that the enemy were advancing and were determined to fight, he answered with the composure of a tactician confident in his skill, "That will be just as we may choose." It was, however, impossible to prevent all skirmishing between the advanced guards of the armies. William was desirous that in such skirmishing nothing might happen which could wound the pride or rouse the vindictive feelings of the nation which he meant to deliver. He therefore, with admirable prudence, placed his British regiments in the situations where there was most risk of collision. The outposts of the royal army were Irish. The consequence was that, in the little combats of this short campaign, the invaders had on their side the hearty sympathy of all Englishmen.

The first of these encounters took place at Wincanton. Mackay's regiment, composed of British soldiers, lay near a body of the king's Irish troops, commanded by their countryman, the gallant Sarsfield. Mackay sent out a small party under a lieutenant named Campbell, to procure horses for the baggage. Campbell found what he wanted at Wincanton, and was just leaving that town on his return, when a strong detachment of Sarsfield's troops approached. The Irish were four to one: but Campbell resolved to fight it out to the last. With a handful of resolute men he took his stand in the road. The rest of his soldiers lined the hedges which overhung the highway on the right and on the left. The enemy came up. "Stand," cried Campbell. "For whom are you?" "I am for King James," answered the leader of the other party. "And I for the Prince of Orange," cried Campbell. "We will prince you," answered the Irishman with a curse. "Fire!" exclaimed Campbell; and a sharp fire was instantly poured in from both the hedges. The king's troops received three well aimed volleys before they could make any return. At length they succeeded in carrying one of the hedges; and would have overpowered the little band which was opposed to them, had not the country people, who mortally hated the Irish, given a false alarm that more of the prince's troops were coming up. Sarsfield recalled his men and fell back; and Campbell proceeded on his march unmolested with the baggage horses. This affair, creditable undoubtedly to the valour and discipline of the prince's army, was magnified by report into a victory won against great odds by British Protestants over Popish barbarians who had been brought from Connaught to oppress our island.

A few hours after this skirmish an event took place which put an end to all risk of a more serious struggle between the armies. Churchill and some of his principal accomplices were assembled at Salisbury. Two of the conspirators, Kirke and Trelawney, had proceeded to Warminster, where their regiments were posted. All was ripe for the execution of the long meditated treason.

Churchill advised the King to visit Warminster, and to inspect the troops stationed there. James assented; and his coach was at the door of the episcopal palace when his nose began to bleed violently. He was forced to postpone his expedition and to put himself under medical treatment. Three days elapsed before the hemorrhage was entirely subdued; and during those three days alarming rumours reached his ears.

It was impossible that a conspiracy so widely spread as that of which Churchill was the head could be kept altogether secret. There was no evidence which could be laid before a jury or a court martial: but strange whispers wandered about the camp. Feversham, who held the chief command, reported that there was a bad spirit in the army. It was hinted to the king that some who were near his person were not his friends, and that it would be a wise precaution to send Churchill and Grafton under a guard to Portsmouth. James rejected this counsel. A propensity to suspicion was not among his vices. Indeed the confidence which he reposed in professions of fidelity and attachment was such as might rather have been expected from a goodhearted and inexperienced stripling than from a politician who was far advanced in life, who had seen much of the world, who had suffered much from villanous arts, and whose own character was by no means a favourable specimen of human nature. It would be difficult to mention any other man who, having himself so little scruple about breaking faith with others, was so slow to believe that others could break faith with him. Nevertheless the reports which he had received of the state of his army disturbed him greatly. He was now no longer impatient for a battle. He even began to think of retreating. On the evening of Saturday, the twenty-fourth of November, he called a council of war. The meeting was attended by those officers against whom he had been most earnestly cautioned. Feversham expressed an opinion that it was desirable to fall back. Churchill argued on the other side. The consultation lasted till midnight. At length the king declared that he had decided for a retreat. Churchill saw or imagined that he was distrusted, and, though gifted with a rare self command, could not conceal his uneasiness. Before the day broke he fled to the prince's quarters, accompanied by Grafton.

Churchill left behind him a letter of explanation. It was written with that decorum which he never failed to preserve in the midst of guilt and dishonor. He acknowledged that he owed everything to the royal favour. Interest, he said, and gratitude impelled him in the same direction. Under no other government could he hope to be so great and prosperous as he had been: but all such considerations must yield to a paramount duty. He was a Protestant; and he could not conscientiously draw his sword against the Protestant cause. As to the rest he would ever be ready to hazard life and fortune in defence of the sacred person and of the lawful rights of his gracious master.

Next morning all was confusion in the royal camp. The king's friends were in dismay. His enemies could not conceal their exultation. The consternation of James was increased by news which arrived on the same day from Warminster. Kirke, who commanded at that post, had refused to obey orders which he had received from Salisbury. There could no longer be any doubt that he too was in league with the Prince of Orange. It was rumoured that he had actually gone over with all his troops to the enemy; and the rumour, though false, was, during some hours, fully believed. A new light flashed on the mind of the unhappy king. He thought that he understood why he had been pressed, a few days before, to visit Warminster. There he would have found himself helpless, at the mercy of the conspirators, and in the vicinity of the hostile outposts. Those who might have attempted to defend him would have been easily overpowered. He would have been carried a prisoner to the head quarters of the invading army. Perhaps some still blacker treason might have been committed; for men who have once engaged in a wicked and perilous enterprise are no longer their own masters, and are often impelled, by a fatality which is part of their just punishment, to crimes such as they would at first have shuddered to contemplate. Surely it was not without the special intervention of some guardian saint that a king devoted to the Catholic Church had, at the very moment when he was blindly hastening to captivity, perhaps to death, been suddenly arrested by what he had then thought a disastrous malady.

All these things confirmed James in the resolution which he had taken on the preceding evening. Orders were given for an immediate retreat. Salisbury was in an uproar. The camp broke up with the confusion of a flight. No man knew whom to trust or whom to obey. The material strength of the army was little diminished: but its moral strength had been destroyed. Many whom shame would have restrained from leading the way to the prince's quarters were eager to imitate an example which they never would have set; and many who would have stood by their king while he appeared to be resolutely advancing against the invaders, felt no inclination to follow a receding standard. . . .

While foes were thus rising up all round the king, friends were fast shrinking from his side. The idea of resistance had become familiar to every mind. Many who had been struck with horror when they heard of the first defections now blamed themselves for having been so slow to discern the signs of the times. There was no longer any difficulty or danger in repairing to William. The king, in calling on the nation to elect representatives, had, by implication, authorised all men to repair to the places where they had votes or interest; and many of those places were already occupied by invaders or insurgents. Clarendon eagerly caught at this opportunity of deserting the falling cause. He knew that his speech in the council of peers had given deadly offence: and he was mortified by finding that he was not to be one of the royal commissioners. He had estates in Wiltshire. He determined that his son, the son of whom he had lately spoken with grief and horror, should be a candidate for that county; and, under pretence of looking after the election, he set out for the West. He was speedily followed by Oxford, and by others who had hitherto disclaimed all connection with the prince's enterprise.

By this time the invaders, steadily though slowly advancing, were within seventy miles of London. Though midwinter was approaching the weather was fine; the way was pleasant; and the turf of Salisbury plain seemed luxuriously smooth to men who had been toiling through the miry ruts of the Devonshire and Somersetshire highways. The route of the army lay close by Stonehenge; and regiment after regiment halted to examine that mysterious ruin, celebrated all over the Continent as the greatest wonder of our island. William entered Salisbury with the same military pomp which he had displayed at Exeter, and was lodged there in the palace which the king had occupied a few days before.

His train was now swelled by the Earls of Clarendon and Oxford, and by other men of high rank, who had, till within a few days, been considered as zealous royalists. Citters also made his appearance at the Dutch head quarters. He had been during some weeks almost a prisoner in his house, near Whitehall, under the constant observation of relays of spies. Yet, in spite of those spies, or perhaps by their help, he had succeeded in obtaining full and accurate intelligence of all that passed in the palace: and now, full fraught with valuable information about men and things, he came to assist the deliberations of William.

Thus far the prince's enterprise had prospered beyond the anticipations of the most sanguine. And now, according to the general law which governs human affairs, prosperity began to produce disunion. The Englishmen assembled at Salisbury were divided into two parties. One party consisted of Whigs who had always regarded the doctrines of passive obedience and of indefeasible hereditary right as slavish superstitions. Many of them had passed years in exile. All had been long shut out from participation in the favours of the crown. They now exulted in the near prospect of greatness and of vengeance. Burning with resentment, flushed with victory and hope, they would hear of no compromise. Nothing less than the deposition of the tyrant would content them: nor can it be disputed that herein they were perfectly consistent. They had exerted themselves, nine years earlier, to exclude him from the throne, because they thought it likely that he would be a bad king. It could therefore scarcely be expected that they would willingly leave him on the throne, now that he had turned out a far worse king than any reasonable man could have anticipated.

On the other hand, not a few of William's followers were zealous Tories, who had, till very recently, held the doctrine of nonresistance in the most absolute form, but whose faith in that doctrine had, for a moment, given way to the strong passions excited by the ingratitude of the king and by the peril of the Church. No situation could be more painful or perplexing than that of the old Cavalier who found himself in arms against the throne. The scruples which had not prevented him from repairing to the Dutch camp began to torment him cruelly as soon as he was there. His mind misgave him that he had committed a crime. At all events he had exposed himself to reproach, by acting in diametrical opposition to the professions of his whole life. He felt insurmountable disgust for his new allies. They were people whom, ever since he could remember, he had been reviling and persecuting, Presbyterians, Independents, Anabaptists, old soldiers of Cromwell, brisk boys of Shaftesbury, accomplices in the Rye House Plot, captains of the Western Insurrection. He naturally wished to find out some salvo which might sooth his conscience, which might vindicate his consistency, and which might put a distinction between him and the crew of schismatical rebels whom he had always despised and abhorred, but with whom he was now in danger of being confounded. He therefore disclaimed, with vehemence, all thought of taking the crown from that anointed head which the ordinance of heaven and the fundamental laws of the realm had made sacred. His dearest wish was to see a reconciliation effected on terms which would not lower the royal dignity. He was no traitor. He was not, in truth, resisting the kingly authority. He was in arms only because he was convinced that the best service which could be rendered to the throne was to rescue his majesty, by a little gentle coercion, from the hands of wicked counsellors.

The evils which the mutual animosity of these factions tended to produce were, to a great extent, averted by the ascendency and by the wisdom of the prince. Surrounded by eager disputants, officious advisers, abject flatterers, vigilant spies, malicious talebearers, he remained serene and inscrutable. He preserved silence while silence was possible. When he was forced to speak, the earnest and peremptory tone in which he uttered his well weighed opinions soon silenced everybody else. Whatever some of his too zealous adherents might say, he uttered not a word indicating any design on the English crown. He was doubtless well aware that between him and that crown were still interposed obstacles which no prudence might be able to surmount, and which a single false step would make insurmountable. His only chance of obtaining the splendid prize was not to seize it rudely, but to wait till, without any appearance of exertion or stratagem on his part, his secret wish should be accomplished by the force of circumstances, by the blunders of his opponents, and by the free choice of the Estates of the Realm. Those who ventured to interrogate him learned nothing, and yet could not accuse him of shuffling. He quietly referred them to his declaration, and assured them that his views had undergone no change since that instrument had been drawn up. So skilfully did he manage his followers that their discord seems rather to have strengthened than to have weakened his hands: but it broke forth with violence when his control was withdrawn, interrupted the harmony of convivial meetings, and did not respect even the sanctity of the house of God. Clarendon, who tried to hide from others and from himself, by an ostentatious display of loyal sentiments, the plain fact that he was a rebel, was shocked to hear some of his new associates laughing over their wine at the royal amnesty which had just been graciously offered to them. They wanted no pardon, they said. They would make the king ask pardon before they had done with him. Still more alarming and disgusting to every good Tory was an incident which happened at Salisbury Cathedral. As soon as the officiating minister began to read the collect for the king, Burnet, among whose many good qualities selfcommand and a fine sense of the becoming cannot be reckoned, rose from his knees, sate down in his stall, and uttered some contemptuous noises which disturbed the devotions of the whole congregation.

In a short time the factions which divided the prince's camp had an opportunity of measuring their strength. The royal commissioners were on their way to him. Several days had elapsed since they had been appointed; and it was thought strange that, in a case of such urgency, there should be such delay. But in truth neither James nor William was desirous that negotiations should speedily commence; for James wished only to gain time sufficient for sending his wife and son into France; and the position of William became every day more commanding. At length the prince caused it to be notified to the commissioners that he would meet them at Hungerford. He probably selected this place because, lying at an equal distance from Salisbury and from Oxford, it was well situated for a rendezvous of his most important adherents. At Salisbury were those noblemen and gentlemen who had accompanied him from Holland or had joined him in the west; and at Oxford were many chiefs of the northern insurrection.

Late on Thursday, the sixth of December, he reached Hungerford. The little town was soon crowded with men of rank and note who came thither from opposite quarters. The prince was escorted by a strong body of troops. The northern lords brought with them hundreds of irregular cavalry, whose accoutrements and horsemanship moved the mirth of men accustomed to the splendour and precision of regular armies.

While the prince lay at Hungerford a sharp encounter took place between two hundred and fifty of his troops and six hundred Irish, who were posted at Reading. The superior discipline of the invaders was signally proved on this occasion. Though greatly outnumbered, they, at one onset, drove the king's forces in confusion through the streets of the town into the market place. There the Irish attempted to rally; but being vigorously attacked in front and fired upon at the same time by the inhabitants from the windows of the neighbouring houses, they soon lost heart, and fled with the loss of their colours and of fifty men. Of the conquerors only five fell. The satisfaction which this news gave to the lords and gentlemen who had joined William was unmixed. There was nothing in what had happened to gall their national feelings. The Dutch had not beaten the English, but had assisted an English town to free itself from the insupportable dominion of the Irish.

On the morning of Saturday, the eighth of December, the king's commissioners reached Hungerford. The prince's body guard was drawn up to receive them with military respect. Bentinck welcomed them, and proposed to conduct them immediately to his master. They expressed a hope that the prince would favour them with a private audience; but they were informed that he had resolved to hear them and answer them in public. They were ushered into his bedchamber, where they found him surrounded by a crowd of noblemen and gentlemen. Halifax, whose rank, age, and abilities entitled him to precedence, was spokesman. The proposition which the commissioners had been instructed to make was that the points in dispute should be referred to the parliament, for which the writs were already sealing, and that in the mean time the prince's army would not come within thirty or forty miles of London. Halifax, having explained that this was the basis on which he and his colleagues were prepared to treat, put into William's hands a letter from the king, and retired. William opened the letter and seemed unusually moved. It was the first letter which he had received from his father in law since they had become avowed enemies. Once they had been on good terms and had written to each other familiarly; nor had they, even when they had begun to regard each other with suspicion and aversion, banished from their correspondence those forms of kindness which persons nearly related by blood and marriage commonly use. The letter which the commissioners had brought was drawn up by a secretary in diplomatic form and in the French language. "I have had many letters from the king," said William, "but they were all in English, and in his own hand." He spoke with a sensibility which he was little in the habit of displaying. Perhaps he thought at that moment how much reproach his enterprise, just, beneficent, and necessary as it was, must bring on him and on the wife who was devoted to him. Perhaps he repined at the hard fate which had placed him in such a situation that he could fulfil his public duties only by breaking through domestic ties, and envied the happier condition of those who are not responsible for the welfare of nations and churches. But such thoughts, if they rose in his mind, were firmly suppressed. He requested the lords and gentlemen whom he had convoked on this occasion to consult together, unrestrained by his presence, as to the answer which ought to be returned. To himself, however, he reserved the power of deciding in the last resort, after hearing their opinion. He then left them, and retired to Littlecote Hall, a manor house situated about two miles off, and renowned down to our own times, not more on account of its venerable architecture and furniture than on account of a horrible and mysterious crime which was perpetrated there in the days of the Tudors.

Before he left Hungerford, he was told that Halifax had expressed a great desire to see Burnet. In this desire there was nothing strange; for Halifax and Burnet had long been on terms of friendship. No two men, indeed, could resemble each other less. Burnet was utterly destitute of delicacy and tact. Halifax's taste was fastidious, and his sense of the ludicrous morbidly quick. Burnet viewed every act and every character through a medium distorted and coloured by party spirit. The tendency of Halifax's mind was always to see the faults of his allies more strongly than the faults of his opponents. Burnet was, with all his infirmities, and through all the vicissitudes of a life passed in circumstances not very favourable to piety, a sincerely pious man. The sceptical and sarcastic Halifax lay under the imputation of infidelity. Halifax therefore often incurred Burnet's indignant censure; and Burnet was often the butt of Halifax's keen and polished pleasantry. Yet they were drawn to each other by a mutual attraction, liked each other's conversation, appreciated each other's abilities, interchanged opinions freely, and interchanged also good offices in perilous times. It was not, however, merely from personal regard that Halifax now wished to see his old acquaintance. The commissioners must have been anxious to know what was the prince's real aim. He had refused to see them in private; and little could be learned from what he might say in a formal and public interview. Almost all those who were admitted to his confidence were men taciturn and impenetrable as himself. Burnet was the only exception. He was notoriously garrulous and indiscreet. Yet circumstances had made it necessary to trust him; and he would doubtless, under the dexterous management of Halifax, have poured out secrets as fast as words. William knew this well, and, when he was informed that Halifax was asking for the doctor, could not refrain from exclaiming, "If they get together there will be fine tattling." Burnet was forbidden to see the commissioners in private; but he was assured in very courteous terms that his fidelity was regarded by the prince as above all suspicion; and, that there might be no ground for complaint, the prohibition was made general.

That afternoon the noblemen and gentlemen whose advice William had asked met in the great room of the principal inn at Hungerford. Oxford was placed in the chair; and the king's overtures were taken into consideration. It soon appeared that the assembly was divided into two parties, a party anxious to come to terms with the king, and a party bent on his destruction. The latter party had the numerical superiority: but it was observed that Shrewsbury, who of all the English nobles was supposed to enjoy the largest share of William's confidence, though a Whig, sided on this occasion with the Tories. After much altercation the question was put. The majority was for rejecting the proposition which the royal commissioners had been instructed to make. The resolution of the assembly was reported to the prince at Littlecote. On no occasion during the whole course of his eventful life did he show more prudence and selfcommand. He could not wish the negotiation to succeed. But he was far too wise a man not to know that, if unreasonable demands made by him should cause it to fail, public feeling would no longer be on his side. He therefore overruled the opinion of his too eager followers, and declared his determination to treat on the basis proposed by the king. Many of the lords and gentlemen assembled at Hungerford remonstrated: a whole day was spent in bickering: but William's purpose was immovable. He declared himself willing to refer all the questions in dispute to the parliament which had just been summoned, and not to advance within forty miles of London. On his side he made some demands which even those who were least disposed to commend him allowed to be moderate. He insisted that the existing statutes should be obeyed till they should be altered by competent authority, and that all persons who held offices without a legal qualification should be forthwith dismissed. The deliberations of the parliament, he justly conceived, could not be free if it was to sit surrounded by Irish regiments while he and his army lay at a distance of several marches. He therefore thought it reasonable that, since his troops were not to advance within forty miles of London on the west, the king's troops should fall back as far to the east. There would thus be round the spot where the Houses were to meet a wide circle of neutral ground. Within that circle, indeed, there were two fastnesses of great importance to the people of the capital, the Tower, which commanded their dwellings, and Tilbury Fort, which commanded their maritime trade. It was impossible to leave these places ungarrisoned. William therefore proposed that they should be temporarily intrusted to the care of the city of London. It might possibly be convenient that, when the parliament assembled, the king should repair to Westminster with a body guard. The prince announced that, in that case, he should claim the right of repairing thither also with an equal number of soldiers. It seemed to him just that, while military operations were suspended, both the armies should be considered as alike engaged in the service of the English nation, and should be alike maintained out of the English revenue. Lastly, he required some guarantee that the king would not take advantage of the armistice for the purpose of introducing a French force into England. The point where there was most danger was Portsmouth. The prince did not however insist that this important fortress should be delivered up to him, but proposed that it should, during the truce, be under the government of an officer in whom both himself and James could confide.

The propositions of William were framed with a punctilious fairness, such as might have been expected rather from a disinterested umpire pronouncing an award than from a victorious prince dictating to a helpless enemy. No fault could be found with them by the partisans of the king. But among the Whigs there was much murmuring. They wanted no reconciliation with the tyrant. They thought themselves absolved from all allegiance to him. They were not disposed to recognise the authority of a parliament convoked by his writ. They were averse to an armistice; and they could not conceive why, if there was to be an armistice, it should be an armistice on equal terms. By all the laws of war the stronger party had a right to take advantage of his strength; and what was there in the character of James to justify any extraordinary indulgence? Those who reasoned thus little knew from how elevated a point of view, and with how discerning an eye the leader whom they censured contemplated the whole situation of England and Europe. They were eager to ruin James, and would therefore either have refused to treat with him on any conditions, or have imposed on him conditions insupportably hard. To the success of William's vast and profound scheme of policy it was necessary that James should ruin himself by rejecting conditions ostentatiously liberal. The event proved the wisdom of the course which the majority of the Englishmen at Hungerford were inclined to condemn.

On Sunday, the ninth of December, the prince's demands were put in writing, and delivered to Halifax. The commissioners dined at Littlecote. A splendid assemblage had been invited to meet them. The old hall, hung with coats of mail which had seen the wars of the Roses, and with portraits of gallants who had adorned the court of Philip and Mary, was now crowded with peers and generals. In such a throng a short question and answer might be exchanged without attracting notice. Halifax seized this opportunity, the first which had presented itself, of extracting all that Burnet knew or thought. "What is it that you want?" said the dexterous diplomatist; "Do you wish to get the king into your power?" "Not at all," said Burnet; "we would not do the least harm to his person." "And if he were to go away?" said Halifax. "There is nothing," said Burnet, "so much to be wished." There can be no doubt that Burnet expressed the general sentiment of the Whigs in the prince's camp. They were all desirous that James should fly from the country: but only a few of the wisest among them understood how important it was that his flight should be ascribed by the nation to his own folly and perverseness, and not to harsh usage and well grounded apprehension. It seems probable that, even in the extremity to which he was now reduced, all his enemies united would have been unable to effect his complete overthrow had he not been his own worst enemy: but, while his commissioners were labouring to save him, he was labouring as earnestly to make all their efforts useless.

His plans were at length ripe for execution. The pretended negotiation had answered its purpose. On the same day on which the three lords reached Hungerford the Prince of Wales arrived at Westminster. It had been intended that he should come over London Bridge; and some Irish troops were sent to Southwark to meet him. But they were received by a great multitude with such hooting and execration that they thought it advisable to retire with all speed. The poor child crossed the Thames at Kingston, and was brought into Whitehall so privately that many believed him to be still at Portsmouth.

To send him and the queen out of the country without delay was now the first object of James. But who could be trusted to manage the escape? Dartmouth was the most loyal of Protestant Tories; and Dartmouth had refused. Dover was a creature of the Jesuits; and even Dover had hesitated. It was not very easy to find an Englishman of rank and honor who would undertake to place the heir apparent of the English crown in the hands of the king of France. In these circumstances, James bethought him of a French nobleman who then resided in London, Antoine, Count of Lauzun. Of this man it has been said that his life was stranger than the dreams of other people. Early in life he had been the intimate associate of Lewis, and had been encouraged to expect the highest employments under the French crown. Then his fortunes had undergone an eclipse. Lewis had driven from him the friend of his youth with bitter reproaches, and had, it was said, scarcely refrained from adding blows. The fallen favourite had been sent prisoner to a fortress: but he had emerged from his confinement, had again enjoyed the smiles of his master, and had gained the heart of one of the greatest ladies in Europe, Anna Maria, daughter of Gaston, Duke of Orleans, grand-daughter of King Henry the Fourth, and heiress of the immense domains of the house of Montpensier. The lovers were bent on marriage. The royal consent was obtained. During a few hours Lauzun was regarded by the court as an adopted member of the house of Bourbon. The portion which the princess brought with her might well have been an object of competition to sovereigns: three great dukedoms, an independent principality with its own mint and with its own tribunals, and an income greatly exceeding the whole revenue of the kingdom of Scotland. But this splendid prospect had been overcast. The match had been broken off. The aspiring suitor had been, during many years, shut up in an Alpine castle. At length Lewis relented. Lauzun was forbidden to appear in the royal presence, but was allowed to enjoy liberty at a distance from the court. He visited England, and was well received at the palace of James and in the fashionable circles of London; for in that age the gentlemen of France were regarded throughout Europe as models of grace; and many chevaliers and viscounts, who had never been admitted to the interior circle at Versailles, found themselves objects of general curiosity and admiration at Whitehall. Lauzun was in every respect the man for the present emergency. He had courage and a sense of honor, had been accustomed to eccentric adventures, and, with the keen observation and ironical pleasantry of a finished man of the world, had a strong propensity to knight errantry. All his national feelings and all his personal interests impelled him to undertake the adventure from which the most devoted subjects of the English crown seemed to shrink. As the guardian, at a perilous crisis, of the Queen of Great Britain and of the Prince of Wales, he might return with honor to his native land; he might once more be admitted to see Lewis dress and dine, and might, after so many vicissitudes, recommence, in the decline of life, the strangely fascinating chase of royal favour.

Animated by such feelings, Lauzun eagerly accepted the high trust which was offered to him. The arrangements for the flight were promptly made: a vessel was ordered to be in readiness at Gravesend: but to reach Gravesend was not easy. The city was in a state of extreme agitation. The slightest cause sufficed to bring a crowd together. No foreigner could appear in the streets without risk of being stopped, questioned, and carried before a magistrate as a Jesuit in disguise. It was, therefore, necessary to take the road on the south of the Thames. No precaution which could quiet suspicion was omitted. The king and queen retired to rest as usual. When the palace had been some time profoundly quiet, James rose and called a servant, who was in attendance. "You will find," said the king, "a man at the door of the antechamber; bring him hither." The servant obeyed, and Lauzun was ushered into the royal bedchamber. "I confide to you," said James, "my queen and my son; every thing must be risked to carry them into France." Lauzun, with a truly chivalrous spirit, returned thanks for the dangerous honor which had been conferred on him, and begged permission to avail himself of the assistance of his friend Saint Victor, a gentleman of Provence, whose courage and faith had been often tried. The services of so valuable an assistant were readily accepted. Lauzun gave his hand to Mary; Saint Victor wrapped up in his warm cloak the ill fated heir of so many kings. The party stole down the back stairs, and embarked in an open skiff. It was a miserable voyage. The night was bleak: the rain fell: the wind roared: the waves were rough: at length the boat reached Lambeth; and the fugitives landed near an inn, where a coach and horses were in waiting. Some time elapsed before the horses could be harnessed. Mary, afraid that her face might be known, would not enter the house. She remained with her child, cowering for shelter from the storm under the tower of Lambeth Church, and distracted by terror whenever the ostler approached her with his lanthern. Two of her women attended her, one who gave suck to the prince, and one whose office was to rock his cradle; but they could be of little use to their mistress; for both were foreigners who could hardly speak the English language, and who shuddered at the rigor of the English climate. The only consolatory circumstance was that the little boy was well, and uttered not a single cry. At length the coach was ready. Saint Victor followed it on horseback. The fugitives reached Gravesend safely, and embarked in the yacht which waited for them. They found there Lord Powis and his wife. Three Irish officers were also on board. These men had been sent thither in order that they might assist Lauzun in any desperate emergency; for it was thought not impossible that the captain of the ship might prove false; and it was fully determined that, on the first suspicion of treachery, he should be stabbed to the heart. There was, however, no necessity for violence. The yacht proceeded down the river with a fair wind; and Saint Victor, having seen her under sail, spurred back with the good news to Whitehall.

On the morning of Monday the tenth of December, the king learned that his wife and son had begun their voyage with a fair prospect of reaching their destination. About the same time a courier arrived at the palace with despatches from Hungerford. Had James been a little more discerning, or a little less obstinate, those despatches would have induced him to reconsider all his plans. The commissioners wrote hopefully. The conditions proposed by the conqueror were strangely liberal. The king himself could not refrain from exclaiming that they were more favourable than he could have expected. He might indeed not unreasonably suspect that they had been framed with no friendly design: but this mattered nothing; for, whether they were offered in the hope that, by closing with them, he would lay the ground for a happy reconciliation, or, as is more likely, in the hope that, by rejecting them, he would exhibit himself to the whole nation as an utterly unreasonable and incorrigible tyrant, his course was equally clear. In either event his policy was to accept them promptly and to observe them faithfully.

But it soon appeared that William had perfectly understood the character with which he had to deal, and, in offering those terms which the Whigs at Hungerford had censured as too indulgent, had risked nothing. The solemn farce by which the public had been amused since the retreat of the royal army from Salisbury was prolonged during a few hours. All the lords who were still in the capital were invited to the palace that they might be informed of the progress of the negotiation which had been opened by their advice. Another meeting of peers was appointed for the following day. The lord mayor and the sheriffs of London were also summoned to attend the king. He exhorted them to perform their duties vigorously, and owned that he had thought it expedient to send his wife and child out of the country, but assured them that he would himself remain at his post. While he uttered this unkingly and unmanly falsehood, his fixed purpose was to depart before daybreak. Already he had intrusted his most valuable moveables to the care of several foreign ambassadors. His most important papers had been deposited with the Tuscan minister. But before the flight there was still something to be done. The tyrant pleased himself with the thought that he might avenge himself on a people who had been impatient of his despotism by inflicting on them at parting all the evils of anarchy. He ordered the great seal and the writs for the new parliament to be brought to his apartment. The writs which could be found he threw into the fire. Those which had been already sent out he annulled by an instrument drawn up in legal form. To his general Feversham he wrote a letter which could be understood only as a command to disband the army. Still, however, the king concealed his intention of absconding even from his chief ministers. Just before he retired he directed Jeffreys to be in the closet early on the morrow; and, while stepping into bed, whispered to Mulgrave that the news from Hungerford was highly satisfactory. Everybody withdrew except the Duke of Northumberland. This young man, a natural son of Charles the Second by the Duchess of Cleveland, commanded a troop of lifeguards, and was a lord of the bedchamber. It seems to have been then the custom of the court that, in the queen's absence, a lord of the bedchamber should sleep on a pallet in the king's room; and it was Northumberland's turn to perform this duty.

At three in the morning of Tuesday the eleventh of December, James rose, took the great seal in his hand, laid his commands on Northumberland not to open the door of the bedchamber till the usual hour, and disappeared through a secret passage; the same passage probably through which Huddleston had been brought to the bedside of the late king. Sir Edward Hales was in attendance with a hackney coach. James was conveyed to Millbank where he crossed the Thames in a small wherry. As he passed Lambeth he flung the great seal into the midst of the stream, where, after many months, it was accidentally caught by a fishing net and dragged up.

At Vauxhall he landed. A carriage and horses had been stationed there for him; and he immediately took the road towards Sheerness, where a hoy belonging to the Custom House had been ordered to await his arrival.

Karl Marx

1818—1883

5

Of all the historians who appear in this series, none has caused more controversy, attracted more followers, or gathered as many detractors as Karl Marx. Considering Marx's influence and the fact that he was a pioneer, if not a very judicious practitioner, of economic history, it is difficult to imagine that with the exception of the *Communist Manifesto* and perhaps a small fraction of *Das Kapital,* his major works were virtually unread during his lifetime. Marx, however, was not an obscure figure in the middle of the nineteenth century. As a political pamphleteer, as a journalist with a truculent pen, as a radical in exile from his native Germany, as an implacable foe to all those who disagreed with him, and as a leader of the International Workingmen's Association, he was well known in the Western World. Today his name and the interpretation of history which bears his name are anathema to some, a cause for argument among many, and the objects of veneration in parts of the world he never knew himself. Much of the heat generated by Marxist studies follows the example of Marx's particular style, for it was not enough for him to state his case. He had to insult and denigrate even those from whom he had learned a good deal in order to establish that his doctrine constituted a science; other socialists, who were also economic and social theorists, were to his mind dreamers, idlers, unconscious pawns of the reactionary forces of bourgeois society.

The year before Marx was born, his father renounced the Jewish religion and adopted the Lutheranism of his neighbors in the German Rhineland. Marx's antipathy to religion is sometimes attributed to a combination of guilt feelings and resentment that he may have felt as a result of his father's conversion. Actually, the elder Marx's inveterate skepticism made this move far less dramatic than it might seem. What probably impressed the young Marx was the repressive atmosphere of the German Restoration after the defeat of Napoleon and the abolition of the French reforms, which included religious toleration. Marx grew up believing that the Europe of his time was hostile as well as reactionary. When he transferred from the University of Bonn to the University of Berlin in 1836, he was a strong and hardened young man, in addition to being a brilliant student.

The dominant intellectual presence at the University of Berlin at that time was Hegel, even though he had died in 1833. His philosophy was taught and debated throughout the University, and it remained a powerful force in German intellectual circles throughout the nineteenth century. Hegel opposed the empiricism and the materialism of the Enlightenment with an elaborate philosophy of history. He maintained that the dynamic factor in the development of peoples and civilizations was not a matter of individual choices or decisive acts. Behind the actual movement of history, Hegel insisted, lay an unfolding spirit that was at once an abstract, rational, and unalterable force constituting the real history of mankind. Such a theory could be interpreted and adapted by students of varying political persuasions. Marx came under the influence of a Hegelian leftist, Moses Hess, who helped him understand how Hegelianism might provide the framework, if not the substance, of a radical political theory.

After a brief career as editor-in-chief of the *Rheinische Zeitung,* which he transformed into an organ of vehement protest against the Prussian government, Marx emigrated to Paris, where, during the years 1843 to 1845, he launched his critique of the conservative interpretation of Hegelianism. Having read the French socialists Fourier and Proudhon, as well as Ludwig Feuerbach's *Theses on Hegelian Philosophy,* Marx, together with Friedrich Engels, his lifelong friend and collaborator, wrote *The German Ideology* in the summer of 1846. In this youthful work the authors claim that "life is not determined by consciousness, but consciousness by life." Hegel was correct in his belief that laws govern history, but those laws themselves, not being the product of ideas or an absolute will, are the product of the material conditions of life. The fabric of the Hegelian dialectic might be preserved, according to Marx and Engels, but it had to be reordered. "In direct contrast to German philosophy," the authors wrote, "which descends from heaven to earth, here we ascend from earth to heaven."

To this early period of Marx's life also belong his *Economic and Philosophical Manuscripts of 1844,* which were not published until the twentieth century, as well as his virulent attack on Proudhon, *The Poverty of Philosophy,* published in 1847. Each of these works represents different aspects of Marx's critique of bourgeois society and of those who would reform it. In the 1844 *Manuscripts,* Marx offers an analysis of the role and function of workingmen in the capitalist system, and concludes that the "filthy self-interest" of the owners of private property is responsible for the alienation of the worker from the product of his labor. Whenever the worker is not needed by the capitalist, "he is shunned like the plague." Proudhon sent Marx a copy of his book *The Philosophy of Poverty* before it reached the public in order to elicit what he believed would be sympathetic advice from a fellow critic of industrial society. What Proudhon received was harsh, biting invective, which became Marx's hallmark throughout the remainder of his life. Marx dismissed Proudhon as totally ignorant of the true nature of the Hegelian dialectic and of the scientific inevitability of revolution. With his naïve reforms, Proudhon, like the other socialists and Utopians, was merely prolonging the existing agony of the vast majority of the population.

With the publication of the *Communist Manifesto,* published just a few weeks before the revolution in Paris in 1848, Marx's name became inextricably bound to the Communist League for which he and Engels had written this daring and confident summary of the meaning of world history. The phrases which open and close this work have become part of a catechism for those who accept Marx's argument that capitalism lives on borrowed time allotted to it by the exploitation of the proletariat. Marx is far more than a historian in the *Manifesto;* he is a prophet, an inciter, a thoroughgoing revolutionary. As far as he is concerned, capitalism contains the kernel of its own destruction; because, as it exploits the proletariat, it organizes it, and thus helps precipitate the inevitable revolution. For those who would alter this process with piecemeal reform and gradual improvement of the condition of the working class, he expresses nothing but contempt. Fruitlessly and destructively these socialists endeavor "to deaden the class struggle and reconcile class antagonisms."

For all his boldness and swagger, Marx proved to be a poor prophet. Within a year after the appearance of the *Manifesto,* the revolution it was supposed to herald had failed, and Marx was living the life of a penurious exile in London. In 1852, he wrote *The Eighteenth Brumaire of Louis Napoleon,* which purports to describe the failure of the revolution in France in 1848, and the establishment of the Second Empire under the nephew of Napoleon Bonaparte. Marx's self-imposed task in this history, as is evident in our selections from it, is to unmask the means by which the bourgeoisie swindled the proletariat during this revolution, thus accounting for its egregious failure. The revolution he constructs is a logical retrogressive development. From a bourgeois monarchy to a bourgeois republic, to the restoration of a bourgeois empire, the propertied class made sure that the proletariat would serve only as a means to their ends, and wind up cheated in the end. But Marx concluded with what was for him a sanguine prophecy: the government of Louis Napoleon would be no more successful than that of his uncle nor would any other regime which attempted to exist in defiance of the inexorable march of history, a process that would finally bring the victory to the proletariat, and an end to the class struggle.

The chief work of Marx's long isolation in London was *Das Kapital.* He provided in this formidable study an elaborate economic theory, and treated it historically. In the first volume, the only one to appear in his lifetime, he applied his economic theories to the rise of the Industrial Revolution. The later volumes, which Engels edited, discuss the methods employed in the capitalist system to sell products and determine wages and profits. He maintained here, as he always had, that the bourgeoisie exploited the proletariat in holding on to the surplus value of labor, the unearned increment which it did not deserve. He predicted that this exploitation as well as the other ills of the capitalist system, including ruthless competition and overproduction, would eventually bring that system to destruction, "when the capitalist husk bursts asunder. The knell of private property sounds. The expropriators are expropriated." At this point, the state, which had been an instrument of oppression, would no longer be needed. The pre-history of mankind would have come to an end.

In London, when he was not at the British Museum library working on *Das Kapital,* or pitifully looking for some work so that his family could eat, he pushed the workers' International in the direction of a single centralized revolution, directed from a common source and toward a common end. Disillusioned by the failure of the Paris Commune of 1871, and heartbroken by the death of his wife, Jenny, Marx went in 1881 to Africa in search of sun and consolation. But he found neither. In 1883, seated in his study in the north of London, he died. He was a powerful indicter of the society that surrounded him, and his memory has been an inspiration to countless social critics, even when those critics no longer accept his philosophy of history. It is also safe to say that his influence on twentieth-century historiography is more pervasive than any other historian's of his time.

Selected Bibliography

A sketchy but lively introduction to Marx is provided by Isaiah Berlin in *Karl Marx: His Life and Environment* (1963). An intelligent and well-informed analysis of Marx's intellectual development may be found in George Lichtheim's *Marxism: An Historical and Critical Study* (1961). M. M. Bober's *Karl Marx's Interpretation of History* (1950) is a formal and sophisticated examination and evaluation of Marx's historical theories. Leonard Krieger studies the changes in Marx's historical works and arrives at some new and interesting conclusions in "Marx and Engels as Historians," in the *Journal of the History of Ideas* XIV:3 (June, 1953), 381–403. Erich Fromm's popular *Marx's Concept of Man* (1961) emphasizes the early works of Marx, and thus greatly exaggerates Marx's humanitarianism.

THE EIGHTEENTH BRUMAIRE OF LOUIS BONAPARTE

I

Hegel remarks somewhere that all facts and personages of great importance in world history occur, as it were, twice. He forgot to add: the first time as tragedy, the second as farce. Caussidière for Danton, Louis Blanc for Robespierre, the *Montagne* of 1848 to 1851 for the *Montagne* of 1793 to 1795, the Nephew for the Uncle. And the same caricature occurs in the circumstances attending the second edition of the eighteenth Brumaire!

Men make their own history, but they do not make it just as they please; they do not make it under circumstances chosen by themselves, but under circumstances directly encountered, given and transmitted from the past. The tradition of all the dead generations weighs like a nightmare on the brain of the living. And just when they seem engaged in revolutionizing themselves and things, in creating something that has never yet existed, precisely in such periods of revolutionary crisis they anxiously conjure up the spirits of the past to their service and borrow from them names, battle cries and costumes in order to present the new scene of world history in this time-honoured disguise and this borrowed language. Thus Luther donned the mask of the Apostle Paul, the Revolution of 1789 to 1814 draped itself alternately as the Roman republic and the Roman empire, and the Revolution of 1848 knew nothing better to do than to parody, now 1789, now the revolutionary tradition of 1793 to 1795. In like manner a beginner who has learnt a new language always translates it back into his mother tongue, but he has assimilated the spirit of the new language and can freely express himself in it only when he finds his way in it without recalling the old and forgets his native tongue in the use of the new.

Consideration of this conjuring up of the dead of world history reveals at once a salient difference. Camille Desmoulins, Danton, Robespierre,

The Eighteenth Brumaire of Louis Bonaparte, New York: International Publishers, 1963, pp. 15–41, 118–135.

Saint-Just, Napoleon, the heroes as well as the parties and the masses of the old French Revolution, performed the task of their time in Roman costume and with Roman phrases, the task of unchaining and setting up modern *bourgeois* society. The first ones knocked the feudal basis to pieces and mowed off the feudal heads which had grown on it. The other created inside France the conditions under which alone free competition could be developed, parcelled landed property exploited and the unchained industrial productive power of the nation employed; and beyond the French borders he everywhere swept the feudal institutions away, so far as was necessary to furnish bourgeois society in France with a suitable up-to-date environment on the European Continent. The new social formation once established, the antediluvian Colossi disappeared and with them resurrected Romanity—the Brutuses, Gracchi, Publicolas, the tribunes, the senators, and Caesar himself. Bourgeois society in its sober reality had begotten its true interpreters and mouthpieces in the Says, Cousins, Royer-Collards, Benjamin Constants and Guizots; its real military leaders sat behind the office desks, and the hog-headed Louis XVIII was its political chief. Wholly absorbed in the production of wealth and in peaceful competitive struggle, it no longer comprehended that ghosts from the days of Rome had watched over its cradle. But unheroic as bourgeois society is, it nevertheless took heroism, sacrifice, terror, civil war and battles of peoples to bring it into being. And in the classically austere traditions of the Roman republic its gladiators found the ideals and the art forms, the self-deceptions that they needed in order to conceal from themselves the bourgeois limitations of the content of their struggles and to keep their enthusiasm on the high plane of the great historical tragedy. Similarly, at another stage of development, a century earlier, Cromwell and the English people had borrowed speech, passions and illusions from the Old Testament for their bourgeois revolution. When the real aim had been achieved, when the bourgeois transformation of English society had been accomplished, Locke supplanted Habakkuk.

Thus the awakening of the dead in those revolutions served the purpose of glorifying the new struggles, not of parodying the old; of magnifying the given task in imagination, not of fleeing from its solution in reality; of finding once more the spirit of revolution, not of making its ghost walk about again.

From 1848 to 1851 only the ghost of the old revolution walked about, from Marrast, the *républicain en gants jaunes,* who disguised himself as the old Bailly, down to the adventurer, who hides his commonplace repulsive features under the iron death mask of Napoleon. An entire people, which had imagined that by means of a revolution it had imparted to itself an accelerated power of motion, suddenly finds itself set back into a defunct epoch and, in order that no doubt as to the relapse may be possible, the old dates arise again, the old chronology, the old names, the old edicts, which had long become a subject of antiquarian erudition, and the old minions of the law, who had seemed long decayed. The nation feels like that mad Englishman in Bedlam who fancies that he lives in the times of the ancient Pharaohs and daily bemoans the hard labour that he must perform in the Ethiopian mines as a gold digger, immured in this subterranean prison, a dimly burning lamp fastened to his head, the overseer of the slaves behind him with a long whip, and at the exits a confused welter of barbarian mercenaries, who understand neither the forced labourers in the mines nor one another, since they speak no common language. "And all this is expected of me," sighs the mad Englishman, "of me, a free-born Briton, in order to make gold for the old Pharaohs." "In order to pay the debts of the Bonaparte family," sighs the French nation. The Englishman, so long as he was in his right mind, could not get rid of the fixed idea of making gold. The French, so long as they were engaged in revolution, could not get rid of the memory of Napoleon, as the election of December 10 proved. They hankered to return from the perils of revolution to the fleshpots of Egypt, and December 2, 1851, was the answer. They have not only a caricature of the old Napoleon, they have the old Napoleon himself, caricatured as he must appear in the middle of the nineteenth century.

The social revolution of the nineteenth century cannot draw its poetry from the past, but only from the future. It cannot begin with itself before it has stripped off all superstition in regard to the past. Earlier revolutions required recollections of past world history in order to drug themselves concerning their own content. In order to arrive at its own content, the revolution of the nineteenth century must let the dead bury their dead. There the phrase went beyond the content; here the content goes beyond the phrase.

The February Revolution was a surprise attack, a *taking* of the old society *unawares,* and the people proclaimed this unexpected *stroke* as a deed of world importance, ushering in a new epoch. On December 2 the February Revolution is conjured away by a cardsharper's trick, and what seems overthrown is no longer the monarchy but the liberal concessions that were wrung from it by centuries of struggle. Instead of *society* having conquered a new content for itself, it seems that the *state* only returned to its oldest form, to the shamelessly simple domination of the sabre and the cowl. This is the answer to the *coup de main* of February 1848, given by the *coup de tête* of December 1851. Easy come, easy go. Meanwhile the interval of time has not passed by unused. During the years 1848 to 1851 French society has made up, and that by an abbreviated because revolutionary method, for the studies and experiences which, in a regular, so to speak, textbook course of development would have had to precede the February Revolution, if it was to be more than a ruffling of the surface. Society now seems to have fallen back behind its point of departure; it has in truth first to create for itself the revolutionary point of departure, the situation, the relations, the conditions under which alone modern revolution becomes serious.

Bourgeois revolutions, like those of the eighteenth century, storm swiftly from success to success; their dramatic effects outdo each other; men and things seem set in sparkling brilliants; ecstasy is the everyday spirit; but they are short-lived; soon they have attained their zenith, and a long crapulent depression lays hold of society before it learns soberly to assimilate the results of its storm-and-stress period. On the other hand, proletarian revolutions, like those of the nineteenth century, criticize themselves constantly, interrupt themselves continually in their own course, come back to the apparently accomplished in order to begin it afresh, deride with unmerciful thoroughness the inadequacies, weaknesses and paltrinesses of their first attempts, seem to throw down their adversary only in order that he may draw new strength from the earth and rise again, more gigantic, before them, recoil ever and anon from the indefinite prodigiousness of their own aims, until a situation has been created which makes all turning back impossible, and the conditions themselves cry out:

> Hic Rhodus, hic salta!
> Here is the rose, here dance!

For the rest, every fairly competent observer, even if he had not followed the course of French developments step by step, must have had a presentiment that an unheard-of fiasco was in store for the revolution. It was enough to hear the self-complacent howl of victory with which Messieurs the Democrats congratulated each other on the expected gracious consequences of the second Sunday in May 1852. In their minds the second Sunday in May 1852 had become a fixed idea, a dogma, like the day on which Christ should reappear and the millennium begin, in the minds of the Chiliasts. As ever, weakness had taken refuge in a belief in miracles, fancied the enemy overcome when he was only conjured away in imagination, and it lost all understanding of the present in a passive glorification of the future that was in store for it and of the deeds it had *in petto* but which it merely did not want to carry out as yet. Those heroes who seek to disprove their demonstrated incapacity by mutually offering each other their sympathy and getting together in a crowd had tied up their bundles, collected their laurel wreaths in advance and were just then engaged in discounting on the exchange market the republics *in partibus* for which they had already providently organized the government personnel with all the calm of their unassuming disposition. December 2 struck them like a thunderbolt from a clear sky, and the peoples that in periods of pusillanimous depression gladly let their inward apprehension be drowned by the loudest bawlers will perchance have convinced themselves that the times are past when the cackle of geese could save the Capitol.

The Constitution, the National Assembly, the dynastic parties, the blue and the red republicans, the heroes of Africa, the thunder from the platform, the sheet lightning of the daily press, the entire literature, the political names and the intellectual reputations, the civil law and the penal code, the *liberté, égalité, fraternité* and the second Sunday in May 1852—all has vanished like a phantasmagoria before the spell of a man whom even his enemies do not make out to be a sorcerer. Universal suffrage seems to have survived only for a moment, in order that with its own hand it may make its last will and testament before the eyes of all the world and declare in the name of the people itself: All that exists deserves to perish.

It is not enough to say, as the French do, that their nation was taken unawares. A nation and a woman are not forgiven the unguarded hour in which the first adventurer that came along could violate them. The riddle is not solved by such turns of speech, but merely formulated differently. It remains to be explained how a nation of thirty-six millions can be surprised and delivered unresisting into captivity by three *chevaliers d'industrie.*

Let us recapitulate in general outline the phases that the French Revolution went through from February 24, 1848, to December 1851.

Three main periods are unmistakable: *the February period;* May 4, 1848, to May 28, 1849: *the period of the constitution of the republic,* or *of the Constituent National Assembly;* May 28, 1849, to December 2, 1851: *the period of the constitutional republic* or *of the Legislative National Assembly.*

The *first period,* from February 24, or the overthrow of Louis Philippe, to May 4, 1848, the meeting of the Constituent Assembly, the *February period* proper, may be described as the *prologue* to the revolution. Its character was officially expressed in the fact that the government improvised by it itself declared that it was *provisional* and, like the government, everything that was mooted, attempted or enunciated during this period proclaimed itself to be only *provisional.* Nothing and nobody ventured to lay claim to the right of existence and of real action. All the elements that had prepared or determined the revolution, the dynastic opposition, the republican bourgeoisie, the democratic-republican petty bourgeoisie and the social-democratic workers, provisionally found their place in the February *government.*

It could not be otherwise. The February days originally intended an electoral reform, by which the circle of the politically privileged among the possessing class itself was to be widened and the exclusive domination of the aristocracy of finance overthrown. When it came to the actual conflict, however, when the people mounted the barricades, the National Guard maintained a passive attitude, the army offered no serious resistance and the monarchy ran away, the republic appeared to be a matter of course. Every party construed it in its own way. Having secured it arms in hand, the proletariat impressed its stamp upon it and proclaimed it to be a *social republic.* There was thus indicated the general content of the modern revolution, a content which was in most singular contradiction to everything that, with the material available, with the degree of education attained by the masses, under the given circumstances and relations, could be immediately realized in practice. On the other hand, the claims of all the remaining elements that had collaborated in the February Revolution were recognized by the lion's share that they obtained in the government. In no period do we, therefore, find a more confused mixture of high-flown phrases and actual uncertainty and clumsiness, of more enthusiastic striving for innovation and more deeply-rooted domination of the old routine, of more apparent harmony of the whole of society and more profound estrangement of its elements. While the Paris proletariat still revelled in the vision of the wide prospects that had opened before it and indulged in seriously-meant discussions on social problems, the old powers of society had grouped themselves, assembled, reflected and found unexpected support in the mass of the nation, the peasants and petty bourgeois, who all at once stormed on to the political stage, after the barriers of the July Monarchy had fallen.

The *second period,* from May 4, 1848, to the end of May 1849, is the period of the *constitution,* the *foundation, of the bourgeois republic.* Directly after the February days not only had the dynastic opposition been surprised by the republicans and the republicans by the Socialists, but all France by Paris. The National Assembly, which met on May 4, 1848, had emerged from the national elections and represented the nation. It was a living protest against the pretensions of the February days and was to reduce the results of the revolution to the bourgeois scale. In vain the Paris proletariat, which immediately grasped the character of this National Assembly, attempted on May 15, a few days after it met, forcibly to negate its existence, to dissolve it, to disintegrate again into its constituent parts the organic form in which the proletariat was threatened by the reacting spirit of the nation. As is known, May 15 had no other result save that of removing Blanqui and his comrades, that is, the real leaders of the proletarian party, from the public stage for the entire duration of the cycle we are considering.

The *bourgeois monarchy* of Louis Philippe can be followed only by a *bourgeois republic,* that is to say, whereas a limited section of the bourgeoisie ruled in the name of the king, the whole of the bourgeoisie will now rule in the name of the people. The demands of the Paris proletariat are utopian nonsense, to which an end must be put. To this declaration of the Constituent National Assembly the Paris proletariat replied with the *June Insurrection,* the most colossal event in the history of European civil wars. The bourgeois republic triumphed. On its side stood the aristocracy of finance, the industrial bourgeoisie, the middle class, the petty bourgeois, the army, the *lumpenproletariat* organized as the Mobile Guard, the intellectual lights, the clergy and the rural population. On the side of the Paris proletariat stood none but itself. More than three thousand insurgents were butchered after the victory, and fifteen thousand were transported without trial. With this defeat the proletariat passes into the *background* of the revolutionary stage. It attempts to press forward again on every occasion, as soon as the movement appears to make a fresh start, but with ever decreased expenditure of strength and always slighter results. As soon as one of the social strata situated above it gets into revolutionary ferment, the proletariat enters into an alliance with it and so shares all the defeats that the different parties suffer, one after another. But these subsequent blows become the weaker, the greater the surface of society over which they are distributed. The more important leaders of the proletariat in the Assembly and in the press successively fall victims to the courts, and ever more equivocal figures come to head it. In part it throws itself into *doctrinaire experiments, exchange banks and workers' associations, hence into a movement in which it renounces the revolutionizing of the old world by means of the latter's own great, combined resources, and seeks, rather, to achieve its salvation behind society's back, in private fashion, within its limited conditions of existence, and hence necessarily suffers shipwreck.* It seems to be unable either to rediscover revolutionary greatness in itself or to win new energy from the connections newly entered into, until *all classes* with which it contended in June themselves lie prostrate beside it. But at least it succumbs with the honours of the great, world-historic struggle; not only France, but all Europe trembles at the June earthquake, while the ensuing defeats of the upper classes are so cheaply bought that they require bare-faced exaggeration by the victorious party to be able to pass for events at all, and become the more ignominious the further the defeated party is removed from the proletarian party.

The defeat of the June insurgents, to be sure, had now prepared, had levelled the ground on which the bourgeois republic could be founded and built up, but it had shown at the same time that in Europe the questions at issue are other than that of "republic or monarchy." It had revealed that here *bourgeois republic* signifies the unlimited despotism of one class over other classes. It had proved that in countries with an old civilization, with a developed formation of classes, with modern conditions of production and with an intellectual consciousness in which all traditional ideas have been dissolved by the work of centuries, *the republic* signifies *in general only the political form of revolution of bourgeois society* and not its *conservative form of life,* as, for example, in the United States of North America, where, though classes already exist, they have not yet become fixed, but continually change and interchange their elements in constant flux, where the modern means of production, instead of coinciding with a stagnant surplus population, rather compensate for the relative deficiency of heads and hands, and where, finally, the feverish, youthful movement of material production, which has to make a new world its own, has left neither time nor opportunity for abolishing the old spirit world.

During the June days all classes and parties had united in the *party of Order* against the proletarian class as the *party of Anarchy,* of Socialism, of Communism. They had "saved" society from *"the enemies of society."* They had given out the watchwords of the old society, *"property, family, religion, order,"* to their army as passwords and had proclaimed to the counter-revolutionary crusaders: "In this sign thou shalt conquer!" From that moment, as soon as one of the numerous parties which had gathered under this sign against the June insurgents seeks to hold the revolutionary battlefield in its own class interest, it goes down before the cry: "Property, family, religion, order." Society is saved just as often as the circle of its rulers contracts, as a more exclusive interest is maintained against a wider one. Every demand of the simplest bourgeois financial reform, of the most ordinary liberalism, of the most formal republicanism, of the most shallow democracy, is simultaneously castigated as an "attempt on society" and stigmatized as "Socialism." And, finally, the high priests of "the religion and order" themselves are driven with kicks from their Pythian tripods, hauled out of their beds in the darkness of night, put in prison-vans, thrown into dungeons or sent into exile; their temple is razed to the ground, their mouths are sealed, their pens broken, their law torn to pieces in the name of religion, of property, of the family, of order. Bourgeois fanatics for order are shot down on their balconies by mobs of drunken soldiers, their domestic sanctuaries profaned, their houses bombarded for amusement—in the name of property, of the family, of religion and of order. Finally, the scum of bourgeois society forms the *holy phalanx of order* and the hero Crapulinski installs himself in the Tuileries as the *"saviour of society."*

II

Let us pick up the threads of the development once more.

The history of the *Constituent National Assembly* since the June days is the *history of the domination and the disintegration of the republican faction of the bourgeoisie,* of that faction which is known by the names of tricolour republicans, pure republicans, political republicans, formalist republicans, etc.

Under the bourgeois monarchy of Louis Philippe it had formed the *official* republican *opposition* and consequently a recognized component part of the political world of the day. It had its representatives in the Chambers and a considerable sphere of influence in the press. Its Paris organ, the *National,* was considered just as respectable in its way as the *Journal des Débats.* Its character corresponded to this position under the constitutional monarchy. It was not a faction of the bourgeoisie held together by great common interests and marked off by specific conditions of production. It was a clique of republican-minded bourgeois, writers, lawyers, officers and officials that owed its influence to the personal antipathies of the country against Louis Philippe, to memories of the old republic, to the republican faith of a number of enthusiasts, above all, however, to *French nationalism,* whose hatred of the Vienna treaties and of the alliance with England it stirred up perpetually. A large part of the following that the *National* had under Louis Philippe was due to this concealed imperialism, which could consequently confront it later, under the republic, as a deadly rival in the person of Louis Bonaparte. It fought the aristocracy of finance, as did all the rest of the bourgeois opposition. Polemics against the budget, which were closely connected in France with fighting the aristocracy of finance, procured popularity too cheaply and material for puritanical leading articles too plentifully, not to be exploited. The industrial bourgeoisie was grateful to it for its slavish defence of the French protectionist system, which it accepted, however, more on national grounds than on grounds of national economy; the bourgeoisie as a whole, for its vicious denunciation of Communism and Socialism. For the rest, the party of the *National* was *purely republican,* that is, it demanded a republican instead of a monarchist form of bourgeois rule and, above all, the lion's share of this rule. Concerning the conditions of this transformation it was by no means clear in its own mind. On the other hand, what was clear as daylight to it and was publicly acknowledged at the reform banquets in the last days of Louis Philippe, was its unpopularity with the democratic petty bourgeois and, in particular, with the revolutionary proletariat. These pure republicans, as is, indeed, the way with pure republicans, were already on the point of contenting themselves in the first instance with a regency of the Duchess of Orleans, when the February Revolution broke out and assigned their best-known representatives a place in the Provisional Government. From the start, they naturally had the confidence of the bourgeoisie and a majority in the Constituent National Assembly. The *socialist* elements of the Provisional Government were excluded forthwith from the Executive Commission which the National Assembly formed when it met, and the party of the *National* took advantage of the outbreak of the June insurrection to discharge the *Executive Commission* also, and therewith to get rid of its closest rivals, the *petty-bourgeois,* or *democratic, republicans* (Ledru-Rollin, etc.). Cavaignac, the general of the bourgeois-republican party who commanded the June massacre, took the place of the Executive Commission with a sort of dictatorial power. Marrast, former editor-in-chief of the *National,* became the perpetual president of the Constituent National Assembly, and the ministries, as well as all other important posts, fell to the portion of the pure republicans.

The republican bourgeois faction, which had long regarded itself as the legitimate heir of the July Monarchy, thus found its fondest hopes exceeded; it attained power, however, not as it had dreamed under Louis Philippe, through a liberal revolt of the bourgeoisie against the throne, but through a rising of the proletariat against capital, a rising laid low with grape-shot. What it had conceived as the *most revolutionary* event turned out in reality to be the *most counter-revolutionary.* The fruit fell into its lap, but it fell from the tree of knowledge, not from the tree of life.

The exclusive *rule of the bourgeois republicans* lasted only from June 24 to December 10, 1848. It is summed up in the *drafting of a republican constitution* and in the *state of siege of Paris.*

The new *Constitution* was at bottom only the republicanized edition of the constitutional Charter of 1830. The narrow electoral qualification of the July Monarchy, which excluded even a large part of the bourgeoisie from political rule, was incompatible with the existence of the bourgeois republic. In lieu of this qualification, the February Revolution had at once proclaimed direct universal suffrage. The bourgeois republicans could not undo this event. They had to content themselves with adding the limiting proviso of a six months' residence in the constituency. The old organization of the administration, of the municipal system, of the judicial system, of the army, etc., continued to exist inviolate, or, where the Constitution changed them, the change concerned the table of contents, not the contents; the name, not the subject matter.

The inevitable general staff of the liberties of 1848, personal liberty, liberty of the press, of speech, of association, of assembly, of education and religion, etc., received a constitutional uniform, which made them invulnerable. For each of these liberties is proclaimed as the *absolute* right of the French *citoyen,* but always with the marginal note that it is unlimited so far as it is not limited by the *"equal rights of others* and the *public safety"* or by "laws" which are intended to mediate just this harmony of the individual liberties with one another and with the public safety. For example: "The citizens have the right of association, of peaceful and unarmed assembly, of petition and of expressing their opinions, whether in the press or in any other way. *The enjoyment of these rights has no limit save the equal rights of others and the public safety."* (Chapter II of the French Constitution, §8.) —"Education is free. Freedom of education shall be *enjoyed* under the conditions fixed by law and under the supreme control of the state." (*Ibidem,* §9.) —"The home of every citizen is inviolable *except* in the forms prescribed by law." (Chapter II, §3.) Etc., etc.—The Constitution, therefore, constantly refers to future *organic* laws which are to put into effect those marginal notes and regulate the enjoyment of these unrestricted liberties in such manner that they will collide neither with one another nor with the public safety. And later, these organic laws were brought into being by the friends of order and all those liberties regulated in such manner that the bourgeoisie in its enjoyment of them finds itself unhindered by the equal rights of the other classes. Where it forbids these liberties entirely to "the others" or permits enjoyment of them under conditions that are just so many police traps, this always happens solely in the interest of *"public safety,"* that is, the safety of the bourgeoisie, as the Constitution prescribes. In the sequel, both sides accordingly appeal with complete justice to the Constitution: the friends of order, who abrogated all these liberties, as well as the democrats, who demanded all of them. For each paragraph of the Constitution contains its own antithesis, its own Upper and Lower House, namely, liberty in the general phrase, abrogation of liberty in the marginal note. Thus, so long as the *name* of freedom was respected and only its actual realization prevented, of course in a legal way, the constitutional existence of liberty remained intact, inviolate, however mortal the blows dealt to its existence *in actual life.*

This Constitution, made inviolable in so ingenious a manner, was nevertheless, like Achilles, vulnerable in one point, not in the heel, but in the head, or rather in the two heads in which it wound up—the *Legislative Assembly,* on the one hand, the *President,* on the other. Glance through the Constitution and you will find that only the paragraphs in which the relationship of the President to the Legislative Assembly is defined are absolute, positive, non-contradictory, and cannot be distorted. For here it was a question of the bourgeois republicans safeguarding themselves. §§45–70 of the Constitution are so worded that the National Assembly can remove the President constitutionally, whereas the President can remove the National Assembly only unconstitutionally, only by setting aside the

Constitution itself. Here, therefore, it challenges its forcible destruction. It not only sanctifies the division of powers, like the Charter of 1830, it widens it into an intolerable contradiction. The *play of the constitutional powers,* as Guizot termed the parliamentary squabble between the legislative and executive power, is in the Constitution of 1848 continually played *va-banque.* On one side are seven hundred and fifty representatives of the people, elected by universal suffrage and eligible for re-election; they form an uncontrollable, indissoluble, indivisible National Assembly, a National Assembly that enjoys legislative omnipotence, decides in the last instance on war, peace and commercial treaties, alone possesses the right of amnesty and, by its permanence, perpetually holds the front of the stage. On the other side is the President, with all the attributes of royal power, with authority to appoint and dismiss his ministers independently of the National Assembly, with all the resources of the executive power in his hands, bestowing all posts and disposing thereby in France of the livelihoods of at least a million and a half people, for so many depend on the five hundred thousand officials and officers of every rank. He has the whole of the armed forces behind him. He enjoys the privilege of pardoning individual criminals, of suspending National Guards, of discharging, with the concurrence of the Council of State, general, cantonal and municipal councils elected by the citizens themselves. Initiative and direction are reserved to him in all treaties with foreign countries. While the Assembly constantly performs on the boards and is exposed to daily public criticism, he leads a secluded life in the Elysian Fields, and that with Article 45 of the Constitution before his eyes and in his heart, crying to him daily: *"Frère, il faut mourir!"* Your power ceases on the second Sunday of the lovely month of May in the fourth year after your election! Then your glory is at an end, the piece is not played twice and if you have debts, look to it betimes that you pay them off with the six hundred thousand francs granted you by the Constitution, unless, perchance, you should prefer to go to Clichy on the second Monday of the lovely month of May!—Thus, whereas the Constitution assigns actual power to the President, it seeks to secure moral power for the National Assembly. Apart from the fact that it is impossible to create a moral power by paragraphs of law, the Constitution here abrogates itself once more by having the President elected by all Frenchmen through direct suffrage. While the votes of France are split up among the seven hundred and fifty members of the National Assembly, they are here, on the contrary, concentrated on a single individual. While each separate representative of the people represents only this or that party, this or that town, this or that bridgehead, or even only the mere necessity of electing some one as the seven hundred and fiftieth, without examining too closely either the cause or the man, *he* is the elect of the nation and the act of his election is the trump that the sovereign people plays once every four years. The elected National Assembly stands in a metaphysical relation, but the elected President in a personal relation, to the nation. The National Assembly, indeed, exhibits in its individual representatives the manifold aspects of the national spirit, but in the President this national spirit finds its incarnation. As against the Assembly, he possesses a sort of divine right; he is President by the grace of the people.

Thetis, the sea goddess, had prophesied to Achilles that he would die in the bloom of youth. The Constitution, which, like Achilles, had its weak spot, had also, like Achilles, its presentiment that it must go to an early death. It was sufficient for the constitution-making pure republicans to cast a glance from the lofty heaven of their ideal republic at the profane world to perceive how the arrogance of the royalists, the Bonapartists, the Democrats, the Communists as well as their own discredit grew daily in the same measure as they approached the completion of their great legislative work of art, without Thetis on this account having to leave the sea and communicate the secret to them. They sought to cheat destiny by a catch in the Constitution, through §111 of it, according to which every motion for a *revision of the Constitution* must be supported by at least three-quarters of the votes, cast in three successive debates between which an entire month must always lie, with the added proviso that not less than five hundred members of the National Assembly must vote. Thereby they merely made the impotent attempt still to exercise a power—when only a parliamentary minority, as which they already saw themselves prophetically in their mind's eye—a power which at the present time, when they commanded a parliamentary majority and all the resources of governmental authority, was slipping daily more and more from their feeble hands.

Finally the Constitution, in a melodramatic paragraph, entrusts itself "to the vigilance and the patriotism of the whole French people and every single Frenchman," after it had previously entrusted in another paragraph the "vigilant" and "patriotic" to the tender, most painstaking care of the High Court of Justice, the *"haute cour,"* invented by it for the purpose.

Such was the Constitution of 1848, which on December 2, 1851, was not overthrown by a head, but fell down at the touch of a mere hat; this hat, to be sure, was a three-cornered Napoleonic hat.

While the bourgeois republicans in the Assembly were busy devising, discussing and voting this Constitution, Cavaignac outside the Assembly maintained the *state of siege of Paris.* The state of siege of Paris was the midwife of the Constituent Assembly in its travail of republican creation. If the Constitution is subsequently put out of existence by bayonets, it must not be forgotten that it was likewise by bayonets, and these turned against the people, that it had to be protected in its mother's womb and by bayonets that it had to be brought into existence. The forefathers of the "respectable republicans" had sent their symbol, the tricolour, on a tour round Europe. They themselves in turn produced an invention that of itself made its way over the whole Continent, but returned to France with ever renewed love until it has now become naturalized in half her Departments—the *state of siege.* A splendid invention, periodically employed in every ensuing crisis in the course of the French Revolution. But barrack and bivouac, which were thus periodically laid on French society's head to compress its brain and render it quiet; sabre and musket, which were periodically allowed to act as judges and administrators, as guardians and censors, to play policeman and do night watchman's duty; moustache and uniform, which were periodically trumpeted forth as the highest wisdom of society and as its rector—were not barrack and bivouac, sabre and musket, moustache and uniform finally bound to hit upon the idea of rather saving society once and for all by proclaiming their own regime as the highest and freeing civil society completely from the trouble of governing itself? Barrack and bivouac, sabre and musket, moustache and uniform were bound to hit upon this idea all the more as they might then also expect better cash payment for their higher services, whereas from the merely periodical state of siege and the transient rescues of society at the bidding of this or that bourgeois faction little of substance was gleaned save some killed and wounded and some friendly bourgeois grimaces. Should not the military at last one day play state of siege in their own interest and for their own benefit, and at the same time besiege the citizens' purses? Moreover, be it noted in passing, one must not forget that *Colonel Bernard,* the same military commission president who under Cavaignac had 15,000 insurgents deported without trial, is at this moment again at the head of the military commissions active in Paris.

Whereas, with the state of siege in Paris, the respectable, the pure republicans planted the nursery in which the praetorians of December 2, 1851, were to grow up, they on the other hand deserve praise for the reason that, instead of exaggerating the national sentiment as under Louis Philippe, they now, when they had command of the national power, crawled before foreign countries, and, instead of setting Italy free, let her be reconquered by Austrians and Neapolitans. Louis Bonaparte's election as President on December 10, 1848, put an end to the dictatorship of Cavaignac and to the Constituent Assembly.

In §44 of the Constitution it is stated: "The President of the French Republic must never have lost his status of a French citizen." The first President of the French republic, L. N. Bonaparte, had not merely lost his status of a French citizen, had not only been an English special constable, he was even a naturalized Swiss.

I have worked out elsewhere the significance of the election of December 10. I will not revert to it here. It is sufficient to remark here that it was a *reaction of the peasants,* who had had to pay the costs of the February Revolution, against the remaining classes of the nation, a *reaction of the country against the town.* It met with great approval in the army, for which the republicans of the *National* had provided neither glory nor additional pay among the big bourgeoisie, which hailed Bonaparte as a bridge to monarchy, among the proletarians and petty bourgeois, who hailed him as a scourge for Cavaignac. I shall have an opportunity later of going more closely into the relationship of the peasants to the French Revolution.

The period from December 20, 1848, until the dissolution of the Constituent Assembly, in May 1849, comprises the history of the downfall of the bourgeois republicans. After having founded a republic for the bourgeoisie, driven the revolutionary proletariat out of the field and reduced the democratic petty bourgeoisie to silence for the time being, they are themselves thrust aside by the mass of the bourgeoisie, which justly impounds this republic as *its property.* This bourgeois mass was, however, *royalist.* One section of it, the large landowners, had ruled during the *Restoration* and was accordingly *Legitimist.* The other, the aristocrats of finance and big industrialists, had ruled during the July Monarchy and was consequently *Orleanist.* The high dignitaries of the army, the university, the church, the bar, the academy and of the press were to be found on either side, though in various proportions. Here, in the bourgeois republic, which bore neither the name *Bourbon* nor the name *Orleans,* but the name *Capital,* they had found the form of state in which they could rule *conjointly.* The June Insurrection had already united them in the "party of Order." Now it was necessary, in the first place, to remove the coterie of bourgeois republicans who still occupied the seats of the National Assembly. Just as brutal as these pure republicans had been in their misuse of physical force against the people, just as cowardly, mealy-mouthed, broken-spirited and incapable of fighting were they now in their retreat, when it was a question of maintaining their republicanism and their legislative rights against the executive power and the royalists. I need not relate here the ignominious history of their dissolution. They did not succumb; they passed out of existence. Their history has come to an end forever, and, both inside and outside the Assembly, they figure in the following period only as memories, memories that seem to regain life whenever the mere name of Republic is once more the issue and as often as the revolutionary conflict threatens to sink down to the lowest level. I may remark in passing that the journal which gave its name to this party, the *National,* was converted to Socialism in the following period.

Before we finish with this period we must still cast a retrospective glance at the two powers, one of which annihilated the other on December 2, 1851, whereas from December 20, 1848, until the exit of the Constituent Assembly, they had lived in conjugal relations. We mean Louis Bonaparte, on the one hand, and the party of the coalesced royalists, the party of Order, of the big bourgeoisie, on the other. On acceding to the presidency, Bonaparte at once formed a ministry of the party of Order, at the head of which he placed Odilon Barrot, the old leader, *nota bene,* of the most liberal faction of the parliamentary bourgeoisie. M. Barrot had at last secured the ministerial portfolio, the spectre of which had haunted him since 1830, and what is more, the premiership in the ministry; but not, as he had imagined under Louis Philippe, as the most advanced leader of the parliamentary opposition, but with the task of putting a parliament to death, and as the confederate of all his arch-enemies, Jesuits and Legitimists. He brought the bride home at last, but only after she had been prostituted. Bonaparte seemed to efface himself completely. This party acted for him.

The very first meeting of the council of ministers resolved on the expedition to Rome, which, it was agreed, should be undertaken behind the back of the National Assembly and the means for which were to be wrested from it by false pretences. Thus they began by swindling the National Assembly and secretly conspiring with the absolutist powers abroad against the revolutionary Roman republic. In the same manner and with the same manoeuvres Bonaparte prepared his *coup* of December 2 against the royalist Legislative Assembly and its constitutional republic. Let us not forget that the same party which formed Bonaparte's ministry on December 20, 1848, formed the majority of the Legislative National Assembly on December 2, 1851.

In August the Constituent Assembly had decided to dissolve only after it had worked out and promulgated a whole series of organic laws that were to supplement the Constitution. On January 6, 1849, the party of Order had a deputy named Rateau move that the Assembly should let the organic laws go and rather decide on its *own dissolution.* Not only the ministry, with Odilon Barrot at its head, but all the royalist members of the National Assembly told it in bullying accents then that its dissolution was necessary for the restoration of credit, for the consolidation of order, for putting an end to the indefinite provisional arrangements and for establishing a definitive state of affairs; that it hampered the productivity of the new government and sought to prolong its existence merely out of malice; that the country was tired of it. Bonaparte took note of all this invective against the legislative power, learnt it by heart and proved to the parliamentary royalists, on December 2, 1851, that he had learnt from them. He reiterated their own catchwords against them.

The Barrot ministry and the party of Order went further. They caused *petitions to the National Assembly* to be made throughout France, in which this body was politely requested to decamp. They thus led the unorganized popular masses into the fire of battle against the National Assembly, the constitutionally organized expression of the people. They taught Bonaparte to appeal against the parliamentary assemblies to the people. At length, on January 29, 1849, the day had come on which the Constituent Assembly was to decide concerning its own dissolution. The National Assembly found the building where its sessions were held occupied by the military; Changarnier, the general of the party of Order, in whose hands the supreme command of the National Guard and troops of the line had been united, held a great military review in Paris, as if a battle were impending, and the royalists in coalition threateningly declared to the Constituent Assembly that force would be employed if it should prove unwilling. It was willing, and only bargained for a very short extra term of life. What was January 29 but the *coup d'état* of December 2, 1851, only carried out by the royalists with Bonaparte against the republican National Assembly? The gentlemen did not observe, or did not wish to observe, that Bonaparte availed himself of January 29, 1849, to have a portion of the troops march past him in front of the Tuileries, and seized with avidity on just this first public summoning of the military power against the parliamentary power to foreshadow Caligula. They, to be sure, saw only their Changarnier.

A motive that particularly actuated the party of Order in forcibly cutting short the duration of the Constituent Assembly's life was the *organic* laws supplementing the Constitution, such as the education law, the law on religious worship, etc. To the royalists in coalition it was most important that they themselves should make these laws and not let them be made by the republicans, who had grown mistrustful. Among these organic laws, however, was also a law on the responsibility of the President of the republic. In 1851 the Legislative Assembly was occupied with the drafting of just such a law, when Bonaparte anticipated this *coup* with the *coup* of December 2. What would the royalists in coalition not have given in their parliamentary winter campaign of 1851 to have found the Responsibility Law ready to hand, and drawn up, at that, by a mistrustful, hostile, republican Assembly!

After the Constituent Assembly had itself shattered its last weapon on January 29, 1849, the Barrot ministry and the friends of order hounded it to death, left nothing undone that could humiliate it and wrested from the impotent, self-despairing Assembly laws that cost it the last remnant of respect in the eyes of the public. Bonaparte, occupied with his fixed Napoleonic idea, was brazen enough to exploit publicly this degradation of the parliamentary power. For when on May 8, 1849, the National Assembly passed a vote of censure of the ministry because of the occupation of Civitavecchia by Oudinot, and ordered it to bring back the Roman expedition to its alleged purpose, Bonaparte published the same evening in the *Moniteur* a letter to Oudinot, in which he congratulated him on his heroic exploits and, in contrast to the ink-slinging parliamentarians, already posed as the generous protector of the army. The royalists smiled at this. They regarded him simply as their dupe. Finally, when Marrast, the President of the Constituent Assembly, believed for a moment that the safety of the National Assembly was endangered and, relying on the Constitution, requisitioned a colonel and his regiment, the colonel declined, cited discipline in his support and referred Marrast to Changarnier, who scornfully refused him with the remark that he did not like *baïonnettes intelligentes.* In November 1851, when the royalists in coalition wanted to begin the decisive struggle with Bonaparte, they sought to put through in their notorious *Quaestors' Bill,* the principle of the direct requisition of troops by the President of the National Assembly. One of their generals, Le Flô, had signed the bill. In vain did Changarnier vote for it and Thiers pay homage to the far-sighted wisdom of the former Constituent Assembly. The *War Minister, Saint-Arnaud,* answered him as Changarnier had answered Marrast—and to the acclamation of the *Montagne!*

Thus the *party of Order,* when it was not yet the National Assembly, when it was still only the ministry, had itself stigmatized the *parliamentary regime.* And it makes an outcry when December 2, 1851, banished this regime from France!

We wish it a happy journey.

VII

On the threshold of the February Revolution, the *social republic* appeared as a phrase, as a prophecy. In the June days of 1848, it was drowned in the blood of the *Paris proletariat,* but it haunts the subsequent acts of the drama like a ghost. The *democratic republic* announces its arrival. On June 13, 1849, it is dissipated together with its *petty bourgeois,* who have taken to their heels, but in its flight it blows its own trumpet with redoubled boastfulness. The *parliamentary republic,* together with the bourgeoisie, takes possession of the entire stage; it enjoys its existence to the full, but December 2, 1851, buries it to the accompaniment of the anguished cry of the royalists in coalition: "Long live the Republic!"

The French bourgeoisie balked at the domination of the working proletariat; it has brought the *lumpenproletariat* to domination, with the chief of the Society of December 10 at the head. The bourgeoisie kept France in breathless fear of the future terrors of red anarchy; Bonaparte discounted this future for it when, on December 4, he had the eminent bourgeois of the Boulevard Montmartre and the Boulevard des Italiens shot down at their windows by the liquor-inspired army of order. It apotheosized the sword; the sword rules it. It destroyed the revolutionary press; its own press has been destroyed. It placed popular meetings under police supervision; its salons are under the supervision of the police. It disbanded the democratic National Guards; its own National Guard is disbanded. It imposed a state of siege; a state of siege is imposed upon it. It supplanted the juries by military commissions; its juries are supplanted by military commissions. It subjected public education to the sway of the priests; the priests subject it to their own education. It transported people without trial; it is being transported without trial. It repressed every stirring in society by means of the state power; every stirring in its society is suppressed by means of the state power. Out of enthusiasm for its purse, it rebelled against its own politicians and men of letters; its politicians and men of letters are swept aside, but its purse is being plundered now that its mouth has been gagged and its pen broken. The bourgeoisie never wearied of crying out to the revolution what Saint Arsenius cried out to the Christians: *"Fuge, tace, quiesce!* Flee, be silent, keep still!" Bonaparte cries to the bourgeoisie: *"Fuge, tace, quiesce!* Flee, be silent, keep still!"

The French bourgeoisie had long ago found the solution to Napoleon's dilemma: *"Dans cinquante ans l'Europe sera républicaine ou cosaque."* It had found the solution to it in the *"république cosaque."* No Circe, by means of black magic, has distorted that work of art, the bourgeois republic, into a monstrous shape. That republic has lost nothing but the semblance of respectability. Present-day France was contained in a finished state within the parliamentary republic. It only required a bayonet thrust for the bubble to burst and the monster to spring forth before our eyes.

Why did the Paris proletariat not rise in revolt after December 2?

The overthrow of the bourgeoisie had as yet been only decreed; the decree had not been carried out. Any serious insurrection of the proletariat would at once have put fresh life into the bourgeoisie, would have reconciled it with the army and ensured a second June defeat for the workers.

On December 4 the proletariat was incited by bourgeois and *épicier* to fight. On the evening of that day several legions of the National Guard promised to appear, armed and uniformed, on the scene of battle. For the bourgeois and the *épicier* had got wind of the fact that in one of his decrees of December 2 Bonaparte abolished the secret ballot and enjoined them to record their "yes" or "no" in the official registers after their names. The resistance of December 4 intimidated Bonaparte. During the night he caused placards to be posted on all the street corners of Paris, announcing the restoration of the secret ballot. The bourgeois and the *épicier* believed that they had gained their end. Those who failed to appear next morning were the bourgeois and the *épicier.*

By a *coup de main* during the night of December 1 to 2, Bonaparte had robbed the Paris proletariat of its leaders, the barricade commanders. An army without officers, averse to fighting under the banner of the *Montagnards* because of the memories of June 1848 and 1849 and May 1850, it left to its vanguard, the secret societies, the task of saving the insurrectionary honour of Paris, which the bourgeoisie had so unresistingly surrendered to the soldiery that, later on, Bonaparte could sneeringly give as his motive for disarming the National Guard—his fear that its arms would be turned against it itself by the anarchists!

"C'est le triomphe complet et définitif du socialisme!" Thus Guizot characterized December 2. But if the overthrow of the parliamentary republic contains within itself the germ of the triumph of the proletarian revolution, its immediate and palpable result was *the victory of Bonaparte over parliament, of the executive power over the legislative power, of force without phrases over the force of phrases.* In parliament the nation made its general will the law, that is, it made the law of the ruling class its general will. Before the executive power it renounces all will of its own and submits to the superior command of an alien will, to authority. The executive power, in contrast to the legislative power, expresses the heteronomy of a nation, in contrast to its autonomy. France, therefore, seems to have escaped the despotism of a class only to fall back beneath the despotism of an individual, and, what is more, beneath the authority of an individual without authority. The struggle seems to be settled in such a way that all classes, equally impotent and equally mute, fall on their knees before the rifle butt.

But the revolution is thoroughgoing. It is still journeying through purgatory. It does its work methodically. By December 2, 1851, it had completed one half of its preparatory work; it is now completing the other half. First it perfected the parliamentary power, in order to be able to overthrow it. Now that it has attained this, it perfects the *executive power,* reduces it to its purest expression, isolates it, sets it up against itself as the sole target, in order to concentrate all its forces of destruction against it. And when it has done this second half of its preliminary work, Europe will leap from its seat and exultantly exclaim: Well grubbed, old mole!

This executive power with its enormous bureaucratic and military organization, with its ingenious state machinery, embracing wide strata, with a host of officials numbering half a million, besides an army of another half million, this appalling parasitic body, which enmeshes the body of French society like a net and chokes all its pores, sprang up in the days of the absolute monarchy, with the decay of the feudal system, which it helped to hasten. The seignorial privileges of the landowners and towns became transformed into so many attributes of the state power, the feudal dignitaries into paid officials and the motley pattern of conflicting medieval plenary powers into the regulated plan of a state authority whose work is divided and centralized as in a factory. The first French Revolution, with its task of breaking all separate local, territorial, urban and provincial powers in order to create the civil unity of the nation, was bound to develop what the absolute monarchy had begun: centralization, but at the same time the extent, the attributes and the agents of governmental power. Napoleon perfected this state machinery. The Legitimist Monarchy and the July Monarchy added nothing but a greater division of labour, growing in the same measure as the division of labour within bourgeois society created new groups of interests, and, therefore, new material for state administration. Every *common* interest was straightway severed from society, counterposed to it as a higher, *general* interest, snatched from the activity of society's members themselves and made an object of government activity, from a bridge, a schoolhouse and the communal property of a village community to the railways, the national wealth and the national university of France. Finally, in its struggle against the revolution, the parliamentary republic found itself compelled to strengthen, along with the repressive measures, the resources and centralization of governmental power. All revolutions perfected this machine instead of smashing it. The parties that contended in turn for domination regarded the possession of this huge state edifice as the principal spoils of the victor.

But under the absolute monarchy, during the first Revolution, under Napoleon, bureaucracy was only the means of preparing the class rule of the bourgeoisie. Under the Restoration, under Louis Philippe, under the parliamentary republic, it was the instrument of the ruling class, however much it strove for power of its own.

Only under the second Bonaparte does the state seem to have made itself completely independent. As against civil society, the state machine has consolidated its position so thoroughly that the chief of the Society of December 10 suffices for its head, an adventurer blown in from abroad, raised on the shield by a drunken soldiery, which he has bought with liquor and sausages, and which he must continually ply with sausage anew. Hence the downcast despair, the feeling of most dreadful humiliation and degradation that oppresses the breast of France and makes her catch her breath. She feels dishonoured.

And yet the state power is not suspended in midair. Bonaparte represents a class, and the most numerous class of French society at that, the *small-holding peasants*.

Just as the Bourbons were the dynasty of big landed property and just as the Orleans were the dynasty of money, so the Bonapartes are the dynasty of the peasants, that is, the mass of the French people. Not the Bonaparte who submitted to the bourgeois parliament, but the Bonaparte who dispersed the bourgeois parliament is the chosen of the peasantry. For three years the towns had succeeded in falsifying the meaning of the election of December 10 and in cheating the peasants out of the restoration of the empire. The election of December 10, 1848, has been consummated only by the *coup d'état* of December 2, 1851.

The small-holding peasants form a vast mass, the members of which live in similar conditions but without entering into manifold relations with one another. Their mode of production isolates them from one another instead of bringing them into mutual intercourse. The isolation is increased by France's bad means of communication and by the poverty of the peasants. Their field of production, the small holding, admits of no division of labour in its cultivation, no application of science and, therefore, no diversity of development, no variety of talent, no wealth of social relationships. Each individual peasant family is almost self-sufficient; it itself directly produces the major part of its consumption and thus acquires its means of life more through exchange with nature than in intercourse with society. A small holding, a peasant and his family; alongside them another small holding, another peasant and another family. A few score of these make up a village, and a few score of villages make up a Department. In this way, the great mass of the French nation is formed by simple addition of homologous magnitudes, much as potatoes in a sack form a sack of potatoes. In so far as millions of families live under economic conditions of existence that separate their mode of life, their interests and their culture from those of the other classes, and put them in hostile opposition to the latter, they form a class. In so far as there is merely a local interconnection among these small-holding peasants, and the identity of their interests begets no community, no national bond and no political organization among them, they do not form a class. They are consequently incapable of enforcing their class interest in their own name, whether through a parliament or through a convention. They cannot represent themselves, they must be represented. Their representative must at the same time appear as their master, as an authority over them, as an unlimited governmental power that protects them against the other classes and sends them rain and sunshine from above. The political influence of the small-holding peasants, therefore, finds its final expression in the executive power subordinating society to itself.

Historical tradition gave rise to the belief of the French peasants in the miracle that a man named Napoleon would bring all the glory back to them. And an individual turned up who gives himself out as the man because he bears the name of Napoleon, in consequence of the *Code*

Napoléon, which lays down that *la recherche de la paternité est interdite.* After a vagabondage of twenty years and after a series of grotesque adventures, the legend finds fulfilment and the man becomes Emperor of the French. The fixed idea of the Nephew was realized, because it coincided with the fixed idea of the most numerous class of the French people.

But, it may be objected, what about the peasant risings in half of France, the raids on the peasants by the army, the mass incarceration and transportation of peasants?

Since Louis XIV, France has experienced no similar persecution of the peasants "on account of demagogic practices."

But let there be no misunderstanding. The Bonaparte dynasty represents not the revolutionary, but the conservative peasant; not the peasant that strikes out beyond the condition of his social existence, the small holding, but rather the peasant who wants to consolidate this holding, not the country folk who, linked up with the towns, want to overthrow the old order through their own energies, but on the contrary those who, in stupefied seclusion within this old order, want to see themselves and their small holdings saved and favoured by the ghost of the empire. It represents not the enlightenment, but the superstition of the peasant; not his judgment, but his prejudice; not his future, but his past; not his modern Cevennes, but his modern Vendée.

The three years' rigorous rule of the parliamentary republic had freed a part of the French peasants from the Napoleonic illusion and had revolutionized them, even if only superficially; but the bourgeoisie violently repressed them, as often as they set themselves in motion. Under the parliamentary republic the modern and the traditional consciousness of the French peasant contended for mastery. This progress took the form of an incessant struggle between the schoolmasters and the priests. The bourgeoisie struck down the schoolmasters. For the first time the peasants made efforts to behave independently in the face of the activity of the government. This was shown in the continual conflict between the *maires* and the prefects. The bourgeoisie deposed the *maires.* Finally, during the period of the parliamentary republic, the peasants of different localities rose against their own offspring, the army. The bourgeoisie punished them with states of siege and punitive expeditions. And this same bourgeoisie now cries out about the stupidity of the masses, the vile multitude, that has betrayed it to Bonaparte. It has itself forcibly strengthened the empire sentiments of the peasant class, it conserved the conditions that form the birthplace of this peasant religion. The bourgeoisie, to be sure, is bound to fear the stupidity of the masses as long as they remain conservative, and the insight of the masses as soon as they become revolutionary.

In the risings after the *coup d'état,* a part of the French peasants protested, arms in hand, against their own vote of December 10, 1848. The school they had gone through since 1848 had sharpened their wits. But they had made themselves over to the underworld of history; history held them to their word, and the majority was still so prejudiced that in precisely the reddest Departments the peasant population voted openly for Bonaparte. In its view, the National Assembly had hindered his progress. He had now merely broken the fetters that the towns had imposed on the will of the countryside. In some parts the peasants even entertained the grotesque notion of a convention side by side with Napoleon.

After the first revolution had transformed the peasants from semi-villeins into freeholders, Napoleon confirmed and regulated the conditions on which they could exploit undisturbed the soil of France which had only just fallen to their lot and slake their youthful passion for property. But what is now causing the ruin of the French peasant is his small holding itself, the division of the land, the form of property which Napoleon consolidated in France. It is precisely the material conditions which made the feudal peasant a small-holding peasant and Napoleon an emperor. Two generations have sufficed to produce the inevitable result: progressive deterioration of agriculture, progressive indebtedness of the agriculturist. The "Napoleonic" form of property, which at the beginning of the nineteenth century was the condition for the liberation and enrichment of the French country folk, has developed in the course of this century into the law of their enslavement and pauperization. And precisely this law is the first of the *"idées napoléoniennes"* which the second Bonaparte has to uphold. If he still shares with the peasants the illusion that the cause of their ruin is to be sought, not in this small-holding property itself, but outside it, in the influence of secondary circumstances, his experiments will burst like soap bubbles when they come in contact with the relations of production.

The economic development of small-holding property has radically changed the relation of the peasants to the other classes of society. Under Napoleon, the fragmentation of the land in the countryside supplemented free competition and the beginning of big industry in the towns. The peasant class was the ubiquitous protest against the landed aristocracy which had just been overthrown. The roots that small-holding property struck in French soil deprived feudalism of all nutriment. Its landmarks formed the natural fortifications of the bourgeoisie against any surprise attack on the part of its old overlords. But in the course of the nineteenth century the feudal lords were replaced by urban usurers; the feudal obligation that went with the land was replaced by the mortgage; aristocratic landed property was replaced by bourgeois capital. The small holding of the peasant is now only the pretext that allows the capitalist to draw profits, interest and rent from the soil, while leaving it to the tiller of the soil himself to see how he can extract his wages. The mortgage debt burdening the soil of France imposes on the French peasantry payment of an amount of interest equal to the annual interest on the entire British national debt. Small-holding property, in this enslavement by capital to which its development inevitably pushes forward, has transformed the mass of the French nation into troglodytes. Sixteen million peasants (including women and children) dwell in hovels, a large number of which have but one opening, others only two and the most favoured only three. And windows are to a house what the five senses are to the head. The bourgeois order, which at the beginning of the century set the state to stand guard over the newly arisen small holding and manured it with laurels, has become a vampire that sucks out its blood and brains and throws it into the alchemistic cauldron of capital. The *Code Napoléon* is now nothing but a *codex* of distraints, forced sales and compulsory auctions. To the four million (including children, etc.) officially recognized paupers, vagabonds, criminals and prostitutes in France must be added five million who hover on the margin of existence and either have their haunts in the countryside itself or, with their rags and their children, continually desert the countryside for the towns and the towns for the countryside. The interests of the peasants, therefore, are no longer, as under Napoleon, in accord with, but in opposition to the interests of the bourgeoisie, to capital. Hence the peasants find their natural ally and leader in the *urban proletariat,* whose task is the overthrow of the bourgeois order. But *strong and unlimited government*—and this is the second *"idée napoléonienne,"* which the second Napoleon has to carry out—is called upon to defend this "material" order by force. This *"ordre matériel"* also serves as the catchword in all of Bonaparte's proclamations against the rebellious peasants.

Besides the mortgage which capital imposes on it, the small holding is burdened by *taxes.* Taxes are the source of life for the bureaucracy, the army, the priests and the court, in short, for the whole apparatus of the executive power. Strong government and heavy taxes are identical. By its very nature, small-holding property forms a suitable basis for an all-powerful and innumerable bureaucracy. It creates a uniform level of relationships and persons over the whole surface of the land. Hence it also permits of uniform action from a supreme centre on all points of this uniform mass. It annihilates the aristocratic intermediate grades between the mass of the people and the state power. On all sides, therefore, it calls forth the direct interference of this state power and the interposition of its immediate organs. Finally, it produces an unemployed surplus population for which there is no place either on the land or in the towns, and which accordingly reaches out for state offices as a sort of respectable alms, and provokes the creation of state posts. By the new markets which he opened at the point of the bayonet, by the plundering of the Continent, Napoleon repaid the compulsory taxes with interest. These taxes were a spur to the industry of the peasant, whereas now they rob his industry of its last resources and complete his inability to resist pauperism. And an enormous bureaucracy, well-gallooned and well-fed, is the *"idée napoléonienne"* which is most congenial of all to the second Bonaparte. How could it be otherwise, seeing that alongside the actual classes of society he is forced to create an artificial caste, for which the maintenance of his regime becomes a bread-and-butter question? Accordingly, one of his first financial operations was the raising of officials' salaries to their old level and the creation of new sinecures.

Another *"idée napoléonienne"* is the domination of the *priests* as an instrument of government. But while in its accord with society, in its dependence on natural forces and its submission to the authority which protected it from above, the small holding that had newly come into being was naturally religious, the small holding that is ruined by debts, at odds with society and authority, and driven beyond its own limitations naturally becomes irreligious. Heaven was quite a pleasing accession to the narrow strip of land just won, more particularly as it makes the weather; it becomes an insult as soon as it is thrust forward as substitute for the small holding. The priest then appears as only the anointed bloodhound of the earthly police—another *"idée napoléonienne."* On the next occasion, the expedition against Rome will take place in France itself, but in a sense opposite to that of M. de Montalembert.

Lastly, the culminating point of the *"idées napoléoniennes"* is the preponderance of the *army.* The army was the *point d'honneur* of the small-holding peasants, it was they themselves transformed into heroes, defending their new possessions against the outer world, glorifying their recently won nationhood, plundering and revolutionizing the world. The uniform was their own state dress; war was their poetry; the small holding, extended and rounded off in imagination, was their fatherland, and patriotism the ideal form of the sense of property. But the enemies against whom the French peasant has now to defend his property are not the Cossacks; they are the *huissiers* and the tax collectors. The small holding lies no longer in the so-called fatherland, but in the register of mortgages. The army itself is no longer the flower of the peasant youth; it is the swamp-flower of the peasant *lumpenproletariat.* It consists in large measure of *remplaçants,* of substitutes, just as the second Bonaparte is himself only a *remplaçant,* the substitute for Napoleon. It now performs its deeds of valour by hounding the peasants in masses like chamois, by doing *gendarme* duty, and if the internal contradictions of his system chase the chief of the Society of December 10 over the French border, his army, after some acts of brigandage, will reap, not laurels, but thrashings.

One sees: *all* "idées napoléoniennes" *are ideas of the undeveloped small holding in the freshness of its youth;* for the small holding that has outlived its day they are an absurdity. They are only the hallucinations of its death struggle, words that are transformed into phrases, spirits transformed into ghosts. But the parody of the empire was necessary to free the mass of the French nation from the weight of tradition and to work out in pure form the opposition between the state power and society. With the progressive undermining of small-holding property, the state structure erected upon it collapses. The centralization of the state that modern society requires arises only on the ruins of the military-bureaucratic government machinery which was forged in opposition to feudalism.

The condition of the French peasants provides us with the answer to the riddle of the *general elections of December 20 and 21,* which bore the second Bonaparte up Mount Sinai, not to receive laws, but to give them.

Manifestly, the bourgeoisie had now no choice but to elect Bonaparte. When the puritans at the Council of Constance complained of the dissolute lives of the popes and wailed about the necessity of moral reform, Cardinal Pierre d'Ailly thundered at them: "Only the devil in person can still save the Catholic Church, and you ask for angels." In like manner, after the *coup d'état,* the French bourgeoisie cried: Only the chief of the Society of December 10 can still save bourgeois society! Only theft can still save property; only perjury, religion; bastardy, the family; disorder, order!

As the executive authority which has made itself an independent power, Bonaparte feels it to be his mission to safeguard "bourgeois order." But the strength of this bourgeois order lies in the middle class. He looks on himself, therefore, as the representative of the middle class and issues decrees in this sense. Nevertheless, he is somebody solely due to the fact that he has broken the political power of this middle class and daily breaks it anew. Consequently, he looks on himself as the adversary of the political and literary power of the middle class. But by protecting its material power, he generates its political power anew. The cause must accordingly be kept alive; but the effect, where it manifests itself, must be done away with. But this cannot pass off without slight confusions of cause and effect, since in their interaction both lose their distinguishing features. New decrees that obliterate the border line. As against the bourgeoisie, Bonaparte looks on himself, at the same time, as the representative of the peasants and of the people in general, who wants to make the lower classes of the people happy within the frame of bourgeois society. New decrees that cheat the "True Socialists" of their statecraft in advance. But, above all, Bonaparte looks on himself as the chief of the Society of December 10, as the representative of the *lumpenproletariat* to which he himself, his *entourage,* his government and his army belong, and whose prime consideration is to benefit itself and draw California lottery prizes from the state treasury. And he vindicates his position as chief of the Society of December 10 with decrees, without decrees and despite decrees.

This contradictory task of the man explains the contradictions of his government, the confused groping about which seeks now to win, now to humiliate first one class and then another and arrays all of them uniformly against him, whose practical uncertainty forms a highly comical contrast to the imperious, categorical style of the government decrees, a style which is faithfully copied from the Uncle.

Industry and trade, hence the business affairs of the middle class, are to prosper in hothouse fashion under the strong government. The grant of innumerable railway concessions. But the Bonapartist *lumpenproletariat* is to enrich itself. The initiated play *tripotage* on the *bourse* with the railway concessions. But no capital is forthcoming for the railways. Obligation of the Bank to make advances on railway shares. But, at the same time, the Bank is to be exploited for personal ends and therefore must be cajoled. Release of the Bank from the obligation to publish its report weekly. Leonine agreement of the Bank with the government. The people are to be given employment. Initiation of public works. But the public works increase the obligations of the people in respect of taxes. Hence reduction of the taxes by an onslaught on the *rentiers,* by conversion of the five per cent bonds to four-and-a-half per cent. But, once more, the middle class must receive a *douceur.* Therefore doubling of the wine tax for the people, who buy it *en détail,* and halving of the wine tax for the middle class, who drink it *en gros.* Dissolution of the actual workers' associations, but promises of miracles of association in the future. The peasants are to be helped. Mortgage banks that expedite their getting into debt and accelerate the concentration of property. But these banks are to be used to make money out of the confiscated estates of the House of Orleans. No capitalist wants to agree to this condition, which is not in the decree, and the mortgage bank remains a mere decree, etc., etc.

Bonaparte would like to appear as the patriarchal benefactor of all classes. But he cannot give to one class without taking from another. Just as at the time of the Fronde it was said of the Duke of Guise that he was the most *obligeant* man in France because he had turned all his estates into his partisans' obligations to him, so Bonaparte would fain be the most *obligeant* man in France and turn all the property, all the labour of France into a personal obligation to himself. He would like to steal the whole of France in order to be able to make a present of her to France or, rather, in order to be able to buy France anew with French money, for as the chief of the Society of December 10 he must needs buy what ought to belong to him. And all the state institutions, the Senate, the Council of State, the legislative body, the Legion of Honour, the soldiers' medals, the washhouses, the public works, the railways, the *état major* of the National Guard to the exclusion of privates, and the confiscated estates of the House of Orleans—all become parts of the institution of purchase. Every place in the army and in the government machine becomes a means of purchase. But the most important feature of this process, whereby France is taken in order to give to her, is the percentages that find their way into the pockets of the head and the members of the Society of December 10 during the turnover. The witticism with which Countess L., the mistress of M. de Morny, characterized the confiscation of the Orleans estates: *"C'est le premier vol de l'aigle"* is applicable to every flight of this *eagle,* which is more like a *raven.* He himself and his adherents call out to one another daily like that Italian Carthusian admonishing the miser who, with boastful display, counted up the goods on which he could yet live for years to come: *"Tu fai conto sopra i beni, bisogna prima far il conto sopra gli anni."* Lest they make a mistake in the years, they count the minutes. A bunch of blokes push their way forward to the court, into the ministries, to the head of the administration and the army, a crowd of the best of whom it must be said that no one knows whence he comes, a noisy, disreputable, rapacious bohème that crawls into galloоned coats with the same grotesque dignity as the high dignitaries of Soulouque. One can visualize clearly this upper stratum of the Society of December 10, if one reflects that *Véron-Crevel* is its preacher of morals and *Granier de Cassagnac* its thinker. When Guizot, at the time of his ministry, utilized this Granier on a hole-and-corner newspaper against the dynastic opposition, he used to boast of him with the quip: *"C'est le roi des drôles,"* "he is the king of buffoons." One would do wrong to recall the Regency or Louis XV in connection with Louis Bonaparte's court and clique. For "often already, France has experienced a government of mistresses; but never before a government of *hommes entretenus."*

Driven by the contradictory demands of his situation and being at the same time, like a conjurer, under the necessity of keeping the public gaze fixed on himself, as Napoleon's substitute, by springing constant surprises, that is to say, under the necessity of executing a *coup d'état en miniature* every day, Bonaparte throws the entire bourgeois economy into confusion, violates everything that seemed inviolable to the Revolution of 1848, makes some tolerant of revolution, others desirous of revolution, and produces actual anarchy in the name of order, while at the same time stripping its halo from the entire state machine, profanes it and makes it at once loathsome and ridiculous. The cult of the Holy Tunic of Treves he duplicates at Paris in the cult of the Napoleonic imperial mantle. But when the imperial mantle finally falls on the shoulders of Louis Bonaparte, the bronze statue of Napoleon will crash from the top of the Vendôme Column.

Jacob Burckhardt 1818—1897

6

Within a decade after the publication of Jacob Burckhardt's *The Civilization of the Renaissance in Italy,* the French historian Hippolyte Taine proclaimed this masterpiece to be "an admirable book, the most complete and philosophical one that has been written on the Italian Renaissance." More than a century has passed since Burckhardt constructed his essay in cultural history, and yet there are few, if any, who would not concur with Taine's estimation of that achievement. It was the unparalleled accomplishment of Burckhardt to have defined in a single work, which he deliberately limited in size and scope, a historical epoch and given that epoch a form and a vitality that have insured its permanent place in the history of civilization in the West.

Before the publication of Burckhardt's *Renaissance* in 1860, there had been numerous attempts at the creation of cultural history, as well as at a definition of the "revival of letters" in Italy. In the century of the Enlightenment, Voltaire, in addition to proclaiming that Italian cultural revival one of the great ages of man, attempted to dislodge the old annalistic historiography and to emphasize cultural history as the clue to understanding the spirit of an age. But Voltaire could only be a pioneer in the writing of cultural history and not a master craftsman like Burckhardt; moreover, he was interested in tracing the origins of the Enlightenment rather than in studying the Renaissance. The seventh volume of Jules Michelet's *History of France* (1855) bore the subtitle *The Renaissance.* Michelet conceived of the Renaissance as a period quite distinct from the Middle Ages and saw it as a spontaneous rebirth without antecedent causes. Michelet's conception was also limited in its failure to recognize Italian precedence in, or to treat anything before or beyond the sixteenth century. Just a year before Burckhardt's *Renaissance* appeared, Georg Voigt's *The Revival of Classical Antiquity* had established the thesis that the characteristic which distinguished the culture of Italy in the period from Petrarch to Michelangelo was the revival of classical learning. His position owed much to humanist historians themselves, who had insisted that the culture of antiquity had helped to lift them from the clutches of the Middle Ages. And countless other historians had treated Italy from the fourteenth to the sixteenth centuries as the center of painting, sculpture, architecture, and scholarship.

No historian before Burckhardt, however, had synthesized all these developments into an organic whole. It was Burckhardt who gave substance and meaning to Michelet's epigram that the Renaissance witnessed the "discovery of the world and of man." *The Civilization of the Renaissance in Italy* was, in the literal sense, an epoch-making work.

This work was also the product of a political outsider. Burckhardt was born and remained for the major part of his life in Basel, Switzerland. Except for his time in the 1830's as a student in Berlin, where he studied under Ranke, and except for his trips to Italy, Burckhardt was content to remain in his native city, which was for the most part spared the revolutions that rent most of the European continent in the mid-nineteenth century. In his youth, Burckhardt found the intellectual atmosphere in Berlin exciting. It was impossible not to be impressed by the Ranke seminar, and the impressionable young scholar became very much caught up in the enthusiasm for the Germanic Middle Ages that the sentimentalism of Romantic art criticism fostered during this period. Two trips to Italy—one in 1846 and another in 1853—as well as an increasing sense of independence, helped him achieve a conversion from Romanticism to Classicism. As a mature historian, he learned to become critical of the limited scope of Ranke and his methods. He later emerged as a prophetic and penetrating critic of German politics. He was proud that his native language was German, because that had been the language of Goethe, who also outgrew the "excesses" of Romanticism. The vulgarity of the Bismarckian state would indeed have repelled Goethe as it would his kindred spirit Burckhardt.

Even his native Basel was not to remain immune from the social upheaval of Europe in mid-century. In 1847, the oligarchical government of Basel was forced to adopt a new constitution, which effectively ended the rule of the patrician families, among whom the Burckhardts had figured prominently. For over a century one of the two burgomasters of Basel had been a Burckhardt. In the new, industrial city of Basel, the greatest member of this aristocratic family retired to two rooms above a baker's shop, where he could contemplate the art and culture of the ageless beauty and harmonious form that he had found in Italy. From what he called his "Archimedean point outside events," he was determined to discover the value for which he said he was willing to perish, "the old culture of Europe."

Burckhardt was first attracted to the culture of the Italian Renaissance as an amateur art historian. He edited and reworked a standard guide to Italian art history and offered a fine analysis of the decline of ancient culture in *The Age of Constantine the Great* in 1853; two years later he published the *Cicerone,* his own enthusiastic handbook on Italian art. These were followed by his brilliant essay, the last major work he ever published. It was in his *History of Greek Civilization,* published after his death, that Burckhardt provided the most direct statement of his method and purpose in writing cultural history. "Our task," he wrote, "is to give the history of the Greek way of thinking and of looking at things, and to strive for perception of the living forces, constructive and destructive, that were active in Greek life. Not by narrative, yet historically, we must consider the Greeks in their essential peculiarity. To this, to the history of Greek spirit, must the entire study be directed."

In *The Civilization of the Renaissance in Italy,* Burckhardt fully realized his goal. He deliberately subtitled this work "an essay." It is not in any sense a comprehensive or narrative history of the period. It is an artfully executed topical discussion which illustrates in a variety of ways the central thesis that the Renaissance marks the beginning of modern times. Burckhardt declared quite boldly that the Italian of the Renaissance was the "first-born among the sons of modern Europe." In striking contrast to the man of the Middle Ages, modern man no longer saw himself as a member of a race, people, party, family or corporation. As an autonomous individual, man now faced life directly without any fixed relationships or obvious responsibilities. It was, according to Burckhardt, during the Renaissance that the full burden of existential freedom was felt for the first time.

We have included as our selection the entire first part of the *Renaissance,* "The State as a Work of Art," because the problems encountered in assuming this new freedom are so vividly illustrated here. While describing the conflicts between popes and emperors, Burckhardt discovers the appearance of the "modern European state spirit . . . free to follow its inclinations." And with these inclinations, he continues, a new factor enters history, "the State as the outcome of reflection and calculation, the State as a work of art." The internecine strife of the Italian republics and the lawlessness of despotic governments bred a new type of uninhibited egomaniac, typified by Cesare Borgia, who "isolates his father, murders his brother, his brother-in-law and other relatives and courtiers" when he finds it expedient. The modern state might be a work of art, but Burckhardt understood all too well that it might also be the work of amoral monsters.

In the second part of his essay, Burckhardt, in his discussion of the development of the individual, gives further evidence of the arrival of modern man. Unfettered by traditional loyalties and the restrictions of conventional morality, the consciousness of the entire personality emerges. This eventually results not only in the desire for fame but in the expression of spiteful will as well. Burckhardt then, in Part Three, takes up the revival of antiquity, which had long been recognized as a vital aspect of the Renaissance. But in his interpretation, this revival is more an effect than a cause of the Renaissance. It was only when Classicism began to fascinate the genius of the Italian people that "the conquest of the modern world" could take place. In the last three sections of the essay, Burckhardt examines how the new individual and the modern state affect the cultural, social, and moral life of the time. He accounts for the interest in science and exploration as well as in festivals and literature as part of the dawning of the modern era.

When, in 1872, Burckhardt was offered Ranke's chair at the University of Berlin, he refused to leave Basel. That same year he wrote to a German official expressing his distaste for the growth of a military and industrial state, and he predicted that "the development of a crafty and enduring tyranny is only in its infancy. It is in Germany that it will grow to maturity." In writing about his favorite period, the historian sought to preserve European culture by making his readers aware of the risks inherent in modern life. Burckhardt saw that there was more to fear than to admire in the supermen, the "terrible simplifiers," of modern time. Burckhardt thus deserves to be remembered as a critic of our era as well as one of its most eloquent historians.

An achievement as remarkable as Burckhardt's *Renaissance* inevitably invites constant criticism and numerous revisions. In the half century that followed its publication, Burckhardt's essay was amplified in detail but unchallenged as a whole. In the first decades of the twentieth century, scholars began to balk at his lack of interest in economics and in the life of the common people. After the Second World War, many medievalists revolted against what they took to be Burckhardt's implicit denigration of the Middle Ages, and they were anxious to place the origins of the Renaissance into their own period of interest. Their arguments may shade Burckhardt's bold analysis, but, in the words of a present-day specialist, "our conception of the Renaissance is Jacob Burckhardt's creation."

Selected Bibliography

The authoritative biography of Burckhardt is Werner Kaegi's *Jacob Burckhardt: Eine Biographie,* 4 vols. (1947–67). Wallace K. Ferguson, in *The Renaissance in Historical Thought* (1948), provides a scholarly discussion of Burckhardt's predecessors, his contribution to the historiography of the Renaissance, as well as his influence on subsequent generations of Renaissance scholars. Hajo Holborn wrote an appreciative "Introduction" to the 1954 edition of Burckhardt's *Renaissance;* and Peter Gay's essay "Burckhardt's *Renaissance:* Between Responsibility and Power," in *The Responsibility of Power: Historical Essays in Honor of Hajo Holborn* (1967), 185–198, Leonard Krieger and Fritz Stern, eds., interprets Burckhardt's dialectic vision of the burdens of modernity. H. R. Trevor-Roper's "Introduction" to some of Burckhardt's lectures, published as *Judgments on History and Historians* (1958), offers some helpful insight into Burckhardt as a critic of his own culture.

THE CIVILIZATION OF THE RENAISSANCE IN ITALY

PART I. THE STATE AS A WORK OF ART

Chapter 1. Introduction

This work bears the title of an essay in the strictest sense of the word. No one is more conscious than the writer with what limited means and strength he has addressed himself to a task so arduous. And even if he could look with greater confidence upon his own researches he would hardly thereby feel more assured of the approval of competent judges. To each eye, perhaps, the outlines of a given civilization present a different picture; and in treating of a civilization which is the mother of our own, and whose influence is still at work among us, it is unavoidable that individual judgment and feeling should tell every moment both on the writer and on the reader. In the wide ocean upon which we venture the possible ways and directions are many; and the same studies which have served for this work might easily, in other hands, not only receive a wholly different treatment and application, but lead also to essentially different conclusions. Such, indeed, is the importance of the subject that it still calls for fresh investigation, and may be studied with advantage from the most varied points of view. Meanwhile we are content if a patient hearing be granted us, and if this book be taken and judged as a whole. It is the most serious difficulty of the history of civilization that a great intellectual process must be broken up into single, and often into what seem arbitrary, categories in order to be in any way intelligible. It was formerly our intention to fill up the gaps in this book by a special work on the art of the Renaissance—an intention, however, which we have been able only to fulfil in part.

The struggle between the Popes and the Hohenstaufen left Italy in a political condition which differed essentially from that of other countries of the West. While in France, Spain, and England the feudal system was so organized that at the close of its existence it was naturally transformed into a unified monarchy, and while in Germany it helped to maintain, at least outwardly, the unity of the Empire, Italy had shaken it off almost entirely. The Emperors of the fourteenth century, even in the most favourable case, were no longer received and respected as feudal lords, but as possible leaders and supporters of powers already in existence; while the Papacy, with its creatures and allies, was strong enough to hinder national unity in the future, not strong enough itself to bring about that unity. Between the two lay a multitude of political units—republics and despots—in part of long standing, in part of recent origin, whose existence was founded simply on their power to maintain it. In them for the first time we detect the modern political spirit of Europe, surrendered freely to its own instincts, often displaying the worst features of an unbridled egoism, outraging every right, and killing every germ of a healthier culture. But wherever this vicious tendency is overcome or in any way compensated a new fact appears in history—the State as the outcome of reflection and calculation, the State as a work of art. This new life displays itself in a hundred forms, both in the republican and in the despotic states, and determines their inward constitution no less than their foreign policy. We shall limit ourselves to the consideration of the completer and more clearly defined type, which is offered by the despotic states.

The internal condition of the despotically governed states had a memorable counterpart in the Norman empire of Lower Italy and Sicily after its transformation by the Emperor Frederick II. Bred amid treason and peril in the neighbourhood of the Saracens, Frederick, the first ruler of the modern type who sat upon a throne, had early accustomed himself, both in criticism and action, to a thoroughly objective treatment of affairs. His acquaintance with the internal condition and administration of the Saracenic states was close and intimate; and the mortal struggle in which he was engaged with the Papacy compelled him, no less than his adversaries, to bring into the field all the resources at his command. Frederick's measures (especially after 1231) are aimed at the complete destruction of the feudal state, at the transformation of the people into a multitude destitute of will and of the means of resistance, but profitable in the utmost degree to the exchequer. He centralized, in a manner hitherto unknown in the West, the whole judicial and political administration by establishing the right of appeal from the feudal courts, which he did not, however, abolish, to the imperial judges. No office was henceforth to be filled by popular election, under penalty of the devastation of the offending district and of the enslavement of its inhabitants. Excise duties were introduced; the taxes, based on a comprehensive assessment, and distributed in accordance with Mohammedan usages, were collected by those cruel and vexatious methods without which, it is true, it is impossible to obtain any money from Orientals. Here, in short, we find not a people, but simply a disciplined multitude of subjects; who were forbidden, for example, to marry out of the country without special permission, and under no circumstances were allowed to study abroad. The

University of Naples was the first we know of to restrict the freedom of study, while the East, in these respects at all events, left its youth unfettered. It was after the example of Mohammedan rulers that Frederick traded on his own account in all parts of the Mediterranean, reserving to himself the monopoly of many commodities, and restricting in various ways the commerce of his subjects. The Fatimite caliphs, with all their esoteric unbelief, were, at least in their earlier history, tolerant of the differences in the religious faith of their people; Frederick, on the other hand, crowned his system of government by a religious inquisition, which will seem the more reprehensible when we remember that in the persons of the heretics he was persecuting the representatives of a free municipal life. Lastly the internal police, and the kernel of the army for foreign service, was composed of Saracens, who had been brought over from Sicily to Nocera and Lucera—men who were deaf to the cry of misery and careless of the ban of the Church. At a later period the subjects, by whom the use of weapons had long been forgotten, were passive witnesses of the fall of Manfred and of the seizure of the government by Charles of Anjou; the latter continued to use the system which he found already at work.

At the side of the centralizing Emperor appeared a usurper of the most peculiar kind: his vicar and son-in-law, Ezzelino da Romano. He stands as the representative of no system of government or administration, for all his activity was wasted in struggles for supremacy in the eastern part of Upper Italy; but as a political type he was a figure of no less importance for the future than his Imperial protector Frederick. The conquests and usurpations which had hitherto taken place in the Middle Ages rested on real or pretended inheritance and other such claims, or else were effected against unbelievers and excommunicated persons. Here for the first time the attempt was openly made to found a throne by wholesale murder and endless barbarities, by the adoption, in short, of any means with a view to nothing but the end pursued. None of his successors, not even Cesare Borgia, rivalled the colossal guilt of Ezzelino; but the example once set was not forgotten, and his fall led to no return of justice among the nations, and served as no warning to future transgressors.

It was in vain at such a time that St. Thomas Aquinas, a born subject of Frederick, set up the theory of a constitutional monarchy, in which the prince was to be supported by an upper house named by himself, and a representative body elected by the people; in vain did he concede to the people the right of revolution. Such theories found no echo outside the lecture-room, and Frederick and Ezzelino were and remain for Italy the great political phenomena of the thirteenth century. Their personality, already half legendary, forms the most important subject of *The Hundred Old Tales,* whose original composition falls certainly within this century. In them Frederick is already represented as possessing the right to do as he pleased with the property of his subjects, and exercises on all, even on criminals, a profound influence by the force of his personality; Ezzelino is spoken of with the awe which all mighty impressions leave behind them. His person became the centre of a whole literature, from the chronicle of eye-witnesses to the half-mythical tragedy of later poets.

Immediately after the fall of Frederick and Ezzelino a crowd of tyrants appeared upon the scene. The struggle between Guelph and Ghibelline was their opportunity. They came forward in general as Ghibelline leaders, but at times and under conditions so various that it is impossible not to recognize in the fact a law of supreme and universal necessity. The means which they used were those already familiar in the party struggles of the past—the banishment of destruction of their adversaries and of their adversaries' households.

Chapter 2. The Tyranny of the Fourteenth Century

The tyrannies, great and small, of the fourteenth century afford constant proof that examples such as these were not thrown away. Their misdeeds cried forth loudly, and have been circumstantially told by historians. As states depending for existence on themselves alone, and scientifically organized with a view to this object, they present to us a higher interest than that of mere narrative.

The deliberate adaptation of means to ends, of which no prince out of Italy had at that time a conception, joined to almost absolute power within the limits of the state, produced among the despots both men and modes of life of a peculiar character. The chief secret of government in the hands of the prudent ruler lay in leaving the incidence of taxation so far as possible where he found it, or as he had first arranged it. The chief sources of income were a land-tax, based on a valuation; definite taxes on articles of consumption and duties on exported and imported goods; together with the private fortune of the ruling house. The only possible increase was derived from the growth of business and of general prosperity. Loans, such as we find in the free cities, were here unknown; a well-planned confiscation was held a preferable means of raising money, provided only that it left public credit unshaken—an end attained, for example, by the truly Oriental practice of deposing and plundering the director of finances.

Out of this income the expenses of the little Court, of the bodyguard, of the mercenary troops, and of the public buildings were met, as well as of the buffoons and men of talent who belonged to the personal attendants of the prince. The illegitimacy of his rule isolated the tyrant and surrounded him with constant danger; the most honourable alliance which he could form was with intellectual merit, without regard to its origin. The liberality of the Northern princes of the thirteenth century was confined to the knights, to the nobility which served and sang. It was otherwise with the Italian despot. With his thirst for fame and his passion for monumental works it was talent, not birth, which he needed. In the company of the poet and the scholar he felt himself in a new position —almost, indeed, in possession of a new legitimacy.

No prince was more famous in this respect than the ruler of Verona, Can Grande della Scala, who numbered among the illustrious exiles whom he entertained at his Court representatives of the whole of Italy. The men of letters were not ungrateful. Petrarch, whose visits at the Courts of such men have been so severely censured, sketched an ideal picture of a prince of the fourteenth century. He demands great things from his patron, the lord of Padua, but in a manner which shows that he holds him capable of them.

> Thou must not be the master, but the father of thy subjects, and must love them as thy children; yea, as members of thy body. Weapons, guards, and soldiers thou mayest employ against the enemy—with thy subjects goodwill is sufficient. By citizens, of course, I mean those who love the existing order; for those who daily desire change are rebels and traitors, and against such a stern justice may take its course.

Here follows, worked out in detail, the purely modern fiction of the omnipotence of the State. The prince is to be independent of his courtiers, but at the same time to govern with simplicity and modesty; he is to take everything into his charge, to maintain and restore churches and public buildings, to keep up the municipal police, to drain the marshes, to look after the supply of wine and corn; he is to exercise a strict justice, so to distribute the taxes that the people can recognize their necessity and the regret of the ruler to be compelled to put his hands in the pockets of others; he is to support the sick and the helpless, and to give his protection and society to distinguished scholars, on whom his fame in after ages will depend.

But whatever might be the brighter sides of the system, and the merits of individual rulers, yet the men of the fourteenth century were not without a more or less distinct consciousness of the brief and uncertain tenure of most of these despotisms. Inasmuch as political institutions like these are naturally secure in proportion to the size of the territory in which they exist, the larger principalities were constantly tempted to swallow up the smaller. Whole hecatombs of petty rulers were sacrificed at this time to the Visconti alone. As a result of this outward danger an inward ferment was in ceaseless activity; and the effect of the situation on the character of the ruler was generally of the most sinister kind.

Absolute power, with its temptations to luxury and unbridled selfishness, and the perils to which he was exposed from enemies and conspirators, turned him almost inevitably into a tyrant in the worst sense of the word. Well for him if he could trust his nearest relations! But where all was illegitimate there could be no regular law of inheritance, either with regard to succession or to the division of the ruler's property; and consequently the heir, if incompetent or a minor, was liable in the interest of the family itself to be supplanted by an uncle or cousin of more resolute character. The acknowledgment or exclusion of the bastards was a fruitful source of contest; and most of these families in consequence were plagued with a crowd of discontented and vindictive kinsmen. This circumstance gave rise to continual outbreaks of treason and to frightful scenes of domestic bloodshed. Sometimes the pretenders lived abroad in exile, and, like the Visconti who practised the fisherman's craft on the Lake of Garda, viewed the situation with patient indifference. When asked by a messenger of his rival when and how he thought of returning to Milan he gave the reply: "By the same means as those by which I was expelled, but not till his crimes have outweighed my own." Sometimes, too, with the view of saving the family, the despot was sacrificed by his relations to the public conscience which he had too grossly outraged. In a few cases the government was in the hands of the whole family, or at least the ruler was bound to take their advice; and here too the distribution of property and influence often led to bitter disputes.

The whole of this system excited the deep and persistent hatred of the Florentine writers of that epoch. Even the pomp and display with which the despot was perhaps less anxious to gratify his own vanity than to impress the popular imagination awakened their keenest sarcasm. Woe to an adventurer if he fell into their hands, like the upstart Doge Aguello of Pisa (1364), who used to ride out with a golden sceptre, and show himself at the window of his house, "as relics are shown," reclining on embroidered drapery and cushions, served like a Pope or emperor by kneeling attendants. More often, however, the old Florentines speak on this subject in a tone of lofty seriousness. Dante saw and characterized well the vulgarity and commonplace which mark the ambition of the new princes. "What mean their trumpets and their bells, their horns and their flutes, but 'Come, hangman—come, vultures'?" The castle of the tyrant, as pictured by the popular mind, is a lofty and solitary building, full of dungeons and listening-tubes, the home of cruelty and misery. Misfortune is foretold to all who enter the service of the despot, who even becomes at last himself an object of pity: he must needs be the enemy of all good and honest men; he can trust no one, and can read in the faces of his subjects the expectation of his fall. "As despotisms rise, grow, and are consolidated, so grows in their midst the hidden element which must produce their dissolution and ruin." But the deepest ground of dislike has not been stated; Florence was then the scene of the richest development of human individuality, while for the despots no other individuality could be suffered to live and thrive but their own and that of their nearest dependents. The control of the individual was rigorously carried out, even down to the establishment of a system of passports.

The astrological superstitions and the religious unbelief of many of the tyrants gave, in the minds of their contemporaries, a peculiar colour to this awful and God-forsaken existence. When the last Carrara could no longer defend the walls and gates of the plague-stricken Padua, hemmed in on all sides by the Venetians (1405), the soldiers of the guard heard him cry to the devil "to come and kill him."

The most complete and instructive type of the tyranny of the fourteenth century is to be found unquestionably among the Visconti of Milan, from the death of the Archbishop Giovanni onward (1354). The family likeness which shows itself between Bernabò and the worst of the Roman Emperors is unmistakable; the most important public object was the prince's boar-hunting; whoever interfered with it was put to death with torture; the terrified people were forced to maintain five thousand boar-hounds, with strict responsibility for their health and safety. The taxes were extorted by every conceivable sort of compulsion; seven daughters of the prince received a dowry of 100,000 gold florins apiece; and an enormous treasure was collected. On the death of his wife (1384) an order was issued "to the subjects" to share his grief, as once they had shared his joy, and to wear mourning for a year. The *coup de main* (1385) by which his nephew Giangaleazzo got him into his power—one of those brilliant plots which make the heart of even late historians beat more quickly—was strikingly characteristic of the man. Giangaleazzo, despised by his relations on account of his religion and his love of science, resolved on vengeance, and, leaving the city under pretext of a pilgrimage, fell upon his unsuspecting uncle, took him prisoner, forced his way back into the city at the head of an armed band, seized on the government, and gave up the palace of Bernabò to general plunder.

In Giangaleazzo that passion for the colossal which was common to most of the despots shows itself on the largest scale. He undertook, at the cost of 300,000 golden florins, the construction of gigantic dikes, to divert in case of need the Mincio from Mantua and the Brenta from Padua, and thus to render these cities defenceless. It is not impossible, indeed, that he thought of draining away the lagoons of Venice. He founded that most wonderful of all convents, the Certosa of Pavia, and the cathedral of Milan, "which exceeds in size and splendour all the churches of Christendom." The palace in Pavia, which his father Galeazzo began, and which he himself finished, was probably by far the most magnificent of the princely dwellings of Europe. There he transferred his famous library and the great collection of relics of the saints, in which he placed a peculiar faith. King Winceslaus made him Duke (1395); he was hoping for nothing less than the kingdom of Italy or the Imperial crown, when (1402) he fell ill and died. His whole territories are said to have paid him in a single year, besides the regular contribution of 1,200,000 gold florins, no less than 800,000 more in extraordinary subsidies. After his death the dominions which he had brought together by every sort of violence fell to pieces; and for a time even the original nucleus could with difficulty be maintained by his successors. What might have become of his sons Giovanni Maria (d. 1412) and Filippo Maria (d. 1417), had they lived in a different country and among other traditions, cannot be said. But as heirs of their house they inherited that monstrous capital of cruelty and cowardice which had been accumulated from generation to generation.

Giovanni Maria, too, is famed for his dogs, which were no longer, however, used for hunting, but for tearing human bodies. Tradition has preserved their names, like those of the bears of the Emperor Valentinian I. In May 1409, when war was going on, and the starving populace cried to him in the streets, *"Pace! Pace!"* he let loose his mercenaries upon them, and two hundred lives were sacrificed; under penalty of the gallows it was forbidden to utter the words *pace* and *guerra,* and the priests were ordered, instead of *dona nobis pacem,* to say *tranquillitatem!* At last a band of conspirators took advantage of the moment when Facino Cane, the chief *condottiere* of the insane ruler, lay ill at Pavia, and cut down Giovanni Maria in the church of S. Gottardo at Milan; the dying Facino on the same day made his officers swear to stand by the heir Filippo Maria, whom he himself urged his wife to take for a second husband. His wife, Beatrice di Tenda, followed his advice. We shall have occasion to speak of Filippo Maria later on.

And in times like these Cola di Rienzi was dreaming of founding on the rickety enthusiasm of the corrupt population of Rome a new state which was to comprise all Italy. By the side of rulers such as those whom we have described he seems no better than a poor deluded fool.

Chapter 3. The Tyranny of the Fifteenth Century

The despotisms of the fifteenth century show an altered character. Many of the less important tyrants, and some of the greater, like the Scala and the Carrara, had disappeared, while the more powerful ones, aggrandized by conquest, had given to their systems each its characteristic development. Naples, for example, received a fresh and stronger impulse from the new Aragonese dynasty. A striking feature of this epoch is the attempt of the *condottieri* to found independent dynasties of their own.

Facts and the actual relations of things, apart from traditional estimates, are alone regarded; talent and audacity win the great prizes. The petty despots, to secure a trustworthy support, begin to enter the service of the larger states, and become themselves *condottieri,* receiving in return for their services money and impunity for their misdeeds, if not an increase of territory. All, whether small or great, must exert themselves more, must act with greater caution and calculation, and must learn to refrain from too wholesale barbarities; only so much wrong is permitted by public opinion as is necessary for the end in view, and this the impartial bystander certainly finds no fault with. No trace is here visible of that half-religious loyalty by which the legitimate princes of the West were supported; personal popularity is the nearest approach we can find to it. Talent and calculation are the only means of advancement. A character like that of Charles the Bold, which wore itself out in the passionate pursuit of impracticable ends, was a riddle to the Italian.

> The Swiss were only peasants, and if they were all killed that would be no satisfaction for the Burgundian nobles who might fall in the war. If the Duke got possession of all Switzerland without a struggle his income would not be five thousand ducats the greater.

The medieval features in the character of Charles, his chivalrous aspirations and ideals, had long become unintelligible to the Italian. The diplomatists of the South, when they saw him strike his officers and yet keep them in his service, when he maltreated his troops to punish them for a defeat, and then threw the blame on his counsellors in the presence of the same troops, gave him up for lost. Louis XI, on the other hand, whose policy surpasses that of the Italian princes in their own style, and who was an avowed admirer of Francesco Sforza, must be placed in all that regards culture and refinement far below these rulers.

Good and evil lie strangely mixed together in the Italian states of the fifteenth century. The personality of the ruler is so highly developed, often of such deep significance, and so characteristic of the conditions and needs of the time that to form an adequate moral judgment on it is no easy task.

The foundation of the system was and remained illegitimate, and nothing could remove the curse which rested upon it. The Imperial approval or investiture made no change in the matter, since the people attached little weight to the fact that the despot had bought a piece of parchment somewhere in foreign countries, or from some stranger passing through his territory. If the Emperor had been good for anything—so ran the logic of uncritical common sense—he would never have let the tyrant rise at all. Since the Roman expedition of Charles IV the Emperors had done nothing more in Italy than sanction a tyranny which had arisen without their help; they could give it no other practical authority than what might flow from an Imperial charter. The whole conduct of Charles in Italy was a scandalous political comedy. Matteo Villani relates how the Visconti escorted him round their territory, and at last out of it; how he went about like a hawker selling his wares (privileges, etc.) for money; what a mean appearance he made in Rome, and how at the end, without even drawing the sword, he returned with replenished coffers across the Alps. Nevertheless, patriotic enthusiasts and poets, full of the greatness of the past, conceived high hopes at his coming, which were afterward dissipated by his pitiful conduct. Petrarch, who had written frequent letters exhorting the Emperor to cross the Alps, to give back to Rome its departed greatness, and to set up a new universal empire, now, when the Emperor, careless of these high-flying projects, had come at last, still hoped to see his dreams realized, strove unweariedly, by speech and writing, to impress the Emperor with them, but was at length driven away from him with disgust when he saw the Imperial authority dishonoured by the submission of Charles to the Pope. Sigismund came, on the first occasion at least (1414), with the good intention of persuading John XXIII to take part in his council; it was on that journey, when Pope and Emperor were gazing from the lofty tower of Cremona on the panorama of Lombardy, that their host, the tyrant Gabino Fondolo, was seized with the desire to throw them both over. On his second visit Sigismund came as a mere adventurer, giving no proof whatever of his Imperial prerogative, except by crowning Beccadelli as a poet; for more than half a year he remained shut up in Siena, like a debtor in gaol, and only with difficulty, and at a later period, succeeded in being crowned in Rome. And what can be thought of Frederick III? His journeys to Italy have the air of holiday-trips or pleasure-tours made at the expense of those who wanted him to confirm their prerogatives, or whose vanity it flattered to entertain an emperor. The latter was the case with Alfonso of Naples, who paid a hundred and fifty thousand florins for the honour of an Imperial visit. At Ferrara, on his second return from Rome (1469), Frederick spent a whole day without leaving his chamber, distributing no fewer than eighty titles; he created knights, counts, doctors, notaries —counts, indeed, of different degrees, as, for instance, counts palatine, counts with the right to create doctors up to the number of five, counts with the right to legitimatize bastards, to appoint notaries and so forth. The Chancellor, however, expected in return for the patents in question a gratuity which was thought excessive at Ferrara. The opinion of Borso, himself created Duke of Modena and Reggio in return for an annual payment of four thousand gold florins, when his Imperial patron was distributing titles and diplomas to all the little Court, is not mentioned. The humanists, then the chief spokesmen of the age, were divided in opinion according to their personal interests, while the Emperor was greeted by some of them with the conventional acclamations of the poets of Imperial Rome. Poggio confessed that he no longer knew what the coronation meant; in the old times only the victorious Imperator was crowned, and then he was crowned with laurel.

With Maximilian I begins not only the general intervention of foreign nations, but a new Imperial policy with regard to Italy. The first step—the investiture of Lodovico il Moro with the duchy of Milan and the exclusion of his unhappy nephew—was not of a kind to bear good fruits. According to the modern theory of intervention, when two parties are tearing a country to pieces a third may step in and take its share, and on this principle the Empire acted. But right and justice were appealed to no longer. When Louis XII was expected in Genoa (1502), and the Imperial eagle was removed from the hall of the ducal palace and replaced by painted lilies, the historian Senarega asked what after all was the meaning of the eagle which so many revolutions had spared, and what claims the Empire had upon Genoa. No one knew more about the matter than the old phrase that Genoa was a *camera imperii.* In fact, nobody in Italy could give a clear answer to any such questions. At length, when Charles V held Spain and the Empire together, he was able by means of Spanish forces to make good Imperial claims; but it is notorious that what he thereby gained turned to the profit not of the Empire, but of the Spanish monarchy.

Closely connected with the political illegitimacy of the dynasties of the fifteenth century was the public indifference to legitimate birth, which to foreigners—for example, to Comines—appeared so remarkable. The two things went naturally together. In Northern countries, as in Burgundy, the illegitimate offspring were provided for by a distinct class of appanages, such as bishoprics and the like; in Portugal an illegitimate line maintained itself on the throne only by constant effort; in Italy, on the contrary, there no longer existed a princely house where, even in the direct line of descent, bastards were not patiently tolerated. The Aragonese monarchs of Naples belonged to the illegitimate line, Aragon itself falling to the lot of the brother of Alfonso I. The great Federigo of Urbino was, perhaps, no Montefeltro at all. When Pius II was on his way to the Congress of Mantua (1459) eight bastards of the house of Este rode to meet him at Ferrara, among them the reigning Duke Borso himself and two illegitimate sons of his illegitimate brother and predecessor Leonello. The latter had also had a lawful wife, herself an illegitimate daughter of Alfonso I of Naples by an African woman. The bastards were often admitted to the succession where the lawful children were minors and the dangers of the situation were pressing; and a rule of seniority became recognized which took no account of pure or impure birth. The fitness of the individual, his worth and his capacity, were of more weight than all the laws and usages which prevailed elsewhere in the West. It was the age, indeed, in which the sons of the Popes were founding dynasties. In the sixteenth century, through the influence of foreign ideas and of the Counter-Reformation, which then began, the whole question was judged more strictly: Varchi discovers that the succession of the legitimate children "is ordered by reason, and is the will of heaven from eternity." Cardinal Ippolito de' Medici founded his claim to the lordship of Florence on the fact that he was perhaps the fruit of a lawful marriage, and at all events son of a gentlewoman, and not, like Duke Alessandro, of a servant-girl. At this time began those morganatic marriages of affection which in the fifteenth century, on grounds either of policy or morality, would have had no meaning at all.

But the highest and the most admired form of illegitimacy in the fifteenth century was presented by the *condottiere,* who, whatever may have been his origin, raised himself to the position of an independent ruler. At bottom, the occupation of Lower Italy by the Normans in the eleventh century was of this character. Such attempts now began to keep the peninsula in a constant ferment.

It was possible for a *condottiere* to obtain the lordship of a district even without usurpation, in the case where his employer, through want of money or troops, provided for him in this way; under any circumstances the *condottiere,* even when he dismissed for the time the greater part of his forces, needed a safe place where he could establish his winter quarters and lay up his stores and provisions. The first example of a captain thus portioned is John Hawkwood, who was invested by Gregory XI with the lordship of Bagnacavallo and Cotignola. When with Alberigo da Barbiano Italian armies and leaders appeared upon the scene the chances of founding a principality, or of increasing one already acquired, became more frequent. The first great bacchanalian outbreak of military ambition took place in the duchy of Milan after the death of Giangaleazzo (1402). The policy of his two sons was chiefly aimed at the destruction of the new despotisms founded by the *condottieri;* and from the greatest of them, Facino Cane, the house of Visconti inherited, together with his widow, a long list of cities, and 400,000 golden florins, not to speak of the soldiers of her first husband whom Beatrice di Tenda brought with her. From henceforth that thoroughly immoral relation between the Governments and their *condottieri* which is characteristic of the fifteenth century became more and more common. An old story—one of those which are true and not true, everywhere and nowhere—describes it as follows. The citizens of a certain town (Siena seems to be meant) had once an officer in their service who had freed them from foreign aggression; daily they took counsel how to recompense him, and concluded that no reward in their power was great enough, not even if they made him lord of the city. At last one of them rose and said, "Let us kill him and then worship him as our patron saint." And so they did, following the example set by the Roman Senate with Romulus. In fact, the *condottieri* had reason to fear none so much as their employers; if they were successful they became dangerous, and were put out of the way like Roberto Malatesta just after the victory he had won for Sixtus IV (1482); if they failed the vengeance of the Venetians on Carmagnola showed to what risks they were exposed (1432). It is characteristic of the moral aspect of the situation that the *condottieri* had often to give their wives and children as hostages, and, notwithstanding this, neither felt nor inspired confidence. They must have been heroes of abnegation, natures like Belisarius himself, not to be cankered by hatred and bitterness; only the most perfect goodness could save them from the most monstrous iniquity. No wonder then if we find them full of contempt for all sacred things, cruel and treacherous to their fellows—men who cared nothing whether or no they died under the ban of the Church. At the same time, and through the force of the same conditions, the genius and capacity of many among them attained the highest conceivable development, and won for them the admiring devotion of their followers; their armies are the first in modern history in which the personal credit of the leader is the one moving power. A brilliant example is shown in the life of Francesco Sforza; no prejudice of birth could prevent him from winning and turning to account when he needed it a boundless devotion from each individual with whom he had to deal; it happened more than once that his enemies laid down their arms at the sight of him, greeting him reverently with uncovered heads, each honouring in him "the common father of the men-at-arms." The race of Sforza has this special interest, that from the very beginning of its history we seem able to trace its endeavours after the crown. The foundation of its fortune lay in the remarkable fruitfulness of the family; Francesco's father, Jacopo, himself a celebrated man, had twenty brothers and sisters, all brought up roughly at Cotignola, near Faenza, amid the perils of one of the endless Romagnole *vendette* between their own house and that of the Pasolini. The family dwelling was a mere arsenal and fortress; the mother and daughters were as warlike as their kinsmen. In his thirteenth year Jacopo ran away and fled to Panicale to the Papal *condottiere* Boldrino—the man who even in death continued to lead his troops, the word of order being given from the bannered tent in which the embalmed body lay, till at last a fit leader was found to succeed him. Jacopo, when he had at length made himself a name in the service of different *condottieri*, sent for his relations, and obtained through them the same advantages that a prince derives from a numerous dynasty. It was these relations who kept the army together when he lay a captive in the Castel dell' Uovo at Naples; his sister took the royal envoys prisoners with her own hands, and saved him by this reprisal from death. It was an indication of the breadth and the range of his plans that in monetary affairs Jacopo was thoroughly trustworthy; even in his defeats he consequently found credit with the bankers. He habitually protected the peasants against the licence of his troops, and reluctantly destroyed or injured a conquered city. He gave his well-known mistress, Lucia, the mother of Francesco, in marriage to another in order to be free from a princely alliance. Even the marriages of his relations were arranged on a definite plan. He kept clear of the impious and profligate life of his contemporaries, and brought up his son Francesco to the three rules: "Let other men's wives alone; strike none of your followers, or, if you do, send the injured man far away; don't ride a hard-mouthed horse, or one that drops his shoe." But his chief source of influence lay in the qualities, if not of a great general, at least of a great soldier. His frame was powerful, and developed by every kind of exercise; his peasant's face and frank manners won general popularity; his memory was marvellous, and after the lapse of years could recall the names of his followers, the number of their horses, and the amount of their pay. His education was purely Italian: he devoted his leisure to the study of history, and had Greek and Latin authors translated for his use. Francesco, his still more famous son, set his mind from the first on founding a powerful state, and through brilliant generalship and a faithlessness which hesitated at nothing got possession of the great city of Milan (1447–50).

His example was contagious. Aeneas Sylvius wrote about this time: "In our change-loving Italy, where nothing stands firm, and where no ancient dynasty exists, a servant can easily become a king." One man in particular, who styled himself "the man of fortune," filled the imagination of the whole country: Jacopo Piccinino, the son of Niccolò. It was a burning question of the day if he too would succeed in founding a princely house. The greater states had an obvious interest in hindering it, and even Francesco Sforza thought it would be all the better if the list of self-made sovereigns were not enlarged. But the troops and captains sent against him, at the time, for instance, when he was aiming at the lordship of Siena, recognized their interest in supporting him: "If it were all over with him, we should have to go back and plough our fields." Even while besieging him at Orbetello they supplied him with provisions; and he got out of his straits with honour. But at last Fate overtook him. All Italy was betting on the result, when (1465), after a visit to Sforza at Milan, he went to King Ferrante at Naples. In spite of the pledges given, and of his high connexions, he was murdered in the Castel dell' Uovo. Even the *condottieri* who had obtained their dominions by inheritance never felt themselves safe. When Roberto Malatesta and Federigo of Urbino died on the same day (1482), the one at Rome, the other at Bologna, it was found that each had recommended his state to the care of the other. Against a class of men who themselves stuck at nothing everything was held to be permissible. Francesco Sforza, when quite young, had married a rich Calabrian heiress, Polissena Russa, Countess of Montalto, who bore him a daughter; an aunt poisoned both mother and child, and seized the inheritance.

From the death of Piccinino onward the foundations of new states by the *condottieri* became a scandal not to be tolerated. The four great Powers, Naples, Milan, the Papacy, and Venice, formed among themselves a political equilibrium which refused to allow of any disturbance. In the States of the Church, which swarmed with petty tyrants, who in part were, or had been, *condottieri,* the nephews of the Popes, since the time of Sixtus IV, monopolized the right to all such undertakings. But at the first sign of a political crisis the soldiers of fortune appeared again upon the scene. Under the wretched administration of Innocent VIII it was near happening that a certain Boccalino, who had formerly served in the Burgundian army, gave himself and the town of Osimo, of which he was master, up to the Turkish forces; fortunately, through the intervention of Lorenzo the Magnificent, he proved willing to be paid off, and took himself away. In 1495, when the wars of Charles VIII had turned Italy upside-down, the *condottiere* Vidovero, of Brescia, made trial of his strength: he had already seized the town of Cesena and murdered many of the nobles and the burghers; but the citadel held out, and he was forced to withdraw. He then, at the head of a band lent him by another scoundrel, Pandolfo Malatesta of Rimini, son of the Roberto already spoken of, and Venetian *condottiere,* wrested the town of Castelnuovo from the Archbishop of Ravenna. The Venetians, fearing that worse would follow, and urged also by the Pope, ordered Pandolfo, "with the kindest intentions," to take an opportunity of arresting his good friend: the arrest was made, though "with great regret," whereupon the order came to bring the prisoner to the gallows. Pandolfo was considerate enough to strangle him in prison, and then show his corpse to the people. The last notable example of such usurpers is the famous Castellan of Musso, who, during the confusion in the Milanese territory which followed the battle of Pavia (1525), improvised a sovereignty on the Lake of Como.

Chapter 4. The Petty Tyrannies

It may be said in general of the despotisms of the fifteenth century that the greatest crimes are most frequent in the smallest states. In these, where the family was numerous and all the members wished to live in a manner befitting their rank, disputes respecting the inheritance were unavoidable. Bernardo Varano of Camerino put (1434) two of his brothers to death, wishing to divide their property among his sons. Where the ruler of a single town was distinguished by a wise, moderate, and humane government, and by zeal for intellectual culture, he was generally a member of some great family, or politically dependent on it. This was the case, for example, with Alessandro Sforza, Prince of Pesaro, brother of the great Francesco, and stepfather of Federigo of Urbino (d. 1473). Prudent in administration, just and affable in his rule, he enjoyed, after years of warfare, a tranquil reign, collected a noble library, and passed his leisure in learned or religious conversation. A man of the same class was Giovanni II Bentivoglio of Bologna (1462–1506), whose policy was determined by that of the Este and the Sforza. What ferocity and bloodthirstiness are found, on the other hand, among the Varani of Camerino, the Malatesta of Rimini, the Manfreddi of Faenza, and above all among the Baglioni of Perugia! We find a striking picture of the events in the last-named family toward the close of the fifteenth century in the admirable historical narratives of Graziani and Materazzo.

The Baglioni were one of those families whose rule never took the shape of an avowed despotism. It was rather a leadership exercised by means of their vast wealth and of their practical influence in the choice of public officers. Within the family one man was recognized as head; but deep and secret jealousy prevailed among the members of the different branches. Opposed to the Baglioni stood another aristocratic party, led by the family of the Oddi. In 1487 Perugia was turned into a camp, and the houses of the leading citizens swarmed with bravoes; scenes of violence were of daily occurrence. At the burial of a German student, who had been assassinated, two colleges took arms against one another; sometimes the bravoes of the different houses even joined battle in the public square. The complaints of the merchants and artisans were vain; the Papal Governors and *nipoti* held their tongues, or took themselves off on the first opportunity. At last the Oddi were forced to abandon Perugia, and the city became a beleaguered fortress under the absolute despotism of the Baglioni, who used even the cathedral as barracks. Plots and surprises were met with cruel vengeance; in 1491, after a hundred and thirty conspirators who had forced their way into the city were killed and hung up at the Palazzo Communale, thirty-five altars were erected in the square, and for three days Mass was performed and processions held to take away the curse which rested on the spot. A nephew of Innocent VIII was in open day run through in the street. A nephew of Alexander VI, who was sent to smooth matters over, was dismissed with public contempt. All the while the two leaders of the ruling house, Guido and Ridolfo, were holding frequent interviews with Suor Colomba of Rieti, a

Dominican nun of saintly reputation and miraculous powers, who under penalty of some great disaster ordered them to make peace—naturally in vain. Nevertheless the chronicle takes the opportunity to point out the devotion and piety of the better men in Perugia during this reign of terror. When in 1494 Charles VIII approached the Baglioni from Perugia and the exiles encamped in and near Assisi conducted the war with such ferocity that every house in the valley was levelled to the ground. The fields lay untilled, the peasants were turned into plundering and murdering savages, the fresh-grown bushes were filled with stags and wolves, and the beasts grew fat on the bodies of the slain, on so-called "Christian flesh." When Alexander VI withdrew (1495) into Umbria before Charles VIII, then returning from Naples, it occurred to him, when at Perugia, that he might now rid himself of the Baglioni once for all; he proposed to Guido a festival or tournament, or something else of the same kind, which would bring the whole family together. Guido, however, was of opinion "that the most impressive spectacle of all would be to see the whole military force of Perugia collected in a body," whereupon the Pope abandoned his project. Soon after the exiles made another attack, in which nothing but the personal heroism of the Baglioni won them the victory. It was then that Simonetto Baglione, a lad of scarcely eighteen, fought in the square with a handful of followers against hundreds of the enemy: he fell at last with more than twenty wounds, but recovered himself when Astorre Baglione came to his help, and, mounting on horseback in gilded armour with a falcon on his helmet, "like Mars in bearing and in deeds, plunged into the struggle."

At that time Raphael, a boy of twelve years of age, was at school under Pietro Perugino. The impressions of these days are perhaps immortalized in the small early pictures of St Michael and St George: something of them, it may be, lives eternally in the great painting of St Michael; and if Astorre Baglione has anywhere found his apotheosis it is in the figure of the heavenly horseman in the *Heliodorus*.

The opponents of the Baglioni were partly destroyed, partly scattered in terror, and were henceforth incapable of another enterprise of the kind. After a time a partial reconciliation took place, and some of the exiles were allowed to return. But Perugia became none the safer or more tranquil: the inward discord of the ruling family broke out in frightful excesses. An opposition was formed against Guido and Ridolfo and their sons Gianpaolo, Simonetto, Astorre, Gismondo, Gentile, Marcantonio, and others by two great-nephews, Grifone and Carlo Barciglia; the latter of the two was also nephew of Varano, Prince of Camerino, and brother of one of the former exiles, Ieronimo della Penna. In vain did Simonetto, warned by sinister presentiment, entreat his uncle on his knees to allow him to put Penna to death; Guido refused. The plot ripened suddenly on the occasion of the marriage of Astorre with Lavinia Colonna, at midsummer 1500. The festival began and lasted several days amid gloomy forebodings, whose deepening effect is admirably described by Matarazzo. Varano fed and encouraged them with devilish ingenuity: he worked upon Grifone by the prospect of undivided authority, and by stories of an imaginary intrigue of his wife Zenobia with Gianpaolo. Finally each conspirator was provided with a victim. (The Baglioni lived all of them in separate houses, mostly on the site of the present castle.) Each received fifteen of the bravoes at hand; the remainder were set on the watch. In the night of July 15 the doors were forced, and Guido, Astorre, Simonetto, and Gismondo were murdered; the others succeeded in escaping.

As the corpse of Astorre lay by that of Simonetto in the street the spectators, "and especially the foreign students," compared him to an ancient Roman, so great and imposing did he seem. In the features of Simonetto could still be traced the audacity and defiance which death itself had not tamed. The victors went round among the friends of the family, and did their best to recommend themselves; they found all in tears and preparing to leave for the country. Meantime the escaped Baglioni collected forces without the city, and on the following day forced their way in, Gianpaolo at their head, and speedily found adherents among others whom Barciglia had been threatening with death. When Grifone fell into their hands near S. Ercolono Gianpaolo handed him over for execution to his followers. Barciglia and Penna fled to Varano, the chief author of the tragedy, at Camerino; and in a moment, almost without loss, Gianpaolo became master of the city.

Atalanta, the still young and beautiful mother of Grifone, who the day before had withdrawn to a country house with the latter's wife Zenobia and two children of Gianpaolo, and more than once had repulsed her son with a mother's curse, now returned with her stepdaughter in search of the dying man. All stood aside as the two women approached, each man shrinking from being recognized as the slayer of Grifone, and dreading the malediction of the mother. But they were deceived: she herself besought her son to pardon him who had dealt the fatal blow, and he died with her blessing. The eyes of the crowd followed the two women reverently as they crossed the square with bloodstained garments. It was Atalanta for whom Raphael afterward painted the world-famed *Deposition,* with which she laid her own maternal sorrows at the feet of a yet higher and holier suffering.

The cathedral, in the immediate neighbourhood of which the greater part of this tragedy had been enacted, was washed with wine and consecrated afresh. The triumphal arch, erected for the wedding, still remained standing, painted with the deeds of Astorre and with the laudatory verses of the narrator of these events, the worthy Matarazzo.

A legendary history, which is simply the reflection of these atrocities, arose out of the early days of the Baglioni. All the members of this family from the beginning were reported to have died an evil death—twenty-seven on one occasion together; their houses were said to have been once before levelled to the ground, and the streets of Perugia paved with the bricks—and more of the same kind. Under Paul III the destruction of their palaces really took place.

For a time they seem to have formed good resolutions, to have brought their own party into order, and to have protected the public officials against the arbitrary acts of the nobility. But the old curse broke out again, like a smouldering fire. Gianpaolo was enticed to Rome under Leo X, and there beheaded; one of his sons, Orazio, who ruled in Perugia for a short time only, and by the most violent means, as the partisan of the Duke of Urbino (himself threatened by the Pope), once more repeated in his own family the horrors of the past. His uncle and three cousins were murdered, whereupon the Duke sent him word that enough had been done. His brother, Malatesta Baglione, the Florentine general, has made himself immortal by the treason of 1530; and Malatesta's son Ridolfo, the last of the house, attained, by the murder of the legate and the public officers in 1534, a brief but sanguinary authority.

Here and there we meet with the names of the rulers of Rimini. Unscrupulousness, impiety, military skill, and high culture have been seldom so combined in one individual as in Sigismondo Malatesta (d. 1467). But the accumulated crimes of such a family must at last outweigh all talent, however great, and drag the tyrant into the abyss. Pandolfo, Sigismondo's nephew, who has been mentioned already, succeeded in holding his ground for the sole reason that the Venetians refused to abandon their *condottiere,* whatever guilt he might be chargeable with; when his subjects (1497), after ample provocation, bombarded him in his castle at Rimini, and afterward allowed him to escape, a Venetian commissioner brought him back, stained as he was with fratricide and every other abomination. Thirty years later the Malatesta were penniless exiles. In 1527, as in the time of Cesare Borgia, a sort of epidemic fell on the petty tyrants; few of them outlived this date, and none to their own good. At Mirandola, which was governed by insignificant princes of the house of Pico, lived in 1533 a poor scholar, Lilio Gregorio Giraldi, who had fled from the sack of Rome to the hospitable hearth of the aged Giovanni Francesco Pico, nephew of the famous Giovanni; the discussions as to the sepulchral monument which the Prince was constructing for himself gave rise to a treatise, the dedication of which bears the date of April in this year. The postscript is a sad one. "In October of the same year the unhappy Prince was attacked in the night and robbed of life and throne by his brother's son; and I myself escaped narrowly, and am now in the deepest misery."

A pseudo-despotism without characteristic features, such as Pandolfo Petrucci exercised from 1490 in Siena, then torn by faction, is hardly worth a closer consideration. Insignificant and malicious, he governed with the help of a professor of jurisprudence and of an astrologer, and frightened his people by an occasional murder. His pastime in the summer months was to roll blocks of stone from the top of Monte Amiata, without caring what or whom they hit. After succeeding, where the most prudent failed, in escaping from the devices of Cesare Borgia, he died at last forsaken and despised. His sons maintained a qualified supremacy for many years afterward.

Chapter 5. The Greater Dynasties

In treating of the chief dynasties of Italy it is convenient to discuss the Aragonese, on account of its special character, apart from the rest. The feudal system, which from the days of the Normans had survived in the form of a territorial supremacy of the barons, gave a distinctive colour to the political constitution of Naples; while elsewhere in Italy, excepting only in the southern part of the ecclesiastical dominion, and in a few other districts, a direct tenure of land prevailed, and no hereditary powers were permitted by the law. The great Alfonso, who reigned in Naples from 1435 onward (d. 1458), was a man of another kind than his real or alleged descendants. Brilliant in his whole existence, fearless in mixing with his people, mild and generous toward his enemies, dignified and affable in intercourse, modest notwithstanding his legitimate royal descent, admired rather than blamed even for his old man's passion for Lucrezia d'Alagna, he had the one bad quality of extravagance, from which, however, the natural consequence followed. Unscrupulous financiers were long omnipotent at Court, till the bankrupt King robbed them of their spoils; a crusade was preached, as a pretext for taxing the clergy; the Jews were forced to save themselves from conversion and other oppressive measures by presents and the payment of regular taxes; when a great earthquake happened in the Abruzzi the survivors were compelled to make good the contributions of the dead. On the other hand, he abolished unreasonable taxes, like that on dice, and aimed at relieving his poorer subjects from the imposts which pressed most heavily upon them. By such means Alfonso was able to entertain distinguished guests with unrivalled splendour; he found pleasure in ceaseless expense, even for the benefit of his enemies, and in rewarding literary work knew absolutely no measure. Poggio received five hundred pieces of gold for translating Xenophon's *Cyropædia.*

Ferrante, who succeeded him, passed as his illegitimate son by a Spanish lady, but was not improbably the son of a half-caste Moor of Valencia. Whether it was his blood or the plots formed against his life by the barons which embittered and darkened his nature, it is certain that he was equalled in ferocity by none among the princes of his time. Restlessly active, recognized as one of the most powerful political minds of the day, and free from the vices of the profligate, he concentrated all his powers, among which must be reckoned profound dissimulation and an irreconcilable spirit of vengeance, on the destruction of his opponents. He had been wounded in every point in which a ruler is open to offence; for the leaders of the barons, though related to him by marriage, were yet the allies of his foreign enemies. Extreme measures became part of his daily policy. The means for this struggle with his barons, and for his external wars, were exacted in the same Mohammedan fashion which Frederick II had introduced: the Government alone dealt in oil and wine; the whole commerce of the country was put by Ferrante into the hands of a wealthy merchant, Francesco Coppola, who had entire control of the anchorage on the coast, and shared the profits with the King. Deficits were made up by forced loans, by executions and confiscations, by open simony, and by contributions levied on the ecclesiastical corporations. Besides hunting, which he practised regardless of all rights of property, his pleasures were of two kinds: he liked to have his opponents near him, either alive in well-guarded prisons, or dead and embalmed, dressed in the costume which they wore in their lifetime. He would chuckle in talking of the captives with his friends, and made no secret whatever of the museum of mummies. His victims were mostly men whom he had got into his power by treachery; some were even seized while guests at the royal table. His conduct to his first minister, Antonello Petrucci, who had grown sick and grey in his service, and from whose increasing fear of death he extorted present after present, was literally devilish. At length the suspicion of complicity with the last conspiracy of the barons gave the pretext for his arrest and execution. With him died Coppola. The way in which all this is narrated in Caracciolo and Porzio makes one's hair stand on end. The elder of the King's sons, Alfonso, Duke of Calabria, enjoyed in later years a kind of coregency with his father. He was a savage, brutal profligate—described by Comines as "the cruellest, worst, most vicious, and basest man ever seen"—who in point of frankness alone had the advantage of Ferrante, and who openly avowed his contempt for religion and its usages. The better and nobler features of the Italian despotisms are not to be found among the princes of this line; all that they possessed of the art and culture of their time served the purposes of luxury or display. Even the genuine Spaniards seem to have almost always degenerated in Italy; but the end of this cross-bred house

(1494 and 1503) gives clear proof of a want of blood. Ferrante died of mental care and trouble; Alfonso accused his brother Federigo, the only honest member of the family, of treason, and insulted him in the vilest manner. At length, though he had hitherto passed for one of the ablest generals in Italy, he lost his head and fled to Sicily, leaving his son, the younger Ferrante, a prey to the French and to domestic treason. A dynasty which had ruled as this had done must at least have sold its life dear, if its children were ever to hope for a restoration. But, as Comines one-sidedly, and yet on the whole rightly, observes on this occasion, "Jamais homme cruel ne fut hardi."

The despotism of the Dukes of Milan, whose government from the time of Giangaleazzo onward was an absolute monarchy of the most thoroughgoing sort, shows the genuine Italian character of the fifteenth century. The last of the Visconti, Filippo Maria (1412–47), is a character of peculiar interest, and of which fortunately an admirable description has been left us. What a man of uncommon gifts and high position can be made by the passion of fear is here shown with what may be called a mathematical completeness. All the resources of the State were devoted to the one end of securing his personal safety, though happily his cruel egoism did not degenerate into a purposeless thirst for blood. He lived in the citadel of Milan, surrounded by magnificent gardens, arbours, and lawns. For years he never set foot in the city, making his excursions only in the country, where lay several of his splendid castles; the flotilla which, drawn by the swiftest horses, conducted him to them along canals constructed for the purpose was so arranged as to allow of the application of the most rigorous etiquette. Whoever entered the citadel was watched by a hundred eyes; it was forbidden even to stand at the window, lest signs should be given to those without. All who were admitted among the personal followers of the Prince were subjected to a series of the strictest examinations; then, once accepted, were charged with the highest diplomatic commissions, as well as with the humblest personal services—both in this Court being alike honourable. And this was the man who conducted long and difficult wars, who dealt habitually with political affairs of the first importance, and every day sent his plenipotentiaries to all parts of Italy. His safety lay in the fact that none of his servants trusted the others, that his *condottieri* were watched and misled by spies, and that the ambassadors and higher officials were baffled and kept apart by artificially nourished jealousies, and in particular by the device of coupling an honest man with a knave. His inward faith too rested upon opposed and contradictory systems; he believed in blind necessity, and in the influence of the stars, and offering prayers at one and the same time to helpers of every sort; he was a student of the ancient authors, as well as of French tales of chivalry. And yet the same man, who would never suffer death to be mentioned in his presence, and caused his dying favourites to be removed from the castle, that no shadow might fall on the abode of happiness, deliberately hastened his own death by closing up a wound, and, refusing to be bled, died at last with dignity and grace.

His stepson and successor, the fortunate *condottiere* Francesco Sforza (1450–66), was perhaps of all the Italians of the fifteenth century the man most after the heart of his age. Never was the triumph of genius and individual power more brilliantly displayed than in him; and those who would not recognize his merit were at least forced to wonder at him as the spoilt child of fortune. The Milanese claimed it openly as an honour to be governed by so distinguished a master; when he entered the city the thronging populace bore him on horseback into the cathedral, without giving him the chance to dismount. Let us listen to the balance-sheet of his life, in the estimate of Pope Pius II, a judge in such matters:

> In 1459, when the Duke came to the congress at Mantua, he was sixty years old; on horseback he looked like a young man; of a lofty and imposing figure, with serious features, calm and affable in conversation, princely in his whole bearing, with a combination of bodily and intellectual gifts unrivalled in our time, unconquered on the field of battle—such was the man who raised himself from a humble position to the control of an empire. His wife was beautiful and virtuous, his children were like the angels of heaven; he was seldom ill, and all his chief wishes were fulfilled. And yet he was not without misfortune. His wife, out of jealousy, killed his mistress; his old comrades and friends, Troilo and Brunoro, abandoned him and went over to King Alfonso; another, Ciarpollone, he was forced to hang for treason; he had to suffer it that his brother Alessandro set the French upon him; one of his sons formed intrigues against him, and was imprisoned; the March of Ancona, which he had won in war, he lost again in the same way. No man enjoys so unclouded a fortune that he has not somewhere to struggle with adversity. He is happy who has but few troubles.

With this negative definition of happiness the learned Pope dismisses the reader. Had he been able to see into the future, or been willing to stop and discuss the consequences of an uncontrolled despotism, one pervading fact would not have escaped his notice—the absence of all guarantee for the future. Those children, beautiful as angels, carefully and thoroughly educated as they were, fell victims when they grew up to the corruption of a measureless egoism. Galeazzo Maria (1466–76), solicitous only of outward effect, took pride in the beauty of his hands, in the high salaries he paid, in the financial credit he enjoyed, in his treasure of two million pieces of gold, in the distinguished people who surrounded him, and in the army and birds of chase which he maintained. He was fond of the sound of his own voice, and spoke well, most fluently, perhaps, when he had the chance of insulting a Venetian ambassador. He was subject to caprices, such as having a room painted with figures in a single night;

and, what was worse, to fits of senseless debauchery and of revolting cruelty to his nearest friends. To a handful of enthusiasts, at whose head stood Giov. Andrea di Lampugnano, he seemed a tyrant too bad to live; they murdered him, and thereby delivered the state into the power of his brothers, one of whom, Lodovico il Moro, threw his nephew into prison, and took the government into his own hands. From this usurpation followed the French intervention and the disasters which befell the whole of Italy.

The Moor is the most perfect type of the despot of that age, and, as a kind of natural product, almost disarms our moral judgment. Notwithstanding the profound immorality of the means he employed, he used them with perfect ingenuousness; no one would probably have been more astonished than himself to learn that for the choice of means as well as of ends a human being is morally responsible; he would rather have reckoned it as a singular virtue that, so far as possible, he had abstained from too free a use of the punishment of death. He accepted as no more than his due the almost fabulous respect of the Italians for his political genius. In 1496 he boasted that the Pope Alexander was his chaplain, the Emperor Maximilian his *condottiere,* Venice his chamberlain, and the King of France his courier, who must come and go at his bidding. With marvellous presence of mind he weighed, even in his last extremity, all possible means of escape, and at length decided, to his honour, to trust to the goodness of human nature; he rejected the proposal of his brother, Cardinal Ascanio, who wished to remain in the citadel of Milan, on the ground of a former quarrel: "Monsignore, take it not ill, but I trust you not, brother though you be"; and appointed to the command of the castle, "that pledge of his return," a man to whom he had always done good, but who nevertheless betrayed him. At home the Moor was a good and useful ruler, and to the last he reckoned on his popularity both in Milan and in Como. In former years (after 1496) he had overstrained the resources of his state, and at Cremona had ordered, out of pure expediency, a respectable citizen who had spoken against the new taxes to be quietly strangled. Since that time, in holding audiences, he kept his visitors away from his person by means of a bar, so that in conversing with him they were compelled to speak at the top of their voices. At his Court, the most brilliant in Europe since that of Burgundy had ceased to exist, immorality of the worst kind was prevalent: the daughter was sold by the father, the wife by the husband, the sister by the brother. The Prince himself was incessantly active, and, as son of his own deeds, claimed relationship with all who, like himself, stood on their personal merits—with scholars, poets, artists, and musicians. The academy which he founded served rather for his own purposes than for the instruction of scholars; nor was it the fame of the distinguished men who surrounded him which he heeded, so much as their society and their services. It is certain that Bramante was scantily paid at first; Leonardo, on the other hand, was up to 1496 suitably remunerated—and besides, what kept him at the Court, if not his own free will? The world lay open to him, as perhaps to no other mortal man of that day; and if proof were wanting of the loftier element in the nature of Lodovico il Moro, it is found in the long stay of the enigmatic master at his Court. That afterward Leonardo entered the service of Cesare Borgia and Francis I was probably due to the interest he felt in the unusual and striking character of the two men.

After the fall of the Moor—he was captured in April 1500 by the French, after his return from his flight to Germany—his sons were badly brought up among strangers, and showed no capacity for carrying out his political testament. The elder, Massimiliano, had no resemblance to him; the younger, Francesco, was at all events not without spirit. Milan, which in those years changed its rulers so often, and suffered so unspeakably in the change, endeavoured to secure itself against a reaction. In 1512 the French, retreating before the arms of Maximilian and the Spaniards, were induced to make a declaration that the Milanese had taken no part in their expulsion, and, without being guilty of rebellion, might yield themselves to a new conqueror. It is a fact of some political importance that in such moments of transition the unhappy city, like Naples at the flight of the Aragonese, was apt to fall a prey to gangs of (often highly aristocratic) scoundrels.

The house of Gonzaga at Mantua and that of Montefeltro of Urbino were among the best ordered and richest in men of ability during the second half of the fifteenth century. The Gonzaga were a tolerably harmonious family; for a long period no murder had been known among them, and their dead could be shown to the world without fear. The Marquis Francesco Gonzaga and his wife, Isabella d'Este, in spite of some few irregularities, were a united and respectable couple, and brought up their sons to be successful and remarkable men at a time when their small but most important state was exposed to incessant danger. That Francesco, either as statesman or as soldier, should adopt a policy of exceptional honesty was what neither the Emperor, nor Venice, nor the King of France could have expected or desired; but certainly since the battle at Taro (1495), so far as military honour was concerned, he felt and acted as an Italian patriot, and imparted the same spirit to his wife. Every deed of loyalty and heroism, such as the defence of Faenza against Cesare Borgia, she felt as a vindication of the honour of Italy. Our judgment of her does not need to rest on the praises of the artists and writers who made the fair princess a rich return for her patronage; her own letters show her to us as a woman of unshaken firmness, full of kindliness and humorous observation. Bembo, Bandello, Ariosto, and Bernardo Tasso sent their works to this Court, small and powerless as it was, and empty as they found its treasury. A more polished and charming circle was not to be seen in Italy since the dissolution (1508) of the old Court of Urbino; and in one respect, in freedom of movement, the society of Ferrara was inferior to that of Mantua. In artistic matters Isabella had an accurate knowledge, and the catalogue of her small but choice collection can be read by no lover of art without emotion.

In the great Federigo (1444–82), whether he were a genuine Montefeltro or not, Urbino possessed a brilliant representative of the princely order. As a *condottiere*—and in this capacity he served kings and Popes for thirty years after he became prince—he shared the political morality of soldiers of fortune, a morality of which the fault does not rest with them alone; as ruler of his little territory he adopted the plan of spending at home the money he had earned abroad, and taxing his people as lightly as possible. Of him and his two successors, Guidobaldo and Francesco Maria, we read: "They erected buildings, furthered the cultivation of the land, lived at home, and gave employment to a large number of people: their subjects loved them." But not only the State, but the Court too, was a work of art and organization, and this in every sense of the word. Federigo had five hundred persons in his service; the arrangements of the Court were as complete as in the capitals of the greatest monarchs, but nothing was wasted; all had its object, and all was carefully watched and controlled. The Court was no scene of vice and dissipation: it served as a school of military education for the sons of other great houses, the thoroughness of whose culture and instruction was made a point of honour by the Duke. The palace which he built, if not one of the most splendid, was classical in the perfection of its plan; there was placed the greatest of his treasures, the celebrated library. Feeling secure in a land where all gained profit or employment from his rule, and where none were beggars, he habitually went unarmed and almost unaccompanied; alone among the princes of his time he ventured to walk in an open park, and to take his frugal meals in an open chamber, while Livy, or in time of fasting some devotional work, was read to him. In the course of the same afternoon he would listen to a lecture on some classical subject, and thence would go to the monastery of the Clarisse and talk of sacred things through the grating with the abbess. In the evening he would overlook the martial exercises of the young people of his Court on the meadow of S. Francesco, known for its magnificent view, and saw to it well that all the feats were done in the most perfect manner. He strove always to be affable and accessible to the utmost degree, visiting the artisans who worked for him in their shops, holding frequent audiences, and, if possible, attending to the requests of each individual on the same day that they were presented. No wonder that the people, as he walked along the street, knelt down and cried: *"Dio ti mantenga, signore!"* He was called by thinking people "the light of Italy."

His gifted son Guidobaldo, visited by sickness and misfortune of every kind, was able at the last (1508) to give his state into the safe hands of his nephew Francesco Maria (nephew also of Pope Julius II), who, at least, succeeded in preserving the territory from any permanent foreign occupation. It is remarkable with what confidence Guidobaldo yielded and fled before Cesare Borgia and Francesco before the troops of Leo X; each knew that his restoration would be all the easier and the more popular the less the country suffered through a fruitless defence. When Lodovico made the same calculation at Milan he forgot the many grounds of hatred which existed against him. The Court of Guidobaldo has been made immortal as the high school of polished manners by Baldassare Castiglione, who represented his eclogue *Thyrsis* before, and in honour of, that society (1506), and who afterward (1518) laid the *scena* of the dialogue of his *Cortigiano* in the circle of the accomplished Duchess Elisabetta Gonzaga.

The government of the family of Este at Ferrara, Modena, and Reggio displays curious contrasts of violence and popularity. Within the palace frightful deeds were perpetrated; a princess was beheaded (1425) for alleged adultery with a stepson; legitimate and illegitimate children fled from the Court, and even abroad their lives were threatened by assassins sent in pursuit of them (1471). Plots from without were incessant; the bastard of a bastard tried to wrest the crown from the lawful heir, Hercules I: this latter is said afterward (1493) to have poisoned his wife on discovering that she, at the instigation of her brother, Ferrante of Naples, was going to poison him. This list of tragedies is closed by the plot of two bastards against their brothers, the ruling Duke Alfonso I and Cardinal Ippolito (1506), which was discovered in time, and punished with imprisonment for life.

The financial system in this state was of the most perfect kind, and necessarily so, since none of the large or second-rate Powers of Italy were exposed to such danger and stood in such constant need of armaments and fortifications. It was the hope of the rulers that the increasing prosperity of the people would keep pace with the increasing weight of taxation, and the Marquis Niccolò (d. 1441) used to express the wish that his subjects might be richer than the people of other countries. If the rapid increase of the population be a measure of the prosperity actually attained, it is certainly a fact of importance that in 1497, notwithstanding the wonderful extension of the capital, no houses were to be let. Ferrara is the first really modern city in Europe; large and well-built quarters sprang up at the bidding of the ruler: here, by the concentration of the official classes and the active promotion of trade, was formed for the first time a true capital; wealthy fugitives from all parts of Italy, Florentines especially, settled and built their palaces at Ferrara. But the indirect taxation, at all events, must have reached a point at which it could only just be borne. The Government, it is true, took measures of alleviation which were also adopted by other Italian despots, such as Galeazzo Maria Sforza: in time of famine corn was brought from a distance, and seems to have been distributed gratuitously; but in ordinary times it compensated itself by the monopoly, if not of corn, of many other of the necessaries of life—fish, salt meat, fruit, and vegetables, which last were carefully planted on and near the walls of the city. The most considerable source of income, however, was the annual sale of public offices, a usage which was common throughout Italy, and about the working of which at Ferrara we have more precise information. We read, for example, that at the new year 1502 the majority of the officials bought their places at *prezzi salati;* public servants of the most various kinds, custom-house officers, bailiffs *(massari),* notaries, *podestà,* judges, and even captains—*i.e.,* lieutenant-governors of provincial towns—are quoted by name. As one of the "devourers of the people" who paid dearly for their places, and who were "hated worse than the devil," Tito Strozzi—let us hope not the famous Latin poet—is mentioned. About the same time every year the Dukes were accustomed to make a round of visits in Ferrara, the so-called *andar per ventura,* in which they took presents from, at any rate, the more wealthy citizens. The gifts, however, did not consist of money, but of natural products.

It was the pride of the Duke for all Italy to know that at Ferrara the soldiers received their pay and the professors of the University their salary not a day later than it was due; that the soldiers never dared lay arbitrary hands on citizen or peasant; that the town was impregnable to assault; and that vast sums of coined money were stored up in the citadel. To keep two sets of accounts seemed unnecessary; the Minister of Finance was at the same time manager of the ducal household. The buildings erected by Borso (1430–71), by Hercules I (till 1505), and by Alfonso I (till 1534) were very numerous, but of small size: they are characteristic of a princely house which, with all its love of splendour—Borso never appeared but in embroidery and jewels—indulged in no ill-considered expense. Alfonso may perhaps have foreseen the fate which was in store for his charming little villas, the Belvedere, with its shady gardens, and Montana, with its fountains and beautiful frescoes.

It is undeniable that the dangers to which these princes were constantly exposed developed in them capacities of a remarkable kind. In so artificial a world only a man of consummate address could hope to succeed; each candidate for distinction was forced to make good his claims by personal merit and show himself worthy of the crown he sought. Their characters are not without dark sides; but in all of them lives something of those qualities which Italy then pursued as its ideal. What European monarch of the time so laboured for his own culture as, for instance, Alfonso I? His travels in France, England, and the Netherlands were undertaken for the purpose of study; by means of them he gained an accurate knowledge of the industry and commerce of these countries. It is ridiculous to reproach him with the turner's work which he practised in his leisure hours, connected as it was with his skill in the casting of cannon, and with the unprejudiced freedom with which he surrounded himself by masters of every art. The Italian princes were not, like their contemporaries in the North, dependent on the society of an aristocracy which held itself to be the only class worth consideration, and which infected the monarch with the same conceit. In Italy the prince was permitted and compelled to know and to use men of every grade in society; and the nobility, though by birth a caste, were forced in social intercourse to stand upon their personal qualifications alone. But this is a point which we shall discuss more fully in the sequel.

The feeling of the Ferrarese toward the ruling house was a strange compound of silent dread, of the truly Italian sense of well-calculated interest, and of the loyalty of the modern subject: personal admiration was transformed into a new sentiment of duty. The city of Ferrara raised in 1451 a bronze equestrian statue to their Prince Niccolò, who had died ten years earlier; Borso (1454) did not scruple to place his own statue, also of bronze, but in a sitting posture, hard by in the market; in addition to which the city, at the beginning of his reign, decreed to him a "marble triumphal pillar." And when he was buried the whole people felt as if God Himself had died a second time. A citizen who, when abroad from Venice, had spoken ill of Borso in public was denounced on his return home, and condemned to banishment and the confiscation of his goods; a loyal subject was with difficulty restrained from cutting him down before the tribunal itself, and with a rope round his neck the offender went to the Duke and begged for a full pardon. The Government was well provided with spies, and the Duke inspected personally the daily list of travellers which the innkeepers were strictly ordered to present. Under Borso, who was anxious to leave no distinguished stranger unhonoured, this regulation served a hospitable purpose; Hercules I used it simply as a measure of precaution. In Bologna too it was then the rule, under Giovanni II Bentivoglio, that every passing traveller who entered at one gate must obtain a ticket in order to go out at another. An unfailing means of popularity was the sudden dismissal of oppressive officials. When Borso arrested in person his chief and confidential counsellors, when Hercules I removed and disgraced a tax-gatherer who for years had been sucking the blood of the people, bonfires were lighted and the bells were pealed in their honour. With one of his servants, however, Hercules let things go too far. The director of the police, or by whatever name we should choose to call him *(capitano di giustizia),* was Gregorio Zampante of Lucca—a native being unsuited for an office of this kind. Even the sons and brothers of the Duke trembled before this man; the fines he inflicted amounted to hundreds and thousands of ducats, and torture was applied even before the hearing of a case: bribes were accepted from wealthy criminals, and their pardon obtained from the Duke by false representations. Gladly would the people have paid any sum to this ruler for sending away the "enemy of God and man." But Hercules had knighted him and made him godfather to his children; and year by year Zampante laid by two thousand ducats. He dared only eat pigeons bred in his own house, and could not cross the street without a band of archers and bravoes. It was time to get rid of him; in 1490 two students and a converted Jew whom he had mortally offended killed him in his house while he was taking his *siesta,* and then rode through the town on horses held in waiting, raising the cry, "Come out! come out! we have slain Zampante!" The pursuers came too late, and found them already safe across the frontier. Of course it now rained satires—some of them in the form of sonnets, others of odes.

It was wholly in the spirit of this system that the sovereign imposed his own respect for useful servants on the Court and on the people. When in 1469 Borso's privy councillor Lodovico Casella died no court of law or place of business in the city, and no lecture-room at the University, was allowed to be open: all had to follow the body to S. Domenico, since the Duke intended to be present. And, in fact, "the first of the house of Este who attended the corpse of a subject" walked, clad in black, after the coffin, weeping, while behind him came the relatives of Casella, each conducted by one of the gentlemen of the Court; the body of the plain citizen was carried by nobles from the church into the cloister, where it was buried. Indeed this official sympathy with princely emotion first came up in the Italian states. At the root of the practice may be a beautiful, humane sentiment; the utterance of it, especially in the poets, is, as a rule, of equivocal sincerity. One of the youthful poems of Ariosto, on the death of Leonora of Aragon, wife of Hercules I, contains besides the inevitable graveyard flowers, which are scattered in the elegies of all ages, some thoroughly modern features.

> This death had given Ferrara a blow which it would not get over for years: its benefactress was now its advocate in heaven, since earth was not worthy of her;

truly, the Angel of Death did not come to her, as to us common mortals, with bloodstained scythe, but fair to behold [*onesta*], and with so kind a face that every fear was allayed.

But we meet, also, with a sympathy of a different kind. Novelists, depending wholly on the favour of their patrons, tell us the love-stories of the prince, even before his death, in a way which, to later times, would seem the height of indiscretion, but which then passed simply as an innocent compliment. Lyrical poets even went so far as to sing the illicit flames of their lawfully married lords—*e.g.,* Angelo Poliziano those of Lorenzo the Magnificent, and Gioviano Pontano, with a singular gusto, those of Alfonso of Calabria. The poem in question betrays unconsciously the odious disposition of the Aragonese ruler; in these things too he must needs be the most fortunate, else woe be to those who are more successful! That the greatest artists—for example, Leonardo—should paint the mistresses of their patrons was no more than a matter of course.

But the house of Este was not satisfied with the praises of others; it undertook to celebrate them itself. In the Palazzo Schifanoja Borso caused himself to be painted in a series of historical representations, and Hercules kept the anniversary of his accession to the throne by a procession which was compared to the feast of Corpus Christi; shops were closed as on Sunday; in the centre of the line walked all the members of the princely house (bastards included), clad in embroidered robes. That the Crown was the fountain of honour and authority, that all personal distinction flowed from it alone, had been long expressed at this Court by the Order of the Golden Spur—an order which had nothing in common with medieval chivalry. Hercules I added to the spur a sword, a gold-laced mantle, and a grant of money, in return for which there is no doubt that regular service was required.

The patronage of art and letters for which this Court has obtained a world-wide reputation was exercised through the University, which was one of the most perfect in Italy, and by the gift of places in the personal or official service of the prince; it involved consequently no additional expense. Bojardo, as a wealthy country gentleman and high official, belonged to this class. At the time when Ariosto began to distinguish himself there existed no Court, in the true sense of the word, either at Milan or Florence, and soon there was none either at Urbino or at Naples. He had to content himself with a place among the musicians and jugglers of Cardinal Ippolito till Alfonso took him into his service. It was otherwise at a later time with Torquato Tasso, whose presence at Court was jealously sought after.

Chapter 6. The Opponents of Tyranny

In face of this centralized authority all legal opposition within the borders of the state was futile. The elements needed for the restoration of a republic had been for ever destroyed, and the field prepared for violence and despotism. The nobles, destitute of political rights, even where they held feudal possessions, might call themselves Guelphs or Ghibellines at will, might dress up their bravoes in padded hose and feathered caps, or how else they pleased; thoughtful men like Machiavelli knew well enough that Milan and Naples were too 'corrupt' for a republic. Strange judgments fall on these two so-called parties, which now served only to give an official sanction to personal and family disputes. An Italian prince, whom Agrippa of Nettesheim advised to put them down, replied that their quarrels brought him in more than twelve thousand ducats a year in fines. And when in 1500, during the brief return of Lodovico il Moro to his states, the Guelphs of Tortona summoned a part of the neighbouring French army into the city, in order to make an end once for all of their opponents, the French certainly began by plundering and ruining the Ghibellines, but finished by doing the same to their hosts, till Tortona was utterly laid waste. In Romagna, the hotbed of every ferocious passion, these two names had long lost all political meaning. It was a sign of the political delusion of the people that they not seldom believed the Guelphs to be the natural allies of the French and the Ghibellines of the Spaniards. It is hard to see that those who tried to profit by this error got much by doing so. France, after all her interventions, had to abandon the peninsula at last, and what became of Spain, after she had destroyed Italy, is known to every reader.

But to return to the despots of the Renaissance. A pure and simple mind, we might think, would perhaps have argued that, since all power is derived from God, these princes, if they were loyally and honestly supported by all their subjects, must in time themselves improve and lose all traces of their violent origin. But from characters and imaginations inflamed by passion and ambition reasoning of this kind could not be expected. Like bad physicians, they thought to cure the disease by removing the symptoms, and fancied that if the tyrant were put to death freedom would follow of itself. Or else, without reflecting even to this extent, they sought only to give a vent to the universal hatred, or to take vengeance for some family misfortune or personal affront. Since the Governments were absolute, and free from all legal restraints, the opposition chose its weapons with equal freedom. Boccaccio declares openly:

> Shall I call the tyrant king or prince, and obey him loyally as my lord? No, for he is the enemy of the commonwealth. Against him I may use arms, conspira-

cies, spies, ambushes, and fraud; to do so is a sacred and necessary work. There is no more acceptable sacrifice than the blood of a tyrant.

We need not occupy ourselves with individual cases; Machiavelli, in a famous chapter of his *Discorsi,* treats of the conspiracies of ancient and modern times from the days of the Greek tyrants downward, and classifies them with cold-blooded indifference according to their various plans and results. We need make but two observations, first on the murders committed in church, and next on the influence of classical antiquity. So well was the tyrant guarded that it was almost impossible to lay hands upon him elsewhere than at solemn religious services; and on no other occasion was the whole family to be found assembled together. It was thus that the Fabrianese murdered (1435) the members of their ruling house, the Chiavistelli, during High Mass, the signal being given by the words of the Creed, "Et incarnatus est." At Milan the Duke Giovanni Maria Visconti (1412) was assassinated at the entrance of the church of S. Gottardo, Galeazzo Maria Sforza (1476) in the church of S. Stefano, and Lodovico il Moro only escaped (1484) the daggers of the adherents of the widowed Duchess Bona through entering the church of Sant' Ambrogio by another door than that by which he was expected. There was no intentional impiety in the act; the assassins of Galeazzo did not fail to pray before the murder to the patron saint of the church, and to listen devoutly to the first Mass. It was, however, one cause of the partial failure of the conspiracy of the Pazzi against Lorenzo and Giuliano de' Medici (1478) that the brigand Montesecco, who had bargained to commit the murder at a banquet, declined to undertake it in the cathedral of Florence. Certain of the clergy "who were familiar with the sacred place, and consequently had no fear," were induced to act in his stead.

As to the imitation of antiquity, the influence of which on moral, and more especially on political, questions we shall often refer to, the example was set by the rulers themselves, who, both in their conception of the state and in their personal conduct, took the old Roman Empire avowedly as their model. In like manner their opponents, when they set to work with a deliberate theory, took pattern by the ancient tyrannicides. It may be hard to prove that in the main point—in forming the resolve itself—they consciously followed a classical example; but the appeal to antiquity was no mere phrase. The most striking disclosures have been left us with respect to the murderers of Galeazzo Sforza—Lampugnani, Olgiati, and Visconti. Though all three had personal ends to serve, yet their enterprise may be partly ascribed to a more general reason. About this time Cola de' Montani, a humanist and professor of eloquence, had awakened among many of the young Milanese nobility a vague passion for glory and patriotic achievements, and had mentioned to Lampugnani and Olgiati his hope of delivering Milan. Suspicion was soon aroused against him: he was banished from the city, and his pupils were abandoned to the fanaticism he had excited. Some ten days before the deed they met together and took a solemn oath in the monastery of S. Ambrogio. "Then," says Olgiati, "in a remote corner I raised my eyes before the picture of the patron saint, and implored his help for ourselves and for all *his* people." The heavenly protector of the city was called on to bless the undertaking, as was afterward St Stephen, in whose church it was fulfilled. Many of their comrades were now informed of the plot, nightly meetings were held in the house of Lampugnani, and the conspirators practised for the murder with the sheaths of their daggers. The attempt was successful, but Lampugnani was killed on the spot by the attendants of the Duke; the others were captured: Visconti was penitent, but Olgiati through all his tortures maintained that the deed was an acceptable offering to God, and exclaimed while the executioner was breaking his ribs, "Courage, Girolamo! thou wilt long be remembered; death is bitter, but glory is eternal."

But however idealistic the object and purpose of such conspiracies may appear, the manner in which they were conducted betrays the influence of that worst of all conspirators, Catiline—a man in whose thoughts freedom had no place whatever. The annals of Siena tell us expressly that the conspirators were students of Sallust, and the fact is indirectly confirmed by the confession of Olgiati. Elsewhere, too, we meet with the name of Catiline, and a more attractive pattern of the conspirator, apart from the end he followed, could hardly be discovered.

Among the Florentines, whenever they got rid of, or tried to get rid of, the Medici, tyrannicide was a practice universally accepted and approved. After the flight of the Medici in 1494 the bronze group of Donatello—Judith with the dead Holofernes—was taken from their collection and placed before the Palazzo della Signoria, on the spot where the *David* of Michelangelo now stands, with the inscription, "Exemplum salutis publicæ cives posuere 1495." No example was more popular than that of the younger Brutus, who, in Dante, lies with Cassius and Judas Iscariot in the lowest pit of hell, because of his treason to the Empire. Pietro Paolo Boscoli, whose plot against Giuliano, Giovanni, and Giulio de' Medici failed (1513), was an enthusiastic admirer of Brutus, and in order to follow his steps only waited to find a Cassius. Such a partner he met with in Agostino Capponi. His last utterances in prison—a striking evidence of the religious feeling of the time—show with what an effort he rid his mind of these classical imaginations in order to die like a Christian. A friend and the confessor both had to assure him that St Thomas Aquinas condemned conspirators absolutely; but the confessor afterward admitted to the same friend that St Thomas drew a distinction and permitted conspiracies against a tyrant who had forced himself on a people against their will. After Lorenzino de' Medici had murdered the Duke Alessandro (1537), and then escaped, an apology for the deed appeared, which is probably his own work, and certainly composed in his interest, and in which he praises tyrannicide as an act of the highest merit; on the supposition that Alessandro was a legitimate Medici, and therefore related to him, if only distantly, he boldly compares himself with Timoleon, who slew his brother for his country's sake. Others, on the same occasion, made use of the comparison with Brutus, and that Michelangelo himself, even late in life, was not unfriendly to ideas of this kind may be inferred from his bust of Brutus in the Uffizi. He left it unfinished, like nearly all his works, but certainly not because the murder of Cæsar was repugnant to his feeling, as the couplet beneath declares.

A popular radicalism in the form in which it is opposed to the monarchies of later times is not to be found in the despotic states of the Renaissance. Each individual protested inwardly against despotism, but was rather disposed to make tolerable or profitable terms with it than to combine with others for its destruction. Things must have been as bad as at Camerino, Fabriano, or Rimini before the citizens united to destroy or expel the ruling house. They knew in most cases only too well that this would but mean a change of masters. The star of the republics was certainly on the decline.

Chapter 7. The Republics: Venice and Florence

The Italian municipalities had, in earlier days, given signal proof of that force which transforms the city into the state. It remained only that these cities should combine in a great confederation; and this idea was constantly recurring to Italian statesmen, whatever differences of form it might from time to time display. In fact, during the struggles of the twelfth and thirteenth centuries great and formidable leagues actually were formed by the cities; and Sismondi (ii, 174) is of opinion that the time of the final armaments of the Lombard confederation against Barbarossa was the moment when a universal Italian league was possible. But the more powerful states had already developed characteristic features which made any such scheme impracticable. In their commercial dealings they shrank from no measures, however extreme, which might damage their competitors; they held their weaker neighbours in a condition of helpless dependence—in short, they all fancied they could get on by themselves without the assistance of the rest, and thus paved the way for future usurpation. The usurper was forthcoming when long conflicts between the nobility and the people, and between the different factions of the nobility, had awakened the desire for a strong government, and when bands of mercenaries ready and willing to sell their aid to the highest bidder had superseded the general levy of the citizens, which party leaders now found unsuited to their purposes. The tyrants destroyed the freedom of most of the cities; here and there they were expelled, but not thoroughly, or only for a short time; and they were always restored, since the inward conditions were favourable to them, and the opposing forces were exhausted.

Among the cities which maintained their independence are two of deep significance for the history of the human race: Florence, the city of incessant movement, which has left us a record of the thoughts and aspirations of each and all who, for three centuries, took part in this movement, and Venice, the city of apparent stagnation and of political secrecy. No contrast can be imagined stronger than that which is offered us by these two, and neither can be compared to anything else which the world has hitherto produced.

Venice recognized itself from the first as a strange and mysterious creation—the fruits of a higher power than human ingenuity. The solemn foundation of the city was the subject of a legend. On March 25, 413, at midday the emigrants from Padua laid the first stone at the Rialto, that they might have a sacred, inviolable asylum amid the devastations of the barbarians. Later writers attributed to the founders the presentiment of the future greatness of the city; M. Antonio Sabellico, who has celebrated the event in the dignified flow of his hexameters, makes the priest, who completes the act of consecration, cry to heaven: "When we hereafter attempt great things grant us prosperity! Now we kneel before a poor altar; but if our vows are not made in vain, a hundred temples, O God, of gold and marble shall arise to Thee." The island-city at the end of the fifteenth century was the jewel-casket of the world. It is so described by the same Sabellico, with its ancient cupolas, its leaning towers, its inlaid marble façades, its compressed splendour, where the richest decoration did not hinder the practical employment of every corner of space. He takes us to the crowded *piazza* before S. Giacometto at the Rialto, where the business of the world is transacted, not amid shouting and confusion, but with the subdued hum of many voices; where in the porticos round the square and in those of the adjoining streets sit hundreds of money-changers and goldsmiths, with endless rows of shops and warehouses above their heads. He describes the great Fondaco of the Germans beyond the bridge, where their goods and their dwellings lay, and before which their ships are drawn up side by side in the canal; higher up is a whole fleet laden with wine and oil, and parallel with it, on the shore swarming with porters, are the vaults of the merchants; then from the Rialto to the Square of St Mark come the inns and the perfumers' cabinets. So he conducts the reader from one quarter of the city to another till he comes at last to the two hospitals which were among those institutions of public utility nowhere so numerous as at Venice. Care for the people, in peace as well as in war, was characteristic of this Government, and its attention to the wounded, even to those of the enemy, excited the admiration of other states. Public institutions of every kind found in Venice their pattern; the pensioning of retired servants was carried out systematically, and included a provision for widows and orphans. Wealth, political security, and acquaintance with other countries had matured the understanding of such questions. These slender fair-haired men, with quiet, cautious steps and deliberate speech, differed but slightly in costume and bearing from one another; ornaments, especially pearls, were reserved for the women and girls. At that time the general prosperity, notwithstanding the losses sustained from the Turks, was still dazzling; the stores of energy which the city possessed, and the prejudice in its favour diffused throughout Europe, enabled it at a much later time to survive the heavy blows which were inflicted by the discovery of the sea route to the Indies, by the fall of the Mamelukes in Egypt, and by the war of the League of Cambray.

Sabellico, born in the neighbourhood of Tivoli, and accustomed to the frank loquacity of the scholars of his day, remarks elsewhere with some astonishment that the young nobles who came of a morning to hear his lectures could not be prevailed on to enter into political discussions: "When I ask them what people think, say, and expect about this or that movement in Italy they all answer with one voice that they know nothing about the matter." Still, in spite of the strict inquisition of the state, much was to be learned from the more corrupt members of the aristocracy by those who were willing to pay enough for it. In the last quarter of the fifteenth century there were traitors among the highest officials; the Popes, the Italian princes, and even second-rate *condottieri* in the service of the Government had informers in their pay, sometimes with regular salaries; things went so far that the Council of Ten found it prudent to conceal important political news from the Council of the Pregadi, and it was even supposed that Lodovico il Moro had control of a definite number of votes among the latter. Whether the hanging of single offenders and the high rewards—such as a life-pension of sixty ducats paid to those who informed against them—were of much avail, it is hard to decide; one of the chief causes of this evil, the poverty of many of the nobility, could not be removed in a day. In 1492 a proposal was urged by two of that order that the State should annually spend seventy thousand ducats for the relief of those poorer nobles who held no public office; the matter was near coming before the Great Council, in which it might have had a majority, when the Council of Ten interfered in time and banished the two proposers for life to Nicosia, in Cyprus. About this time a Soranzo was hung, though not at Venice itself, for sacrilege, and a Contarini put in chains for burglary; another of the same family came in 1499 before the Signoria, and complained that for many years he had been without an office, that he had only sixteen ducats a year and nine children, that his debts amounted to sixty ducats, that he knew no trade and had lately been turned on to the streets. We can understand why some of the wealthier nobles built houses, sometimes whole rows of them, to provide free lodging for their needy comrades. Such works figure in wills among deeds of charity.

But if the enemies of Venice ever founded serious hopes upon abuses of this kind they were greatly in error. It might be thought that the commercial activity of the city, which put within reach of the humblest a rich reward for their labour, and the colonies on the Eastern shores of the Mediterranean would have diverted from political affairs the dangerous elements of society. But had not the political history of Genoa, notwithstanding similar advantages, been of the stormiest? The cause of the stability of Venice lies rather in a combination of circumstances which were found in union nowhere else. Unassailable from its position, it had been able from the beginning to treat of foreign affairs with the fullest and calmest reflection, and ignore nearly altogether the parties which divided the rest of Italy, to escape the entanglement of permanent alliances, and to set the highest price on those which it thought fit to make. The keynote of the Venetian character was, consequently, a spirit of proud and contemptuous isolation, which, joined to the hatred felt for the city by the other states of Italy, gave rise to a strong sense of solidarity within. The inhabitants meanwhile were united by the most powerful ties of interest in dealing both with the colonies and with the possessions on the mainland, forcing the population of the latter—that is, of all the towns up to Bergamo—to buy and sell in Venice alone. A power which rested on means so artificial could only be maintained by internal harmony and unity; and this conviction was so widely diffused among the citizens that the conspirator found few elements to work upon. And the discontented, if there were such, were held so far apart by the division between the noble and the burgher that a mutual understanding was not easy. On the other hand, within the ranks of the nobility itself travel, commercial enterprise, and the incessant wars with the Turks saved the wealthy and dangerous from that fruitful source of conspiracies—idleness. In these wars they were spared, often to a criminal extent, by the general in command, and the fall of the city was predicted by a Venetian Cato if this fear of the nobles "to give one another pain" should continue at the expense of justice. Nevertheless this free movement in the open air gave the Venetian aristocracy, as a whole, a healthy bias.

And when envy and ambition called for satisfaction an official victim was forthcoming, and legal means and authorities were ready. The moral torture which for years the Doge Francesco Foscari (d. 1457) suffered before the eyes of all Venice is a frightful example of a vengeance possible only in an aristocracy. The Council of Ten, which had a hand in everything, which disposed without appeal of life and death, of financial affairs and military appointments, which included the Inquisitors among its number, and which overthrew Foscari, as it had overthrown so many powerful men before—this council was yearly chosen afresh from the whole governing body, the *Gran Consilio,* and was consequently the most direct expression of its will. It is not probable that serious intrigues occurred at these elections, as the short duration of the office and the accountability which followed rendered it an object of no great desire. But violent and mysterious as the proceedings of this and other authorities might be, the genuine Venetian courted rather than fled their sentence, not only because the republic had long arms, and if it could not catch him might punish his family, but because in most cases it acted from rational motives and not from a thirst for blood. No state, indeed, has ever exercised a greater moral influence over its subjects, whether abroad or at home. If traitors were to be found among the Pregadi, there was ample compensation for this in the fact that every Venetian away from home was a born spy for his Government. It was a matter of course that the Venetian cardinals at Rome sent home news of the transactions of the secret Papal consistories. Cardinal Domenico Grimani had the dispatches which Ascanio Sforza was sending to his brother Lodovico il Moro intercepted in the neighbourhood of Rome (1500), and forwarded them to Venice; his father, then exposed to a serious accusation, claimed public credit for this service of his son before the *Gran Consilio*—in other words, before all the world.

The conduct of the Venetian Government to the *condottieri* in its pay has been spoken of already. The only further guarantee of their fidelity which could be obtained lay in their great number, by which treachery was made as difficult as its discovery was easy. In looking at the Venetian army list one is only surprised that among forces of such miscellaneous composition any common action was possible. In the catalogue for the campaign of 1495 we find 15,526 horsemen, broken up into a number of small divisions. Gonzaga of Mantua alone had as many as 1200, and Gioffredo Borgia 740; then follow six officers with a contingent of 600 to 700, ten with 400, twelve with 200 to 400, fourteen or thereabouts with 100 to 200, nine with 80, six with 50 to 60, and so forth. These forces were partly composed of old Venetian troops, partly of veterans led by Venetian city or country nobles; the majority of the leaders were, however, princes and rulers of cities or their relatives. To these forces must be added 24,000 infantry—we are not told how they were raised or commanded—with 3300 additional troops, who probably belonged to the special services. In time of peace the cities of the mainland were wholly unprotected or occupied by insignificant garrisons. Venice relied, if not exactly on the loyalty, at least on the good sense of its subjects; in the war of the League of Cambray (1509) it absolved them, as is well known, from their oath of allegiance, and let them compare the amenities of a foreign occupation with the mild government to which they had been accustomed. As there had been no treason in their desertion of St Mark, and consequently no punishment was to be feared, they returned to their old masters with the utmost eagerness. This war, we may remark parenthetically, was the result of a century's outcry against the Venetian desire for aggrandizement. The Venetians, in fact, were not free from the mistake of those over-clever people who will credit their opponents with no irrational and inconsiderate conduct. Misled by this optimism, which is, perhaps, a peculiar weakness of aristocracies, they had utterly ignored not only the preparations of Mohammed II for the capture of Constantinople, but even the armaments of Charles VIII, till the unexpected blow fell at last. The League of Cambray was an event of the same character, in so far as it was clearly opposed to the interest of the two chief members, Louis XII and Julius II. The hatred of all Italy against the victorious city seemed to be concentrated in the mind of the Pope, and to have blinded him to the evils of foreign intervention; and as to the policy of Cardinal d'Amboise and his king, Venice ought long before to have recognized it as a piece of malicious imbecility, and to have been thoroughly on its guard. The other members of the League took part in it from that envy which may be a salutary corrective to great wealth and power, but which in itself is a beggarly sentiment. Venice came out of the conflict with honour, but not without lasting damage.

A Power whose foundations were so complicated, whose activity and interests filled so wide a stage, cannot be imagined without a systematic oversight of the whole, without a regular estimate of means and burdens, of profits and losses. Venice can fairly make good its claim to be the birthplace of statistical science, together, perhaps, with Florence, and followed by the more enlightened despotisms. The feudal state of the Middle Ages knew of nothing more than catalogues of signorial rights and possessions *(urbaria);* it looked on production as a fixed quantity, which it approximately is, so long as we have to do with landed property only. The towns, on the other hand, throughout the West must from very early times have treated production, which with them depended on industry and commerce, as exceedingly variable; but even in the most flourishing times of the Hanseatic League they never got beyond a simple commercial balance-sheet. Fleets, armies, political power, and influence fall under the debit and credit of a trader's ledger. In the Italian states a clear political consciousness, the pattern of Mohammedan administration, and the long and active exercise of trade and commerce combined to produce for the first time a true science of statistics. The absolute monarchy of Frederick II in Lower Italy was organized with the sole object of securing a concentrated power for the death-struggle in which he was engaged. In Venice, on the contrary, the supreme objects were the enjoyment of life and power, the increase of inherited advantages, the creation of the most lucrative forms of industry, and the opening of new channels for commerce.

The writers of the time speak of these things with the greatest freedom. We learn that the population of the city amounted in 1422 to 190,000 souls; the Italians were, perhaps, the first to reckon, not according to hearths, or men able to bear arms, or people able to walk, and so forth, but according to *animæ,* and thus to get the most neutral basis for further calculation. About this time, when the Florentines wished to form an alliance with Venice against Filippo Maria Visconti, they were for the moment refused, in the belief, resting on accurate commercial returns, that a war between Venice and Milan—that is, between seller and buyer—was foolish. Even if the Duke simply increased his army the Milanese, through the heavier taxation they must pay, would become worse customers.

> Better let the Florentines be defeated, and then, used as they are to the life of a free city, they will settle with us and bring their silk and woollen industry with them, as the Lucchese did in their distress.

The speech of the dying Doge Mocenigo (1423) to a few of the senators whom he had sent for to his bedside is still more remarkable. It contains the chief elements of a statistical account of the whole resources of Venice. I cannot say whether or where a thorough elucidation of this perplexing document exists; by way of illustration, the following facts may be quoted. After repaying a war-loan of four million ducats the public debt *(il monte)* still amounted to six million ducats; the current trade reached (so it seems) ten millions, which yielded, the text informs us, a profit of four millions. The 3000 *navigli,* the 300 *navi,* and the 45 galleys were manned respectively by 17,000, 8000, and 11,000 seamen (more than 200 for each galley). To these must be added 16,000 shipwrights. The houses in Venice were valued at seven millions, and brought in a rent of half a million. There were 1000 nobles whose income ranged from 70 to 4000 ducats. In another passage the ordinary income of the State in that same year is put at 1,100,000 ducats; through the disturbance of trade caused by the wars it sank about the middle of the century to 800,000 ducats.

If Venice, by this spirit of calculation, and by the practical turn which she gave it, was the first fully to represent one important side of modern political life, in that culture, on the other hand, which Italy then prized most highly she did not stand in the front rank. The literary impulse in general was here wanting, and especially that enthusiasm for classical antiquity which prevailed elsewhere. The aptitude of the Venetians, says Sabellico, for philosophy and eloquence was in itself not less remarkable than for commerce and politics; but this aptitude was neither developed in themselves nor rewarded in strangers as it was rewarded elsewhere in Italy. Filelfo, summoned to Venice not by the State, but by private individuals, soon found his expectations deceived; and George of Trebizond, who in 1459 laid the Latin translation of Plato's laws at the feet of the Doge, and was appointed professor of philology with a yearly salary of a hundred and fifty ducats, and finally dedicated his *Rhetoric* to the Signoria, soon left the city in dissatisfaction. Literature, in fact, like the rest at Venice, had mostly a practical end in view. If, accordingly, we look through the history of Venetian literature which Francesco Sansovino has appended to his well-known book we shall find in the fourteenth century almost nothing but history and special works on theology, jurisprudence, and medicine; and in the fifteenth century, till we come to Ermolao Barbaro and Aldo Manucci, humanistic culture is, for a city of such importance, most scantily represented. Similarly we find comparatively few traces of the passion, elsewhere so strong, for collecting books and manuscripts; and the valuable texts which formed part of Petrarch's legacies were so badly preserved that soon all traces of them were lost. The library which Cardinal Bessarion bequeathed to the State (1468) narrowly escaped dispersion and destruction. Learning was certainly cultivated at the University of Padua, where, however, the physicians and the jurists—the latter as the authors of legal opinions—received by far the highest pay. The share of Venice in the poetical creations of the country was long insignificant, till, at the beginning of the sixteenth century, her deficiencies were made good. Even the art of the Renaissance was imported into the city from without, and it was not before the end of the fifteenth century that she learned to move in this field with independent freedom and strength. But we find more striking instances still of intellectual backwardness. This Government, which had the clergy so thoroughly in its control, which reserved to itself the appointment to all important ecclesiastical offices, and which, one time after another, dared to defy the Court of Rome, displayed an official piety of a most singular kind. The bodies of saints and other relics imported from Greece after the Turkish conquest were bought at the greatest sacrifices and received by the Doge in solemn procession. For the coat without a seam it was decided (1455) to offer 10,000 ducats, but it was not to be had.

These measures were not the fruit of any popular excitement, but of the tranquil resolutions of the heads of the Government, and might have been omitted without attracting any comment, and at Florence, under similar circumstances, would certainly have been omitted. We shall say nothing of the piety of the masses, and of their firm belief in the indulgences of an Alexander VI. But the State itself, after absorbing the Church to a degree unknown elsewhere, had in truth a certain ecclesiastical element in its composition, and the Doge, the symbol of the State, appeared in twelve great processions *(andate)* in a half-clerical character. They were almost all festivals in memory of political events, and competed in splendour with the great feasts of the Church; the most brilliant of all, the famous marriage with the sea, fell on Ascension Day.

The most elevated political thought and the most varied forms of human development are found united in the history of Florence, which in this sense deserves the name of the first modern state in the world. Here the whole people are busied with what in the despotic cities is the affair of a single family. That wondrous Florentine spirit, at once keenly critical and artistically creative, was incessantly transforming the social and political condition of the state, and as incessantly describing and judging the change. Florence thus became the home of political doctrines and theories, of experiments and sudden changes, but also, like Venice, the home of statistical science, and, alone and above all other states in the world, the home of historical representation in the modern sense of the phrase. The spectacle of ancient Rome and a familiarity with its leading writers were not without influence; Giovanni Villani confesses that he received the first impulse to his great work at the jubilee of 1300, and began it immediately on his return home. Yet how many among the 200,000 pilgrims of that year may have been like him in gifts and tendencies, and still did not write the history of their native cities! For not all of them could encourage themselves with the thought: "Rome is sinking; my native city is rising, and ready to achieve great things, and therefore I wish to relate its past history, and hope to continue the story to the present time, and as long as my life shall last." And besides the witness to its past, Florence obtained through its historians something further—a greater fame than fell to the lot of any other city of Italy.

Our present task is not to write the history of this remarkable state, but merely to give a few indications of the intellectual freedom and independence for which the Florentines were indebted to this history.

In no other city of Italy were the struggles of political parties so bitter, of such early origin, and so permanent. The descriptions of them, which belong, it is true, to a somewhat later period, give clear evidence of the superiority of Florentine criticism.

And what a politician is the great victim of these crises, Dante Alighieri, matured alike by home and by exile! He uttered his scorn of the incessant changes and experiments in the constitution of his native city in verses of adamant, which will remain proverbial so long as political events of the same kind recur; he addressed his home in words of defiance and yearning which must have stirred the hearts of his countrymen. But his thoughts ranged over Italy and the whole world; and if his passion for the Empire, as he conceived it, was no more than an illusion, it must yet be admitted that the youthful dreams of a new-born political speculation are in his case not without a poetical grandeur. He is proud to be the first who had trod this path, certainly in the footsteps of Aristotle, but in his own way independently. His ideal Emperor is a just and humane judge, dependent on God only, the heir of the universal sway of Rome, to which belonged the sanction of nature, of right, and of the will of God. The conquest of the world was, according to this view, rightful, resting on a divine judgment between Rome and the other nations of the earth, and God gave His approval to this empire since under it He became Man, submitting at His birth to the census of the Emperor Augustus, and at His death to the judgment of Pontius Pilate. We may find it hard to appreciate these and other arguments of the same kind, but Dante's passion never fails to carry us with him. In his letters he appears as one of the earliest publicists, and is perhaps the first layman to publish political tracts in this form. He began early. Soon after the death of Beatrice he addressed a pamphlet on the state of Florence "to the great ones of the earth," and the public utterances of his later years, dating from the time of his banishment, are all directed to emperors, princes, and cardinals. In these letters and in his book *De Vulgari Eloquentia* the feeling, bought with such bitter pains, is constantly recurring that the exile may find elsewhere than in his native place an intellectual home in language and culture which cannot be taken from him. On this point we shall have more to say in the sequel.

To the two Villani, Giovanni as well as Matteo, we owe not so much deep political reflection as fresh and practical observations, together with the elements of Florentine statistics and important notices of other states. Here too trade and commerce had given the impulse to economical as well as political science. Nowhere else in the world was such accurate information to be had on financial affairs. The wealth of the Papal Court at Avignon, which at the death of John XXII amounted to twenty-five millions of gold florins, would be incredible on any less trustworthy authority. Here only, at Florence, do we meet with colossal loans like that which the King of England contracted from the Florentine houses of Bardi and Peruzzi, who lost to his Majesty the sum of 1,365,000 gold florins (1338)—their own money and that of their partners—and nevertheless recovered from the shock. Most important facts are here recorded as to the condition of Florence at this time: the public income (over 300,000 gold florins) and expenditure; the population of the city, here only roughly estimated, according to the consumption of bread in *bocche—i.e.,* mouths—put at 90,000, and the population of the whole territory; the excess of 300 to 500 male children among the 5800 to 6000 annually baptized; the school-children, of whom 8000 to 10,000 learned reading, 1000 to 1200 in six schools arithmetic; and besides these 600 scholars who were taught Latin grammar and logic in four schools. Then follow the statistics of the churches and monasteries; of the hospitals, which held more than a thousand beds; of the wool trade, with its most valuable details; of the mint, the provisioning of the city, the public officials, and so on. Incidentally we learn many curious facts; how, for instance, when the public funds *(il monte)* were first established, in the year 1353, the Franciscans spoke from the pulpit in favour of the measure, the Dominicans and Augustinians against it. The economical results of the Black Death were and could be observed and described nowhere else in all Europe as in this city. Only a Florentine could have left it on record how it was expected that the scanty population would have made everything cheap, and how instead of that labour and commodities doubled in price; how the common people at first would do no work at all, but simply give themselves up to enjoyment; how in the city itself servants and maids were not to be had except at extravagant wages; how the peasants would only till the best lands, and left the rest uncultivated; and how the enormous legacies bequeathed to the poor at the time of the plague seemed afterward useless, since the poor had either died or had ceased to be poor. Lastly, on the occasion of a great bequest, by which a childless philanthropist left six *danari* to every beggar in the city, the attempt is made to give a comprehensive statistical account of Florentine mendicancy.

This statistical view of things was at a later time still more highly cultivated at Florence. The noteworthy point about it is that, as a rule, we can perceive its connexion with the higher aspects of history, with art, and with culture in general. An inventory of 1422 mentions, within the compass of the same document, the seventy-two exchange offices which surrounded the "Mercato Nuovo"; the amount of coined money in circulation (two million golden florins); the then new industry of gold-spinning; the silk wares; Filippo Brunellesco, then busy in digging classical architecture from its grave; and Leonardo Aretino, secretary of the republic, at work at the revival of ancient literature and eloquence; lastly it speaks of the general prosperity of the city, then free from political conflicts, and of the good fortune of Italy, which had rid itself of foreign mercenaries. The Venetian statistics quoted above, which date from about the same year, certainly give evidence of larger property and profits and of a more extensive scene of action; Venice had long been mistress of the seas before Florence sent out its first galleys (1422) to Alexandria. But no reader can fail to recognize the higher spirit of the Florentine documents. These and similar lists recur at intervals of ten years, systematically arranged and tabulated, while elsewhere we find at best occasional notices. We can form an approximate estimate of the property and the business of the first Medici; they paid for charities, public buildings, and taxes from 1434 to 1471 no less than 633,755 gold florins, of which more than 400,000 fell to Cosimo alone, and Lorenzo the Magnificent was delighted that the money had been so well spent. In 1472 we have again a most important and in its way complete view of the commerce and trades of this city, some of which may be wholly or partly reckoned among the fine arts—such as those which had to do with damasks and gold or silver embroidery, with wood-carving and *intarsia,* with the sculpture of arabesques in marble and sandstone, with portraits in wax, and with jewellery and work in gold. The inborn talent of the Florentines for the systematization of outward life is shown by their books on agriculture, business, and domestic economy, which are markedly superior to those of other European people in the fifteenth century. It has been rightly decided to publish selections of these works, although no little study will be needed to extract clear and definite results from them. At all events, we have no difficulty in recognizing the city, where dying parents begged the Government in their wills to fine their sons 1000 florins if they declined to practise a regular profession.

For the first half of the sixteenth century probably no state in the world possesses a document like the magnificent description of Florence by Varchi. In descriptive statistics, as in so many things besides, yet another model is left to us, before the freedom and greatness of the city sank into the grave.

This statistical estimate of outward life is, however, uniformly accompanied by the narrative of political events to which we have already referred.

Florence not only existed under political forms more varied than those of the free states of Italy and of Europe generally, but it reflected upon them far more deeply. It is a faithful mirror of the relations of individuals and classes to a variable whole. The pictures of the great civic democracies in France and in Flanders, as they are delineated in Froissart, and the narratives of the German chroniclers of the fourteenth century, are in truth of high importance; but in comprehensiveness of thought and in the rational development of the story, none will bear comparison with the Florentines. The rule of the nobility, the tyrannies, the struggles of the middle class with the proletariate, limited and unlimited democracy, pseudo-democracy, the primacy of a single house, the theocracy of

Savonarola, and the mixed forms of government which prepared the way for the Medicean despotism—all are so described that the inmost motives of the actors are laid bare to the light. At length Machiavelli in his Florentine history (down to 1492) represents his native city as a living organism and its development as a natural and individual process; he is the first of the moderns who has risen to such a conception. It lies without our province to determine whether and in what points Machiavelli may have done violence to history, as is notoriously the case in his life of Castruccio Castracane—a fancy picture of the typical despot. We might find something to say against every line of the *Istorie Fiorentine,* and yet the great and unique value of the whole would remain unaffected. And his contemporaries and successors, Jacopo Pitti, Guicciardini, Segni, Varchi, Vettori, what a circle of illustrious names! And what a story it is which these masters tell us! The great and memorable drama of the last decades of the Florentine republic is here unfolded. The voluminous record of the collapse of the highest and most original life which the world could then show may appear to one but as a collection of curiosities, may awaken in another a devilish delight at the shipwreck of so much nobility and grandeur, to a third may seem like a great historical assize; for all it will be an object of thought and study to the end of time. The evil which was for ever troubling the peace of the city was its rule over once powerful and now conquered rivals like Pisa—a rule of which the necessary consequence was a chronic state of violence. The only remedy, certainly an extreme one and which none but Savonarola could have persuaded Florence to accept, and that only with the help of favourable chances, would have been the well-timed resolution of Tuscany into a federal union of free cities. At a later period this scheme, then no more than the dream of a past age, brought (1548) a patriotic citizen of Lucca to the scaffold. From this evil and from the ill-starred Guelph sympathies of Florence for a foreign prince, which familiarized it with foreign intervention, came all the disasters which followed. But who does not admire the people, which was wrought up by its venerated preacher to a mood of such sustained loftiness that for the first time in Italy it set the example of sparing a conquered foe, while the whole history of its past taught nothing but vengeance and extermination? The glow which melted patriotism into one with moral regeneration may seem, when looked at from a distance, to have soon passed away; but its best results shine forth again in the memorable siege of 1529–30. They were "fools," as Guicciardini then wrote, who drew down this storm upon Florence, but he confesses himself that they achieved things which seemed incredible; and when he declares that sensible people would have got out of the way of the danger he means no more than that Florence ought to have yielded itself silently and ingloriously into the hands of its enemies. It would no doubt have preserved its splendid suburbs and gardens and the lives and prosperity of countless citizens; but it would have been the poorer by one of its greatest and most ennobling memories.

In many of their chief merits the Florentines are the pattern and the earliest type of Italians and modern Europeans generally; they are so also in many of their defects. When Dante compares the city which was always mending its constitution with the sick man who is continually changing his posture to escape from pain, he touches with the comparison a permanent feature of the political life of Florence. The great modern fallacy that a constitution can be made, can be manufactured by a combination of existing forces and tendencies, was constantly cropping up in stormy times; even Machiavelli is not wholly free from it. Constitutional artists were never wanting who by an ingenious distribution and division of political power, by indirect elections of the most complicated kind, by the establishment of nominal offices, sought to found a lasting order of things, and to satisfy or to deceive the rich and the poor alike. They naïvely fetch their examples from classical antiquity, and borrow the party names *ottimati, aristocrazia,* as a matter of course. The world since then has become used to these expressions and given them a conventional European sense, whereas all former party names were purely national, and either characterized the cause at issue or sprang from the caprice of accident. But how a name colours or discolours a political cause!

But of all who thought it possible to construct a state the greatest beyond all comparison was Machiavelli. He treats existing forces as living and active, takes a large and an accurate view of alternative possibilities, and seeks to mislead neither himself nor others. No man could be freer from vanity or ostentation; indeed, he does not write for the public, but either for princes and administrators or for personal friends. The danger for him does not lie in an affection of genius or in a false order of ideas, but rather in a powerful imagination which he evidently controls with difficulty. The objectivity of his political judgment is sometimes appalling in its sincerity; but it is the sign of a time of no ordinary need and peril when it was a hard matter to believe in right, or to credit others with just dealing. Virtuous indignation at his expense is thrown away upon us who have seen in what sense political morality is understood by the statesmen of our own century. Machiavelli was at all events able to forget himself in his cause. In truth, although his writings, with the exception of very few words, are altogether destitute of enthusiasm, and although the Florentines themselves treated him at last as a criminal, he was a patriot in the fullest meaning of the word. But free as he was, like most of his contemporaries, in speech and morals, the welfare of the State was yet his first and last thought.

His most complete programme for the construction of a new political system at Florence is set forth in the memorial to Leo X, composed after the death of the younger Lorenzo de' Medici, Duke of Urbino (d. 1519), to whom he had dedicated his *Prince.* The State was by that time in extremities and utterly corrupt, and the remedies proposed are not always morally justifiable; but it is most interesting to see how he hopes to set up the republic in the form of a moderate democracy, as heiress to the Medici. A more ingenious scheme of concessions to the Pope, to the Pope's various adherents, and to the different Florentine interests cannot be imagined; we might fancy ourselves looking into the works of a clock. Principles, observations, comparisons, political forecasts, and the like are to be found in numbers in the *Discorsi,* among them flashes of wonderful insight. He recognizes, for example, the law of a continuous though not uniform development in republican institutions, and requires the constitution to be flexible and capable of change, as the only means of dispensing with bloodshed and banishments. For a like reason, in order to guard against private violence and foreign interference—"the death of all freedom"—he wishes to see introduced a judicial procedure *(accusa)* against hated citizens, in place of which Florence had hitherto had nothing but the court of scandal. The tardy and involuntary decisions, which at critical moments play so important a part in republican states, are characterized with a masterly hand. Once, it is true, he is misled by his imagination and the pressure of events into unqualified praise of the people, which chooses its officers, he says, better than any prince, and which can be cured of its errors by "good advice." With regard to the government of Tuscany, he has no doubt that it belongs to his native city, and maintains in a special *Discorso* that the reconquest of Pisa is a question of life or death; he deplores that Arezzo, after the rebellion of 1502, was not razed to the ground; he admits in general that Italian republics must be allowed to expand freely and add to their territory in order to enjoy peace at home, and not to be themselves attacked by others, but declares that Florence had always begun at the wrong end, and from the first made deadly enemies of Pisa, Lucca, and Siena, while Pistoja, "treated like a brother," had voluntarily submitted to her.

It would be unreasonable to draw a parallel between the few other republics which still existed in the fifteenth century and this unique city—the most important workshop of the Italian and, indeed, of the modern European spirit. Siena suffered from the gravest organic maladies, and its relative prosperity in art and industry must not mislead us on this point. Aeneas Sylvius looks with longing from his native town over to the "merry" German Imperial cities, where life is embittered by no confiscations of land and goods, by no arbitrary officials, and by no political factions. Genoa scarcely comes within range of our task, as before the time of Andrea Doria it took almost no part in the Renaissance. Indeed, the inhabitant of the Riviera was proverbial among Italians for his contempt of all higher culture. Party conflicts here assumed so fierce a character, and disturbed so violently the whole course of life, that we can hardly understand how, after so many revolutions and invasions, the Genoese ever contrived to return to an endurable condition. Perhaps it was owing to the fact that nearly all who took part in public affairs were at the same time almost without exception active men of business. The example of Genoa shows in a striking manner with what insecurity wealth and vast commerce, and with what internal disorder the possession of distant colonies, are compatible.

Lucca is of small significance in the fifteenth century.

Chapter 8. The Foreign Policy of the Italian States

As the majority of the Italian states were in their internal constitution works of art—that is, the fruit of reflection and careful adaptation—so was their relation to one another and to foreign countries also a work of art. That nearly all of them were the result of recent usurpations was a fact which exercised as fatal an influence in their foreign as in their internal policy. Not one of them recognized another without reserve; the same play of chance which had helped to found and consolidate one dynasty might upset another. Nor was it always a matter of choice with the despot whether to keep quiet or not. The necessity of movement and aggrandizement is common to all illegitimate powers. Thus Italy became the scene of a "foreign policy" which gradually, as in other countries also, acquired the position of a recognized system of public law. The purely objective treatment of international affairs, as free from prejudice as from moral scruples, attained a perfection which sometimes is not without a certain beauty and grandeur of its own. But as a whole it gives us the impression of a bottomless abyss.

Intrigues, armaments, leagues, corruption, and treason make up the outward history of Italy at this period. Venice in particular was long accused on all hands of seeking to conquer the whole peninsula, or gradually so to reduce its strength that one state after another must fall into her hands. But on a closer view it is evident that this complaint did not come from the people, but rather from the courts and official classes, which were commonly abhorred by their subjects, while the mild government of Venice had secured for it general confidence. Even Florence, with its restive subject cities, found itself in a false position with regard to Venice, apart from all commercial jealousy and from the progress of Venice in Romagna. At last the League of Cambray actually did strike a serious blow at the state which all Italy ought to have supported with united strength.

The other states also were animated by feelings no less unfriendly, and were at all times ready to use against one another any weapon which their evil conscience might suggest. Lodovico il Moro, the Aragonese Kings of Naples, and Sixtus IV—to say nothing of the smaller Powers—kept Italy in a state of constant and perilous agitation. It would have been well if the atrocious game had been confined to Italy; but it lay in the nature of the case that intervention and help should at last be sought from abroad—in particular from the French and the Turks.

The sympathies of the people at large were throughout on the side of France. Florence had never ceased to confess with shocking *naïveté* its old Guelph preference for the French. And when Charles VIII actually appeared on the south of the Alps all Italy accepted him with an enthusiasm which to himself and his followers seemed unaccountable. In the imagination of the Italians, to take Savonarola for an example, the ideal picture of a wise, just, and powerful saviour and ruler was still living, with the difference that he was no longer the Emperor invoked by Dante, but the Capetian King of France. With his departure the illusion was broken; but it was long before all understood how completely Charles VIII, Louis XII, and Francis I had mistaken their true relation to Italy and by what inferior motives they were led. The princes, for their part, tried to make use of France in a wholly different way. When the Franco-English wars came to an end, when Louis XI began to cast about his diplomatic nets on all sides, and Charles of Burgundy to embark on his foolish adventures, the Italian Cabinets came to meet them at every point. It became clear that the intervention of France was only a question of time, even though the claims on Naples and Milan had never existed, and that the old interference with Genoa and Piedmont was only a type of what was to follow. The Venetians, in fact, expected it as early as 1642. The mortal terror of the Duke Galeazzo Maria of Milan during the Burgundian war, in which he was apparently the ally of Charles as well as of Louis, and consequently had reason to dread an attack from both, is strikingly shown in his correspondence. The plan of an equilibrium of the four chief Italian Powers, as understood by Lorenzo the Magnificent, was but the assumption of a cheerful, optimistic spirit, which had outgrown both the recklessness of an experimental policy and the superstitions of Florentine Guelphism, and persisted in hoping the best. When Louis XI offered him aid in the war against Ferrante of Naples and Sixtus IV he replied: "I cannot set my own advantage above the safety of all Italy; would to God it never came into the mind of the French kings to try their strength in this country! Should they ever do so, Italy is lost." For the other princes, the King of France was alternately a bugbear to themselves and their enemies, and they threatened to call him in whenever they saw no more convenient way out of their difficulties. The Popes, in their turn, fancied that they could make use of France without any danger to themselves, and even Innocent VIII imagined that he could withdraw to sulk in the North and return as a conqueror to Italy at the head of a French army.

Thoughtful men, indeed, foresaw the foreign conquest long before the expedition of Charles VIII. And when Charles was back again on the other side of the Alps it was plain to every eye that an era of intervention had begun. Misfortune now followed on misfortune; it was understood too late that France and Spain, the two chief invaders, had become great European Powers, that they would be no longer satisfied with verbal homage, but would fight to the death for influence and territory in Italy. They had begun to resemble the centralized Italian states, and, indeed, to copy them, only on a gigantic scale. Schemes of annexation or exchange of territory were for a time indefinitely multiplied. The end, as is well known, was the complete victory of Spain, which, as sword and shield of the Counter-Reformation, long held the Papacy among its other subjects. The melancholy reflections of the philosophers could only show them how those who had called in the barbarians all came to a bad end.

Alliances were at the same time formed with the Turks too, with as little scruple or disguise; they were reckoned no worse than any other political expedients. The belief in the unity of Western Christendom had at various times in the course of the Crusades been seriously shaken, and Frederick II had probably outgrown it. But the fresh advance of the Oriental nations, the need and the ruin of the Greek Empire, had revived the old feeling, though not in its former strength, throughout Western Europe. Italy, however, was a striking exception to this rule. Great as was the terror felt for the Turks and the actual danger from them, there was yet scarcely a Government of any consequence which did not conspire against other Italian states with Mohammed II and his successors. And when they did not do so, they still had the credit of it; nor was it worse than the sending of emissaries to poison the cisterns of Venice, which was the charge brought against the heirs of Alfonso, King of Naples. From a scoundrel like Sigismondo Malatesta nothing better could be expected than that he should call the Turks into Italy. But the Aragonese monarchs of Naples, from whom Mohammed—at the instigation, we read, of other Italian Governments, especially of Venice—had once wrested Otranto (1480), afterward hounded on the Sultan Bajazet II against the Venetians. The same charge was brought against Lodovico il Moro. "The blood of the slain, and the misery of the prisoners in the hands of the Turks, cry to God for vengeance against him," says the State historian. In Venice, where the Government was informed of everything, it was known that Giovanni Sforza, ruler of Pesaro, the cousin of the Moor, had entertained the Turkish ambassadors on their way to Milan. The two most respectable among the Popes of the fifteenth century, Nicholas V and Pius II, died in the deepest grief at the progress of the Turks, the latter, indeed, amid the preparations for a crusade which he was hoping to lead in person; their successors embezzled the contributions sent for this purpose from all parts of Christendom, and degraded the indulgences granted in return for them into a private commercial speculation. Innocent VIII consented to be gaoler to the fugitive Prince Djem for a salary paid by the prisoner's brother, Bajazet II, and Alexander VI supported the steps taken by Lodovico il Moro in Constantinople to further a Turkish assault upon Venice (1498), whereupon the latter threatened him with a Council. It is clear that the notorious alliance between Francis I and Soliman II was nothing new or unheard of.

Indeed, we find instances of whole populations to whom it seemed no particular crime to go over bodily to the Turks. Even if it were only held out as a threat to oppressive Governments, this is at least a proof that the idea had become familiar. As early as 1480 Battista Mantovano gives us clearly to understand that most of the inhabitants of the Adriatic coast foresaw something of this kind, and that Ancona in particular desired it. When Romagna was suffering from the oppressive Government of Leo X a deputy from Ravenna said openly to the legate, Cardinal Giulio de' Medici: "Monsignore, the honourable Republic of Venice will not have us, for fear of a dispute with the Holy See; but if the Turk comes to Ragusa we will put ourselves into his hands."

It was a poor but not wholly groundless consolation for the enslavement of Italy then begun by the Spaniards that the country was at least secured from the relapse into barbarism, which would have awaited it under the Turkish rule. By itself, divided as it was, it could hardly have escaped this fate.

If, with all these drawbacks, the Italian statesmanship of this period deserves our praise, it is only on the ground of its practical and unprejudiced treatment of those questions which were not affected by fear, passion, or malice. Here was no feudal system after the Northern fashion, with its artificial scheme of rights; but the power which each possessed he held in practice as in theory. Here was no attendant nobility to foster in the mind of the prince the medieval sense of honour, with all its strange consequences; but princes and counsellors were agreed in acting according to the exigencies of the particular case and to the end they had in view. Toward the men whose services were used and toward allies, come from what quarter they might, no pride of caste was felt which could possibly estrange a supporter; and the class of the *condottieri,* in which birth was a matter of indifference, shows clearly enough in what sort of hands the real power lay; and lastly, the Government, in the hands of an enlightened despot, had an incomparably more accurate acquaintance with its own country and that of its neighbours than was possessed by Northern contemporaries, and estimated the economical and moral capacities of friend and foe down to the smallest particular. The rulers were, notwithstanding grave errors, born masters of statistical science. With such men negotiation was possible; it might be presumed that they would be convinced and their opinion modified when practical reasons were laid before them. When the great Alfonso of Naples was (1434) a prisoner of Filippo Maria Visconti he was able to satisfy his gaoler that the rule of the house of Anjou instead of his own at Naples would make the French masters of Italy; Filippo Maria set him free without ransom and made an alliance with him. A Northern prince would scarcely have acted in the same way, certainly not one whose morality in other respects was like that of Visconti. What confidence was felt in the power of self-interest is shown by the celebrated visit which Lorenzo the Magnificent, to the universal astonishment of the Florentines, paid the faithless Ferrante at Naples—a man who would be certainly tempted to keep him a prisoner, and was by no means too scrupulous to do so. For to arrest a powerful monarch, and then to let him go alive, after extorting his signature and otherwise insulting him, as Charles the Bold did to Louis XI at Péronne (1468), seemed madness to the Italians; so that Lorenzo was expected to come back covered with glory, or else not to come back at all. The art of political persuasion was at this time raised to a point—especially by the Venetian ambassadors—of which Northern nations first obtained a conception from the Italians, and of which the official addresses give a most imperfect idea. These are mere pieces of humanistic rhetoric. Nor, in spite of an otherwise ceremonious etiquette, was there in case of need any lack of rough and frank speaking in diplomatic intercourse. A man like Machiavelli appears in his *legazioni* in an almost pathetic light. Furnished with scanty instructions, shabbily equipped, and treated as an agent of inferior rank, he never loses his gift of free and wide observation or his pleasure in picturesque description. From that time Italy was and remained the country of political *istruzioni* and *relazioni.* There was doubtless plenty of diplomatic ability in other states, but Italy alone at so early a period has preserved documentary evidence of it in considerable quantity. The long dispatch on the last period of the life of Ferrante of Naples (January 17, 1494), written by the hand of Pontano and addressed to the Cabinet of Alexander VI, gives us the highest opinion of this class of political writing, although it is only quoted incidentally and as one of many written. And how many other dispatches, as important and as vigorously written, in the diplomatic intercourse of this and later times still remain unknown or unedited!

A special division of this work will treat of the study of man individually and nationally, which among the Italians went hand in hand with the study of the outward conditions of human life.

Chapter 9. War as a Work of Art

It must here be briefly indicated by what steps the art of war assumed the character of a product of reflection. Throughout the countries of the West the education of the individual soldier in the Middle Ages was perfect within the limits of the then prevalent system of defence and attack: nor was there any want of ingenious inventors in the arts of besieging and of fortification. But the development both of strategy and of tactics was hindered by the character and duration of military service, and by the ambition of the nobles, who disputed questions of precedence in the face of the enemy, and through simple want of discipline caused the loss of great battles like Crécy and Maupertuis. Italy, on the contrary, was the first country to adopt the system of mercenary troops, which demanded a wholly different organization; and the early introduction of firearms did its part in making war a democratic pursuit not only because the strongest castles were unable to withstand a bombardment, but because the skill of the engineer, of the gun-founder, and of the artillerist—men belonging to another class than the nobility—was now of the first importance in a campaign. It was felt, with regret, that the value of the individual, which had been the soul of the small and admirably organized bands of mercenaries, would suffer from these novel means of destruction, which did their work at a distance; and there were *condottieri* who opposed to the utmost the introduction at least of the musket, which had been lately invented in Germany. We read that Paolo Vitelli, while recognizing and himself adopting the cannon, put out the eyes and cut off the hands of the captured *schioppettieri* of the enemy, because he held it unworthy that a gallant, and it might be noble, knight should be wounded and laid low by a common, despised foot-soldier. On the whole, however, the new discoveries were accepted and turned to useful account, till the Italians became the teachers of all Europe, both in the building of fortifications and in the means of attacking them. Princes like Federigo of Urbino and Alfonso of Ferrara acquired a mastery of the subject compared to which the knowledge even of Maximilian I appears superficial. In Italy, earlier than elsewhere, there existed a comprehensive science and art of military affairs; here, for the first time, that impartial delight is taken in able generalship for its own sake, which might, indeed, be expected from the frequent change of party and from the wholly unsentimental mode of action of the *condottieri.* During the Milano-Venetian war of 1451 and 1452, between Francesco Sforza and Jacopo Piccinino, the headquarters of the latter were attended by the scholar Gian Antonio Porcello dei Pandoni, commissioned by Alfonso of Naples to write a report of the campaign. It is written, not in the purest, but in a fluent Latin, a little too much in the style of the humanistic bombast of the day, is modelled on Cæsar's *Commentaries,* and interspersed with speeches, prodigies, and the like. Since for the past hundred years it had been seriously disputed whether Scipio Africanus or Hannibal was the greater, Piccinino through the whole book must needs be called Scipio and Sforza Hannibal. But something positive had to be reported too respecting the Milanese army; the sophist presented himself to Sforza, was led along the ranks, praised highly all that he saw, and promised to hand it down to posterity. Apart from him the Italian literature of the day is rich in descriptions of wars and strategic devices, written for the use of educated men in general as well as of specialists, while the contemporary narratives of Northerners, such as the *Burgundian Wars* by Diebold Schilling, still retain the shapelessness and matter-of-fact dryness of a mere chronicle. The greatest *dilettante* who has ever treated in that character of military affairs was then busy writing his *Arte della Guerra.* But the development of the individual soldier found its most complete expression in those public and solemn conflicts between one or more pairs of combatants which were practised long before the famous *Challenge of Barletta* (1503). The victor was assured of the praises of poets and scholars, which were denied to the Northern warrior. The result of these combats was no longer regarded as a divine judgment, but as a triumph of personal merit, and to the minds of the spectators seemed to be both the decision of an exciting competition and a satisfaction for the honour of the army or the nation.

It is obvious that this purely rational treatment of warlike affairs allowed, under certain circumstances, of the worst atrocities, even in the absence of a strong political hatred, as, for instance, when the plunder of a city had been promised to the troops. After the four days' devastation of Piacenza, which Sforza was compelled to permit to his soldiers (1447), the town long stood empty, and at last had to be peopled by force. Yet outrages like these were nothing compared with the misery which was afterward brought upon Italy by foreign troops, and most of all by the Spaniards, in whom perhaps a touch of Oriental blood, perhaps familiarity with the spectacles of the Inquisition, had unloosed the devilish element of human nature. After seeing them at work at Prato, Rome, and elsewhere it is not easy to take any interest of the higher sort in Ferdinand the Catholic and Charles V, who knew what these hordes were, and yet unchained them. The mass of documents which are gradually brought to light from the cabinets of these rulers will always remain an important source of historical information; but from such men no fruitful political conception can be looked for.

Francis Parkman 1823—1893

7

During the commemorative service held at Harvard University in his honor, Professor John Fiske said of Francis Parkman that his work of almost fifty years, the history of *France and England in North America,* "was a book for all mankind and for all time." Funeral panegyrics are often extravagant, especially when uttered by grateful associates, and the one offered on this occasion was no exception. Parkman had been a dedicated Overseer at Harvard and a Fellow of the Corporation for many years after his graduation; however, his life's work was not a book designed to please, or even one fair-minded about all mankind. The eight exquisitely written volumes that make up his account of the struggle of France and England for supremacy in the New World express a point of view and an attitude that offended many when the books were published, and probably infuriate at least as many readers today.

Yet it is for the foregoing reason that this work is of great interest and importance —it represents a peculiarly American, or rather Bostonian and Anglo-Saxon, interpretation of the adventures and turmoil involved in the conquest of a continent. Parkman's history deserves its status as a classic not only because it articulates the mentality of the Federalist oligarchy of New England in the nineteenth century but because it is, in addition, a beautiful book. No American historian has ever matched Parkman's consummate skill as a literary artist. His bias is as obvious as is his ability to write vividly, movingly, and poetically.

In his brief *Autobiography,* Parkman recorded that it was early in his sophomore year at Harvard that he conceived the plan of writing "the story of what was then known as the 'Old French War,' that is, the war that ended in the conquest of Canada. . . . My theme fascinated me, and I was haunted with wilderness images day and night. . . . I enlarged the plan to include the whole course of the American conflict between France and England, or, in other words, the history of the American forest." It was, indeed, his love of the American wilderness which inspired a work that would occupy him for the rest of his life and which made that work the artistic achievement that it was. Before college and during all of his summer vacations from Cambridge, he ventured forth to the American forest, first through New England by horseback, keeping a journal in which he described the forest, the crags, and the cliffs that enchanted him; then to the northern lakes, including Lake Champlain, where much of his history was to take place; and finally up the inland waterways, along the St. Lawrence to Quebec. After graduation he joined his cousin in an extraordinary adventure for young Bostonian gentlemen: they set off to see the frontier, observe the Indians, explore the Ohio Valley, and follow the Oregon Trail, *terra incognita.*

The Oregon Trail first appeared serially in the *Knickerbocker Magazine* in 1847. Parkman's journals furnished the firsthand material for the articles, and his discipline and skill as a literary craftsman produced descriptions that conjure up a closeness to nature that is generally the accomplishment of the poet. As a thunderstorm arrives, Parkman writes, "the old familiar black heads of thunder clouds rise above the horizon, and the same deep muttering of distant thunder that had become the ordinary accompaniment of our afternoon's journey began to fall hoarsely over the prairie. . . . Suddenly from the densest fold of the cloud, the flash leaped out, quivering again and again down to the edge of the prairie . . ." *The Oregon Trail* is obviously a work of great adventure and excitement; it is also the work of a "Boston Brahmin," "the Harvard snob," who developed a condescending interest in the savage Indian and in the crude trapper, as well as an absolute loathing for the middle-class settler. In many ways we are fortunate to have Parkman's impressions unfiltered by the sociological jargon and uncensored by the liberal superego of later generations.

Perhaps the most extraordinary aspects of Parkman's career as a historian were the tremendous nervous strain and physical pain he endured while writing his history. From his teen-age years to the very end of his life he was intermittently plagued by terrible headaches, insomnia, and semi-blindness. In a letter to his friend Reverend Henri Raymond Casgrain, Parkman described his private hell: "The trouble comes from an abnormal state or partial paralysis of certain arteries of the brain. Whatever it is, it is a nuisance of the first order, and a school of patience by which Job himself might have profited. . . . Providence permitting I will spite the devil yet." After an initial encounter with the "enemy," as he personified his affliction, his family sent the young man on a tour of Europe, which he enjoyed and which helped relieve the symptoms. As an adult, after the death of his wife and son, he went to Paris to consult with a famous specialist, but no one could cure the disease. The historian himself found the only respite from his suffering: work. The devil could never be sufficiently spited, but the torments he inflicted could from time to time be held in abeyance by Parkman's will to write history.

Fearing that he would not live long enough to execute the complete design of *France and England in North America,* he did not begin his narrative with the French colonization of Canada, but rather with the dramatic attempt of the Indians in 1763 to drive the European settlers back to the line of the Appalachians. Parkman published his interpretation of the last great Indian offensive in 1851 and entitled it *The Conspiracy of Pontiac.* His conclusion that the uprising was an irresponsible plot initiated by the redoubtable Indian chief has been challenged by modern research and condemned by present-day sensitivity to the plight of the American Indian, but his story was, as always, moving and heroic.

When the Civil War broke out, Parkman cursed his private "enemy" for preventing him from fighting for the Union. He wrote letters to the newspapers endorsing the cause of his class and section of the country, and with renewed energy turned again to his history. He sent for bundles of manuscripts from Parisian archives, and was able to make several journeys to Europe in search of documents between the years 1868 and 1887. When he was too ill to read, he had his sources read to him; and when the pain of arthritis deprived him of his ability to take pen in hand, he dictated his work or employed a wire device to enable him to write. In 1865, *Pioneers of France in the New World* was published, and the remaining six volumes appeared at uneven intervals until the year before his death.

The theme of Parkman's story is the victory of English liberty over French absolutism in the New World. To him the survival of French Canada would have been nothing short of a miracle. He wrote in *The Old Régime in Canada* (1874), from which we have taken our selections, that "an ignorant population sprung from a brave and active race, but trained to subjection and dependence through centuries of feudal and monarchical despotism, was planted in the wilderness . . . and told to go and grow and flourish. . . . Freedom is for those who are fit for it; the rest will lose it, or turn it to corruption." Such a clearly defined and confidently stated thesis calls for little comment, but it invites a good deal of criticism for its failure to account for the complexities that made the English victorious over the French. Parkman's confidence was guided by his conviction that "England imposed by the sword on reluctant Canada the boon of rational and ordered liberty." The entire multi-volume history is infused with Parkman's exuberance for his subject, as is evident from our first selection, which depicts Champlain's arrival at Quebec.

When Parkman could take some time from his history, and when he was well enough, he pursued his interest in horticulture and wrote some articles about his experiments in his garden. He also turned out newspaper articles in an effort to stem the trend in the Republic toward what he believed to be excessive democracy. He proudly believed in a limited suffrage based on merit, and in the cultivation of an educated class that could govern the nation and stave off the ever present threat of demagoguery.

There is no small amount of irony in the title of the last volume of Parkman's history, *Half-Century of Conflict.* For most of his life he struggled against an insidious "enemy," and although he finally lost the conflict, he surely set a very high standard of historical scholarship and secured for himself an incomparable place in the history of historical prose.

Selected Bibliography

A useful introduction to Parkman is Richard Sonderegger's *Francis Parkman* (1951), published in the *Historiadores de América* series. Mason Wade's biography, *Francis Parkman: Heroic Historian* (1942), is complete, critical, and lucid. Howard Doughty's *Francis Parkman* (1962) is sound and interesting, but adds little to Wade's work. Otto A. Pease has, with good cause and reasonable success, written a detailed monograph on Parkman's style, entitled *Parkman's History: The Historian as Literary Artist* (1968).

THE OLD RÉGIME IN CANADA

Chapter 9. 1608, 1609. Champlain at Quebec

A lonely ship sailed up the St. Lawrence. The white whales floundering in the Bay of Tadoussac, and the wild duck diving as the foaming prow drew near,—there was no life but these in all that watery solitude, twenty miles from shore to shore. The ship was from Honfleur, and was commanded by Samuel de Champlain. He was the Aeneas of a destined people, and in her womb lay the embryo life of Canada.

De Monts, after his exclusive privilege of trade was revoked and his Acadian enterprise ruined, had, as we have seen, abandoned it to Poutrincourt. Perhaps would it have been well for him had he abandoned with it all Transatlantic enterprises; but the passion for discovery and the noble ambition of founding colonies had taken possession of his mind. These, rather than a mere hope of gain, seem to have been his controlling motives; yet the profits of the fur-trade were vital to the new designs he was meditating, to meet the heavy outlay they demanded, and he solicited and obtained a fresh monopoly of the traffic for one year.

Champlain was, at the time, in Paris; but his unquiet thoughts turned westward. He was enamoured of the New World, whose rugged charms had seized his fancy and his heart; and as explorers of Arctic seas have pined in their repose for polar ice and snow, so did his restless thoughts revert to the fog-wrapped coasts, the piny odors of forests, the noise of waters, the sharp and piercing sunlight, so dear to his remembrance. He longed to unveil the mystery of that boundless wilderness, and plant the Catholic faith and the power of France amid its ancient barbarism.

Five years before, he had explored the St. Lawrence as far as the rapids above Montreal. On its banks, as he thought, was the true site for a settlement,—a fortified post, whence, as from a secure basis, the waters of the vast interior might be traced back towards their sources, and a western route discovered to China and Japan. For the fur-trade, too, the innumerable streams that descended to the great river might all be closed against foreign intrusion by a single fort at some commanding point, and made tributary to a rich and permanent commerce; while—and this was nearer to his heart, for he had often been heard to say that the saving of a soul was worth more than the conquest of an empire—

countless savage tribes, in the bondage of Satan, might by the same avenues be reached and redeemed.

De Monts embraced his views; and, fitting out two ships, gave command of one to the elder Pontgravé, of the other to Champlain. The former was to trade with the Indians and bring back the cargo of furs which, it was hoped, would meet the expense of the voyage. To Champlain fell the harder task of settlement and exploration.

Pontgravé, laden with goods for the Indian trade of Tadoussac, sailed from Honfleur on the fifth of April, 1608. Champlain, with men, arms, and stores for the colony, followed, eight days later. On the fifteenth of May he was on the Grand Bank; on the thirtieth he passed Gaspé, and on the third of June neared Tadoussac. No living thing was to be seen. He anchored, lowered a boat, and rowed into the port, round the rocky point at the southeast, then, from the fury of its winds and currents, called La Pointe de Tous les Diables. There was life enough within, and more than he cared to find. In the still anchorage under the cliffs lay Pontgravé's vessel, and at her side another ship, which proved to be a Basque fur-trader.

Pontgravé, arriving a few days before, had found himself anticipated by the Basques, who were busied in a brisk trade with bands of Indians cabined along the borders of the cove. He displayed the royal letters, and commanded a cessation of the prohibited traffic; but the Basques proved refractory, declared that they would trade in spite of the King, fired on Pontgravé with cannon and musketry, wounded him and two of his men, and killed a third. They then boarded his vessel, and carried away all his cannon, small arms, and ammunition, saying that they would restore them when they had finished their trade and were ready to return home.

Champlain found his comrade on shore, in a disabled condition. The Basques, though still strong enough to make fight, were alarmed for the consequences of their conduct, and anxious to come to terms. A peace, therefore, was signed on board their vessel; all differences were referred to the judgment of the French courts, harmony was restored, and the choleric strangers betook themselves to catching whales.

This port of Tadoussac was long the centre of the Canadian fur-trade. A desolation of barren mountains closes round it, betwixt whose ribs of rugged granite, bristling with savins, birches, and firs, the Saguenay rolls its gloomy waters from the northern wilderness. Centuries of civilization have not tamed the wildness of the place; and still, in grim repose, the mountains hold their guard around the waveless lake that glistens in their shadow, and doubles, in its sullen mirror, crag, precipice, and forest.

Near the brink of the cove or harbor where the vessels lay, and a little below the mouth of a brook which formed one of the outlets of this small lake, stood the remains of the wooden barrack built by Chauvin eight years before. Above the brook were the lodges of an Indian camp, — stacks of poles covered with birch-bark. They belonged to an Algonquin horde, called *Montagnais,* denizens of surrounding wilds, and gatherers of their only harvest,—skins of the moose, caribou, and bear; fur of the beaver, marten, otter, fox, wild-cat, and lynx. Nor was this all, for there were intermediate traders betwixt the French and the shivering bands who roamed the weary stretch of stunted forest between the head-waters of the Saguenay and Hudson's Bay. Indefatigable canoe-men, in their birchen vessels, light as egg-shells, they threaded the devious tracks of countless rippling streams, shady by-ways of the forest, where the wild duck scarcely finds depth to swim; then descended to their mart along those scenes of picturesque yet dreary grandeur which steam has made familiar to modern tourists. With slowly moving paddles, they glided beneath the cliff whose shaggy brows frown across the zenith, and whose base the deep waves wash with a hoarse and hollow cadence; and they passed the sepulchral Bay of the Trinity, dark as the tide of Acheron,—a sanctuary of solitude and silence: depths which, as the fable runs, no sounding line can fathom, and heights at whose dizzy verge the wheeling eagle seems a speck.

Peace being established with the Basques, and the wounded Pontgravé busied, as far as might be, in transferring to the hold of his ship the rich lading of the Indian canoes, Champlain spread his sails, and again held his course up the St. Lawrence. Far to the south, in sun and shadow, slumbered the woody mountains whence fell the countless springs of the St. John, behind tenantless shores, now white with glimmering villages, —La Chenaie, Granville, Kamouraska, St. Roche, St. Jean, Vincelot, Berthier. But on the north the jealous wilderness still asserts its sway, crowding to the river's verge its walls, domes, and towers of granite; and, to this hour, its solitude is scarcely broken.

Above the point of the Island of Orleans, a constriction of the vast channel narrows it to less than a mile, with the green heights of Point Levi on one side, and on the other the cliffs of Quebec. Here, a small stream, the St. Charles, enters the St. Lawrence, and in the angle betwixt them rises the promontory, on two sides a natural fortress. Between the cliffs and the river lay a strand covered with walnuts and other trees. From this strand, by a rough passage gullied downward from the place where Prescott Gate now guards the way, one might climb the heights to the broken plateau above, now burdened with its ponderous load of churches, convents, dwellings, ramparts, and batteries. Thence, by a gradual ascent, the rock sloped upward to its highest summit, Cape Diamond, looking down on the St. Lawrence from a height of three hundred and fifty feet. Here the citadel now stands; then the fierce sun fell on the bald, baking rock, with its crisped mosses and parched lichens. Two centuries and a half have quickened the solitude with swarming life, covered the deep bosom of the river with barge and steamer and gliding sail, and reared cities and villages on the site of forests; but nothing can destroy the surpassing grandeur of the scene.

On the strand between the water and the cliffs Champlain's axemen fell to their work. They were pioneers of an advancing host,—advancing, it is true, with feeble and uncertain progress,—priests, soldiers, peasants, feudal scutcheons, royal insignia: not the Middle Age, but engendered of it by the stronger life of modern centralization, sharply stamped with a parental likeness, heir to parental weakness and parental force.

In a few weeks a pile of wooden buildings rose on the brink of the St. Lawrence, on or near the site of the market-place of the Lower Town of Quebec. The pencil of Champlain, always regardless of proportion and perspective, has preserved its likeness. A strong wooden wall, surmounted by a gallery loopholed for musketry, enclosed three buildings, containing quarters for himself and his men, together with a courtyard, from one side of which rose a tall dove-cot, like a belfry. A moat surrounded the whole, and two or three small cannon were planted on salient platforms towards the river. There was a large storehouse near at hand, and a part of the adjacent ground was laid out as a garden.

In this garden Champlain was one morning directing his laborers, when Têtu, his pilot, approached him with an anxious countenance, and muttered a request to speak with him in private. Champlain assenting, they withdrew to the neighboring woods, when the pilot disburdened himself of his secret. One Antoine Natel, a locksmith, smitten by conscience or fear, had revealed to him a conspiracy to murder his commander and deliver Quebec into the hands of the Basques and Spaniards then at Tadoussac. Another locksmith, named Duval, was author of the plot, and, with the aid of three accomplices, had befooled or frightened nearly all the company into taking part in it. Each was assured that he should make his fortune, and all were mutually pledged to poniard the first betrayer of the secret. The critical point of their enterprise was the killing of Champlain. Some were for strangling him, some for raising a false alarm in the night and shooting him as he came out from his quarters.

Having heard the pilot's story, Champlain, remaining in the woods, desired his informant to find Antoine Natel, and bring him to the spot. Natel soon appeared, trembling with excitement and fear, and a close examination left no doubt of the truth of his statement. A small vessel, built by Pontgravé at Tadoussac, had lately arrived, and orders were now given that it should anchor close at hand. On board was a young man in whom confidence could be placed. Champlain sent him two bottles of wine, with a direction to tell the four ringleaders that they had been given him by his Basque friends at Tadoussac, and to invite them to share the good cheer. They came aboard in the evening, and were seized and secured. "Voyla donc mes galants bien estonnez," writes Champlain.

It was ten o'clock, and most of the men on shore were asleep. They were wakened suddenly, and told of the discovery of the plot and the arrest of the ringleaders. Pardon was then promised them, and they were dismissed again to their beds, greatly relieved; for they had lived in trepidation, each fearing the other. Duval's body, swinging from a gibbet, gave wholesome warning to those he had seduced; and his head was displayed on a pike, from the highest roof of the buildings, food for birds and a lesson to sedition. His three accomplices were carried by Pontgravé to France, where they made their atonement in the galleys.

It was on the eighteenth of September that Pontgravé set sail, leaving Champlain with twenty-eight men to hold Quebec through the winter. Three weeks later, and shores and hills glowed with gay prognostics of approaching desolation,—the yellow and scarlet of the maples, the deep purple of the ash, the garnet hue of young oaks, the crimson of the tupelo at the water's edge, and the golden plumage of birch saplings in the fissures of the cliff. It was a short-lived beauty. The forest dropped its festal robes. Shrivelled and faded, they rustled to the earth. The crystal air and laughing sun of October passed away, and November sank upon the shivering waste, chill and sombre as the tomb.

A roving band of Montagnais had built their huts near the buildings, and were busying themselves with their autumn eel-fishery, on which they greatly relied to sustain their miserable lives through the winter. Their slimy harvest being gathered, and duly smoked and dried, they gave it for safe-keeping to Champlain, and set out to hunt beavers. It was deep in the winter before they came back, reclaimed their eels, built their birch cabins again, and disposed themselves for a life of ease, until famine or their enemies should put an end to their enjoyments. These were by no means without alloy. While, gorged with food, they lay dozing on piles of branches in their smoky huts, where, through the crevices of the thin birch bark, streamed in a cold capable at times of congealing mercury, their slumbers were beset with nightmare visions of Iroquois forays, scalpings, butcherings, and burnings. As dreams were their oracles, the camp was wild with fright. They sent out no scouts and placed no guard; but, with each repetition of these nocturnal terrors, they came flocking in a body to beg admission within the fort. The women and children were allowed to enter the yard and remain during the night, while anxious fathers and jealous husbands shivered in the darkness without.

On one occasion, a group of wretched beings was seen on the farther bank of the St. Lawrence, like wild animals driven by famine to the borders of the settler's clearing. The river was full of drifting ice, and there was no crossing without risk of life. The Indians, in their desperation, made the attempt; and midway their canoes were ground to atoms among the tossing masses. Agile as wild-cats, they all leaped upon a huge raft of ice, the squaws carrying their children on their shoulders, a feat at which Champlain marvelled when he saw their starved and emaciated condition. Here they began a wail of despair; when happily the pressure of other masses thrust the sheet of ice against the northern shore. They landed and soon made their appearance at the fort, worn to skeletons and horrible to look upon. The French gave them food, which they devoured with a frenzied avidity, and, unappeased, fell upon a dead dog left on the snow by Champlain for two months past as a bait for foxes. They broke this carrion into fragments, and thawed and devoured it, to the disgust of the spectators, who tried vainly to prevent them.

This was but a severe access of the periodical famine which, during winter, was a normal condition of the Algonquin tribes of Acadia and the Lower St. Lawrence, who, unlike the cognate tribes of New England, never tilled the soil, or made any reasonable provision against the time of need.

One would gladly know how the founders of Quebec spent the long hours of their first winter; but on this point the only man among them, perhaps, who could write, has not thought it necessary to enlarge. He himself beguiled his leisure with trapping foxes, or hanging a dead dog from a tree and watching the hungry martens in their efforts to reach it. Towards the close of winter, all found abundant employment in nursing themselves or their neighbors, for the inevitable scurvy broke out with virulence. At the middle of May, only eight men of the twenty-eight were alive, and of these half were suffering from disease.

This wintry purgatory wore away; the icy stalactites that hung from the cliffs fell crashing to the earth; the clamor of the wild geese was heard; the bluebirds appeared in the naked woods; the water-willows were covered with their soft caterpillar-like blossoms; the twigs of the swamp maple were flushed with ruddy bloom; the ash hung out its black tufts; the shad-bush seemed a wreath of snow; the white stars of the bloodroot gleamed among dank, fallen leaves; and in the young grass of the wet meadows the marsh-marigolds shone like spots of gold.

Great was the joy of Champlain when, on the fifth of June, he saw a sailboat rounding the Point of Orleans, betokening that the spring had brought with it the longed for succors. A son-in-law of Pontgravé, named Marais, was on board, and he reported that Pontgravé was then at Tadoussac, where he had lately arrived. Thither Champlain hastened, to take counsel with his comrade. His constitution or his courage had defied the scurvy. They met, and it was determined betwixt them, that, while Pontgravé remained in charge of Quebec, Champlain should enter at once on his long-meditated explorations, by which, like La Salle seventy years later, he had good hope of finding a way to China.

But there was a lion in the path. The Indian tribes, to whom peace was unknown, infested with their scalping parties the streams and pathways of the forest, and increased tenfold its inseparable risks. The after career of Champlain gives abundant proof that he was more than indifferent to all such chances; yet now an expedient for evading them offered itself, so consonant with his instincts that he was glad to accept it.

During the last autumn, a young chief from the banks of the then unknown Ottawa had been at Quebec; and, amazed at what he saw, he had begged Champlain to join him in the spring against his enemies. These enemies were a formidable race of savages,—the Iroquois, or Five Confederate Nations, who dwelt in fortified villages within limits now embraced by the State of New York, and who were a terror to all the surrounding forests. They were deadly foes of their kindred the Hurons, who dwelt on the lake which bears their name, and were allies of Algonquin bands on the Ottawa. All alike were tillers of the soil, living at ease when compared with the famished Algonquins of the Lower St. Lawrence.

By joining these Hurons and Algonquins against their Iroquois enemies, Champlain might make himself the indispensable ally and leader of the tribes of Canada, and at the same time fight his way to discovery in regions which otherwise were barred against him. From first to last it was the policy of France in America to mingle in Indian politics, hold the balance of power between adverse tribes, and envelop in the network of her power and diplomacy the remotest hordes of the wilderness. Of this policy the Father of New France may perhaps be held to have set a rash and premature example. Yet while he was apparently following the dictates of his own adventurous spirit, it became evident, a few years later, that under his thirst for discovery and spirit of knight-errantry lay a consistent and deliberate purpose. That it had already assumed a definite shape is not likely; but his after course makes it plain that, in embroiling himself and his colony with the most formidable savages on the continent, he was by no means acting so recklessly as at first sight would appear.

Chapter 10. Lake Champlain

It was past the middle of June, and the expected warriors from the upper country had not come,—a delay which seems to have given Champlain little concern, for, without waiting longer, he set out with no better allies than a band of Montagnais. But, as he moved up the St. Lawrence, he saw, thickly clustered in the bordering forest, the lodges of an Indian camp, and, landing, found his Huron and Algonquin allies. Few of them had ever seen a white man, and they surrounded the steel-clad strangers in speechless wonder. Champlain asked for their chief, and the staring throng moved with him towards a lodge where sat, not one chief, but two; for each band had its own. There were feasting, smoking, and speeches; and, the needful ceremony over, all descended together to Quebec; for the strangers were bent on seeing those wonders of architecture, the fame of which had pierced the recesses of their forests.

On their arrival, they feasted their eyes and glutted their appetites; yelped consternation at the sharp explosions of the arquebuse and the roar of the cannon; pitched their camps, and bedecked themselves for their war-dance. In the still night, their fire glared against the black and jagged cliff, and the fierce red light fell on tawny limbs convulsed with frenzied gestures and ferocious stampings; on contorted visages, hideous with paint; on brandished weapons, stone war-clubs, stone hatchets, and stone-pointed lances; while the drum kept up its hollow boom, and the air was split with mingled yells.

The war-feast followed, and then all embarked together. Champlain was in a small shallop, carrying, besides himself, eleven men of Pont-gravé's party, including his son-in-law Marais and the pilot La Routte. They were armed with the arquebuse,—a matchlock or firelock somewhat like the modern carbine, and from its shortness not ill suited for use in the forest. On the twenty-eighth of June they spread their sails and held their course against the current, while around them the river was alive with canoes, and hundreds of naked arms plied the paddle with a steady, measured sweep. They crossed the Lake of St. Peter, threaded the devious channels among its many islands, and reached at last the mouth of the Rivière des Iroquois, since called the Richelieu, or the St. John. Here, probably on the site of the town of Sorel, the leisurely warriors encamped for two days, hunted, fished, and took their ease, regaling their allies with venison and wild-fowl. They quarrelled, too; three fourths of their number seceded, took to their canoes in dudgeon, and paddled towards their homes, while the rest pursued their course up the broad and placid stream.

Walls of verdure stretched on left and right. Now, aloft in the lonely air rose the cliffs of Belœil, and now, before them, framed in circling forests, the Basin of Chambly spread its tranquil mirror, glittering in the sun. The shallop outsailed the canoes. Champlain, leaving his allies behind, crossed the basin and tried to pursue his course; but, as he listened in the stillness, the unwelcome noise of rapids reached his ear, and, by glimpses through the dark foliage of the Islets of St. John he could see the gleam of snowy foam and the flash of hurrying waters. Leaving the boat by the shore in charge of four men, he went with Marais, La Routte, and five others, to explore the wild before him. They pushed their way through the damps and shadows of the wood, through thickets and tangled vines, over mossy rocks and mouldering logs. Still the hoarse surging of the rapids followed them; and when, parting the screen of foliage, they looked out upon the river, they saw it thick set with rocks where, plunging over ledges, gurgling under drift-logs, darting along clefts, and boiling in chasms, the angry waters filled the solitude with monotonous ravings.

Champlain retraced his steps. He had learned the value of an Indian's word. His allies had promised him that his boat could pass unobstructed throughout the whole journey. "It afflicted me," he says, "and troubled me exceedingly to be obliged to return without having seen so great a lake, full of fair islands and bordered with the fine countries which they had described to me."

When he reached the boat, he found the whole savage crew gathered at the spot. He mildly rebuked their bad faith, but added, that, though they had deceived him, he, as far as might be, would fulfil his pledge. To this end, he directed Marais, with the boat and the greater part of the men, to return to Quebec, while he, with two who offered to follow him, should proceed in the Indian canoes.

The warriors lifted their canoes from the water, and bore them on their shoulders half a league through the forest to the smoother stream above. Here the chiefs made a muster of their forces, counting twenty-four canoes and sixty warriors. All embarked again, and advanced once more, by marsh, meadow, forest, and scattered islands,—then full of game, for it was an uninhabited land, the war-path and battle-ground of hostile tribes. The warriors observed a certain system in their advance. Some were in front as a vanguard; others formed the main body; while an equal number were in the forests on the flanks and rear, hunting for the subsistence of the whole; for, though they had a provision of parched maize pounded into meal, they kept it for use when, from the vicinity of the enemy, hunting should become impossible.

Late in the day they landed and drew up their canoes, ranging them closely, side by side. Some stripped sheets of bark, to cover their camp sheds; others gathered wood, the forest being full of dead, dry trees; others felled the living trees, for a barricade. They seem to have had steel axes, obtained by barter from the French; for in less than two hours they had made a strong defensive work, in the form of a half-circle, open on the river side, where their canoes lay on the strand, and large enough to enclose all their huts and sheds. Some of their number had gone forward as scouts, and, returning, reported no signs of an enemy. This was the extent of their precaution, for they placed no guard, but all, in full security, stretched themselves to sleep,—a vicious custom from which the lazy warrior of the forest rarely departs.

They had not forgotten, however, to consult their oracle. The medicine-man pitched his magic lodge in the woods, formed of a small stack of poles, planted in a circle and brought together at the tops like stacked muskets. Over these he placed the filthy deer-skins which served him for a robe, and, creeping in at a narrow opening, hid himself from view. Crouched in a ball upon the earth, he invoked the spirits in mumbling inarticulate tones; while his naked auditory, squatted on the ground like apes, listened in wonder and awe. Suddenly, the lodge moved, rocking with violence to and fro,—by the power of the spirits, as the Indians thought, while Champlain could plainly see the tawny fist of the medicine-man shaking the poles. They begged him to keep a watchful eye on the peak of the lodge, whence fire and smoke would presently issue; but with the best efforts of his vision, he discovered none. Meanwhile the medicine-man was seized with such convulsions, that, when his divination was over, his naked body streamed with perspiration. In loud, clear tones, and in an unknown tongue, he invoked the spirit, who was understood to be present in the form of a stone, and whose feeble and squeaking accents were heard at intervals, like the wail of a young puppy.

In this manner they consulted the spirit—as Champlain thinks, the Devil—at all their camps. His replies, for the most part, seem to have given them great content; yet they took other measures, of which the military advantages were less questionable. The principal chief gathered bundles of sticks, and, without wasting his breath, stuck them in the earth in a certain order, calling each by the name of some warrior, a few taller than the rest representing the subordinate chiefs. Thus was indicated the position which each was to hold in the expected battle. All gathered round and attentively studied the sticks, ranged like a child's wooden soldiers, or the pieces on a chessboard; then, with no further instruction, they formed their ranks, broke them, and reformed them again and again with excellent alacrity and skill.

Again the canoes advanced, the river widening as they went. Great islands appeared, leagues in extent,—Isle à la Motte, Long Island, Grande Isle; channels where ships might float and broad reaches of water stretched between them, and Champlain entered the lake which preserves his name to posterity. Cumberland Head was passed, and from the opening of the great channel between Grande Isle and the main he could look forth on the wilderness sea. Edged with woods, the tranquil flood spread southward beyond the sight. Far on the left rose the forest ridges of the Green Mountains, and on the right the Adirondacks,—haunts in these later years of amateur sportsmen from counting-rooms or college halls. Then the Iroquois made them their hunting-ground; and beyond, in the valleys of the Mohawk, the Onondaga, and the Genesee, stretched the long line of their five cantons and palisaded towns.

At night they encamped again. The scene is a familiar one to many a tourist; and perhaps, standing at sunset on the peaceful strand, Champlain saw what a roving student of this generation has seen on those same shores, at that same hour,—the glow of the vanished sun behind the western mountains, darkly piled in mist and shadow along the sky; near at hand, the dead pine, mighty in decay, stretching its ragged arms athwart the burning heaven, the crow perched on its top like an image carved in jet; and aloft, the nighthawk, circling in his flight, and, with a strange whirring sound, diving through the air each moment for the insects he makes his prey.

The progress of the party was becoming dangerous. They changed their mode of advance and moved only in the night. All day they lay close in the depth of the forest, sleeping, lounging, smoking tobacco of their own raising, and beguiling the hours, no doubt, with the shallow banter and obscene jesting with which knots of Indians are wont to amuse their leisure. At twilight they embarked again, paddling their cautious way till the eastern sky began to redden. Their goal was the rocky promontory where Fort Ticonderoga was long afterward built. Thence, they would pass the outlet of Lake George, and launch their canoes again on that Como of the wilderness, whose waters, limpid as a fountain-head, stretched far southward between their flanking mountains. Landing at the future site of Fort William Henry, they would carry their canoes through the forest to the river Hudson, and, descending it, attack perhaps some outlying town of the Mohawks. In the next century this chain of lakes and rivers became the grand highway of savage and civilized war, linked to memories of momentous conflicts.

The allies were spared so long a progress. On the morning of the twenty-ninth of July, after paddling all night, they hid as usual in the forest on the western shore, apparently between Crown Point and Ticonderoga. The warriors stretched themselves to their slumbers, and Champlain, after walking till nine or ten o'clock through the surrounding woods, returned to take his repose on a pile of spruce-boughs. Sleeping, he dreamed a dream, wherein he beheld the Iroquois drowning in the lake; and, trying to rescue them, he was told by his Algonquin friends that they were good for nothing, and had better be left to their fate. For some time past he had been beset every morning by his superstitious allies, eager to learn about his dreams; and, to this moment, his unbroken slumbers had failed to furnish the desired prognostics. The announcement of this auspicious vision filled the crowd with joy, and at nightfall they embarked, flushed with anticipated victories.

It was ten o'clock in the evening, when, near a projecting point of land, which was probably Ticonderoga, they descried dark objects in motion on the lake before them. These were a flotilla of Iroquois canoes, heavier and slower than theirs, for they were made of oak bark. Each party saw the other, and the mingled war-cries pealed over the darkened water. The Iroquois, who were near the shore, having no stomach for an aquatic battle, landed, and, making night hideous with their clamors, began to barricade themselves. Champlain could see them in the woods, laboring like beavers, hacking down trees with iron axes taken from the Canadian tribes in war, and with stone hatchets of their own making. The allies remained on the lake, a bowshot from the hostile barricade, their canoes made fast together by poles lashed across. All night they danced with as much vigor as the frailty of their vessels would permit, their throats making amends for the enforced restraint of their limbs. It was agreed on both sides that the fight should be deferred till daybreak; but meanwhile a commerce of abuse, sarcasm, menace, and boasting gave unceasing exercise to the lungs and fancy of the combatants,—"much," says Champlain, "like the besiegers and besieged in a beleaguered town."

As day approached, he and his two followers put on the light armor of the time. Champlain wore the doublet and long hose then in vogue. Over the doublet he buckled on a breastplate, and probably a back-piece, while his thighs were protected by cuisses of steel, and his head by a plumed casque. Across his shoulder hung the strap of his bandoleer, or ammunition-box; at his side was his sword, and in his hand his arquebuse. Such was the equipment of this ancient Indian-fighter, whose exploits date eleven years before the landing of the Puritans at Plymouth, and sixty-six years before King Philip's War.

Each of the three Frenchmen was in a separate canoe, and, as it grew light, they kept themselves hidden, either by lying at the bottom, or covering themselves with an Indian robe. The canoes approached the shore, and all landed without opposition at some distance from the Iroquois, whom they presently could see filing out of their barricade,—tall, strong men, some two hundred in number, the boldest and fiercest warriors of North America. They advanced through the forest with a steadiness which excited the admiration of Champlain. Among them could be seen three chiefs, made conspicuous by their tall plumes. Some bore shields of wood and hide, and some were covered with a kind of armor made of tough twigs interlaced with a vegetable fibre supposed by Champlain to be cotton.

The allies, growing anxious, called with loud cries for their champion, and opened their ranks that he might pass to the front. He did so, and, advancing before his red companions in arms, stood revealed to the gaze of the Iroquois, who, beholding the warlike apparition in their path, stared in mute amazement. "I looked at them," says Champlain, "and they looked at me. When I saw them getting ready to shoot their arrows at us, I levelled my arquebuse, which I had loaded with four balls, and aimed straight at one of the three chiefs. The shot brought down two, and wounded another. On this, our Indians set up such a yelling that one could not have heard a thunder-clap, and all the while the arrows flew thick on both sides. The Iroquois were greatly astonished and frightened to see two of their men killed so quickly, in spite of their arrow-proof armor. As I was reloading, one of my companions fired a shot from the woods, which so increased their astonishment that, seeing their chiefs dead, they abandoned the field and fled into the depth of the forest." The allies dashed after them. Some of the Iroquois were killed, and more were taken. Camp, canoes, provisions, all were abandoned, and many weapons flung down in the panic flight. The victory was complete.

At night, the victors led out one of the prisoners, told him that he was to die by fire, and ordered him to sing his death-song if he dared. Then they began the torture, and presently scalped their victim alive, when Champlain, sickening at the sight, begged leave to shoot him. They refused, and he turned away in anger and disgust; on which they called him back and told him to do as he pleased. He turned again, and a shot from his arquebuse put the wretch out of misery.

The scene filled him with horror; but a few months later, on the Place de la Grève at Paris, he might have witnessed tortures equally revolting and equally vindictive, inflicted on the regicide Ravaillac by the sentence of grave and learned judges.

The allies made a prompt retreat from the scene of their triumph. Three or four days brought them to the mouth of the Richelieu. Here they separated; the Hurons and Algonquins made for the Ottawa, their homeward route, each with a share of prisoners for future torments. At parting, they invited Champlain to visit their towns and aid them again in their wars, an invitation which this paladin of the woods failed not to accept.

The companions now remaining to him were the Montagnais. In their camp on the Richelieu, one of them dreamed that a war party of Iroquois was close upon them; on which, in a torrent of rain, they left their huts, paddled in dismay to the islands above the Lake of St. Peter, and hid themselves all night in the rushes. In the morning they took heart, emerged from their hiding-places, descended to Quebec, and went thence to Tadoussac, whither Champlain accompanied them. Here the squaws, stark naked, swam out to the canoes to receive the heads of the dead Iroquois, and, hanging them from their necks, danced in triumph along the shore. One of the heads and a pair of arms were then bestowed on Champlain,—touching memorials of gratitude, which, however, he was by no means to keep for himself, but to present to the King.

Thus did New France rush into collision with the redoubted warriors of the Five Nations. Here was the beginning, and in some measure doubtless the cause, of a long suite of murderous conflicts, bearing havoc and flame to generations yet unborn. Champlain had invaded the tiger's den; and now, in smothered fury, the patient savage would lie biding his day of blood.

Chapter 19. 1663–1763. The Rulers of Canada

The government of Canada was formed in its chief features after the government of a French province. Throughout France the past and the present stood side by side. The kingdom had a double administration; or, rather, the shadow of the old administration and the substance of the new. The government of provinces had long been held by the high nobles, often kindred to the Crown; and hence, in former times, great perils had arisen, amounting during the civil wars to the danger of dismemberment. The high nobles were still governors of provinces; but here, as elsewhere, they had ceased to be dangerous. Titles, honors, and ceremonial they had in abundance; but they were deprived of real power. Close beside them was the royal intendant, an obscure figure, lost amid the vainglories of the feudal sunset, but in the name of the King holding the reins of government,— a check and a spy on his gorgeous colleague. He was the King's agent; of modest birth, springing from the legal class; owing his present to the King, and dependent on him for his future; learned in the law and trained to administration. It was by such instruments that the powerful centralization of the monarchy enforced itself throughout the kingdom, and, penetrating beneath the crust of old prescriptions, supplanted without seeming to supplant them. The courtier noble looked down in the pride of rank on the busy man in black at his side; but this man in black, with the troop of officials at his beck, controlled finance, the royal courts, public works, and all the administrative business of the province.

The governor-general and the intendant of Canada answered to those of a French province. The governor, excepting in the earliest period of the colony, was a military noble,—in most cases bearing a title and sometimes of high rank. The intendant, as in France, was usually drawn from the *gens de robe,* or legal class. The mutual relations of the two officers were modified by the circumstances about them. The governor was superior in rank to the intendant; he commanded the troops, conducted relations with foreign colonies and Indian tribes, and took precedence on all occasions of ceremony. Unlike a provincial governor in France, he had great and substantial power. The King and the minister, his sole masters, were a thousand leagues distant, and he controlled the whole military force. If he abused his position, there was no remedy but in appeal to the court, which alone could hold him in check. There were local governors at Montreal and Three Rivers; but their power was carefully curbed, and they were forbidden to fine or imprison any person without authority from Quebec.

The intendant was virtually a spy on the governor-general, of whose proceedings and of everything else that took place he was required to make report. Every year he wrote to the minister of state one, two, three, or four letters, often forty or fifty pages long, filled with the secrets of the colony, political and personal, great and small, set forth with a minuteness often interesting, often instructive, and often excessively tedious. The governor, too, wrote letters of pitiless length; and each of the colleagues was jealous of the letters of the other. In truth, their relations to each other were so critical, and perfect harmony so rare, that they might almost be described as natural enemies. The court, it is certain, did not desire their perfect accord; nor, on the other hand, did it wish them to quarrel: it aimed to keep them on such terms that, without deranging the machinery of administration, each should be a check on the other.

The governor, the intendant, and the supreme council or court were absolute masters of Canada under the pleasure of the King. Legislative, judicial, and executive power, all centred in them. We have seen already the very unpromising beginnings of the supreme council. It had consisted at first of the governor, the bishop, and five councillors chosen by them. The intendant was soon added, to form the ruling triumvirate; but the appointment of the councillors, the occasion of so many quarrels, was afterwards exercised by the King himself. Even the name of the council underwent a change in the interest of his autocracy, and he commanded that it should no longer be called the *Supreme*, but only the *Superior* Council. The same change had just been imposed on all the high tribunals of France. Under the shadow of the *fleur-de-lis*, the King alone was to be supreme.

In 1675 the number of councillors was increased to seven, and in 1703 it was again increased to twelve; but the character of the council or court remained the same. It issued decrees for the civil, commercial, and financial government of the colony, and gave judgment in civil and criminal causes according to the royal ordinances and the *Coutume de Paris*. It exercised also the function of registration borrowed from the parliament of Paris. That body, it will be remembered, had no analogy whatever with the English parliament. Its ordinary functions were not legislative, but judicial; and it was composed of judges hereditary under certain conditions. Nevertheless, it had long acted as a check on the royal power through its right of registration. No royal edict had the force of law till entered upon its books, and this custom had so deep a root in the monarchical constitution of France, that even Louis XIV., in the flush of his power, did not attempt to abolish it. He did better; he ordered his decrees to be registered, and the humbled parliament submissively obeyed. In like manner all edicts, ordinances, or declarations relating to Canada were entered on the registers of the superior council at Quebec. The order of registration was commonly affixed to the edict or other mandate, and nobody dreamed of disobeying it.

The council or court had its attorney-general, who heard complaints, and brought them before the tribunal if he thought necessary; its secretary, who kept its registers, and its *huissiers* or attendant officers. It sat once a week; and, though it was the highest court of appeal, it exercised at first original jurisdiction in very trivial cases. It was empowered to establish subordinate courts or judges throughout the colony. Besides these, there was a judge appointed by the King for each of the three districts into which Canada was divided,—those of Quebec, Three Rivers, and Montreal. To each of the three royal judges were joined a clerk and an attorney-general, under the supervision and control of the attorney-general of the superior court, to which tribunal appeal lay from all the subordinate jurisdictions. The jurisdiction of the seigniors within their own limits has already been mentioned. They were entitled by the terms of their grants to the exercise of "high, middle, and low justice"; but most of them were practically restricted to the last of the three,—that is, to petty disputes between the *habitants,* involving not more than sixty sous, or offences for which the fine did not exceed ten sous. Thus limited, their judgments were often useful in saving time, trouble, and money to the disputants. The corporate seigniors of Montreal long continued to hold a feudal court in form, with attorney-general, clerk, and *huissier;* but very few other seigniors were in a condition to imitate them. Added to all these tribunals was the bishop's court at Quebec, to try causes held to be within the province of the Church.

The office of judge in Canada was no sinecure. The people were of a litigious disposition,—partly from their Norman blood; partly, perhaps, from the idleness of the long and tedious winter, which gave full leisure for gossip and quarrel; and partly from the very imperfect manner in which titles had been drawn and the boundaries of grants marked out, whence ensued disputes without end between neighbor and neighbor.

"I will not say," writes the satirical La Hontan, "that Justice is more chaste and disinterested here than in France; but, at least, if she is sold, she is sold cheaper. We do not pass through the clutches of advocates, the talons of attorneys, and the claws of clerks. These vermin do not infest Canada yet. Everybody pleads his own cause. Our Themis is prompt, and she does not bristle with fees, costs, and charges. The judges have only four hundred francs a year,—a great temptation to look for law in the bottom of the suitor's purse. Four hundred francs! Not enough to buy a cap and gown; so these gentry never wear them."

Thus far La Hontan. Now let us hear the King himself. "The greatest disorder which has hitherto existed in Canada," writes Louis XIV. to the intendant Meules, "has come from the small degree of liberty which the officers of justice have had in the discharge of their duties, by reason of the violence to which they have been subjected, and the part they have been obliged to take in the continual quarrels between the governor and the intendant; insomuch that justice having been administered by cabal and animosity, the inhabitants have hitherto been far from the tranquillity and repose which cannot be found in a place where everybody is compelled to take side with one party or another."

Nevertheless, on ordinary local questions between the *habitants,* justice seems to have been administered on the whole fairly; and judges of all grades often interposed in their personal capacity to bring parties to an agreement without a trial. From head to foot, the government kept its attitude of paternity.

Beyond and above all the regular tribunals, beyond and above the council itself, was the independent jurisdiction lodged in the person of the King's man, the intendant. His commission empowered him, if he saw fit, to call any cause whatever before himself for judgment; and he judged exclusively the cases which concerned the King, and those involving the relations of seignior and vassal. He appointed subordinate judges, from whom there was appeal to him; but from his decisions, as well as from those of the superior council, there was no appeal but to the King in his council of state.

On any Monday morning one would have found the superior council in session in the antechamber of the governor's apartment, at the Château St. Louis. The members sat at a round table. At the head was the governor, with the bishop on his right, and the intendant on his left. The councillors sat in the order of their appointment, and the attorney-general also had his place at the board. As La Hontan says, they were not in judicial robes, but in their ordinary dress, and all but the bishop wore swords. The want of the cap and gown greatly disturbed the intendant Meules; and he begs the minister to consider how important it is that the councillors, in order to inspire respect, should appear in public in long black robes, which on occasions of ceremony they should exchange for robes of red. He thinks that the principal persons of the colony would thus be induced to train up their children to so enviable a dignity; "and," he concludes, "as none of the councillors can afford to buy red robes, I hope that the King will vouchsafe to send out nine such. As for the black robes, they can furnish those themselves." The King did not respond, and the nine robes never arrived.

The official dignity of the council was sometimes exposed to trials against which even red gowns might have proved an insufficient protection. The same intendant urges that the tribunal ought to be provided immediately with a house of its own. "It is not decent," he says, "that it should sit in the governor's antechamber any longer. His guards and valets make such a noise that we cannot hear one another speak. I have continually to tell them to keep quiet, which causes them to make a thousand jokes at the councillors as they pass in and out." As the governor and the council were often on ill terms, the official head of the colony could not always be trusted to keep his attendants on their good behavior. The minister listened to the complaint of Meules, and adopted his suggestion that the government should buy the old brewery of Talon,—a large structure of mingled timber and masonry on the banks of the St. Charles. It was at an easy distance from the château; passing the Hôtel Dieu and descending the rock, one reached it by a walk of a few minutes. It was accordingly repaired, partly rebuilt, and fitted up to serve the double purpose of a lodging for the intendant and a court-house. Henceforth the transformed brewery was known as the Palace of the Intendant, or the Palace of Justice; and here the council and inferior courts long continued to hold their sessions.

Some of these inferior courts appear to have needed a lodging quite as much as the council. The watchful Meules informs the minister that the royal judge for the district of Quebec was accustomed in winter, with a view to saving fuel, to hear causes and pronounce judgment by his own fireside, in the midst of his children, whose gambols disturbed the even distribution of justice.

The superior council was not a very harmonious body. As its three chiefs—the man of the sword, the man of the church, and the man of the law—were often at variance, the councillors attached themselves to one party or the other, and hot disputes sometimes ensued. The intendant, though but third in rank, presided at the sessions, took votes, pronounced judgment, signed papers, and called special meetings. This matter of the presidency was for some time a source of contention between him and the governor, till the question was set at rest by a decree of the King.

The intendants in their reports to the minister do not paint the council in flattering colors. One of them complains that the councillors, being busy with their farms, neglect their official duties. Another says that they are all more or less in trade. A third calls them uneducated persons of slight account, allied to the chief families and chief merchants in Canada, in whose interest they make laws; and he adds, that, as a year and a half or even two years usually elapse before the answer to a complaint is received from France, they take advantage of this long interval to the injury of the King's service. These and other similar charges betray the continual friction between the several branches of the government.

The councillors were rarely changed, and they usually held office for life. In a few cases the King granted to the son of a councillor yet living the right of succeeding his father when the charge should become vacant. It was a post of honor and not of profit, at least of direct profit. The salaries were very small, and coupled with a prohibition to receive fees.

Judging solely by the terms of his commission, the intendant was the ruling power in the colony. He controlled all expenditure of public money, and not only presided at the council, but was clothed in his own person with independent legislative as well as judicial power. He was authorized to issue ordinances having the force of law whenever he thought necessary, and, in the words of his commission, "to order everything as he shall see just and proper." He was directed to be present at councils of war, though war was the special province of his colleague, and to protect soldiers and all others from official extortion and abuse; that is, to protect them from the governor. Yet there were practical difficulties in the way of his apparent power. The King, his master, was far away; but official jealousy was busy around him, and his patience was sometimes put to the proof. Thus the royal judge of Quebec had fallen into irregularities. "I can do nothing with him," writes the intendant; "he keeps on good terms with the governor and council, and sets me at naught." The governor had, as he thought, treated him amiss. "You have told me," he writes to the minister, "to bear everything from him and report to you"; and he proceeds to recount his grievances. Again, "the attorney-general is bold to insolence, and needs to be repressed. The King's interposition is necessary." He modestly adds that the intendant is the only man in Canada whom his Majesty can trust, and that he ought to have more power.

These were far from being his only troubles. The enormous powers with which his commission clothed him were sometimes retrenched by contradictory instructions from the King; for this government, not of laws but of arbitrary will, is marked by frequent inconsistencies. When he quarrelled with the governor, and the governor chanced to have strong friends at court, his position became truly pitiable. He was berated as an imperious master berates an offending servant. "Your last letter is full of nothing but complaints." "You have exceeded your authority." "Study to know yourself, and to understand clearly the difference there is between a governor and an intendant." "Since you failed to comprehend the difference between you and the officer who represents the King's person, you are in danger of being often condemned, or rather of being recalled; for his Majesty cannot endure so many petty complaints, founded on nothing but a certain *quasi* equality between the governor and you, which you assume, but which does not exist." "Meddle with nothing beyond your functions." "Take good care to tell me nothing but the truth." "You ask too many favors for your adherents." "You must not spend more than you have authority to spend, or it will be taken out of your pay." In short, there are several letters from the minister Colbert to his colonial man-of-all-work, which, from beginning to end, are one continued scold.

The luckless intendant was liable to be held to account for the action of natural laws. "If the population does not increase in proportion to the pains I take," writes the King to Duchesneau, "you are to lay the blame on yourself for not having executed my principal order [to promote marriages], and for having failed in the principal object for which I sent you to Canada."

A great number of ordinances of intendants are preserved. They were usually read to the people at the doors of churches after mass, or sometimes by the curé from his pulpit. They relate to a great variety of subjects,—regulation of inns and markets, poaching, preservation of game, sale of brandy, rent of pews, stray hogs, mad dogs, tithes, matrimonial quarrels, fast driving, wards and guardians, weights and measures, nuisances, value of coinage, trespass on lands, building churches, observance of Sunday, preservation of timber, seignior and vassal, settlement of boundaries, and many other matters. If a curé with some of his parishioners reported that his church or his house needed repair or rebuilding, the intendant issued an ordinance requiring all the inhabitants of the parish, "both those who have consented and those who have not consented," to contribute materials and labor, on pain of fine or other penalty. The militia captain of the *côte* was to direct the work and see that each parishioner did his due part, which was determined by the extent of his farm; so, too, if the *grand voyer,* an officer charged with the superintendence of highways, reported that a new road was wanted or that an old one needed mending, an ordinance of the intendant set the whole neighborhood at work upon it, directed, as in the other case, by the captain of militia. If children were left fatherless, the intendant ordered the curé of the parish to assemble their relations or friends for the choice of a guardian. If a *censitaire* did not clear his land and live on it, the intendant took it from him and gave it back to the seignior.

Chimney-sweeping having been neglected at Quebec, the intendant commands all householders promptly to do their duty in this respect, and at the same time fixes the pay of the sweep at six sous a chimney. Another order forbids quarrelling in church. Another assigns pews in due order of precedence to the seignior, the captain of militia, and the wardens. The intendant Raudot, who seems to have been inspired even more than the others with the spirit of paternal intervention, issued a mandate to the effect, that, whereas the people of Montreal raise too many horses, which prevents them from raising cattle and sheep, "being therein ignorant of their true interest. . . . Now, therefore, we command that each inhabitant of the *côtes* of this government shall hereafter own no more than two horses, or mares, and one foal,—the same to take effect after the sowing-season of the ensuing year, 1710, giving them time to rid themselves of their horses in excess of said number, after which they will be required to kill any of such excess that may remain in their possession." Many other ordinances, if not equally preposterous, are equally stringent; such, for example, as that of the intendant Bigot, in which, with a view of promoting agriculture, and protecting the morals of the farmers by saving them from the temptations of cities, he proclaims to them: "We prohibit and forbid you to remove to this town [Quebec] under any pretext whatever, without our permission in writing, on pain of being expelled and sent back to your farms, your furniture and goods confiscated, and a fine of fifty livres laid on you for the benefit of the hospitals. And, furthermore, we forbid all inhabitants of the city to let houses or rooms to persons coming from the country, on pain of a fine of a hundred livres, also applicable to the hospitals." At about the same time a royal edict, designed to prevent the undue subdivision of farms, forbade the country people, except such as were authorized to live in villages, to build a house or barn on any piece of land less than one and a half arpents wide and thirty arpents long; while a subsequent ordinance of the intendant commands the immediate demolition of certain houses built in contravention of the edict.

The spirit of absolutism is everywhere apparent. "It is of very great consequence," writes the intendant Meules, "that the people should not be left at liberty to speak their minds." Hence public meetings were jealously restricted. Even those held by parishioners under the eye of the curé to estimate the cost of a new church seem to have required a special license from the intendant. During a number of years a meeting of the principal inhabitants of Quebec was called in spring and autumn by the council to discuss the price and quality of bread, the supply of firewood, and other similar matters. The council commissioned two of its members to preside at these meetings, and on hearing their report took what action it thought best. Thus, after the meeting held in February, 1686, it issued a decree, in which, after a long and formal preamble, it solemnly ordained "that besides white-bread and light brown-bread, all bakers shall hereafter make dark brown-bread whenever the same shall be required." Such assemblies, so controlled, could scarcely, one would think, wound the tenderest susceptibilities of authority; yet there was evident distrust of them, and after a few years this modest shred of self-government is seen no more. The syndic, too, that functionary whom the people of the towns were at first allowed to choose, under the eye of the authorities, was conjured out of existence by a word from the King. Seignior, *cen-*

sitaire, and citizen were prostrate alike in flat subjection to the royal will. They were not free even to go home to France. No inhabitant of Canada, man or woman, could do so without leave; and several intendants express their belief that without this precaution there would soon be a falling off in the population.

In 1671 the council issued a curious decree. One Paul Dupuy had been heard to say that there is nothing like righting one's self, and that when the English cut off the head of Charles I. they did a good thing, with other discourse to the like effect. The council declared him guilty of speaking ill of royalty in the person of the King of England, and uttering words tending to sedition. He was condemned to be dragged from prison by the public executioner, and led in his shirt, with a rope about his neck and a torch in his hand, to the gate of the Château St. Louis, there to beg pardon of the King; thence to the pillory of the Lower Town to be branded with a *fleur-de-lis* on the cheek, and set in the stocks for half an hour; then to be led back to prison, and put in irons "till the information against him shall be completed."

If irreverence to royalty was thus rigorously chastised, irreverence to God was threatened with still sharper penalties. Louis XIV., ever haunted with the fear of the Devil, sought protection against him by his famous edict against swearing, duly registered on the books of the council at Quebec. "It is our will and pleasure," says this pious mandate, "that all persons convicted of profane swearing or blaspheming the name of God, the most Holy Virgin his mother, or the saints, be condemned for the first offence to a pecuniary fine according to their possessions and the greatness and enormity of the oath and blasphemy; and if those thus punished repeat the said oaths, then for the second, third, and fourth time they shall be condemned to a double, triple, and quadruple fine; and for the fifth time, they shall be set in the pillory on Sunday or other festival days, there to remain from eight in the morning till one in the afternoon, exposed to all sorts of opprobrium and abuse, and be condemned besides to a heavy fine; and for the sixth time, they shall be led to the pillory, and there have the upper lip cut with a hot iron; and for the seventh time, they shall be led to the pillory and have the lower lip cut; and if, by reason of obstinacy and inveterate bad habit, they continue after all these punishments to utter the said oaths and blasphemies, it is our will and command that they have the tongue completely cut out, so that thereafter they cannot utter them again." All those who should hear anybody swear were further required to report the fact to the nearest judge within twenty-four hours, on pain of fine.

This is far from being the only instance in which the temporal power lends aid to the spiritual. Among other cases, the following is worth mentioning: Louis Gaboury, an inhabitant of the island of Orleans, charged with eating meat in Lent without asking leave of the priest, was condemned by the local judge to be tied three hours to a stake in public, and then led to the door of the chapel, there on his knees, with head bare and hands clasped, to ask pardon of God and the King. The culprit appealed to the council, which revoked the sentence and imposed only a fine.

The due subordination of households had its share of attention. Servants who deserted their masters were to be set in the pillory for the first offence, and whipped and branded for the second; while any person harboring them was to pay a fine of twenty francs. On the other hand, nobody was allowed to employ a servant without a license.

In case of heinous charges, torture of the accused was permitted under the French law; and it was sometimes practised in Canada. Condemned murderers and felons were occasionally tortured before being strangled; and the dead body, enclosed in a kind of iron cage, was left hanging for months at the top of Cape Diamond, a terror to children and a warning to evil-doers. Yet, on the whole, Canadian justice, tried by the standard of the time, was neither vindictive nor cruel.

In reading the voluminous correspondence of governors and intendants, the minister and the King, nothing is more apparent than the interest with which, in the early part of his reign, Louis XIV. regarded his colony. One of the faults of his rule is the excess of his benevolence; for not only did he give money to support parish priests, build churches, and aid the seminary, the Ursulines, the missions, and the hospitals; but he established a fund destined, among other objects, to relieve indigent persons, subsidized nearly every branch of trade and industry, and in other instances did for the colonists what they would far better have learned to do for themselves.

Meanwhile, the officers of government were far from suffering from an excess of royal beneficence. La Hontan says that the local governor of Three Rivers would die of hunger if, besides his pay, he did not gain something by trade with the Indians; and that Perrot, local governor of Montreal, with one thousand crowns of salary, traded to such purpose that in a few years he made fifty thousand crowns. This trade, it may be observed, was in violation of the royal edicts. The pay of the governor-general varied from time to time. When La Potherie wrote, it was twelve thousand francs a year, besides three thousand which he received in his capacity of local governor of Quebec. This would hardly tempt a Frenchman of rank to expatriate himself; and yet some at least of the governors came out to the colony for the express purpose of mending their fortunes. Indeed, the higher nobility could scarcely, in time of peace, have other motives for going there; the court and the army were their element, and to be elsewhere was banishment. We shall see hereafter by what means they sought compensation for their exile in Canadian forests.

Loud complaints sometimes found their way to Versailles. A memorial addressed to the regent duke of Orleans, immediately after the King's death, declares that the ministers of state, who have been the real managers of the colony, have made their creatures and relations governors and intendants, and set them free from all responsibility. High colonial officers, pursues the writer, come home rich, while the colony languishes almost to perishing. As for lesser offices, they were multiplied to satisfy needy retainers, till lean and starving Canada was covered with official leeches, sucking, in famished desperation, at her bloodless veins.

The whole system of administration centred in the King, who, to borrow the formula of his edicts, "in the fulness of our power and our certain knowledge," was supposed to direct the whole machine, from its highest functions to its pettiest intervention in private affairs. That this theory, like all extreme theories of government, was an illusion, is no fault of Louis XIV. Hard-working monarch as he was, he spared no pains to guide his distant colony in the paths of prosperity. The prolix letters of governors and intendants were carefully studied; and many of the replies, signed by the royal hand, enter into details of surprising minuteness. That the King himself wrote these letters is incredible; but in the early part of his reign he certainly directed and controlled them. At a later time, when more absorbing interests engrossed him, he could no longer study in person the long-winded despatches of his Canadian officers. They were usually addressed to the minister of state, who caused abstracts to be made from them for the King's use, and perhaps for his own. The minister, or the minister's secretary, could suppress or color as he or those who influenced him saw fit.

In the latter half of his too long reign, when cares, calamities, and humiliations were thickening around the King, another influence was added to make the theoretical supremacy of his royal will more than ever a mockery. That prince of annalists, Saint-Simon, has painted Louis XIV. ruling his realm from the bedchamber of Madame de Maintenon,—seated with his minister at a small table beside the fire, the King in an arm-chair, the minister on a stool, with his bag of papers on a second stool near him. In another arm-chair, at another table on the other side of the fire, sat the sedate favorite, busy to all appearance with a book or a piece of tapestry, but listening to everything that passed. "She rarely spoke," says Saint-Simon, "except when the King asked her opinion, which he often did; and then she answered with great deliberation and gravity. She never, or very rarely, showed a partiality for any measure, still less for any person; but she had an understanding with the minister, who never dared do otherwise than she wished. Whenever any favor or appointment was in question, the business was settled between them beforehand. She would send to the minister that she wanted to speak to him, and he did not dare bring the matter on the carpet till he had received her orders." Saint-Simon next recounts the subtle methods by which Maintenon and the minister, her tool, beguiled the King to do their will, while never doubting that he was doing his own. "He thought," concludes the annalist, "that it was he alone who disposed of all appointments; while in reality he disposed of very few indeed, except on the rare occasions when he had taken a fancy to somebody, or when somebody whom he wanted to favor had spoken to him in behalf of somebody else."

Add to all this the rarity of communication with the distant colony. The ships from France arrived at Quebec in July, August, or September, and returned in November. The machine of Canadian government, wound up once a year, was expected to run unaided at least a twelvemonth. Indeed, it was often left to itself for two years, such was sometimes the tardiness of the overburdened government in answering the despatches of its colonial agents. It is no matter of surprise that a writer well versed in its affairs calls Canada the "country of abuses."

Chapter 24. 1663–1763. Canadian Absolutism

Not institutions alone, but geographical position, climate, and many other conditions unite to form the educational influences that, acting through successive generations, shape the character of nations and communities.

It is easy to see the nature of the education, past and present, which wrought on the Canadians and made them what they were. An ignorant population, sprung from a brave and active race, but trained to subjection and dependence through centuries of feudal and monarchical despotism, was planted in the wilderness by the hand of authority, and told to grow and flourish. Artificial stimulants were applied, but freedom was withheld. Perpetual intervention of government,—regulations, restrictions, encouragements sometimes more mischievous than restrictions, a constant uncertainty what the authorities would do next, the fate of each man resting less with himself than with another, volition enfeebled, self-reliance paralyzed,—the condition, in short, of a child held always under the rule of a father, in the main well-meaning and kind, sometimes generous, sometimes neglectful, often capricious, and rarely very wise,—such were the influences under which Canada grew up. If she had prospered, it would have been sheer miracle. A man, to be a man, must feel that he holds his fate, in some good measure, in his own hands.

But this was not all. Against absolute authority there was a counter influence, rudely and wildly antagonistic. Canada was at the very portal of the great interior wilderness. The St. Lawrence and the Lakes were the highway to that domain of savage freedom; and thither the disfranchised, half-starved seignior, and the discouraged *habitant* who could find no market for his produce naturally enough betook themselves. Their lesson of savagery was well learned, and for many a year a boundless license and a stiff-handed authority battled for the control of Canada. Nor, to the last, were Church and State fairly masters of the field. The French rule was drawing towards its close when the intendant complained that though twenty-eight companies of regular troops were quartered in the colony, there were not soldiers enough to keep the people in order. One cannot but remember that in a neighboring colony, far more populous, perfect order prevailed, with no other guardians than a few constables chosen by the people themselves.

Whence arose this difference, and other differences equally striking, between the rival colonies? It is easy to ascribe them to a difference of political and religious institutions; but the explanation does not cover the ground. The institutions of New England were utterly inapplicable to the population of New France, and the attempt to apply them would have wrought nothing but mischief. There are no political panaceas, except in the imagination of political quacks. To each degree and each variety of public development there are corresponding institutions, best answering the public needs; and what is meat to one is poison to another. Freedom is for those who are fit for it; the rest will lose it, or turn it to corruption. Church and State were right in exercising authority over a people which had not learned the first rudiments of self-government. Their fault was not that they exercised authority, but that they exercised too much of it, and, instead of weaning the child to go alone, kept him in perpetual leading-strings, making him, if possible, more and more dependent, and less and less fit for freedom.

In the building up of colonies, England succeeded and France failed. The cause lies chiefly in the vast advantage drawn by England from the historical training of her people in habits of reflection, forecast, industry, and self-reliance,—a training which enabled them to adopt and maintain an invigorating system of self-rule, totally inapplicable to their rivals.

The New England colonists were far less fugitives from oppression than voluntary exiles seeking the realization of an idea. They were neither peasants nor soldiers, but a substantial Puritan yeomanry, led by Puritan gentlemen and divines in thorough sympathy with them. They were neither sent out by the King, governed by him, nor helped by him. They grew up in utter neglect, and continued neglect was the only boon they asked. Till their increasing strength roused the jealousy of the

Crown, they were virtually independent,—a republic, but by no means a democracy. They chose their governor and all their rulers from among themselves, made their own government and paid for it, supported their own clergy, defended themselves, and educated themselves. Under the hard and repellent surface of New England society lay the true foundations of a stable freedom,—conscience, reflection, faith, patience, and public spirit. The cement of common interests, hopes, and duties compacted the whole people like a rock of conglomerate; while the people of New France remained in a state of political segregation, like a basket of pebbles held together by the enclosure that surrounds them.

It may be that the difference of historical antecedents would alone explain the difference of character between the rival colonies; but there are deeper causes, the influence of which went far to determine the antecedents themselves. The Germanic race, and especially the Anglo-Saxon branch of it, is peculiarly masculine, and, therefore, peculiarly fitted for self-government. It submits its action habitually to the guidance of reason, and has the judicial faculty of seeing both sides of a question. The French Celt is cast in a different mould. He sees the end distinctly, and reasons about it with an admirable clearness; but his own impulses and passions continually turn him away from it. Opposition excites him; he is impatient of delay, is impelled always to extremes, and does not readily sacrifice a present inclination to an ultimate good. He delights in abstractions and generalizations, cuts loose from unpleasing facts, and roams through an ocean of desires and theories.

While New England prospered and Canada did not prosper, the French system had at least one great advantage. It favored military efficiency. The Canadian population sprang in great part from soldiers, and was to the last systematically reinforced by disbanded soldiers. Its chief occupation was a continual training for forest war; it had little or nothing to lose, and little to do but fight and range the woods. This was not all. The Canadian government was essentially military. At its head was a soldier nobleman, often an old and able commander; and those beneath him caught his spirit and emulated his example. In spite of its political nothingness, in spite of poverty and hardship, and in spite even of trade, the upper stratum of Canadian society was animated by the pride and fire of that gallant *noblesse* which held war as its only worthy calling, and prized honor more than life. As for the *habitant,* the forest, lake, and river were his true school; and here, at least, he was an apt scholar. A skilful woodsman, a bold and adroit canoe-man, a willing fighter in time of need, often serving without pay, and receiving from government only his provisions and his canoe, he was more than ready at any time for any hardy enterprise; and in the forest warfare of skirmish and surprise there were few to match him. An absolute government used him at will, and experienced leaders guided his rugged valor to the best account.

The New England man was precisely the same material with that of which Cromwell formed his invincible "Ironsides"; but he had very little forest experience. His geographical position cut him off completely from the great wilderness of the interior. The sea was his field of action. Without the aid of government, and in spite of its restrictions, he built up a prosperous commerce, and enriched himself by distant fisheries, neglected by the rivals before whose doors they lay. He knew every ocean from Greenland to Cape Horn, and the whales of the north and of the south had no more dangerous foe. But he was too busy to fight without good cause; and when he turned his hand to soldiering, it was only to meet some pressing need of the hour. The New England troops in the early wars were bands of raw fishermen and farmers, led by civilians, decorated with military titles, and subject to the slow and uncertain action of legislative bodies. The officers had not learned to command, nor the men to obey. The remarkable exploit of the capture of Louisburg, the strongest fortress in America, was the result of mere audacity and hardihood, backed by the rarest good luck.

One great fact stands out conspicuous in Canadian history,—the Church of Rome. More even than the royal power, she shaped the character and the destinies of the colony. She was its nurse and almost its mother; and, wayward and headstrong as it was, it never broke the ties of faith that held it to her. It was these ties which, in the absence of political franchises, formed under the old régime the only vital coherence in the population. The royal government was transient; the Church was permanent. The English conquest shattered the whole apparatus of civil administration at a blow, but it left her untouched. Governors, intendants, councils, and commandants, all were gone; the principal seigniors fled the colony; and a people who had never learned to control themselves or help themselves were suddenly left to their own devices. Confusion, if not anarchy, would have followed but for the parish priests, who, in a character of double paternity, half spiritual and half temporal, became more than ever the guardians of order throughout Canada.

This English conquest was the grand crisis of Canadian history. It was the beginning of a new life. With England came Protestantism, and the Canadian Church grew purer and better in the presence of an adverse faith. Material growth; an increased mental activity; an education, real though fenced and guarded; a warm and genuine patriotism,—all date from the peace of 1763. England imposed by the sword on reluctant Canada the boon of rational and ordered liberty. Through centuries of striving she had advanced from stage to stage of progress, deliberate and calm,—never breaking with her past, but making each fresh gain the base of a new success,—enlarging popular liberties while bating nothing of that height and force of individual development which is the brain and heart of civilization; and now, through a hard-earned victory, she taught the conquered colony to share the blessings she had won. A happier calamity never befell a people than the conquest of Canada by the British arms.

Henry Adams

1838—1918

8

When Henry Adams was busily at work on his nine-volume *History of the United States During the Jefferson and Madison Administrations,* he wrote to Francis Parkman with great confidence that "the purely mechanical development of the human mind in society must appear in a great democracy so clearly, for want of disturbing elements, that in another generation psychology, physiology, and history will join in proving man to have as fixed and necessary development as that of a tree; and almost as unconscious." During the last twenty-five years of his life, Adams became quite pessimistic about the possibilities of scientific history and, in fact, declared his own historical work to be an abject failure; but until his period of apparent self-denigration set in, he believed as strongly as any social theorist in his century that the laws which govern the natural sciences could be applied to the study of present and past human society. While his *History* may have fallen short of the goal of uncovering the workings of the mechanism of the human mind or of the cosmos, it did mark the zenith of scientific history in America in the nineteenth century, and it is for this reason that the work is being included in this series.

Two vastly influential figures in the nineteenth century provided the background for Adams' belief in the application of the techniques of the natural sciences to history. The French sociologist Auguste Comte stimulated a whole school of positivist thinkers who agreed with him that it was possible to discover the fixed laws which govern human society in the same way as the world of nature is ruled by physical laws. Comte and his votaries believed that an understanding of the laws of society would enable the state to control the direction of history. Charles Darwin's discoveries in his study of evolution provided biological analogies that were freely transposed to the realm of social theory by Herbert Spencer in America. Darwin impressed upon his audience that he had found the key to understanding the evolutionary process, and the elaborate illustrations which fill the pages of *Origin of Species* led many an excited reader to the mistaken conclusion that there was no longer any mystery concerning the history of the species, a conclusion which Darwin himself vainly sought to discourage. When, as a young man, Adams wrote to his brother that "my philosophy teaches me, and I firmly believe it, that the laws which govern animated beings will be ultimately found to be at the bottom the same with those of inanimate nature," he called attention to the impact of these intellectual giants on his own generation.

Adams was born into a family that was not only conscious of the history of America but that had actually made a good deal of it. In *The Education of Henry Adams,* that impressive and disturbing autobiography, the author remarked that in the Quincy Church in Boston he was able to sit "behind a President grandfather and to read over his head the tablet in memory of a President great-grandfather." A distinguished and a very wealthy family may have helped Adams to find his vocation eventually; but, until the age of thirty, his career was governed by filial duties exacted by a patrician family. After being graduated from Harvard he traveled to Europe, but he failed to pursue his intention of studying civil law in Berlin. Upon return to his native Boston, he did begin a legal education in the office of Judge Horace Gray, but he interrupted his apprenticeship to follow his father as a personal secretary—first to Washington, when Charles Francis Adams was elected to Congress in 1858, then to London as part of the legation when his father was made Ambassador to England. It was not until 1868 that Adams was free to choose a career for himself.

For two years, from 1868 to 1870, Adams was active in reform journalism, contributing articles to the *North American Review,* the *Nation,* and the *New York Post* as well as to the British periodicals *Edinburgh Review* and *Westminster Review.* As an observer of the Washington scene, he expressed contempt for the corrupt administration of Ulysses S. Grant and for the party hacks who were appointed to important positions. In 1870, Adams, delighted with his appointment as Assistant Professor of History at Harvard, gladly abandoned journalism and began to teach, first medieval history, for such was his assignment, then to conduct a graduate seminar where he taught some of the first professional history students to be trained in an American university.

Out of this seminar came, in 1876, *Essays in Anglo-Saxon Law,* in which Adams and his pupils traced the origins of English legal institutions. In 1877, Adams published a selection of Federalist documents of the early national period, *Documents Relating to New England Federalism, 1800–1815.* In 1879, he presented an edition of the papers of Albert Gallatin, who had been Thomas Jefferson's Secretary of the Treasury, as well as an admirable political biography of Gallatin, whom he respected for his pragmatic politics and his sound fiscal policies. Except for a brief and frustrating attempt to aid the Liberal Republican reform movement in 1876, Adams during this period of his life spent five hours a day writing history and made numerous trips to London, Paris, and Madrid in search of documents.

By any standard, except the one set by its author, Adams' *History,* published from 1889 to 1894, is an outstanding achievement. The first six chapters, from which we have drawn our selections, are the first sustained attempt in America at social history. In these chapters Adams renders a vivid picture of the American people in 1800. With an interest in geography and demography, Adams contrasts the physical aspects of the American continent with those of Europe. He considers travel, trade, and manufacturing during this period; and he shows how these activities varied among the several states. He concludes that one of the forces working against the Union was the "disproportion between the physical obstacles and the material means for overcoming them" in the different sections of the country. In addition, he uses representative types of character to contrast opposing mentalities in various parts of the country. Thomas Jefferson, for example, is referred to as representing "the hopes of science and the prejudices of Virginia." The bulk of the nine volumes is a detailed account, based on extensive documentary research, of the political, military, and diplomatic history of the period. Throughout, Adams uses the metaphors of natural science in discussing the course of American history. Unfortunately he was unable to realize his aim as he stated it at the end of his work: "Sound the depths of the democratic ocean, measure its currents, foretell its storms, or fix its relations to the system of nature."

Just three years after the publication of the last volume of the *History,* Adams confessed that it had been his unfulfilled dream to "apply Darwin's method to the facts of history." Human nature and human history simply could not be studied as if they were integral parts of a mechanical universe. He could not, in his own words, "fix for a familiar moment a necessary sequence of human movement," because the behavior of the human animal defies any mechanistic mold that might be placed on it, a fact which Adams came to realize quite movingly in his later years. However, if Adams failed to write history in what he believed to be the tradition of Comte or Darwin, he certainly succeeded in applying the rigorous methods of Ranke. In recounting political and diplomatic activities, he demonstrated what one critic has correctly called "a splendid devotion to, and a rigorous regard for, truth as the ultimate end of history." His *History* is significantly different from the literary histories that preceded it. In contrast to Parkman, for example, Adams shows a greater interest in his sources, demands far more from his reader, since he is reluctant to draw obvious conclusions or persuade by means of dramatic episodes and sweeping generalizations. If Adams did not himself know how to integrate the data of social science effectively, he at least was an inspiration to later historians who could.

Adams spent the last years of his life explaining his failure as a historian. He dismissed his belief in science as part of the naïve and crude fashion of the vulgar, materialistic nineteenth century. He claimed that his family, his background, and his education blinded him to emotions, intuition, and instinct. In his *Mont-Saint-Michel and Chartres* he embraced the spirituality of the Middle Ages, personified in the Virgin, as the true source of life's vital energies. Those energies, he insisted in the final chapters of *The Education of Henry Adams,* were quickly dissipating; and in his last essays he predicted that Western civilization would soon join the Adams family in a rapid decline. Adams himself declined into the worst excesses of *fin de siècle* pessimism, and even into thinly veiled anti-Semitism. He at one and the same time excused and glamorized his own failure as the failure of a century.

In the *Education,* looking retrospectively at his life, Adams wrote, "All the historian won was a vehement wish to escape. He saw his education complete, and was sorry he ever began it. As a matter of taste, he greatly preferred his eighteenth-century education when God was a father and nature a mother, and all was for the best in a scientific universe." His discovery in *Mont-Saint-Michel* that in the Virgin "man had found the door of escape" is pathetic. There was no noble fight in struggling to have been born six centuries earlier. There is, fortunately for us, his *History,* which has a secure place in the history of American history and which remains the most complete account of the politics of the first two decades of the nineteenth century.

Selected Bibliography

The first two installments of Ernest Samuel's biography of Adams—*The Young Henry Adams* (1948) and *Henry Adams: The Middle Years* (1958)—are definitive for the period through the writing of the *History.* William H. Jordy's *Henry Adams: Scientific Historian* (1952) is a fine monograph, which does more than trace Adams' scientific theories of history. The long bibliographical essay is complete, up to the date of the publication of the study. George Hochfield's *Henry Adams: An Introduction and Interpretation* (1962) is helpful and lucidly written. A somewhat dated essay, "Henry Adams," by Henry Steele Commager, in *The Marcus W. Jernegan Essays in American Historiography* (1937), is still an arresting commentary on the importance of Adams as a historical figure, if not as a historian. Michael Kraus's estimation of the place of Adams in American historiography in his *A History of American History* (1937) is well-reasoned and eloquently stated. As a commentary on his own life and times, Adams' autobiography, available in many editions, should not be missed.

HISTORY OF THE UNITED STATES DURING THE JEFFERSON AND MADISON ADMINISTRATIONS

Chapter 1

According to the census of 1800, the United States of America contained 5,308,483 persons. In the same year the British Islands contained upwards of fifteen millions; the French Republic, more than twenty-seven millions. Nearly one fifth of the American people were negro slaves; the true political population consisted of four and a half million free whites, or less than one million able-bodied males, on whose shoulders fell the burden of a continent. Even after two centuries of struggle the land was still untamed; forest covered every portion, except here and there a strip of cultivated soil; the minerals lay undisturbed in their rocky beds, and more than two thirds of the people clung to the seaboard within fifty miles of tide-water, where alone the wants of civilized life could be supplied. The centre of population rested within eighteen miles of Baltimore, north and east of Washington. Except in political arrangement, the interior was little more civilized than in 1750, and was not much easier to penetrate than when La Salle and Hennepin found their way to the Mississippi more than a century before.

A great exception broke this rule. Two wagon-roads crossed the Alleghany Mountains in Pennsylvania,—one leading from Philadelphia to Pittsburg; one from the Potomac to the Monongahela; while a third passed through Virginia southwestward to the Holston River and Knoxville in Tennessee, with a branch through the Cumberland Gap into Kentucky. By these roads and by trails less passable from North and South Carolina, or by water-ways from the lakes, between four and five hundred thousand persons had invaded the country beyond the Alleghanies. At Pittsburg and on the Monongahela existed a society, already old, numbering seventy or eighty thousand persons, while on the Ohio River the settlements had grown to an importance which threatened to force a difficult problem on the union of the older States. One hundred and eighty thousand whites, with forty thousand negro slaves, made Kentucky the largest community west of the mountains; and about ninety thousand whites and fourteen thousand slaves were scattered over Tennessee. In the territory north of the Ohio less progress had been made. A New England colony existed at Marietta; some fifteen thousand people were gathered at Cincinnati; half-way between the two, a small town had grown up at Chillicothe, and other villages or straggling cabins were to be found elsewhere; but the whole Ohio territory contained only forty-five thousand inhabitants. The entire population, both free and slave, west of the mountains, reached not yet half a million; but already they were partly disposed to think themselves, and the old thirteen States were not altogether unwilling to consider them, the germ of an independent empire, which was to find its outlet, not through the Alleghanies to the seaboard, but by the Mississippi River to the Gulf.

Nowhere did eastern settlements touch the western. At least one hundred miles of mountainous country held the two regions everywhere apart. The shore of Lake Erie, where alone contact seemed easy, was still unsettled. The Indians had been pushed back to the Cuyahoga River, and a few cabins were built on the site of Cleveland; but in 1800, as in 1700, this intermediate region was only a portage where emigrants and merchandise were transferred from Lake Erie to the Muskingum and Ohio valleys. Even western New York remained a wilderness: Buffalo was not laid out; Indian titles were not extinguished; Rochester did not exist; and the county of Onondaga numbered a population of less than eight thousand. In 1799 Utica contained fifty houses, mostly small and temporary. Albany was still a Dutch city, with some five thousand inhabitants; and the tide of immigration flowed slowly through it into the valley of the Mohawk, while another stream from Pennsylvania, following the Susquehanna, spread toward the Genesee country.

The people of the old thirteen States, along the Atlantic seaboard, thus sent westward a wedge-shaped mass of nearly half a million persons, penetrating by the Tennessee, Cumberland, and Ohio rivers toward the western limit of the Union. The Indians offered sharp resistance to this invasion, exacting life for life, and yielding only as their warriors perished. By the close of the century the wedge of white settlements, with its apex at Nashville and its flanks covered by the Ohio and Tennessee rivers, nearly split the Indian country in halves. The northern half—consisting of the later States of Wisconsin, Michigan, Illinois, Indiana, and one third of Ohio—contained Wyandottes and Shawanese, Miamis, Kickapoos, and other tribes, able to send some five thousand warriors to hunt or fight. In the southern half, powerful confederacies of Creeks, Cherokees, Chickasaws, and Choctaws lived and hunted where the States of Mississippi, Alabama, and the western parts of Georgia, Tennessee, and Kentucky were to extend; and so weak was the State of Georgia, which claimed the southwestern territory for its own, that a well-concerted movement of Indians might without much difficulty have swept back its white population of one hundred thousand toward the ocean or across the Savannah River. The Indian power had been broken in halves, but each half was still terrible to the colonists on the edges of their vast domain, and was used as a political weapon by the Governments whose territory bounded the Union on the north and south. The governors-general of Canada intrigued with the northwestern Indians, that they might hold in check any aggression from Washington; while the Spanish governors of West Florida and Louisiana maintained equally close relations with the Indian confederacies of the Georgia territory.

With the exception that half a million people had crossed the Alleghanies and were struggling with difficulties all their own, in an isolation like that of Jutes or Angles in the fifth century, America, so far as concerned physical problems, had changed little in fifty years. The old landmarks remained nearly where they stood before. The same bad roads and difficult rivers, connecting the same small towns, stretched into the same forests in 1800 as when the armies of Braddock and Amherst pierced the western and northern wilderness, except that these roads extended a few miles farther from the seacoast. Nature was rather man's master than his servant, and the five million Americans struggling with the untamed continent seemed hardly more competent to their task than the beavers and buffalo which had for countless generations made bridges and roads of their own.

Even by water, along the seaboard, communication was as slow and almost as irregular as in colonial times. The wars in Europe caused a sudden and great increase in American shipping employed in foreign commerce, without yet leading to general improvement in navigation. The ordinary sea-going vessel carried a freight of about two hundred and fifty tons; the largest merchant ships hardly reached four hundred tons; the largest frigate in the United States navy, the "line-of-battle ship in disguise," had a capacity of fifteen hundred and seventy-six tons. Elaborately rigged as ships or brigs, the small merchant craft required large crews and were slow sailers; but the voyage to Europe was comparatively more comfortable and more regular than the voyage from New York to Albany, or through Long Island Sound to Providence. No regular packet plied between New York and Albany. Passengers waited till a sloop was advertised to sail; they provided their own bedding and supplies; and within the nineteenth century Captain Elias Bunker won much fame by building the sloop "Experiment," of one hundred and ten tons, to start regularly on a fixed day for Albany, for the convenience of passengers only, supplying beds, wine, and provisions for the voyage of one hundred and fifty miles. A week on the North River or on the Sound was an experience not at all unknown to travellers.

While little improvement had been made in water-travel, every increase of distance added to the difficulties of the westward journey. The settler who after buying wagon and horses hauled his family and goods across the mountains, might buy or build a broad flat-bottomed ark, to float with him and his fortunes down the Ohio, in constant peril of upsetting or of being sunk; but only light boats with strong oars could mount the stream, or boats forced against the current by laboriously poling in shallow water. If he carried his tobacco and wheat down the Mississippi to the Spanish port of New Orleans, and sold it, he might return to his home in Kentucky or Ohio by a long and dangerous journey on horseback through the Indian country from Natchez to Nashville, or he might take ship to Philadelphia, if a ship were about to sail, and again cross the Alleghanies. Compared with river travel, the sea was commonly an easy and safe highway. Nearly all the rivers which penetrated the interior were unsure, liable to be made dangerous by freshets, and both dangerous and impassable by drought; yet such as they were, these streams made the main paths of traffic. Through the mountainous gorges of the Susquehanna the produce of western New York first found an outlet; the Cuyahoga and Muskingum were the first highway from the Lakes to the Ohio; the Ohio itself, with its great tributaries the Cumberland and the Tennessee, marked the lines of western migration; and every stream which could at high water float a boat was thought likely to become a path for commerce. As General Washington, not twenty years earlier, hoped that the brawling waters of the Cheat and Youghiogheny might become the channel of trade between Chesapeake Bay and Pittsburg, so the Americans of 1800 were prepared to risk life and property on any streamlet that fell foaming down either flank of the Alleghanies. The experience of mankind proved trade to be dependent on water communications, and as yet Americans did not dream that the experience of mankind was useless to them.

If America was to be developed along the lines of water communication alone, by such means as were known to Europe, Nature had decided that the experiment of a single republican government must meet extreme difficulties. The valley of the Ohio had no more to do with that of the Hudson, the Susquehanna, the Potomac, the Roanoke, and the Santee, than the valley of the Danube with that of the Rhone, the Po, or the Elbe. Close communication by land could alone hold the great geographical divisions together either in interest or in fear. The union of New England with New York and Pennsylvania was not an easy task even as a problem of geography, and with an ocean highway; but the union of New England with the Carolinas, and of the seacoast with the interior, promised to be a hopeless undertaking. Physical contact alone could make one country of these isolated empires, but to the patriotic American of 1800, struggling for the continued existence of an embryo nation, with machinery so inadequate, the idea of ever bringing the Mississippi River, either by land or water, into close contact with New England, must have seemed wild. By water, an Erie Canal was already foreseen; by land, centuries of labor could alone conquer those obstacles which Nature permitted to be overcome.

In the minds of practical men, the experience of Europe left few doubts on this point. After two thousand years of public labor and private savings, even despotic monarchs, who employed the resources of their subjects as they pleased, could in 1800 pass from one part of their European dominions to another little more quickly than they might have done in the age of the Antonines. A few short canals had been made, a few bridges had been built, an excellent post-road extended from Madrid to St. Petersburg; but the heavy diligence that rumbled from Calais to Paris required three days for its journey of one hundred and fifty miles, and if travellers ventured on a trip to Marseilles they met with rough roads and hardships like those of the Middle Ages. Italy was in 1800 almost as remote from the north of Europe as when carriage-roads were first built. Neither in time nor in thought was Florence or Rome much nearer to London in Wordsworth's youth than in the youth of Milton or Gray. Indeed, such changes as had occurred were partly for the worse, owing to the violence of revolutionary wars during the last ten years of the eighteenth century. Horace Walpole at his life's close saw about him a world which in many respects was less civilized than when as a boy he made the grand tour of Europe.

While so little had been done on the great highways of European travel, these highways were themselves luxuries which furnished no sure measure of progress. The post-horses toiled as painfully as ever through the sand from Hamburg to Berlin, while the coach between York and London rolled along an excellent road at the rate of ten miles an hour; yet neither in England nor on the Continent was the post-road a great channel of commerce. No matter how good the road, it could not compete with water, nor could heavy freights in great quantities be hauled long distances without extravagant cost. Water communication was as necessary for European commerce in 1800 as it had been for the Phoenicians and Egyptians; the Rhine, the Rhone, the Danube, the Elbe, were still the true commercial highways, and except for government post-roads, Europe was as dependent on these rivers in the eighteenth century as in the thirteenth. No certainty could be offered of more rapid progress in the coming century than in the past; the chief hope seemed to lie in the construction of canals.

While Europe had thus consumed centuries in improving paths of trade, until merchandise could be brought by canal a few score miles from the Rhone to the Loire and Seine, to the Garonne and the Rhine, and while all her wealth and energy had not yet united the Danube with other river systems, America was required to construct, without delay, at least three great roads and canals, each several hundred miles long, across mountain ranges, through a country not yet inhabited, to points where no great markets existed,—and this under constant peril of losing her political union, which could not even by such connections be with certainty secured. After this should be accomplished, the Alleghanies must still remain between the eastern and western States, and at any known rate of travel Nashville could not be reached in less than a fortnight or three weeks from Philadelphia. Meanwhile the simpler problem of bringing New England nearer to Virginia and Georgia had not advanced even with the aid of a direct ocean highway. In becoming politically independent of England, the old thirteen provinces developed little more commercial intercourse with each other in proportion to their wealth and population than they had maintained in colonial days. The material ties that united them grew in strength no more rapidly than the ties which bound them to Europe. Each group of States lived a life apart.

Even the lightly equipped traveller found a short journey no slight effort. Between Boston and New York was a tolerable highway, along which, thrice a week, light stage-coaches carried passengers and the mail, in three days. From New York a stage-coach started every week-day for Philadelphia, consuming the greater part of two days in the journey; and the road between Paulus Hook, the modern Jersey City, and Hackensack, was declared by the newspapers in 1802 to be as bad as any other part of the route between Maine and Georgia. South of Philadelphia the road was tolerable as far as Baltimore, but between Baltimore and the new city of Washington it meandered through forests; the driver chose the track which seemed least dangerous, and rejoiced if in wet seasons he reached Washington without miring or upsetting his wagon. In the Northern States, four miles an hour was the average speed for any coach between Bangor and Baltimore. Beyond the Potomac the roads became steadily worse, until south of Petersburg even the mails were carried on horseback. Except for a stage-coach which plied between Charleston and Savannah, no public conveyance of any kind was mentioned in the three southernmost States.

The stage-coach was itself a rude conveyance, of a kind still familiar to experienced travellers. Twelve persons, crowded into one wagon, were jolted over rough roads, their bags and parcels, thrust inside, cramping their legs, while they were protected from the heat and dust of midsummer and the intense cold and driving snow of winter only by leather flaps buttoned to the roof and sides. In fine, dry weather this mode of travel was not unpleasant, when compared with the heavy vehicles of

Europe and the hard English turnpikes; but when spring rains drew the frost from the ground the roads became nearly impassable, and in winter, when the rivers froze, a serious peril was added, for the Susquehanna or the North River at Paulus Hook must be crossed in an open boat,—an affair of hours at best, sometime leading to fatal accidents. Smaller annoyances of many kinds were habitual. The public, as a rule, grumbled less than might have been expected, but occasionally newspapers contained bitter complaints. An angry Philadelphian, probably a foreigner, wrote in 1796 that, "with a few exceptions, brutality, negligence, and filching are as naturally expected by people accustomed to travelling in America, as a mouth, a nose, and two eyes are looked for in a man's face." This sweeping charge, probably unjust, and certainly supported by little public evidence, was chiefly founded on the experience of an alleged journey from New York:

> At Bordentown we went into a second boat where we met with very sorry accommodation. This was about four o'clock in the afternoon. We had about twenty miles down the Delaware to reach Philadelphia. The captain, who had a most provoking tongue, was a boy about eighteen years of age. He and a few companions despatched a dozen or eighteen bottles of porter. We ran three different times against other vessels that were coming up the stream. The women and children lay all night on the bare boards of the cabin floor. . . . We reached Arch Street wharf about eight o'clock on the Wednesday morning, having been about sixteen hours on a voyage of twenty miles.

In the Southern States the difficulties and perils of travel were so great as to form a barrier almost insuperable. Even Virginia was no exception to this rule. At each interval of a few miles the horseman found himself stopped by a river, liable to sudden freshets, and rarely bridged. Jefferson in his frequent journeys between Monticello and Washington was happy to reach the end of the hundred miles without some vexatious delay. "Of eight rivers between here and Washington," he wrote to his Attorney-General in 1801, "five have neither bridges nor boats."

Expense caused an equally serious obstacle to travel. The usual charge in the Northern States was six cents a mile by stage. In the year 1796, according to Francis Baily, President of the Royal Astronomical Society, three or four stages ran daily from Baltimore to Philadelphia, the fare six dollars, with charges amounting to two dollars and a quarter a day at the inns on the road. Baily was three days in making the journey. From Philadelphia to New York he paid the same fare and charges, arriving in one day and a half. The entire journey of two hundred miles cost him twenty-one dollars. He remarked that travelling on the main lines of road in the settled country was about as expensive as in England, and when the roads were good, about as rapid. Congress allowed its members six dollars for every twenty miles travelled. The actual cost, including hotel expenses, could hardly have fallen below ten cents a mile.

Heavy traffic never used stage routes if it could find cheaper. Commerce between one State and another, or even between the seaboard and the interior of the same State, was scarcely possible on any large scale unless navigable water connected them. Except the great highway to Pittsburg, no road served as a channel of commerce between different regions of the country. In this respect New England east of the Connecticut was as independent of New York as both were independent of Virginia, and as Virginia in her turn was independent of Georgia and South Carolina. The chief value of inter-State communication by land rested in the postal system; but the post furnished another illustration of the difficulties which barred progress. In the year 1800 one general mail-route extended from Portland in Maine to Louisville in Georgia, the time required for the trip being twenty days. Between New York and Petersburg in Virginia was a daily service; between New York and Boston, and also between Petersburg and Augusta, the mail was carried thrice a week. Branching from the main line at New York, a mail went to Canandaigua in ten days; from Philadelphia another branch line went to Lexington in sixteen days, to Nashville in twenty-two days. Thus more than twenty thousand miles of post-road, with nine hundred post-offices, proved the vastness of the country and the smallness of the result: for the gross receipts for postage in the year ending Oct. 1, 1801, were only $320,000.

Throughout the land the eighteenth century ruled supreme. Only within a few years had the New Englander begun to abandon his struggle with a barren soil, among granite hills, to learn the comforts of easier existence in the valleys of the Mohawk and Ohio; yet the New England man was thought the shrewdest and most enterprising of Americans. If the Puritans and the Dutch needed a century or more to reach the Mohawk, when would they reach the Mississippi? The distance from New York to the Mississippi was about one thousand miles; from Washington to the extreme southwestern military post, below Natchez, was about twelve hundred. Scarcely a portion of western Europe was three hundred miles distant from some sea, but a width of three hundred miles was hardly more than an outskirt of the United States. No civilized country had yet been required to deal with physical difficulties so serious, nor did experience warrant conviction that such difficulties could be overcome.

If the physical task which lay before the American people had advanced but a short way toward completion, little more change could be seen in the economical conditions of American life. The man who in the year 1800 ventured to hope for a new era in the coming century, could lay his hand on no statistics that silenced doubt. The machinery of production showed no radical difference from that familiar to ages long past. The Saxon farmer of the eighth century enjoyed most of the comforts known to Saxon farmers of the eighteenth. The eorls and ceorls of Offa and Ecgbert could not read or write, and did not receive a weekly newspaper with such information as newspapers in that age could supply; yet neither their houses, their clothing, their food and drink, their agricultural tools and methods, their stock, nor their habits were so greatly altered or improved by time that they would have found much difficulty in accommodating their lives to that of their descendants in the eighteenth century. In this respect America was backward. Fifty or a hundred miles inland more than half the houses were log-cabins, which might or might not enjoy the luxury of a glass window. Throughout the South and West houses showed little attempt at luxury; but even in New England the ordinary farmhouse was hardly so well built, so spacious, or so warm as that of a well-to-do contemporary of Charlemagne. The cloth which the farmer's family wore was still homespun. The hats were manufactured by the village hatter; the clothes were cut and made at home; the shirts, socks, and nearly every other article of dress were also home-made. Hence came a marked air of rusticity which distinguished country from town,—awkward shapes of hat, coat, and trousers, which gave to the Yankee caricature those typical traits that soon disappeared almost as completely as coats of mail and steel head-pieces. The plough was rude and clumsy; the sickle as old as Tabal Cain, and even the cradle not in general use; the flail was unchanged since the Aryan exodus; in Virginia, grain was still commonly trodden out by horses. Enterprising gentlemen-farmers introduced threshing-machines and invented scientific ploughs; but these were novelties. Stock was as a rule not only unimproved, but ill cared for. The swine ran loose; the cattle were left to feed on what pasture they could find, and even in New England were not housed until the severest frosts, on the excuse that exposure hardened them. Near half a century afterward a competent judge asserted that the general treatment of cows in New England was fair matter of presentment by a grand jury. Except among the best farmers, drainage, manures, and rotation of crops were uncommon. The ordinary cultivator planted his corn as his father had planted it, sowing as much rye to the acre, using the same number of oxen to plough, and getting in his crops on the same day. He was even known to remove his barn on account of the manure accumulated round it, although the New England soil was never so rich as to warrant neglect to enrich it. The money for which he sold his wheat and chickens was of the Old World; he reckoned in shillings or pistareens, and rarely handled an American coin more valuable than a large copper cent.

At a time when the wealth and science of London and Paris could not supply an article so necessary as a common sulphur-match, the backwardness of remote country districts could hardly be exaggerated. Yet remote districts were not the only sufferers. Of the whole United States New England claimed to be the most civilized province, yet New England was a region in which life had yet gained few charms of sense and few advantages over its rivals. Wilson, the ornithologist, a Pennsylvania Scotchman, a confirmed grumbler, but a shrewd judge, and the most thorough of American travellers, said in 1808: "My journey through almost the whole of New England has rather lowered the Yankees in my esteem. Except a few neat academies, I found their schoolhouses equally ruinous and deserted with ours; fields covered with stones; stone fences; scrubby oaks and pine-trees; wretched orchards; scarcely one grain-field in twenty miles; the taverns along the road dirty, and filled with loungers brawling about lawsuits and politics; the people snappish and extortioners, lazy, and two hundred years behind the Pennsylvanians in agricultural improvements." The description was exaggerated, for Wilson forgot to speak of the districts where fields were not covered with stones, and where wheat could be grown to advantage. Twenty years earlier, Albert Gallatin, who knew Pennsylvania well, having reached Hartford on his way to Boston, wrote: "I have seen nothing in America equal to the establishments on the Connecticut River." Yet Wilson's account described the first general effect of districts in the New England States, where agriculture was backward and the country poor. The houses were thin wooden buildings, not well suited to the climate; the churches were unwarmed; the clothing was poor; sanitary laws were few, and a bathroom or a soil-pipe was unknown. Consumption, typhoid, scarlet fever, diphtheria, and rheumatic fevers were common; habits of drinking were still a scourge in every family, and dyspepsia destroyed more victims than were consumed by drink. Population increased slowly, as though the conditions of life were more than usually hard. A century earlier, Massachusetts was supposed to contain sixty thousand inhabitants. Governor Hutchinson complained that while the other colonies quadrupled their numbers, Massachusetts failed to double its population in fifty years. In 1790 the State contained 378,000 people, not including the province of Maine; in 1800 the number rose to 423,000, which showed that a period of more rapid growth had begun, for the emigration into other States was also large.

A better measure of the difficulties with which New England struggled was given by the progress of Boston, which was supposed to have contained about eighteen thousand inhabitants as early as 1730, and twenty thousand in 1770. For several years after the Revolution it numbered less than twenty thousand, but in 1800 the census showed twenty-five thousand inhabitants. In appearance, Boston resembled an English market-town, of a kind even then old-fashioned. The footways or sidewalks were paved, like the crooked and narrow streets, with round cobblestones, and were divided from the carriage way only by posts and a gutter. The streets were almost unlighted at night, a few oil-lamps rendering the darkness more visible and the rough pavement rougher. Police hardly existed. The system of taxation was defective. The town was managed by selectmen, the elected instruments of town-meetings whose jealousy of granting power was even greater than their objection to spending money, and whose hostility to city government was not to be overcome.

Although on all sides increase of ease and comfort was evident, and roads, canals, and new buildings, public and private, were already in course of construction on a scale before unknown, yet in spite of more than a century and a half of incessant industry, intelligent labor, and pinching economy Boston and New England were still poor. A few merchants enjoyed incomes derived from foreign trade, which allowed them to imitate in a quiet way the style of the English mercantile class; but the clergy and the lawyers, who stood at the head of society, lived with much economy. Many a country clergyman, eminent for piety and even for hospitality, brought up a family and laid aside some savings on a salary of five hundred dollars a year. President Dwight, who knew well the class to which he belonged, eulogizing the life of Abijah Weld, pastor of Attleborough, declared that on a salary of two hundred and twenty dollars a year Mr. Weld brought up eleven children, besides keeping a hospitable house and maintaining charity to the poor.

On the Exchange a few merchants had done most of the business of Boston since the peace of 1783, but a mail thrice a week to New York, and an occasional arrival from Europe or the departure of a ship to China, left ample leisure for correspondence and even for gossip. The habits of the commercial class had not been greatly affected by recent prosperity. Within ten or fifteen years before 1800 three Banks had been created to supply the commercial needs of Boston. One of these was a branch Bank of the United States, which employed there whatever part of its capital it could profitably use; the two others were local Banks, with capital of $1,600,000, toward which the State subscribed $400,000. Altogether the banking capital of Boston might amount to two millions and a half. A number of small Banks, representing in all about two and a half millions more, were scattered through the smaller New England towns. The extraordinary prosperity caused by the French wars opened to Boston a new career. Wealth and population were doubling; the exports and imports of New England were surprisingly large, and the shipping was greater than that of New York and Pennsylvania combined; but Boston had already learned, and was to learn again, how fleeting were the riches that depended on foreign commerce, and conservative habits were not easily changed by a few years of accidental gain.

Of manufactures New England had many, but none on a large scale. The people could feed or clothe themselves only by household industry; their whale-oil, salt fish, lumber, and rum were mostly sent abroad; but they freighted coasters with turners' articles, home-made linens and cloths, cheese, butter, shoes, nails, and what were called Yankee Notions of all sorts, which were sent to Norfolk and the Southern ports, and often peddled from the deck, as goods of every sort were peddled on the flat-boats of the Ohio. Two or three small mills spun cotton with doubtful success; but England supplied ordinary manufactures more cheaply and better than Massachusetts could hope to do. A tri-weekly mail and a few coasting sloops provided for the business of New England with domestic ports. One packet sloop plied regularly to New York.

The State of New York was little in advance of Massachusetts and Maine. In 1800 for the first time New York gained the lead in population by the difference between 589,000 and 573,000. The valuation of New York for the direct tax in 1799 was $100,000,000; that of Massachusetts was $84,000,000. New York was still a frontier State, and although the city was European in its age and habits, travellers needed to go few miles from the Hudson in order to find a wilderness like that of Ohio and Tennessee. In most material respects the State was behind New England; outside the city was to be seen less wealth and less appearance of comfort. The first impression commonly received of any new country was from its inns, and on the whole few better tests of material condition then existed. President Dwight, though maintaining that the best old-fashioned inns of New England were in their way perfect, being in fact excellent private houses, could not wholly approve what he called the modern inns, even in Connecticut; but when he passed into New York he asserted that everything suffered an instant change for the worse. He explained that in Massachusetts the authorities were strict in refusing licenses to any but respectable and responsible persons, whereas in New York licenses were granted to any one who would pay for them,—which caused a multiplication of dram-shops, bad accommodations, and a gathering of loafers and tipplers about every tavern porch, whose rude appearance, clownish manners, drunkenness, swearing, and obscenity confirmed the chief of Federalist clergymen in his belief that democracy had an evil influence on morals.

Far more movement was to be seen, and accumulation was more rapid than in colonial days; but little had yet been done for improvement, either by Government or by individuals, beyond some provision for extending roads and clearing watercourses behind the advancing settlers. If Washington Irving was right, Rip Van Winkle, who woke from his long slumber about the year 1800, saw little that was new to him, except the head of President Washington where that of King George had once hung, and strange faces instead of familiar ones. Except in numbers, the city was relatively no farther advanced than the country. Between 1790 and 1800 its population rose from 33,000 to 60,000; and if Boston resembled an old-fashioned English market-town, New York was like a foreign seaport, badly paved, undrained, and as foul as a town surrounded by the tides could be. Although the Manhattan Company was laying wooden pipes for a water supply, no sanitary regulations were enforced, and every few years—as in 1798 and 1803—yellow fever swept away crowds of victims, and drove the rest of the population, panic stricken, into the highlands. No day-police existed; constables were still officers of the courts; the night-police consisted of two captains, two deputies, and seventy-two men. The estimate for the city's expenses in 1800 amounted to $130,000. One marked advantage New York enjoyed over Boston, in the possession of a city government able to introduce reforms. Thus, although still mediæval in regard to drainage and cleanliness, the town had taken advantage of recurring fires to rebuild some of the streets with brick sidewalks and curbstones. Travellers dwelt much on this improvement, which only New York and Philadelphia had yet adopted, and Europeans agreed that both had the air of true cities: that while Boston was the Bristol of America, New York was the Liverpool, and Philadelphia the London.

In respect to trade and capital, New York possessed growing advantages, supplying half New Jersey and Connecticut, a part of Massachusetts, and all the rapidly increasing settlements on the branches of the Hudson; but no great amount of wealth, no considerable industry or new creation of power was yet to be seen. Two Banks, besides the branch Bank of the United States, supplied the business wants of the city, and employed about the same amount of capital in loans and discounts as was required for Boston. Besides these city institutions but two other Banks existed in the State,—at Hudson and at Albany.

The proportion of capital in private hands seemed to be no larger. The value of exports from New York in 1800 was but $14,000,000; the net revenue on imports for 1799 was $2,373,000, against $1,607,000 collected in Massachusetts. Such a foreign trade required little capital, yet these values represented a great proportion of all the exchanges. Domestic manufactures could not compete with foreign, and employed little bank credit. Speculation was slow, mostly confined to lands which required patience to exchange or sell. The most important undertakings were turnpikes, bridges such as Boston built across the Charles, or new blocks of houses; and a canal, such as Boston designed to the Merrimac, overstrained the resources of capital. The entire banking means of the United States in 1800 would not have answered the stock-jobbing purposes of one great operator of Wall Street in 1875. The nominal capital of all the Banks, including the Bank of the United States, fell short of $29,000,000. The limit of credit was quickly reached, for only the richest could borrow more than fifteen or twenty thousand dollars at a time, and the United States Government itself was gravely embarrassed whenever obliged to raise money. In 1798 the Secretary of the Treasury could obtain five million dollars only by paying eight per cent interest for a term of years; and in 1814 the Government was forced to stop payments for the want of twenty millions.

The precise value of American trade was uncertain, but in 1800 the gross exports and imports of the United States may have balanced at about seventy-five million dollars. The actual consumption of foreign merchandise amounted perhaps to the value of forty or fifty million dollars, paid in wheat, cotton, and other staples, and by the profits on the shipping employed in carrying West India produce to Europe. The amount of American capital involved in a trade of fifty millions, with credits of three, six, and nine months, must have been small, and the rates of profit large.

As a rule American capital was absorbed in shipping or agriculture, whence it could not be suddenly withdrawn. No stock-exchange existed, and no broker exclusively engaged in stock-jobbing, for there were few stocks. The national debt, of about eighty millions, was held abroad, or as a permanent investment at home. States and municipalities had not learned to borrow. Except for a few banks and insurance offices, turnpikes, bridges, canals, and land-companies, neither bonds nor stocks were known. The city of New York was so small as to make extravagance difficult; the Battery was a fashionable walk, Broadway a country drive, and Wall Street an uptown residence. Great accumulations of wealth had hardly begun. The Patroon was still the richest man in the State. John Jacob Astor was a fur-merchant living where the Astor House afterward stood, and had not yet begun those purchases of real estate which secured his fortune. Cornelius Vanderbilt was a boy six years old, playing about his father's ferry-boat at Staten Island. New York city itself was what it had been for a hundred years past,—a local market.

As a national capital New York made no claim to consideration. If Bostonians for a moment forgot their town-meetings, or if Virginians overcame their dislike for cities and pavements, they visited and admired, not New York, but Philadelphia. "Philadelphia," wrote the Duc de Liancourt, "is not only the finest city in the United States, but may be deemed one of the most beautiful cities in the world." In truth, it surpassed any of its size on either side of the Atlantic for most of the comforts and some of the elegancies of life. While Boston contained twenty-five thousand inhabitants and New York sixty thousand, the census of

1800 showed that Philadelphia was about the size of Liverpool,—a city of seventy thousand people. The repeated ravages of yellow fever roused there a regard for sanitary precautions and cleanliness; the city, well paved and partly drained, was supplied with water in wooden pipes, and was the best-lighted town in America; its market was a model, and its jail was intended also for a model,—although the first experiment proved unsuccessful, because the prisoners went mad or idiotic in solitary confinement. In and about the city flourished industries considerable for the time. The iron-works were already important; paper and gunpowder, pleasure carriages and many other manufactures, were produced on a larger scale than elsewhere in the Union. Philadelphia held the seat of government until July, 1800, and continued to hold the Bank of the United States, with its capital of ten millions, besides private banking capital to the amount of five millions more. Public spirit was more active in Pennsylvania than in New York. More roads and canals were building; a new turnpike ran from Philadelphia to Lancaster, and the great highway to Pittsburg was a more important artery of national life than was controlled by any other State. The exports of Pennsylvania amounted to $12,000,000, and the custom-house produced $1,350,000. The State contained six hundred thousand inhabitants,—a population somewhat larger than that of New York.

Of all parts of the Union, Pennsylvania seemed to have made most use of her national advantages; but her progress was not more rapid than the natural increase of population and wealth demanded, while to deal with the needs of America, man's resources and his power over Nature must be increased in a ratio far more rapid than that which governed his numbers. Nevertheless, Pennsylvania was the most encouraging spectacle in the field of vision. Baltimore, which had suddenly sprung to a population and commerce greater than those of Boston, also offered strong hope of future improvement; but farther South the people showed fewer signs of change.

The city of Washington, rising in a solitude on the banks of the Potomac, was a symbol of American nationality in the Southern States. The contrast between the immensity of the task and the paucity of means seemed to challenge suspicion that the nation itself was a magnificent scheme like the federal city, which could show only a few log-cabins and negro quarters where the plan provided for the traffic of London and the elegance of Versailles. When in the summer of 1800 the government was transferred to what was regarded by most persons as a fever-stricken morass, the half-finished White House stood in a naked field overlooking the Potomac, with two awkward Department buildings near it, a single row of brick houses and a few isolated dwellings within sight, and nothing more; until across a swamp, a mile and a half away, the shapeless, unfinished Capitol was seen, two wings without a body, ambitious enough in design to make more grotesque the nature of its surroundings. The conception proved that the United States understood the vastness of their task, and were willing to stake something on their faith in it. Never did hermit or saint condemn himself to solitude more consciously than Congress and the Executive in removing the government from Philadelphia to Washington: the discontented men clustered together in eight or ten boarding-houses as near as possible to the Capitol, and there lived, like a convent of monks, with no other amusement or occupation than that of going from their lodgings to the Chambers and back again. Even private wealth could do little to improve their situation, for there was nothing which wealth could buy; there were in Washington no shops or markets, skilled labor, commerce, or people. Public efforts and lavish use of public money could alone make the place tolerable; but Congress doled out funds for this national and personal object with so sparing a hand, that their Capitol threatened to crumble in pieces and crush Senate and House under the ruins, long before the building was complete.

A government capable of sketching a magnificent plan, and willing to give only a half-hearted pledge for its fulfilment; a people eager to advertise a vast undertaking beyond their present powers, which when completed would become an object of jealousy and fear,—this was the impression made upon the traveller who visited Washington in 1800, and mused among the unraised columns of the Capitol upon the destiny of the United States. As he travelled farther south his doubts were strengthened, for across the Potomac he could detect no sign of a new spirit. Manufactures had no existence. Alexandria owned a bank with half a million of capital, but no other was to be found between Washington and Charleston, except the branch Bank of the United States at Norfolk, nor any industry to which loans and discounts could safely be made. Virginia, the most populous and powerful of all the States, had a white population of 514,000, nearly equal to that of Pennsylvania and New York, besides about 350,000 slaves. Her energies had pierced the mountains and settled the western territory before the slow-moving Northern people had torn themselves from the safer and more comfortable life by the seaboard; but the Virginia ideal was patriarchal, and an American continent on the Virginia type might reproduce the virtues of Cato, and perhaps the eloquence of Cicero, but was little likely to produce anything more practical in the way of modern progress. The Shenandoah Valley rivalled Pennsylvania and Connecticut in richness and skill of husbandry; but even agriculture, the favorite industry in Virginia, had suffered from the competition of Kentucky and Tennessee, and from the emigration which had drawn away fully one hundred thousand people. The land was no longer very productive. Even Jefferson, the most active-minded and sanguine of all Virginians,—the inventor of the first scientific plough, the importer of the first threshing-machine known in Virginia, the experimenter with a new drilling-machine, the owner of one hundred and fifty slaves and ten thousand acres of land, whose negroes were trained to carpentry, cabinet-making, house-building, weaving, tailoring, shoe-making,—claimed to get from his land no more than six or eight bushels of wheat to an acre, and had been forced to abandon the more profitable cultivation of tobacco. Except in a few favored districts like the Shenandoah Valley, land in Virginia did not average eight bushels of wheat to an acre. The cultivation of tobacco had been almost the sole object of land-owners, and even where the lands were not exhausted, a bad system of agriculture and the force of habit prevented improvement.

The great planters lavished money in vain on experiments to improve their crops and their stock. They devoted themselves to the task with energy and knowledge; but they needed a diversity of interests and local markets, and except at Baltimore these were far from making their appearance. Neither the products, the markets, the relative amount of capital, nor the machinery of production had perceptibly changed. "The Virginians are not generally rich," said the Duc de Liancourt, "especially in net revenue. Thus one often finds a well-served table, covered with silver, in a room where for ten years half the window panes have been missing, and where they will be missed for ten years more. There are few houses in a passable state of repair, and of all parts of the establishment those best cared for are the stables." Wealth reckoned in slaves or land was plenty; but the best Virginians, from President Washington downward, were most outspoken in their warnings against the Virginia system both of slavery and agriculture.

The contrast between Virginia and Pennsylvania was the subject of incessant comment.

> In Pennsylvania [said Robert Sutcliffe, an English Friend who published travels made in 1804–1806] we meet great numbers of wagons drawn by four or more fine fat horses, the carriages firm and well made, and covered with stout good linen, bleached almost white; and it is not uncommon to see ten or fifteen together travelling cheerfully along the road, the driver riding on one of his horses. Many of these come more than three hundred miles to Philadelphia from the Ohio, Pittsburg, and other places, and I have been told by a respectable Friend, a native of Philadelphia, that more than one thousand covered carriages frequently come to Philadelphia market. . . . The appearance of things in the Slave States is quite the reverse of this. We sometimes meet a ragged black boy or girl driving a team consisting of a lean cow and a mule; sometimes a lean bull or an ox and a mule; and I have seen a mule, a bull, and a cow each miserable in its appearance, composing one team, with a half-naked black slave or two

> riding or driving as occasion suited. The carriage or wagon, if it may be called such, appeared in as wretched a condition as the team and its driver. Sometimes a couple of horses, mules, or cows would be dragging a hogshead of tobacco, with a pivot or axle driven into each end of the hogshead, and something like a shaft attached, by which it was drawn or rolled along the road. I have seen two oxen and two slaves pretty fully employed in getting along a single hogshead; and some of these come from a great distance inland.

In the middle of these primitive sights, Sutcliffe was startled by a contrast such as Virginia could always show. Between Richmond and Fredericksburg,—"In the afternoon, as our road lay through the woods, I was surprised to meet a family party travelling along in as elegant a coach as is usually met with in the neighborhood of London, and attended by several gayly dressed footmen."

The country south of Virginia seemed unpromising even to Virginians. In the year 1796 President Washington gave to Sir John Sinclair his opinion upon the relative value of American lands. He then thought the valley of Virginia the garden of America; but he would say nothing to induce others to settle in more southern regions.

> The uplands of North and South Carolina and Georgia are not dissimilar in soil [he wrote], but as they approach the lower latitudes are less congenial to wheat, and are supposed to be proportionably more unhealthy. Towards the seaboard of all the Southern States, and farther south more so, the lands are low, sandy, and unhealthy; for which reason I shall say little concerning them, for as I should not choose to be an inhabitant of them myself, I ought not to say anything that would induce others to be so. . . . I understand that from thirty to forty dollars per acre may be denominated the medium price in the vicinity of the Susquehanna in the State of Pennsylvania, from twenty to thirty on the Potomac in what is called the Valley, . . . and less, as I have noticed before, as you proceed southerly.

Whatever was the cause, the State of North Carolina seemed to offer few temptations to immigrants or capital. Even in white population ranking fifth among the sixteen States, her 478,000 inhabitants were unknown to the world. The beautiful upper country attracted travellers neither for pleasure nor for gain, while the country along the seacoast was avoided except by hardy wanderers. The grumbling Wilson, who knew every nook and corner of the United States, and who found New England so dreary, painted this part of North Carolina in colors compared with which his sketch of New England was gay. "The taverns are the most desolate and beggarly imaginable; bare, bleak, and dirty walls, one or two old broken chairs and a bench form all the furniture. The white females seldom make their appearance. At supper you sit down to a meal the very sight of which is sufficient to deaden the most eager appetite, and you are surrounded by half-a-dozen dirty, half-naked blacks, male and female, whom any man of common scent might smell a quarter of a mile off. The house itself is raised upon props four or five feet, and the space below is left open for the hogs, with whose charming vocal performance the wearied traveller is serenaded the whole night long." The landscape pleased him no better,—"immense solitary pine savannahs through which the road winds among stagnant ponds; dark, sluggish creeks of the color of brandy, over which are thrown high wooden bridges without railings," crazy and rotten.

North Carolina was relatively among the poorest States. The exports and imports were of trifling value, less than one tenth of those returned for Massachusetts, which were more than twice as great as those of North Carolina and Virginia together. That under these conditions America should receive any strong impulse from such a quarter seemed unlikely; yet perhaps for the moment more was to be expected from the Carolinas than from Virginia. Backward as these States in some respects were, they possessed one new element of wealth which promised more for them than anything Virginia could hope. The steam-engines of Watt had been applied in England to spinning, weaving, and printing cotton; an immense demand had risen for that staple, and the cotton-gin had been simultaneously invented. A sudden impetus was given to industry; land which had been worthless and estates which had become bankrupt acquired new value, and in 1800 every planter was growing cotton, buying negroes, and breaking fresh soil. North Carolina felt the strong flood of prosperity, but South Carolina, and particularly the town of Charleston, had most to hope. The exports of South Carolina were nearly equal in value to those of Massachusetts or Pennsylvania; the imports were equally large. Charleston might reasonably expect to rival Boston, New York, Philadelphia, and Baltimore. In 1800 these cities still stood, as far as concerned their foreign trade, within some range of comparison; and between Boston, Baltimore, and Charleston, many plausible reasons could be given for thinking that the last might have the most brilliant future. The three towns stood abreast. If Charleston had but about eighteen thousand inhabitants, this was the number reported by Boston only ten years before, and was five thousand more than Baltimore then boasted. Neither Boston nor Baltimore saw about them a vaster region to supply, or so profitable a staple to export. A cotton crop of two hundred thousand pounds sent abroad in 1791 grew to twenty millions in 1801, and was to double again by 1803. An export of fifty thousand bales was enormous, yet was only the beginning. What use might not Charleston, the only considerable town in the entire South, make of this golden flood?

The town promised hopefully to prove equal to its task. Nowhere in the Union was intelligence, wealth, and education greater in proportion to numbers than in the little society of cotton and rice planters who ruled

South Carolina; and they were in 1800 not behind—they hoped soon to outstrip—their rivals. If Boston was building a canal to the Merrimac, and Philadelphia one along the Schuylkill to the Susquehanna, Charleston had nearly completed another which brought the Santee River to its harbor, and was planning a road to Tennessee which should draw the whole interior within reach. Nashville was nearer to Charleston than to any other seaport of the Union, and Charleston lay nearest to the rich trade of the West Indies. Not even New York seemed more clearly marked for prosperity than this solitary Southern city, which already possessed banking capital in abundance, intelligence, enterprise, the traditions of high culture and aristocratic ambition, all supported by slave-labor, which could be indefinitely increased by the African slave-trade.

If any portion of the United States might hope for a sudden and magnificent bloom, South Carolina seemed entitled to expect it. Rarely had such a situation, combined with such resources, failed to produce some wonderful result. Yet as Washington warned Sinclair, these advantages were counterbalanced by serious evils. The climate in summer was too relaxing. The sun was too hot. The seacoast was unhealthy, and at certain seasons even deadly to the whites. Finally, if history was a guide, no permanent success could be prophesied for a society like that of the low country in South Carolina, where some thirty thousand whites were surrounded by a dense mass of nearly one hundred thousand negro slaves. Even Georgia, then only partially settled, contained sixty thousand slaves and but one hundred thousand whites. The cotton States might still argue that if slavery, malaria, or summer heat barred civilization, all the civilization that was ever known must have been blighted in its infancy; but although the future of South Carolina might be brilliant, like that of other oligarchies in which only a few thousand free-men took part, such a development seemed to diverge far from the path likely to be followed by Northern society, and bade fair to increase and complicate the social and economical difficulties with which Americans had to deal.

A probable valuation of the whole United States in 1800 was eighteen hundred million dollars, equal to $328 for each human being, including slaves; or $418 to each free white. This property was distributed with an approach to equality, except in a few of the Southern States. In New York and Philadelphia a private fortune of one hundred thousand dollars was considered handsome, and three hundred thousand was great wealth. Inequalities were frequent; but they were chiefly those of a landed aristocracy. Equality was so far the rule that every white family of five persons might be supposed to own land, stock, or utensils, a house and furniture, worth about two thousand dollars; and as the only considerable industry was agriculture, their scale of life was easy to calculate,—taxes amounting to little or nothing, and wages averaging about a dollar a day.

Not only were these slender resources, but they were also of a kind not easily converted to the ready uses required for rapid development. Among the numerous difficulties with which the Union was to struggle, and which were to form the interest of American history, the disproportion between the physical obstacles and the material means for overcoming them was one of the most striking.

Theodor Mommsen 1817—1903

9

The life and historical achievements of Theodor Mommsen represent many of the finest qualities of nineteenth-century historiography, as we have presented them in this volume. Mommsen was, first of all, the most skilled and professional scholar of his time and, in addition, one of the most productive and versatile historians of all time. In addition to history, he was a master of no fewer than five ancillary fields, including epigraphy, numismatics, civil and constitutional law, archeology, and early Italian philology. His historical bibliography alone approaches 1,500 entries, to say nothing of his contributions to the multi-volume publication of Latin inscriptions, an undertaking which he directed for over twenty years. At universities in Leipzig, Zurich, and Berlin, he inspired scores of students to pursue the profession of history. He was himself a model for those students, not only as a professional historian dedicated to the critical tradition of Niebuhr and Ranke, but also as an artist capable of writing historical prose that eventually brought him the Nobel Prize for Literature. Any reader of his *History of Rome* will be quickly convinced that Mommsen can equal Macaulay or Parkman at their rhetorical best. Not since Gibbon had critical skill and literary flair met in such a felicitous combination. Finally, Mommsen was a political animal, in the best sense of the term. Courageous, outspoken, and liberal, he protested the abuses of Bismarck's Germany and anticipated the tragic course of German history in the twentieth century.

Mommsen was born in the province of Schleswig-Holstein, which was German in language and culture, but which remained under nominal Danish control until 1866. The son of a poor pastor, Mommsen first demonstrated his abilities as a scholar when he studied jurisprudence at the University of Kiel. The study of Roman constitutional law was the predominant element in his legal education, and it remained a central interest for him as he began to write history. After receiving his degree in law in 1844, Mommsen traveled to Italy on a scholarship from the Danish government. He remained in Italy for three years, collecting and studying Latin inscriptions, a task which occupied him for most of his life. He also produced almost ninety articles about these inscriptions, a distinction which secured him an appointment as a special professor at Leipzig in 1848. During this period, Mommsen involved himself in behalf of the liberal cause of 1848, chiefly as the editor of the *Schleswig-Holsteinische Zeitung* from April through July of that crucial and ultimately frustrating year in German history. The revolution was a bleak failure and Mommsen suffered for having taken an active role in it. In 1850, he was relieved of his post at Leipzig. The following year he moved to Zurich to teach and live.

Before his forced departure from Leipzig, Mommsen had contracted to write the work that would bring him immediate fame throughout Europe: *The History of Rome.* From 1854 to 1856, he published in successive years the first three volumes of this brilliant history, from its origins to the end of the Republic. The aim of this history was, in Mommsen's own words, "to bring a more vivid knowledge of classical antiquity to wider circles." He succeeded in this and in a good deal more. In tracing the early history of Rome, he effectively revised the work of Niebuhr, whose reputation was then sacrosanct but who was mistaken in his reliance, no matter how critical, on old legends and myths. Mommsen considered the most reliable data to be those derived from non-literary sources, such as inscriptions, coins, and artifacts. The fusion of archeology and jurisprudence with traditional political narrative distinguished his treatment of ancient history from all of its predecessors.

Mommsen approaches Gibbon in the depth of historical vision, and in the firm grasp of his sources and in supreme artistry, but in at least one respect Mommsen's history surpasses the great *Decline and Fall of the Roman Empire.* Mommsen had no Tillemont to rely on, and he did not need one. He was quite willing and able to do his own digging; he was in a position both to write history and to prepare its materials, to find the inscriptions, decipher them, and then to incorporate them into a larger historical synthesis. In the work of Mommsen it is possible to discern how the professionalization of history in the nineteenth century enabled the science of history to grow upon the foundations laid in the century of the Enlightenment.

The History of Rome is also the work of a frustrated liberal. In the penultimate chapter of the third volume, "The Old Republic and the New Monarchy," from which we have taken our selection, Mommsen venerates Julius Caesar as "the entire and perfect man." Now Caesar helped destroy the Republic and became himself an emperor and an autocrat, but Mommsen saw the Republic in its last days as degenerate, crippled by administrative failure, and perpetually threatened by imminent anarchy. Out of this arose a leader strong enough to preserve the Roman state and eliminate a host of ineffectual opponents. Mommsen sees Cato, Pompey, and Cicero as ancient prototypes of the garrulous and incompetent politicians who were, he believed, responsible for the disaster of 1848.

Mommsen's admiration for Caesar is sometimes misunderstood. He later wrote that "Caesar and Roman Imperialism are in truth a more bitter censure of modern autocracy than could be written by the hand of man," and he could never bring himself to write an internal history of the Julio-Claudian court. When the German Caesar arrived on the scene in 1862, his name was Bismarck, who later attempted to silence Mommsen. To Mommsen, Caesar preserved civil order and civilization during those last hectic days of the Republic. This is evident in his moving conclusion to the third volume: "There was in the world, as Caesar found it, much of the noble heritage of past centuries and an infinite abundance of pomp and glory, but little spirit, still less taste, and least of all true delight in life. It was indeed an old world; and even the richly gifted patriotism of Caesar could not make it young again. . . . But yet with him there came to the sorely harassed peoples on the Mediterranean a tolerable evening after the sultry noon; and when at length after a long historical night the new day dawned once more for the peoples, and fresh nations in free self-movement commenced their race towards new and higher goals, there were found among them not a few in which the seed sown by Caesar had sprung up, and which owed, as they still owe, to him their national individuality."

The fourth volume of *The History of Rome* was never published. One can only imagine why the subject matter of this volume, the intrigues of Augustus and Tiberius, did not detain the historian. Mommsen preferred to write a fifth volume instead, one dealing with Roman administration of its provinces from Caesar to Diocletian. In some ways the final volume was a more impressive achievement than the earlier ones. Here Mommsen extended his historical investigation of the long and peaceful administration of the empire with skill and erudition unprecedented in classical scholarship. He used the most remote and obscure texts, as well as thousands of inscriptions, to demonstrate how the Romans exerted their authority across three continents.

In 1887, Mommsen followed up his interest in Roman government of the Western World with his *Römisches Staatsrecht,* "Roman Constitutional Law." In this remarkable work, Mommsen brought to fruition his abilities as a legal scholar of the highest order. He examined legal texts as well as inscriptions with the minute care worthy of the most learned lawyer; and he combined his training in jurisprudence with the historian's understanding of the principles that governed the evolution of the Roman constitution.

After his Italian sojourn, Mommsen published a volume of Latin inscriptions, and then suggested to the Prussian Academy that a formal project be undertaken to edit, organize, and publish all extant inscriptions. The Academy agreed and appointed Mommsen director. It was a colossal enterprise. Under Mommsen's supervision, investigators were sent to Egypt, Asia Minor, Syria, and North Africa, as well as throughout Western Europe. Mommsen believed that every staff member should if at all possible see the stone, or an original manuscript if the inscription could not be found. He insisted that forgeries and false inscriptions be printed side by side with the real ones so that they might never again be confused. The result of these labors was the monumental *Corpus Inscriptionum Latinarum,* which began to appear in 1863. For more than twenty years, with consistent efficiency, Mommsen kept a close watch over the work of his collaborators. The result is a series of folio volumes which occupy more than eight feet of shelf space in historical libraries. Mommsen believed that in the absence of written records these inscriptions were essential to understanding the history of the ancient world, and no one has ever doubted him. In his own historical works, Mommsen treated familiar subjects with fresh insight and new materials; in the

Corpus, he created a new body of historical research.

After the Franco-Prussian War, Mommsen's protests against the Prussian government became increasingly vigorous. In 1881, he was elected to the Reichstag, where he became an outspoken critic of Bismarck. After one particularly bitter altercation, Bismarck sued Mommsen for libeling the government, but the historian was acquitted. Mommsen not only opposed the government's economic policies, especially the protective tariff, he also spoke out with authority and passion against incipient anti-Semitic propaganda, which was then taking hold at the University of Berlin. A devoted teacher, a popular lecturer, and a prodigious scholar, Mommsen deplored the decay of his university and of the imperial Germany. In his rectoral address of 1874, he predicted that the anti-Semitic movement would destroy the very purpose for which the University existed: "the unfettered search for truth." When in 1902 he received the Nobel Prize, he asked his audience not to applaud. The times, he said, were too grave.

Mommsen's career is an inspiration to all professional students of history, both for his contribution to historiography and for his simple, honest humanity. Moreover, his own works refute any notion that in the writing of history there exists any incompatibility between art and science.

Selected Bibliography

For a long time we have been deprived of a complete biography of Mommsen, because he stipulated in his will that his private papers were to be impounded for thirty years after his death. In Hitler's Germany there was not much interest in them, and subsequently most of them were burned during the bombing of Berlin in 1944. However, Lothar Wickert did examine some of these papers before they were destroyed and he is incorporating his knowledge of them into his authoritative but uninspired *Theodor Mommsen: Eine Biographie,* Vol. I: *Lehrjahre 1817–1844* (1959), Vol. II: *Wanderjahre: Frankreich und Italien* (1964), Vol. III: *Wanderjahre: Leipzig, Zürich, Breslau, Berlin* (1969). The series is not yet complete. Another recent study of Mommsen, which considers the Germany of his time, is Alfred Heuss's *Theodor Mommsen und das 19. Jahrhundert* (1956). W. Ward Fowler includes an appreciative essay on Mommsen in his *Roman Essays and Interpretations* (1920); and a brief but astute article, "Theodor Mommsen," was published shortly after the historian's death by F. Haverfield, in the *English Historical Review* XIV (January, 1904), 80–89. Albert Wucher's *Theodor Mommsen: Geschichtschreibung und Politik* (1956) is an admiring but independent and intelligent appraisal from a liberal perspective.

HISTORY OF ROME

VOLUME III

Chapter 11. The Old Republic and the New Monarchy

The new monarch of Rome, the first ruler over the whole domain of Romano-Hellenic civilization, Gaius Julius Caesar, was in his fifty-sixth year (born 12 July 652?) when the battle at Thapsus, the last link in a long chain of momentous victories, placed the decision as to the future of the world in his hands. Few men have had their elasticity so thoroughly put to the proof as Caesar—the sole creative genius produced by Rome, and the last produced by the ancient world, which accordingly moved on in the path that he marked out for it until its sun went down. Sprung from one of the oldest noble families of Latium—which traced back its lineage to the heroes of the Iliad and the kings of Rome, and in fact to the Venus-Aphrodite common to both nations—he spent the years of his boyhood and early manhood as the genteel youth of that epoch were wont to spend them. He had tasted the sweetness as well as the bitterness of the cup of fashionable life, had recited and declaimed, had practised literature and made verses in his idle hours, had prosecuted love-intrigues of every sort, and got himself initiated into all the mysteries of shaving, curls, and ruffles pertaining to the toilette-wisdom of the day, as well as into the still more mysterious art of always borrowing and never paying. But the flexible steel of that nature was proof against even these dissipated and flighty courses; Caesar retained both his bodily vigour and his elasticity of mind and of heart unimpaired. In fencing and in riding he was a match for any of his soldiers, and his swimming saved his life at Alexandria; the incredible rapidity of his journeys, which usually for the sake of gaining time were performed by night—a thorough contrast to the procession-like slowness with which Pompeius moved from one place to another—was the astonishment of his contemporaries and not the least among the causes of his success. The mind was like the body. His remarkable power of intuition revealed itself in the precision and practicability of all his arrangements, even where he gave orders without having seen with his own eyes. His memory was matchless, and it was easy for him to carry on several occupations simultaneously with equal self-possession. Although a gentleman, a man of genius, and a monarch, he had still a heart. So long as he lived, he cherished the purest veneration for his worthy mother Aurelia (his father having died early); to his wives and above all to his daughter Julia he devoted an honourable affection, which was not without reflex influence even on political affairs. With the ablest and most excellent men of his time, of high and of humbler rank, he maintained noble relations of mutual fidelity, with each after his kind. As he himself never abandoned any of his partisans after the pusillanimous and unfeeling manner of Pompeius, but adhered to his friends—and that not merely from calculation—through good and bad times without wavering, several of these, such as Aulus Hirtius and Gaius Matius, gave, even after his death, noble testimonies of their attachment to him.

If in a nature so harmoniously organized any one aspect of it may be singled out as characteristic, it is this—that he stood aloof from all ideology and everything fanciful. As a matter of course, Caesar was a man of passion, for without passion there is no genius; but his passion was never stronger than he could control. He had had his season of youth, and song, love, and wine had taken lively possession of his spirit; but with him they did not penetrate to the inmost core of his nature. Literature occupied him long and earnestly; but, while Alexander could not sleep for thinking of the Homeric Achilles, Caesar in his sleepless hours mused on the inflections of the Latin nouns and verbs. He made verses, as everybody then did, but they were weak; on the other hand he was interested in subjects of astronomy and natural science. While wine was and continued to be with Alexander the destroyer of care, the temperate Roman, after the revels of his youth were over, avoided it entirely. Around him, as around all those whom the full lustre of woman's love has dazzled in youth, fainter gleams of it continued imperishably to linger; even in later years he had love-adventures and successes with women, and he retained a certain foppishness in his outward appearance, or, to speak more correctly, the pleasing consciousness of his own manly beauty. He carefully covered the baldness, which he keenly felt, with the laurel chaplet that he wore in public in his later years, and he would doubtless have surrendered some of his victories, if he could thereby have brought back his youthful locks. But, however much even when monarch he enjoyed the society of women, he only amused himself with them, and allowed them no manner of influence over him; even his much-censured relation to queen Cleopatra was only contrived to mask a weak point in his political position.

Caesar was thoroughly a realist and a man of sense; and whatever he undertook and achieved was pervaded and guided by the cool sobriety which constitutes the most marked peculiarity of his genius. To this he owed the power of living energetically in the present, undisturbed either by recollection or by expectation; to this he owed the capacity of acting at any moment with collected vigour, and of applying his whole genius even to the smallest and most incidental enterprise; to this he owed the many-sided power with which he grasped and mastered whatever understanding can comprehend and will can compel; to this he owed the self-possessed ease with which he arranged his periods as well as projected his campaigns; to this he owed the "marvellous serenity" which remained steadily with him through good and evil days; to this he owed the complete independence, which admitted of no control by favourite or by mistress, or even by friend. It resulted, moreover, from this clearness of judgment that Caesar never formed to himself illusions regarding the power of fate and the ability of man; in his case the friendly veil was lifted up, which conceals from man the inadequacy of his working. Prudently as he laid his plans and considered all possibilities, the feeling was never absent from his breast that in all things fortune, that is to say accident, must bestow success; and with this may be connected the circumstance that he so often played a desperate game with destiny, and in particular again and again hazarded his person with daring indifference. As indeed occasionally men of predominant sagacity betake themselves to a pure game of hazard, so there was in Caesar's rationalism a point at which it came in some measure into contact with mysticism.

Gifts such as these could not fail to produce a statesman. From early youth, accordingly, Caesar was a statesman in the deepest sense of the term, and his aim was the highest which man is allowed to propose to himself—the political, military, intellectual, and moral regeneration of his own deeply decayed nation, and of the still more deeply decayed Hellenic nation intimately akin to his own. The hard school of thirty years' experience changed his views as to the means by which this aim was to be reached; his aim itself remained the same in the times of his hopeless humiliation and of his unlimited plenitude of power, in the times when as demagogue and conspirator he stole towards it by paths of darkness, and in those when, as joint possessor of the supreme power and then as monarch, he worked at his task in the full light of day before the eyes of the world. All the measures of a permanent kind that proceeded from him at the most various times assume their appropriate places in the great building-plan. We cannot therefore properly speak of isolated achievements of Caesar; he did nothing isolated. With justice men commend Caesar the orator for his masculine eloquence, which, scorning all the arts of the advocate, like a clear flame at once enlightened and warmed. With justice men admire in Caesar the author the inimitable simplicity of the composition, the unique purity and beauty of the language. With justice the greatest masters of war of all times have praised Caesar the general, who, in a singular degree disregarding routine and tradition, knew always how to find out the mode of warfare by which in the given case the enemy was conquered, and which was thus in the given case the right one; who with the certainty of divination found the proper means for every end; who after defeat stood ready for battle like William of Orange, and ended the campaign invariably with victory; who managed that element of warfare, the treatment of which serves to distinguish military genius from the mere ordinary ability of an officer—the rapid movement of masses—with unsurpassed perfection, and found the guarantee of victory not in the massiveness of his forces but in the celerity of their movements, not in long preparation but in rapid and daring action even with inadequate means. But all these were with Caesar mere secondary matters; he was no doubt a great orator, author, and general, but he became each of these merely because he was a consummate statesman. The soldier more especially played in him altogether an accessory part, and it is one of the principal peculiarities by which he is distinguished from Alexander, Hannibal, and Napoleon, that he began his political activity not as an officer, but as a demagogue. According to his original plan he had purposed to reach his object, like Pericles and Gaius Gracchus, without force of arms, and throughout eighteen years he had as leader of the popular party moved exclusively amid political plans and intrigues—until, reluctantly convinced of the necessity for a military support, he, when already forty years of age, put himself at the head of an army. It was natural that he should even afterwards remain still more statesman than general—just like Cromwell, who also transformed himself from a leader of opposition into a military chief and democratic king, and who in general, little as the prince of Puritans seems to resemble the dissolute Roman, is yet in his development as well as in the objects which he aimed at and the results which he achieved of all statesmen perhaps the most akin to Caesar. Even in his mode of warfare this improvised generalship may still be recognized; the enterprises of Napoleon against Egypt and against England do not more clearly exhibit the artillery-lieutenant who had risen by service to command than the similar enterprises of Caesar exhibit the demagogue metamorphosed into a general. A regularly trained officer would hardly have been prepared, through political considerations of a not altogether stringent nature, to set aside the best-founded military scruples in the way in which Caesar did on several occasions, most strikingly in the case of his landing in Epirus. Several of his acts are therefore censurable from a military point of view; but what the general loses, the statesman gains. The task of the statesman is universal in its nature like Caesar's genius; if he undertook things the most varied and most remote one from another, they had all without exception a bearing on the one great object to which with infinite fidelity and consistency he devoted himself; and of the manifold aspects and directions of his great activity he never preferred one to another. Although a master of the art of war, he yet from statesmanly considerations did his utmost to avert civil strife and, when it nevertheless began, to earn laurels stained as little as possible by blood. Although the founder of a military monarchy, he yet, with an energy unexampled in history, allowed no hierarchy of marshals or government of praetorians to come into existence. If he had a preference for any one form of services rendered to the state, it was for the sciences and arts of peace rather than for those of war.

The most remarkable peculiarity of his action as a statesman was its perfect harmony. In reality all the conditions for this most difficult of all human functions were united in Caesar. A thorough realist, he never allowed the images of the past or venerable tradition to disturb him; for him nothing was of value in politics but the living present and the law of reason, just as in his character of grammarian he set aside historical and antiquarian research and recognized nothing but on the one hand the living *usus loquendi* and on the other hand the rule of symmetry. A born ruler, he governed the minds of men as the wind drives the clouds, and compelled the most heterogeneous natures to place themselves at his service—the plain citizen and the rough subaltern, the genteel matrons of Rome and the fair princesses of Egypt and Mauretania, the brilliant cavalry-officer and the calculating banker. His talent for organization was marvellous; no statesman has ever compelled alliances, no general has ever collected an army out of unyielding and refractory elements with such decision, and kept them together with such firmness, as Caesar displayed in constraining and upholding his coalitions and his legions; never did regent judge his instruments and assign each to the place appropriate for him with so acute an eye.

He was monarch; but he never played the king. Even when absolute lord of Rome, he retained the deportment of the party-leader; perfectly pliant and smooth, easy and charming in conversation, complaisant towards every one, it seemed as if he wished to be nothing but the first among his peers. Caesar entirely avoided the blunder into which so many men otherwise on an equality with him have fallen, of carrying into politics the military tone of command; however much occasion his disagreeable relations with the senate gave for it, he never resorted to outrages such as was that of the eighteenth Brumaire. Caesar was monarch; but he was never seized with the giddiness of the tyrant. He is perhaps the only one among the mighty ones of the earth, who in great matters and little never acted according to inclination or caprice, but always without exception according to his duty as ruler, and who, when he looked back on his life, found doubtless erroneous calculations to deplore, but no false step of passion to regret. There is nothing in the history of Caesar's life, which even on a small scale can be compared with those poetico-sensual ebullitions—such as the murder of Kleitos or the burning of Persepolis—which the history of his great predecessor in the east records. He is, in fine, perhaps the only one of those mighty ones, who has preserved to the end of his career the statesman's tact of discriminating between the possible and the impossible, and has not broken down in the task which for greatly gifted natures is the most difficult of all—the task of recognizing, when on the pinnacle of success, its natural limits. What was possible he performed, and never left the possible good undone for the sake of the impossible better, never disdained at least to mitigate by palliatives evils that were incurable. But where he recognized that fate had spoken, he always obeyed. Alexander on the Hypanis, Napoleon at Moscow, turned back because they were compelled to do so, and were indignant at destiny for bestowing even on its favourites merely limited successes; Caesar turned back voluntarily on the Thames and on the Rhine; and thought of carrying into effect even at the Danube and the Euphrates not unbounded plans of world-conquest, but merely well-considered frontier-regulations.

Such was this unique man, whom it seems so easy and yet is so infinitely difficult to describe. His whole nature is transparent clearness; and tradition preserves more copious and more vivid information about him than about any of his peers in the ancient world. Of such a personage our conceptions may well vary in point of shallowness or depth, but they cannot be, strictly speaking, different; to every not utterly perverted inquirer the grand figure has exhibited the same essential features, and yet no one has succeeded in reproducing it to the life. The secret lies in its perfection. In his character as a man as well as in his place in history, Caesar occupies a position where the great contrasts of existence meet and balance each other. Of mighty creative power and yet at the same time of the most penetrating judgment; no longer a youth and not yet an old man; of the highest energy of will and the highest capacity of execution; filled with republican ideals and at the same time born to be a king; a Roman in the deepest essence of his nature, and yet called to reconcile and combine in himself as well as in the outer world the Roman and the Hellenic types of culture—Caesar was the entire and perfect man. Accordingly we miss in him more than in any other historical personage what are called characteristic features, which are in reality nothing else than deviations from the natural course of human development. What in Caesar passes for such at the first superficial glance is, when more closely observed, seen to be the peculiarity not of the individual, but of the epoch of culture or of the nation; his youthful adventures, for instance, were common to him with all his more gifted contemporaries of like position, his unpoetical but strongly logical temperament was the temperament of Romans in general. It formed part also of Caesar's full humanity that he was in the highest degree influenced by the conditions of time and place; for there is no abstract humanity—the living man cannot but occupy a place in a given nationality and in a definite line of culture. Caesar was a perfect man just because he more than any other placed himself amidst the currents of his time, and because he more than any other possessed the essential peculiarity of the Roman nation—practical aptitude as a citizen—in perfection: for his Hellenism in fact was only the Hellenism which had been long intimately blended with the Italian nationality. But in this very circumstance lies the difficulty, we may perhaps say the impossibility, of depicting Caesar to the life. As the artist can paint everything save only consummate beauty, so the historian, when once in a thousand years he encounters the perfect, can only be silent regarding it. For normality admits doubtless of being expressed, but it gives us only the negative notion of the absence of defect; the secret of nature, whereby in her most finished manifestations normality and individuality are combined, is beyond expression. Nothing is left for us but to deem those fortunate who beheld this perfection, and to gain some faint conception of it from the reflected lustre which rests imperishably on the works that were the creation of this great nature. These also, it is true, bear the stamp of the time. The Roman hero himself stood by the side of his youthful Greek predecessor not merely as an equal, but as a superior; but the world had meanwhile become old and its youthful lustre had faded. The action of Caesar was no longer, like that of Alexander, a joyous marching onward towards a goal indefinitely remote; he built on, and out of, ruins, and was content to establish himself as tolerably and as securely as possible within the ample but yet definite bounds once assigned to him. With reason therefore the delicate poetic tact of the nations has not troubled itself about the unpoetical Roman, and on the other hand has invested the son of Philip with all the golden lustre of poetry, with all the rainbow hues of legend. But with equal reason the political life of the nations has during thousands of years again and again reverted to the lines which Caesar drew; and the fact, that the peoples to whom the world belongs still at the present day designate the highest of their monarchs by his name, conveys a warning deeply significant and, unhappily, fraught with shame.

If the old, in every respect vicious, state of things was to be successfully got rid of and the commonwealth was to be renovated, it was necessary first of all that the country should be practically tranquillized and that the ground should be cleared from the rubbish with which since the recent catastrophe it was everywhere strewed. In this work Caesar set out from the principle of the reconciliation of the hitherto subsisting parties or, to put it more correctly—for, where the antagonistic principles are irreconcilable, we cannot speak of real reconciliation—from the principle that the arena, on which the nobility and the populace had hitherto contended with each other, was to be abandoned by both parties, and that both were to meet together on the ground of the new monarchical constitution. First of all therefore all the older quarrels of the republican past were regarded as done away for ever and irrevocably. While Caesar gave orders that the statues of Sulla which had been thrown down by the mob of the capital on the news of the battle of Pharsalus should be re-erected, and thus recognized the fact that it became history alone to sit in judgment on that great man, he at the same time cancelled the last remaining effects of Sulla's exceptional laws, recalled from exile those who had been banished in the times of the Cinnan and Sertorian troubles, and restored to the children of those outlawed by Sulla their forfeited privilege of eligibility to office. In like manner all those were restored, who in the preliminary stage of the recent catastrophe had lost their seat in the senate or their civil existence through sentence of the censors or political process, especially through the impeachments raised on the basis of the exceptional laws of 702. Those alone who had put to death the proscribed for money remained, as was reasonable, still under attainder; and Milo, the most daring *condottiere* of the senatorial party, was excluded from the general pardon.

Far more difficult than the settlement of these questions which already belonged substantially to the past was the treatment of the parties confronting each other at the moment—on the one hand Caesar's own democratic adherents, on the other hand the overthrown aristocracy. That the former should be, if possible, still less satisfied than the latter with Caesar's conduct after the victory and with his summons to abandon the old standing-ground of party, was to be expected. Caesar himself desired doubtless on the whole the same issue which Gaius Gracchus had contemplated; but the designs of the Caesarians were no longer those of the Gracchans. The Roman popular party had been driven onward in gradual progression from reform to revolution, from revolution to anarchy, from anarchy to a war against property; they celebrated among themselves the memory of the reign of terror and now adorned the tomb of Catilina, as formerly that of the Gracchi, with flowers and garlands; they had placed themselves under Caesar's banner, because they expected him to do for them what Catilina had not been able to accomplish. But as it speedily became plain that Caesar was very far from intending to be the testamentary executor of Catilina, and that the utmost which debtors might expect from him was some alleviations of payment and modifications of procedure, indignation found loud vent in the inquiry, For whom then had the popular party conquered, if not for the people?

and the rabble of this description, high and low, out of pure chagrin at the miscarriage of their politico-economic Saturnalia began first to coquet with the Pompeians, and then even during Caesar's absence of nearly two years from Italy (Jan. 706–autumn 707) to instigate there a second civil war within the first.

The praetor Marcus Caelius Rufus, a good aristocrat and bad payer of debts, of some talent and much culture, as a vehement and fluent orator hitherto in the senate and in the Forum one of the most zealous champions for Caesar, proposed to the people—without being instructed from any higher quarter to do so—a law which granted to debtors a respite of six years free of interest, and then, when he was opposed in this step, proposed a second law which even cancelled all claims arising out of loans and current house rents; whereupon the Caesarian senate deposed him from his office. It was just on the eve of the battle of Pharsalus, and the balance in the great contest seemed to incline to the side of the Pompeians; Rufus entered into communication with the old senatorian band-leader Milo, and the two contrived a counter-revolution, which inscribed on its banner partly the republican constitution, partly the cancelling of creditors' claims and the manumission of slaves. Milo left his place of exile Massilia, and called the Pompeians and the slave-herdsmen to arms in the region of Thurii; Rufus made arrangements to seize the town of Capua by armed slaves. But the latter plan was detected before its execution and frustrated by the Capuan militia; Quintus Pedius, who advanced with a legion into the territory of Thurii, scattered the band making havoc there; and the fall of the two leaders put an end to the scandal (706).

Nevertheless there was found in the following year (707) a second fool, the tribune of the people, Publius Dolabella, who, equally insolvent but far from being equally gifted with his predecessor, introduced afresh his law as to creditors' claims and house rents, and with his colleague Lucius Trebellius began on that point once more—it was the last time—the demagogic war; there were serious frays between the armed bands on both sides and various street-riots, till the commandant of Italy Marcus Antonius ordered the military to interfere, and soon afterwards Caesar's return from the east completely put an end to the preposterous proceedings. Caesar attributed to these brainless attempts to revive the projects of Catilina so little importance, that he tolerated Dolabella in Italy and indeed after some time even received him again into favour. Against a rabble of this sort, which had nothing to do with any political question at all, but solely with a war against property—as against gangs of banditti—the mere existence of a strong government is sufficient; and Caesar was too great and too considerate to busy himself with the apprehensions which the Italian alarmists felt regarding these communists of that day, and thereby unduly to procure a false popularity for his monarchy.

While Caesar thus might leave, and actually left, the late democratic party to the process of decomposition which had already in its case advanced almost to the utmost limit, he had on the other hand, with reference to the former aristocratic party possessing a far greater vitality, not to bring about its dissolution—which time alone could accomplish—but to pave the way for and initiate it by a proper combination of repression and conciliation. Among minor measures, Caesar, even from a natural sense of propriety, avoided exasperating the fallen party by empty sarcasm; he did not triumph over his conquered fellow-burgesses; he mentioned Pompeius often and always with respect, and caused his statue overthrown by the people to be re-erected at the senate-house, when the latter was restored, in its earlier distinguished place. To political prosecutions after the victory Caesar assigned the narrowest possible limits. No investigation was instituted into the various communications which the constitutional party had held even with nominal Caesarians; Caesar threw the piles of papers found in the enemy's headquarters at Pharsalus and Thapsus into the fire unread, and spared himself and the country from political processes against individuals suspected of high treason. Further, all the common soldiers who had followed their Roman or provincial officers into the contest against Caesar came off with impunity. The sole exception made was in the case of those Roman burgesses, who had taken service in the army of the Numidian king Juba; their property was confiscated by way of penalty for their treason. Even to the officers of the conquered party Caesar had granted unlimited pardon up to the close of the Spanish campaign of 705; but he became convinced that in this he had gone too far, and that the removal at least of the leaders among them was inevitable. The rule by which he was thenceforth guided was, that every one who after the capitulation of Ilerda had served as an officer in the enemy's army or had sat in the opposition-senate, if he survived the close of the struggle, forfeited his property and his political rights, and was banished from Italy for life; if he did not survive the close of the struggle, his property at least fell to the state; but any one of these, who had formerly accepted pardon from Caesar and was once more found in the ranks of the enemy, thereby forfeited his life. These rules were however materially modified in the execution. The sentence of death was actually executed only against a very few of the numerous backsliders. In the confiscation of the property of the fallen not only were the debts attaching to the several portions of the estate as well as the claims of the widows for their dowries paid off, as was reasonable, but a portion of the paternal estate was left also to the children of the deceased. Lastly not a few of those, who in consequence of those rules were liable to banishment and confiscation of property, were at once pardoned entirely or got off with fines, like the African capitalists who were impressed as members of the senate of Utica. And even the others almost without exception got their freedom and property restored to them, if they could only prevail on themselves to petition Caesar to that effect; on several who declined to do so, such as the consular Marcus Marcellus, pardon was even conferred unasked, and ultimately in 710 a general amnesty was issued for all who were still unrecalled.

The republican opposition submitted to be pardoned; but it was not reconciled. Discontent with the new order of things and exasperation against the unwonted ruler were general. For open political resistance there was indeed no farther opportunity—it was hardly worth taking into account, that some oppositional tribunes on occasion of the question of title acquired for themselves the republican crown of martyrdom by a demonstrative intervention against those who had called Caesar king—but republicanism found expression all the more decidedly as an opposition of sentiment, and in secret agitation and plotting. Not a hand stirred when the Imperator appeared in public. There was abundance of wall-placards and sarcastic verses full of bitter and telling popular satire against the new monarchy. When a comedian ventured on a republican allusion, he was saluted with the loudest applause. The praise of Cato formed the fashionable theme of oppositional pamphleteers, and their writings found a public all the more grateful because even literature was no longer free. Caesar indeed combated the republicans even now on their own field; he himself and his abler confidants replied to the Cato-literature with Anticatones, and the republican and Caesarian scribes fought round the dead hero of Utica like the Trojans and Hellenes round the dead body of Patroclus; but as a matter of course in this conflict—where the public thoroughly republican in its feelings was judge—the Caesarians had the worst of it. No course remained but to overawe the authors; on which account men well known and dangerous in a literary point of view, such as Publius Nigidius Figulus and Aulus Caecina, had more difficulty in obtaining permission to return to Italy than other exiles, while the oppositional writers tolerated in Italy were subjected to a practical censorship, the restraints of which were all the more annoying that the measure of punishment to be dreaded was utterly arbitrary. The underground machinations of the overthrown parties against the new monarchy will be more fitly set forth in another connection. Here it is sufficient to say that risings of pretenders as well as of republicans were incessantly brewing throughout the Roman empire; that the flames of civil war kindled now by the Pompeians, now by the republicans, again burst forth brightly at various places; and that in the capital there was perpetual conspiracy against the life of the monarch. But Caesar could not be induced by these plots even to surround himself permanently with a body-guard, and usually contented himself with making known the detected conspiracies by public placards.

However much Caesar was wont to treat all things relating to his personal safety with daring indifference, he could not possibly conceal from himself the very serious danger with which this mass of malcontents threatened not merely himself but also his creations. If nevertheless, disregarding all the warning and urgency of his friends, he without deluding himself as to the implacability of the very opponents to whom he showed mercy, persevered with marvellous composure and energy in the course of pardoning by far the greater number of them, he did so neither from the chivalrous magnanimity of a proud, nor from the sentimental clemency of an effeminate, nature, but from the correct statesmanly consideration that vanquished parties are disposed of more rapidly and with less public injury by their absorption within the state than by any attempt to extirpate them by proscription or to eject them from the commonwealth by banishment. Caesar could not for his high objects dispense with the constitutional party itself, which in fact embraced not the aristocracy merely but all the elements of a free and national spirit among the Italian burgesses; for his schemes, which contemplated the renovation of the antiquated state, he needed the whole mass of talent, culture, hereditary and self-acquired distinction, which this party embraced; and in this sense he may well have named the pardoning of his opponents the finest reward of victory. Accordingly the most prominent chiefs of the defeated parties were indeed removed, but full pardon was not withheld from the men of the second and third rank and especially of the younger generation; they were not, however, allowed to sulk in passive opposition, but were by more or less gentle pressure induced to take an active part in the new administration, and to accept honours and offices from it. As with Henry the Fourth and William of Orange, so with Caesar his greatest difficulties began only after the victory. Every revolutionary conqueror learns by experience that, if after vanquishing his opponents he would not remain like Cinna and Sulla a mere party-chief, but would like Caesar, Henry the Fourth, and William of Orange substitute the welfare of the commonwealth for the necessarily one-sided programme of his own party, for the moment all parties, his own as well as the vanquished, unite against the new chief; and the more so, the more great and pure his idea of his new vocation. The friends of the constitution and the Pompeians, though doing homage with the lips to Caesar, bore yet in heart a grudge either at monarchy or at least at the dynasty; the degenerate democracy was in open rebellion against Caesar from the moment of its perceiving that Caesar's objects were by no means its own; even the personal adherents of Caesar murmured, when they found that their chief was establishing instead of a state of *condottieri* a monarchy equal and just towards all, and that the portions of gain accruing to them were to be diminished by the accession of the vanquished. This settlement of the commonwealth was acceptable to no party, and had to be imposed on his associates no less than on his opponents. Caesar's own position was now in a certain sense more imperilled than before the victory; but what he lost, the state gained. By annihilating the parties and not simply sparing the partisans but allowing every man of talent or even merely of good descent to attain to office irrespective of his political past, he gained for his great building all the working power extant in the state; and not only so, but the voluntary or compulsory participation of men of all parties in the same work led the nation also over imperceptibly to the newly prepared ground. The fact that this reconciliation of the parties was for the moment only external and that they were for the present much less agreed in adherence to the new state of things than in hatred against Caesar, did not mislead him; he knew well that antagonisms lose their keenness when brought into such outward union, and that only in this way can the statesman anticipate the work of time, which alone is able finally to heal such a strife by laying the old generation in the grave. Still less did he inquire who hated him or meditated his assassination. Like every genuine statesman he served not the people for reward—not even for the reward of their love—but sacrificed the favour of his contemporaries for the blessing of posterity, and above all for the permission to save and renew his nation.

In attempting to give a detailed account of the mode in which the transition was effected from the old to the new state of things, we must first of all recollect that Caesar came not to begin, but to complete. The plan of a new policy suited to the times, long ago projected by Gaius Gracchus, had been maintained by his adherents and successors with more or less of spirit and success, but without wavering. Caesar, from the outset and as it were by hereditary right the head of the popular party, had for thirty years borne aloft its banner without ever changing or even so much as concealing his colours; he remained democrat even when monarch. As he accepted without limitation, apart of course from the preposterous projects of Catilina and Clodius, the heritage of his party; as he displayed the bitterest, even personal, hatred to the aristocracy and the genuine aristocrats; and as he retained unchanged the essential ideas of Roman democracy, viz. alleviation of the burdens of debtors, transmarine colonization, gradual equalization of the differences of rights among the classes belonging to the state, emancipation of the executive power from the senate: his monarchy was so little at variance with democracy, that democracy on the contrary only attained its completion and fulfilment by means of that monarchy. For this monarchy was not the Oriental despotism of divine right, but a monarchy such as Gaius Gracchus wished to found, such as Pericles and Cromwell founded—the representation of the nation by the man in whom it puts supreme and unlimited confidence. The ideas, which lay at the foundation of Caesar's work, were so far not strictly new; but to him belongs their realization, which after all is everywhere the main matter; and to him pertains the grandeur of execution, which would probably have surprised the brilliant projector himself if he could have seen it, and which has impressed, and will always impress, every one to whom it has been presented in the living reality or in the mirror of history—to whatever historical epoch or whatever shade of politics he may belong—according to the measure of his ability to comprehend human and historical greatness, with deep and ever-deepening emotion and admiration.

At this point however it is proper expressly once for all to claim what the historian everywhere tacitly presumes, and to protest against the custom—common to simplicity and perfidy—of using historical praise and historical censure, dissociated from the given circumstances, as phrases of general application, and in the present case of construing the judgment as to Caesar into a judgment as to what is called Caesarism. It is true that the history of past centuries ought to be the instructress of the present; but not in the vulgar sense, as if one could simply by turning over the leaves discover the conjunctures of the present in the records of the past, and collect from these the symptoms for a political diagnosis and the specifics for a prescription; it is instructive only so far as the observation of older forms of culture reveals the organic conditions of civilization generally—the fundamental forces everywhere alike, and the manner of their combination everywhere different—and leads and encourages men, not to unreflecting imitation, but to independent reproduction. In this sense the history of Caesar and of Roman Imperialism, with all the unsurpassed greatness of the master-worker, with all the historical necessity of the work, is in truth a sharper censure of modern autocracy than could be written by the hand of man. According to the same law of nature in virtue of which the smallest organism infinitely surpasses the most artistic machine, every constitution however defective which gives play to the free self-determination of a majority of citizens infinitely surpasses the most brilliant and humane absolutism; for the former is capable of development and therefore living, the latter is what it is and therefore dead. This law of nature has verified itself in the Roman absolute military monarchy and verified itself all the more completely, that, under the impulse of its creator's genius and in the absence of all material complications from without, that monarchy developed itself more purely and freely than any similar state. From Caesar's time, as the sequel will show and Gibbon has shown long ago, the Roman system had only an external coherence and received only a mechanical extension, while internally it became even with him utterly withered and dead. If in the early stages of the autocracy and above all in Caesar's own soul the hopeful dream of a combination of free popular development and absolute rule was still cherished, the government of the highly gifted emperors of the Julian house soon taught men in a terrible form how far it was possible to hold fire and water in the same vessel. Caesar's work was necessary and salutary, not because it was or could be fraught with blessing in itself, but because—with the national organization of antiquity, which was based on slavery and was utterly a stranger to republican-constitutional representation, and in presence of the legitimate urban constitution which in the course of five hundred years had ripened into oligarchic absolutism—absolute military monarchy was the copestone logically necessary and the least of evils. When once the slave-holding aristocracy in Virginia and the Carolinas shall have carried matters as far as their congeners in the Sullan Rome, Caesarism will there too be legitimized at the bar of the spirit of history; where it appears under other conditions of development, it is at once a caricature and a usurpation. But history will not submit to curtail the true Caesar of his due honour, because her verdict may in the presence of bad Caesars lead simplicity astray and may give to roguery occasion for lying and fraud. She too is a Bible, and if she cannot any more than the Bible hinder the fool from misunderstanding and the devil from quoting her, she too will be able to bear with, and to requite, them both.

The position of the new supreme head of the state appears formally, at least in the first instance, as a dictatorship. Caesar took it up at first after his return from Spain in 705, but laid it down again after a few days, and waged the decisive campaign of 706 simply as consul—this was the office his tenure of which was the primary occasion for the outbreak of the civil war. But in the autumn of this year after the battle of Pharsalus he reverted to the dictatorship and had it repeatedly entrusted to him, at first for an undefined period, but from the 1st January 709 as an annual office, and then in January or February 710 for the duration of his life, so that he in the end expressly dropped the earlier reservation as to his laying down the office and gave formal expression to its tenure for life in the new title of *dictator perpetuus.* This dictatorship, both in its first ephemeral and in its second enduring tenure, was not that of the old constitution, but—what was coincident with this merely in the name—the supreme exceptional office as arranged by Sulla; an office, the functions of which were fixed, not by the constitutional ordinances regarding the supreme single magistracy, but by special decree of the people, to such an effect that the holder received, in the commission to project laws and to regulate the commonwealth, an official prerogative *de jure* unlimited which superseded the republican partition of powers. Those were merely applications of this general prerogative to the particular case, when the holder of power was further entrusted by separate acts with the right of deciding on war and peace without consulting the senate and the people, with the independent disposal of armies and finances, and with the nomination of the provincial governors. Caesar could accordingly *de jure* assign to himself even such prerogatives as lay outside of the proper functions of the magistracy and even outside of the province of state-powers at all; and it appears almost as a concession on his part, that he abstained from nominating the magistrates instead of the Comitia and limited himself to claiming a binding right of proposal for a proportion of the praetors and of the lower magistrates; and that he moreover had himself empowered by special decree of the people for the creation of patricians, which was not at all allowable according to use and wont.

For other magistracies in the proper sense there remained alongside of this dictatorship no room; Caesar did not take up the censorship as such, but he doubtless exercised censorial rights—particularly the important right of nominating senators—after a comprehensive fashion.

He held the consulship frequently alongside of the dictatorship, once even without colleague; but he by no means attached it permanently to his person, and he gave no effect to the calls addressed to him to undertake it for five or even for ten years in succession.

Caesar had no need to have the superintendence of worship now committed to him, since he was already *pontifex maximus.* As a matter of course the membership of the college of augurs was conferred on him, and generally an abundance of old and new honorary rights, such as the title of a "father of the fatherland," the designation of the month of his birth by the name which it still bears of Julius, and other manifestations of the incipient courtly tone which ultimately ran into utter deification. Two only of the arrangements deserve to be singled out: namely that Caesar was placed on the same footing with the tribunes of the people as regards their special personal inviolability, and that the appellation of Imperator was permanently attached to his person and borne by him as a title alongside of his other official designations.

Men of judgment will not require any proof, either that Caesar intended to engraft on the commonwealth his supreme power, and this not merely for a few years or even as a personal office for an indefinite period somewhat like Sulla's regency, but as an essential and permanent organ; or that he selected for the new institution an appropriate and simple designation; for, if it is a political blunder to create names without substantial meaning, it is scarcely a less error to set up the substance of plenary power without a name. Only it is not easy to determine what definitive formal shape Caesar had in view; partly because in this period of transition the ephemeral and the permanent buildings are not clearly discriminated from each other, partly because the devotion of his clients which already anticipated the nod of their master loaded him with a multitude—offensive doubtless to himself—of decrees of confidence and laws conferring honours. Least of all could the new monarchy attach itself to the consulship, just on account of the collegiate character that could not well be separated from this office; Caesar also evidently laboured to degrade this hitherto supreme magistracy into an empty title, and subsequently, when he undertook it, he did not hold it through the whole year, but before the year expired gave it away to personages of secondary rank. The dictatorship came practically into prominence most frequently and most definitely, but probably only because Caesar wished to use it in the significance which it had of old in the constitutional machinery—as an extraordinary presidency for surmounting extraordinary crises. On the other hand it was far from recommending itself as an expression for the new monarchy, for the magistracy was inherently clothed with an exceptional and unpopular character, and it could hardly be expected of the representative of the democracy that he should choose for its permanent organization that form, which the most gifted champion of the opposing party had created for his own ends.

The new name of Imperator, on the other hand, appears in every respect by far more appropriate for the formal expression of the monarchy; just because it is in this application new, and no definite outward occasion for its introduction is apparent. The new wine might not be put into old bottles; here is a new name for the new thing, and that name most pregnantly sums up what the democratic party had already expressed in the Gabinian law, only with less precision, as the function of its chief—the concentration and perpetuation of official power *(imperium)* in the hands of a popular chief independent of the senate. We find on Caesar's coins, especially those of the last period, alongside of the dictatorship the title of Imperator prevailing, and in Caesar's law as to political crimes the monarch seems to have been designated by this name. Accordingly the following times, though not immediately, connected the monarchy with the name of Imperator. To lend to this new office at once a democratic and religious sanction, Caesar probably intended to associate with it once for all on the one hand the tribunician power, on the other the supreme pontificate.

That the new organization was not meant to be restricted merely to the lifetime of its founder, is beyond doubt; but he did not succeed in settling the especially difficult question of the succession, and it must remain an undecided point whether he had it in view to institute some sort of form for the election of a successor, such as had subsisted in the case of the original kingly office, or whether he wished to introduce for the supreme office not merely the tenure for life but also the hereditary character, as his adopted son subsequently maintained. It is not improbable that he had the intention of combining in some measure the two systems, and of arranging the succession, similarly to the course followed by Cromwell and by Napoleon, in such a way that the ruler should be succeeded in rule by his son, but, if he had no son, or the son should not seem fitted for the succession, the ruler should of his free choice nominate his successor in the form of adoption.

In point of state law the new office of Imperator was based on the position which the consuls or proconsuls occupied outside of the *pomerium,* so that primarily the military command, but, along with this, the supreme judicial and consequently also the administrative power, were included in it. But the authority of the Imperator was qualitatively superior to the consular-proconsular, in so far as the former was not limited as respected time or space, but was held for life and operative also in the capital; as the Imperator could not, while the consul could, be checked by colleagues of equal power; and as all the restrictions placed in course of time on the original supreme official power—especially the obligation to give place to the *provocatio* and to respect the advice of the senate—did not apply to the Imperator.

In a word, this new office of Imperator was nothing else than the primitive regal office re-established; for it was those very restrictions—as respected the temporal and local limitation of power, the collegiate arrangement, and the co-operation of the senate or the community that was necessary for certain cases—which distinguished the consul from the king. There is hardly a trait of the new monarchy which was not found in the old: the union of the supreme military, judicial, and administrative authority in the hands of the prince; a religious presidency over the commonwealth; the right of issuing ordinances with binding power; the reduction of the senate to a council of state; the revival of the patriciate and of the praefecture of the city. But still more striking than these analogies is the internal similarity of the monarchy of Servius Tullius and the monarchy of Caesar; if those old kings of Rome with all their plenitude of power had yet been rulers of a free community and themselves the protectors of the commons against the nobility, Caesar too had not come to destroy liberty but to fulfil it, and primarily to break the intolerable yoke of the aristocracy. Nor need it surprise us that Caesar, anything but a political antiquary, went back five hundred years to find the model for his new state; for, seeing that the highest office of the Roman commonwealth had remained at all times a kingship restricted by a number of special laws, the idea of the regal office itself had by no means become obsolete. At very various periods and from very different sides—in the decemviral power, in the Sullan regency, and in Caesar's own dictatorship—there had been during the republic a practical recurrence to it; indeed by a certain logical necessity, whenever an exceptional power seemed requisite there emerged, in contradistinction to the usual limited *imperium,* the unlimited *imperium* which was simply nothing else than the regal power.

Lastly, outward considerations also recommended this recurrence to the former kingly position. Mankind have infinite difficulty in reaching new creations, and therefore cherish the once developed forms as sacred heirlooms. Accordingly Caesar very judiciously connected himself with Servius Tullius, in the same way as subsequently Charlemagne connected himself with Caesar, and Napoleon attempted at least to connect himself with Charlemagne. He did so, not in a circuitous way and secretly, but, as well as his successors, in the most open manner possible; it was indeed the very object of this connection to find a clear, national and popular form of expression for the new state. From ancient times there stood on the Capitol the statues of those seven kings, whom the conventional history of Rome was wont to bring on the stage; Caesar ordered his own to be erected beside them as the eighth. He appeared publicly in the costume of the old kings of Alba. In his new law as to political crimes the principal variation from that of Sulla was, that there was placed alongside of the collective community, and on a level with it, the Imperator as the living and personal expression of the people. In the formula used for political oaths there was added to the Jovis and the Penates of the Roman people the Genius of the Imperator. The outward badge of monarchy was, according to the view univerally diffused in antiquity, the image of the monarch on the coins; from the year 710 the head of Caesar appears on those of the Roman state.

There could accordingly be no complaint at least on the score that Caesar left the public in the dark as to his view of his position; as distinctly and as formally as possible he came forward not merely as monarch, but as very king of Rome. It is possible even, although not exactly probable, and at any rate of subordinate importance, that he had it in view to designate his official power not with the new name of Imperator, but directly with the old one of King. Even in his lifetime many of his enemies as of his friends were of opinion that he intended to have himself expressly nominated king of Rome; several indeed of his most vehement adherents suggested to him in different ways and at different times that he should assume the crown; most strikingly of all, Marcus Antonius, when he as consul offered the diadem to Caesar before all the people (15 Feb. 710). But Caesar rejected these proposals without exception at once. If he at the same time took steps against those who made use of these incidents to stir republican opposition, it by no means follows from this that he was not in earnest with his rejection. The assumption that these invitations took place at his bidding, with the view of preparing the multitude for the unwonted spectacle of the Roman diadem, utterly misapprehends the mighty power of the sentimental opposition with which Caesar had to reckon, and which could not be rendered more compliant, but on the contrary necessarily gained a broader basis, through such a public recognition of its warrant on the part of Caesar himself. It may have been the uncalled-for zeal of vehement adherents alone that occasioned these incidents; it may be also, that Caesar merely permitted or even suggested the scene with Antonius, in order to put an end in as marked a manner as possible to the inconvenient gossip by a declinature which took place before the eyes of the burgesses and was inserted by his command even in the calendar of the state and could not, in fact, be well revoked. The probability is that Caesar, who appreciated alike the value of a convenient formal designation and the antipathies of the multitude which fasten more on the names than on the essence of things, was resolved to avoid the name of king as tainted with an ancient curse and as more familiar to the Romans of his time when applied to the despots of the east than to their own Numa and Servius, and to appropriate the substance of the regal office under the title of Imperator.

But, whatever may have been the definitive title present to his thoughts, the sovereign ruler was there, and accordingly the court established itself at once with all its due accompaniments of pomp, insipidity, and emptiness. Caesar appeared in public not in the robe of the consuls which was bordered with purple stripes, but in the robe wholly of purple which was reckoned in antiquity as the proper regal attire, and received, seated on his golden chair and without rising from it, the solemn procession of the senate. The festivals in his honour commemorative of birthday, of victories, and of vows, filled the calendar. When Caesar came to the capital, his principal servants marched forth in troops to great distances so as to meet and escort him. To be near to him began to be of such importance, that the rents rose in the quarter of the city where he dwelt. Personal interviews with him were rendered so difficult by the multitude of individuals soliciting audience, that Caesar found himself compelled in many cases to communicate even with his intimate friends in writing, and that persons even of the highest rank had to wait for hours in the antechamber. People felt, more clearly than was agreeable to Caesar himself, that they no longer approached a fellow-citizen. There arose a monarchical aristocracy, which was in a remarkable manner at once new and old, and which had sprung out of the idea of casting into the shade the aristocracy of the oligarchy by that of royalty, the nobility by the patriciate. The patrician body still subsisted, although without essential privileges as an order, in the character of a close aristocratic guild; but as it could receive no new *gentes* it had dwindled away more and more in the course of centuries, and in the time of Caesar there were not more than fifteen or sixteen patrician *gentes* still in existence. Caesar, himself sprung from one of them, got the right of creating new patrician *gentes* conferred on the Imperator by decree of the people, and so established, in contrast to the republican nobility, the new aristocracy of the patriciate, which most happily combined all the requisites of a monarchical aristocracy—the charm of antiquity, entire dependence on the government, and total insignificance. On all sides the new sovereignty revealed itself.

Under a monarch thus practically unlimited there could hardly be scope for a constitution at all—still less for a continuance of the hitherto existing commonwealth based on the legal co-operation of the burgesses, the senate, and the several magistrates. Caesar fully and definitely reverted to the tradition of the regal period; the burgess-assembly remained—what it had already been in that period—by the side of and with the king the supreme and ultimate expression of the will of the sovereign people, the senate was brought back to its original destination of giving advice to the ruler when he requested it; and lastly the ruler concentrated in his person anew the whole magisterial authority, so that there existed no other independent state-official by his side any more than by the side of the kings of the earliest times.

For legislation the democratic monarch adhered to the primitive maxim of Roman state-law, that the community of the people in concert with the king convoking them had alone the power of organically regulating the commonwealth; and he had his constitutive enactments regularly sanctioned by decree of the people. The free energy and the authority half-moral, half-political, which the yea or nay of those old warrior-assemblies had carried with it, could not indeed be again instilled into the so-called comitia of this period; the co-operation of the burgesses in legislation, which in the old constitution had been extremely limited but real and living, was in the new practically an unsubstantial shadow. There was therefore no need of special restrictive measures against the comitia; many years' experience had shown that every government—the oligarchy as well as the monarch—easily kept on good terms with this formal sovereign. These Caesarian comitia were an important element in the Caesarian system and indirectly of practical significance, only in so far as they served to retain in principle the sovereignty of the people and to constitute an energetic protest against sultanism.

But at the same time—as is not only obvious of itself, but is also distinctly attested—the other maxim also of the oldest state-law was revived by Caesar himself, and not merely for the first time by his successors; viz. that what the supreme, or rather sole, magistrate commands is unconditionally valid so long as he remains in office, and that, while legislation no doubt belongs only to the king and the burgesses in concert, the royal edict is equivalent to law at least till the demission of its author.

While the democratic king thus conceded to the community of the people at least a formal share in the sovereignty, it was by no means his intention to divide his authority with what had hitherto been the governing body, the college of senators. The senate of Caesar was to be—in a quite different way from the later senate of Augustus—nothing but a supreme council of state, which he made use of for advising with him beforehand as to laws, and for the issuing of the more important administrative ordinances through it, or at least under its name—for cases in fact occurred where decrees of senate were issued, of which none of the senators recited as present at their preparation had any cognizance. There were no material difficulties of form in reducing the senate to its original deliberative position, which it had overstepped more *de facto* than *de jure;* but in this case it was necessary to protect himself from practical resistance, for the Roman senate was as much the headquarters of the opposition to Caesar as the Attic Areopagus was of the opposition to Pericles. Chiefly for this reason the number of senators, which had hitherto amounted at most to six hundred in its normal condition and had been greatly reduced by the recent crises, was raised by extraordinary supplement to nine hundred; and at the same time, to keep it at least up to this mark, the number of quaestors to be nominated annually, that is of members annually admitted to the senate, was raised from twenty to forty. The extraordinary filling up of the senate was undertaken by the monarch alone. In the case of the ordinary additions he secured to himself a permanent influence through the circumstance, that the electoral colleges were bound by law to give their votes to the first twenty candidates for the quaestorship who were provided with letters of recommendation from the monarch; besides, the crown was at liberty to confer the honorary rights attaching to the quaestorship or to any office superior to it, and consequently a seat in the senate in particular, by way of exception even on individuals not qualified. The selection of the extraordinary members who were added naturally fell in the main on adherents of the new order of things, and introduced, along with *equites* of respectable standing, various dubious and plebeian personages into the proud corporation—former senators who had been erased from the roll by the censor or in consequence of a judicial sentence, foreigners from Spain and Gaul who had to some extent to learn their Latin in the senate, men lately subaltern officers who had not previously received even the equestrian ring, sons of freedmen or of such as followed dishonourable trades, and other elements of a like kind. The exclusive circles of the nobility, to whom this change in the personal composition of the senate naturally gave the bitterest offence, saw in it an intentional depreciation of the very institution itself. Caesar was not capable of such a self-destructive policy; he was as determined not to let himself be governed by his council as he was convinced of the necessity of the institute in itself. They might more correctly have discerned in this proceeding the intention of the monarch to take away from the senate its former character of an exclusive representation of the oligarchic aristocracy, and to make it once more—what it had been in the regal period—a state-council representing all classes of persons belonging to the state through their most intelligent elements, and not necessarily excluding the man of humble birth or even the foreigner; just as those earliest kings introduced non-burgesses, Caesar introduced non-Italians into his senate.

While the rule of the nobility was thus set aside and its existence undermined, and while the senate in its new form was merely a tool of the monarch, autocracy was at the same time most strictly carried out in the administration and government of the state, and the whole executive was concentrated in the hands of the monarch. First of all, the Imperator naturally decided in person every question of any moment. Caesar was able to carry personal government to an extent which we puny men can hardly conceive, and which is not to be explained solely from the unparalleled rapidity and decision of his working, but has moreover its ground in a more general cause. When we see Caesar, Sulla, Gaius Gracchus, and Roman statesmen in general displaying throughout an activity which transcends our notions of human powers of working, the reason lies, not in any change that human nature has undergone since that time, but in the change which has taken place since then in the organization of the household. The Roman house was a machine, in which even the mental powers of the slaves and freedmen yielded their produce to the master; a master, who knew how to govern these, worked as it were with countless minds. It was the *beau ideal* of bureaucratic centralization; which our counting-house system strives indeed zealously to imitate, but remains as far behind its prototype as the modern power of capital is inferior to the ancient system of slavery. Caesar knew how to profit by this advantage; wherever any post demanded special confidence, we see him filling it up on principle—so far as other considerations at all permit —with his slaves, freedmen, or clients of humble birth. His works as a whole show what an organizing genius like his could accomplish with such an instrument; but to the question, how in detail these marvellous feats were achieved, we have no adequate answer. Bureaucracy resembles a manufactory also in this respect, that the work done does not appear as that of the individual who has worked at it, but as that of the manufactory which stamps it. This much only is quite clear, that Caesar in his work had no helper at all who exerted a personal influence over it or was even so much as initiated into the whole plan; he was not only the sole master, but he worked also without skilled associates, merely with common labourers. . . .

Such were the foundations of the Mediterranean monarchy of Caesar. For the second time in Rome the social question had reached a crisis, at which the antagonisms not only appeared to be, but actually were, in the form of their exhibition, insoluble and, in the form of their expression, irreconcilable. On the former occasion Rome had been saved by the fact that Italy was merged in Rome and Rome in Italy, and in the new enlarged and altered home those old antagonisms were not reconciled, but fell into abeyance. Now Rome was once more saved by the fact that the countries of the Mediterranean were merged in it or became prepared for merging; the war between the Italian poor and rich, which in the old Italy could only end with the destruction of the nation, had no longer a battle-field or a meaning in the Italy of three continents. The Latin colonies closed the gap which threatened to swallow up the Roman community in the fifth century; the deeper chasm of the seventh century was filled by the Transalpine and transmarine colonizations of Gaius Gracchus and Caesar. For Rome alone history not merely performed miracles, but also repeated its miracles, and twice cured the internal crisis, which in the state itself was incurable, by regenerating the state. There was doubtless much corruption in this regeneration; as the union of Italy was accomplished over the ruins of the Samnite and Etruscan nations, so the Mediterranean monarchy built itself on the ruins of countless states and tribes once living and vigorous; but it was a corruption out of which sprang a fresh growth, part of which remains green at the present day. What was pulled down for the sake of the new building, was merely the secondary nationalities which had long since been marked out for destruction by the levelling hand of civilization. Caesar, wherever he came forward as a destroyer, only carried out the pronounced verdict of historical development; but he protected the germs of culture, where and as he found them, in his own land as well as among the sister nation of the Hellenes. He saved and renewed the Roman type; and not only did he spare the Greek type, but with the same self-relying genius with which he accomplished the renewed foundation of Rome he undertook also the regeneration of the Hellenes, and resumed the interrupted work of the great Alexander, whose image, we may well believe, never was absent from Caesar's soul. He solved these two great tasks not merely side by side, but the one by means of the other. The two great essentials of humanity—general and individual development, or state and culture—once in embryo united in those old Graeco-Italians feeding their flocks in primeval simplicity far from the coasts and islands of the Mediterranean, had become dissevered when these were parted into Italians and

Hellenes, and had thenceforth remained apart for many centuries. Now the descendant of the Trojan prince and the Latin king's daughter created out of a state without distinctive culture and a cosmopolitan civilization a new whole, in which state and culture again met together at the acme of human existence in the rich fulness of blessed maturity and worthily filled the sphere appropriate to such an union.

The outlines have thus been set forth, which Caesar drew for this work, according to which he laboured himself, and according to which posterity—for many centuries confined to the paths which this great man marked out—endeavoured to prosecute the work, if not with the intellect and energy, yet on the whole in accordance with the intentions, of the illustrious master. Little was finished; much even was merely begun. Whether the plan was complete, those who venture to vie in thought with such a man may decide; we observe no material defect in what lies before us—every single stone of the building enough to make a man immortal, and yet all combining to form one harmonious whole. Caesar ruled as king of Rome for five years and a half, not half as long as Alexander; in the intervals of seven great campaigns, which allowed him to stay not more than fifteen months altogether in the capital of his empire, he regulated the destinies of the world for the present and the future, from the establishment of the boundary-line between civilization and barbarism down to the removal of the pools of rain in the streets of the capital, and yet retained time and composure enough attentively to follow the prize-pieces in the theatre and to confer the chaplet on the victor with improvised verses. The rapidity and self-precision with which the plan was executed prove that it had been long meditated thoroughly and all its parts settled in detail; but, even thus, they remain not much less wonderful than the plan itself. The outlines were laid down and thereby the new state was defined for all coming time; the boundless future alone could complete the structure. So far Caesar might say, that his aim was attained; and this was probably the meaning of the words which were sometimes heard to fall from him—that he had "lived enough." But precisely because the building was an endless one, the master as long as he lived restlessly added stone to stone, with always the same dexterity and always the same elasticity busy at his work, without ever overturning or postponing, just as if there were for him merely a to-day and no to-morrow. Thus he worked and created as never did any mortal before or after him; and as a worker and creator he still, after wellnigh two thousand years, lives in the memory of the nations—the first, and withal unique, Imperator Caesar.

Frederic William Maitland

1850—1906

10

We close this volume with a selection from a historian who earned the respect and won the admiration of his colleagues throughout the Western World: Frederic William Maitland. For his devotion to his vocation, the fine qualities of his own works, and his intense awareness and understanding of the skills and temperament required of the professional historian, Maitland has, in fact, often been called the historian's historian. But to limit thus the range of his appeal is to do great injustice to his captivating style, which makes all that he has written on subjects as abstruse and technical as exist in history delightful reading, even for non-specialists.

Maitland believed that it was the historian's proper assignment not only to discover what men have done and what they have said in the past but also to determine as far as possible what they have thought. To achieve this aim, the historian must conquer the almost insurmountable barriers of time and place which separate him from his subject. Somehow, methods must be found which permit him to penetrate the meaning of documents written in terms we can no longer fully understand. Since Maitland's time, historians have borrowed the tools of the other social sciences to help in this enormous undertaking. Maitland himself found the study of law to be his entry into the mentality of the Middle Ages.

One of the earliest and most enduring influences that helped mold Maitland into the historian that he became was that of his grandfather, the Reverend Samuel Roffey Maitland, who was librarian to the archbishop of Canterbury and the author of several distinguished books on ecclesiastical history, including *The Dark Ages* (1844). The elder Maitland convinced his grandson that the greatest single obstacle to historical knowledge was the fallacy of anachronism: the application of modern language and concepts to the life of the Middle Ages. As difficult as the task may be, the historian must try to divest himself of the associations and circumstances that constitute his own frame of reference if he hopes to achieve the goal of understanding the mentality of a distant age. The young Maitland went to Cambridge with lofty aims in view; and he worked hard, being graduated first in his class in 1872. The same year, he decided on a career in law and entered Lincoln's Inn. In 1876, he was called to the bar. His associates in the legal profession immediately recognized his exceptional talent and speculated that he would one day become one of England's most celebrated judges. But this was not to be.

His conversion from the practice of law to the study of history was largely the result of a chance meeting with, and the profound influence of, the Russian medievalist Paul Vinogradoff. Maitland later wrote to Vinogradoff of their meeting in 1884: "I often think what an extraordinary piece of luck for me it was that you and I met upon a 'Sunday tramp.' That day determined the rest of my life." Vinogradoff, who was in England in search of materials for a medieval history, impressed Maitland with the importance and vastness of the unexplored treasures for the historian at the Public Record Office in London.

The first fruit of Maitland's exploration of the Record Office was an edition of a thirteenth-century Plea Roll in 1884, *Pleas for the Crown for the County of Glouster,* a work which he dedicated to Vinogradoff and which brought Maitland an appointment as Reader of English Law at Cambridge. In 1887, he published an edition entitled *Bracton's Notebook,* three volumes of notes by a thirteenth-century scholar and jurist, with long excerpts from the official Plea Rolls. In the concluding comments for the "Introduction" to this book, Maitland, in a way that could be only his, explains the importance of this mine of information: "English law is case law, the Plea Rolls contain the ultimate authorities of our law. What would we not give for a book by a medieval lawyer containing a selection of such cases, especially if that lawyer were a great judge and made his selection while the law was still flexible. Such a book chance has preserved to us; it is *Bracton's Notebook.*"

Because he was interested in writing the type of history that would allow, in his own words, "by slow degrees the thoughts of our forefathers, their common thoughts about common things to become thinkable once more," Maitland undertook to edit and publish volume upon volume of documents that might help us to decipher the vocabulary and to comprehend what appears to moderns as the mysterious Middle Ages. He became literary director of the Selden Society upon its founding in 1887 and remained its prime mover until his death. Twenty-one volumes of medieval legal documents were published during that time, eight of them his work. To furnish these volumes with their brilliant introductions, Maitland mastered the Anglo-French language as it was spoken in the courts of England in the thirteenth and fourteenth centuries, and he developed skills as a paleographer, grammarian, orthographer, and phoneticist.

In his inaugural lecture as Downing Professor of the Laws of England at Cambridge in 1888, Maitland explained the current antipathy between legal and historical thinking and how he proposed to close the gap. "What is really required of the practising lawyer," he told his audience, "is not, save in the rarest cases, a knowledge of medieval law as it was in the Middle Ages, but rather a knowledge of medieval law as interpreted by modern courts to suit modern facts. . . . That process by which old principles and old phrases are charged with a new content is from the lawyer's point of view an evolution of the true intent and meaning of the old law; from the historian's point of view it is almost of necessity a process of perversion and misunderstanding." But when used by the historian, the law can provide an invaluable clue to understanding the past, in the most significant and revealing ways. "Think for a moment," he continued, "what lies concealed within the hard rind of legal history. Legal documents are the best, often the only, evidence we have for social and economic history, for the history of morality, for the history of practical religion. On such a point as village life the evidence is inexhaustible, but no one will extract its meaning who has not the patience to master an extremely formal system of pleading and procedure, who is not familiar with a whole scheme of actions with repulsive names." For the remainder of his life, both as a historian and as an editor, he made invaluable contributions to our knowledge of the Middle Ages by decoding and interpreting legal documents.

The History of English Law Before the Time of Edward I was published jointly by Maitland and Sir Frederick Pollock in 1895, although, as Pollock says in the "Preface," the two-volume masterpiece of legal analysis and historical scholarship was mainly the work of Maitland alone. The authors explain the insularity of the English legal tradition by the absence of Roman influence on the laws of medieval England. "Our law," they wrote, "was never obliterated by a wholesale importation of Roman elements, as in Germany." Most of the two volumes are devoted to an analysis of Angevin law, including a discussion of the many varieties of land tenure, which, though necessarily technical in nature, is enlivened by Maitland's typically alert, even humorous style.

Two years later, Maitland completed a pioneering work on local history: *Domesday Book and Beyond.* This is an impressive example of inverse reasoning, in which Maitland proceeds from the known to the unknown, insisting that there was no homogeneous manorial system before the Norman Conquest, but rather several varieties of landholding, none of them familiar in modern legal terminology. In the third and final section of the book, Maitland had to explain the medieval system of land measurement, a subject that would ordinarily try the patience of the most specialized reader; with Maitland the task was pleasurable enough, largely because of his own awareness of the human problems involved in such matters. With wit and charm, he approaches what he called "that dreary, intricate, inhuman subject of Domesday measurements, the hide and carucate and sulung, the virgate, bovate and yoke."

In his Ford lectures, published as *Township and Borough* (1898), Maitland demonstrated the same delightful sense of humor in grappling with the complexities of the origins of privileges of towns and boroughs, using the records available at Oxford and Cambridge. He explains the anomalous legal status of Cambridge in the Middle Ages, a town which had no lord but a king. "The city of Washington is not in any of the United States of North America. Why not? Because it is the moot-stow of the great Republic. The *civitas* of Cambridge is not in any of the hundreds. Why not? Because it is the moot-stow of the republic of Cambridgeshire, a phrase which is 800 years old."

Maitland did not confine his historical work to editing legal documents and explicating legal terms. He could, when he wished, write narrative history as well, as is evidenced in his outstanding article for the *Cambridge Modern History,* "The Elizabethan Settlement and the Scottish Reformation," where he discusses the Reformation compromise with clarity and learning. Our own selection, an essay on the "History of English Law," which was originally written for the supplement to the tenth edition of the *Encyclopaedia Britannica* in 1902, is an incisive example of how the most technically trained historical mind can produce literature that is learned as well as accessible to a wide audience.

Maitland was neither very wealthy nor in good health for most of his life. His early death, in 1906, brought sadness to the academic community and eulogies from historians in Europe and America. One of his Cambridge colleagues remarked that "out of his sufferings he won a deeper sympathy for men, and a broader view of things." George Macaulay Trevelyan, who was inspired by Maitland's work, revealed the contribution of this great scholar when he wrote that Maitland used his legal abilities "to open the mind of medieval man, and to reveal the nature and growth of his institutions."

Selected Bibliography

A moderately sized and vividly written biography of Maitland was written by his brother-in-law, H. A. L. Fisher: *Frederic William Maitland* (1910). Two lectures and a bibliography, *Frederic William Maitland* (1908), by A. L. Smith, are insightful and helpful. Robert Livingston Schuyler's presidential address, "The Historical Spirit Incarnate: Frederic William Maitland," published in the *American Historical Review* LVII:2 (January, 1952), 303–322, is a fine tribute by one historian to another. To no one's surprise, Marc Bloch asked one of his associates to write an essay on Maitland for the *Annales.* Gabriel Le Bras's "Le sens de la vie dans l'histoire du droit: l'œuvre de F. W. Maitland," *Annales d'histoire économique et sociale* VII (July 15, 1930), 387–404, establishes that Maitland had the ability to accomplish what he desired: to make legal history a part of the social history of the Middle Ages. A recent well-written and informative study of Maitland is H. E. Bell's *Maitland: A Critical Examination and Assessment* (1965). C. H. S. Fifoot in *Frederic William Maitland* (1971) uses—for the first time—family papers to produce an intimate biography.

THE HISTORY OF ENGLISH LAW BEFORE THE TIME OF EDWARD I

In English jurisprudence "legal memory" is said to extend as far as, but no further than the coronation of Richard I (3 September 1189). This is a technical doctrine concerning prescriptive rights, but is capable of expressing an important truth. For the last seven centuries, little more or less, the English law, which is now overshadowing a large share of the earth, has had not only an extremely continuous, but a matchlessly well-attested history, and, moreover, has been the subject matter of rational exposition. Already in 1194 the daily doings of a tribunal which was controlling and moulding the whole system were being punctually recorded in letters yet legible, and from that time onwards it is rather the enormous bulk than any dearth of available materials that prevents us from tracing the transformation of every old doctrine and the emergence and expansion of every new idea. If we are content to look no further than the text-books—the books written by lawyers for lawyers—we may read our way backwards to Blackstone (d. 1780), Hale (d. 1676), Coke (d. 1634), Fitzherbert (d. 1538), Littleton (d. 1481), Bracton (d. 1268), Glanvill (d. 1190), until we are in the reign of Henry of Anjou, and yet shall perceive that we are always reading of one and the same body of law, though the little body has become great, and the ideas that were few and indefinite have become many and explicit.

Beyond these seven lucid centuries lies a darker period. Nearly six centuries will still divide us from the dooms of Aethelberht (*c.* 600), and nearly seven from the *Lex Salica* (*c.* 500). We may regard the Norman conquest of England as marking the confluence of two streams of law. The one we may call French or Frankish. If we follow it upwards we pass through the capitularies of Carlovingian emperors and Merovingian kings until we see Chlodwig and his triumphant Franks invading Gaul, submitting their Sicambrian necks to the yoke of the imperial religion, and putting their traditional usages into written Latin. The other rivulet we may call Anglo-Saxon. Pursuing it through the code of Canute (d.

Encyclopaedia Britannica, 10th ed., supplement (1902), vol. XXVIII, pp. 246–53; 11th ed. vol. IX, pp. 600–7.

1035) and the ordinances of Alfred (*c.* 900) and his successors, we see Ine publishing laws in the newly converted Wessex (*c.* 690), and, almost a century earlier, Aethelberht doing the same in the newly converted Kent (*c.* 600). This he did, says Beda, in accordance with Roman precedents. Perhaps from the Roman missionaries he had heard tidings of what the Roman emperor had lately been doing far off in New Rome. We may at any rate notice with interest that in order of time Justinian's law-books fall between the *Lex Salica* and the earliest Kentish dooms; also that the great pope who sent Augustine to England is one of the very few men who between Justinian's day and the eleventh century lived in the Occident and yet can be proved to have known the Digest. In the Occident the time for the Germanic "folk-laws" *(Leges Barbarorum)* had come, and a Canon law, ambitious of independence, was being constructed, when in the Orient the lord of church and state was "enucleating" all that was to live of the classical jurisprudence of pagan Rome. It was but a brief interval between Gothic and Lombardic domination that enabled him to give law to Italy: Gaul and Britain were beyond his reach.

The Anglo-Saxon laws that have come down to us (and we have no reason to fear the loss of much beyond some dooms of the Mercian Offa) are best studied as members of a large Teutonic family. Those that proceed from the Kent and Wessex of the seventh century are closely related to the continental folk-laws. Their next of kin seem to be the *Lex Saxonum* and the laws of the Lombards. Then, though the eighth and ninth centuries are unproductive, we have from Alfred (*c.* 900) and his successors a series of edicts which strongly resemble the Frankish capitularies —so strongly that we should see a clear case of imitation, were it not that in Frankland the age of legislation had come to its disastrous end long before Alfred was king. This, it may be noted, gives to English legal history a singular continuity from Alfred's day to our own. The king of the English was expected to publish laws at a time when hardly any one else was attempting any such feat, and the English dooms of Canute the Dane are probably the most comprehensive statutes that were issued in the Europe of the eleventh century. No genuine laws of the sainted Edward have descended to us, and during his reign England seems but too likely to follow the bad example of Frankland, and become a loose congeries of lordships. From this fate it was saved by the Norman duke, who, like Canute before him, subdued a land in which kings were still expected to publish laws.

In the study of early Germanic law—a study which now for some considerable time has been scientifically prosecuted in Germany—the Anglo-Saxon dooms have received their due share of attention. A high degree of racial purity may be claimed on their behalf. Celtic elements have been sought for in them, but have never been detected. At certain points, notably in the regulation of the blood-feud and the construction of a tariff of atonements, the law of one rude folk will always be somewhat like the law of another; but the existing remains of old Welsh and old Irish law stand far remoter from the dooms of Æthelberht and Ine than stand the edicts of Rothari and Liutprand, kings of the Lombards. Indeed, it is very dubious whether distinctively Celtic customs play any considerable part in the evolution of that system of rules of Anglian, Scandinavian and Frankish origin which becomes the law of Scotland. Within England itself, though for a while there was fighting enough between the various Germanic folks, the tribal differences were not so deep as to prevent the formation of a common language and a common law. Even the strong Scandinavian strain seems to have rapidly blended with the Anglian. It amplified the language and the law, but did not permanently divide the country. If, for example, we can today distinguish between *law* and *right,* we are debtors to the Danes; but very soon *law* is not distinctive of eastern or *right* of western England. In the first half of the twelfth century a would-be expounder of the law of England had still to say that the country was divided between the Wessex law, the Mercian law, and the Danes' law, but he had also to point out that the law of the king's own court stood apart from and above all partial systems. The local customs were those of shires and hundreds, and shaded off into each other. We may speak of more Danish and less Danish counties; it was a matter of degree; for rivers were narrow and hills were low. England was meant by nature to be the land of one law.

Then as to Roman law. In England and elsewhere Germanic law developed in an atmosphere that was charged with traditions of the old world, and many of these traditions had become implicit in the Christian religion. It might be argued that all that we call progress is due to the influence exercised by Roman civilisation; that, were it not for this, Germanic law would never have been set in writing; and that theoretically unchangeable custom would never have been supplemented or superseded by express legislation. All this and much more of the same sort might be said; but the survival in Britain, or the reintroduction into England, of anything that we should dare to call Roman jurisprudence would be a different matter. Eyes, carefully trained, have minutely scrutinised the Anglo-Saxon legal texts without finding the least trace of a Roman rule outside the ecclesiastical sphere. Even within that sphere modern research is showing that the church-property-law of the Middle Ages, the law of the ecclesiastical "benefice," is permeated by Germanic ideas. This is true of Gaul and Italy, and yet truer of an England in which Christianity was for a while extinguished. Moreover, the laws that were written in England were, from the first, written in the English tongue; and this gives them a unique value in the eyes of students of Germanic folk-law, for even the very ancient and barbarous *Lex Salica* is a Latin document, though many old Frankish words are enshrined in it. Also we notice—and this is of grave importance—that in England there are no vestiges of any "Romani" who are being suffered to live under their own law by their Teutonic rulers. On the Continent we may see Gundobad, the Burgundian, publishing one law-book for the Burgundians and another for the Romani who own his sway. A book of laws, excerpted chiefly from the Theodosian code, was issued by Alaric the Visigoth for his Roman subjects before the days of Justinian, and this book (the so-called *Breviarium Alarici* or *Lex Romana Visigothorum*) became for a long while the chief representative of Roman law in Gaul. The Frankish king in his expansive realm ruled over many men whose law was to be found not in the *Lex Salica* or *Lex Ribuaria,* but in what was called the *Lex Romana.* "A system of personal law" prevailed: the *homo Romanus* handed on his Roman law to his children, while Frankish or Lombardic, Swabian or Saxon law would run in the blood of the *homo barbarus.* Of all this we hear nothing in England. Then on the mainland of Europe Roman and barbarian law could not remain in juxtaposition without affecting each other. On the one hand we see distinctively Roman rules making their way into the law of the victorious tribes, and on the other hand we see a decay and debasement of jurisprudence which ends in the formation of what modern historians have called a Roman "vulgar-law" *(Vulgärrecht).* For a short age which centres round the year 800 it seemed possible that Frankish kings, who were becoming Roman emperors, would be able to rule by their capitularies nearly the whole of the Christian Occident. The dream vanished before fratricidal wars, heathen invaders, centrifugal feudalism, and a centripetal church which found its law in the newly concocted forgeries of the Pseudo-Isidore (*c.* 850). The "personal laws" began to transmute themselves into local customs, and the Roman vulgar-law began to look like the local custom of those districts where the Romani were the preponderating element in the population. Meanwhile, the Norse pirates subdued a large tract of what was to be northern France—a land where Romani were few. Their restless and boundless vigour these Normans retained; but they showed a wonderful power of appropriating whatever of alien civilisation came in their way. In their language, religion and law, they had become French many years before they subdued England. It is a plausible opinion that among them there lived some sound traditions of the Frankish monarchy's best days, and that Norman dukes, rather than German emperors or kings of the French, are the truest spiritual heirs of Charles the Great.

The Norman Age

In our own day German historians are wont to speak of English law as a "daughter" of French or Frankish law. This tendency derived its main impulse from H. Brunner's proof that the germ of trial by jury, which cannot be found in the Anglo-Saxon laws, can be found in the prerogative procedure of the Frankish kings. We must here remember that during a long age English lawyers wrote in French and even thought in French, and that to this day most of the technical terms of the law, more especially of the private law, are of French origin. Also it must be allowed that when English law has taken shape in the thirteenth century it is very like one of the *coutumes* of northern France. Even when linguistic difficulties have been surmounted, the Saxon Mirror of Eike von Repgow will seem far less familiar to an Englishman than the so-called Establishments of St. Louis. This was the outcome of a slow process which fills more than a century (1066–1189), and was in a great measure due to the reforming energy of Henry II, the French prince who, in addition to England, ruled a good half of France. William the Conqueror seems to have intended to govern Englishmen by English law. After the tyranny of Rufus, Henry I promised a restoration of King Edward's law: that is, the law of the Confessor's time *(Lagam Eadwardi regis vobis reddo).* Various attempts were then made, mostly, so it would seem, by men of French birth, to state in a modern and practicable form the *laga Eadwardi* which was thus restored. The result of their labours is an intricate group of legal tracts which has been explored of late years by Dr Liebermann. The best of these has long been known as the *Leges Henrici Primi,* and aspires to be a comprehensive law-book. Its author, though he had some foreign sources at his command, such as the *Lex Ribuaria* and an epitome of the Breviary of Alaric, took the main part of his matter from the code of Canute and the older English dooms. Neither the Conqueror nor either of his sons had issued many ordinances: the invading Normans had little, if any, written law to bring with them, and had invaded a country where kings had been lawgivers. Moreover, there was much in the English system that the Conqueror was keenly interested in retaining —especially an elaborate method of taxing the land and its holders. The great product of Norman government, the grandest feat of government that the world had seen for a long time past, the compilation of *Domesday Book,* was a conservative effort, an attempt to fix upon every landholder, French or English, the amount of geld that was due from his predecessor in title. Himself the rebellious vassal of the French king, the duke of the Normans, who had become king of the English, knew much of disruptive feudalism, and had no mind to see England that other France which it had threatened to become in the days of his pious but incompetent cousin. The sheriffs, though called *vice-comites,* were to be the king's officers; the shire-moots might be called county courts, but were not to be the courts of counts. Much that was sound and royal in English public law was to be preserved if William could preserve it.

Royal Justice

The gulf that divides the so-called *Leges Henrici* (*c.* 1115) from the textbook ascribed to Ranulf Glanvill (*c.* 1188) seems at first sight very wide. The one represents a not easily imaginable chaos and clash of old rules and new; it represents also a stage in the development of feudalism which in other countries is represented chiefly by a significant silence. The other is an orderly, rational book, which through all the subsequent centuries will be readily understood by English lawyers. Making no attempt to tell us what goes on in the local courts, its author, who may be Henry II's chief justiciar, Ranulf Glanvill, or may be Glanvill's nephew, Hubert Walter, fixes our attention on a novel element which is beginning to subdue all else to its powerful operation. He speaks to us of the justice that is done by the king's own court. Henry II had opened the doors of his French-speaking court to the mass of his subjects. Judges chosen for their ability were to sit there, term after term; judges were to travel in circuits through the land, and in many cases the procedure by way of "an inquest of the country," which the Norman kings had used for the ascertainment of their fiscal rights, was to be at the disposal of ordinary litigants. All this had been done in a piecemeal, experimental fashion by ordinances that were known as "assizes." There had not been, and was not to be, any enunciation of a general principle inviting all who were wronged to bring in their own words their complaints to the king's audience. The general prevalence of feudal justice, and of the world-old methods of supernatural probation (ordeals, battle, oaths sworn with oath-helpers), was to be theoretically respected; but in exceptional cases, which would soon begin to devour the rule, a royal remedy was to be open to anyone who could frame his case within the compass of some carefully worded and prescript formula. With allusion to a remote stage in the history of Roman law, a stage of which Henry's advisers can have known little or nothing, we may say that a "formulary system" is established which will preside over English law until modern times. Certain actions, each with a name of its own, are open to litigants. Each has its own formula set forth in its original (or, as we might say, originating) writ; each has its own procedure and its appropriate mode of trial. The litigant chooses his writ, his action, and must stand or fall by his choice. Thus a book about royal justice tends to become, and Glanvill's book already is, a commentary on original writs.

The precipitation of English law in so coherent a form as that which it has assumed in Glanvill's book is not to be explained without reference to the revival of Roman jurisprudence in Italy. Out of a school of Lombard lawyers at Pavia had come Lanfranc the Conqueror's adviser, and the Lombardists had already been studying Justinian's Institutes. Then at length the Digest came by its rights. About the year 1100 Irnerius was teaching at Bologna, and from all parts of the West men were eagerly flocking to hear the new gospel of civilisation. About the year 1149 Vacarius was teaching Roman law in England. The rest of a long life he spent here, and faculties of Roman and Canon law took shape in the nascent University of Oxford. Whatever might be the fate of Roman law in England, there could be no doubt that the Canon law, which was crystallising in the *Decretum Gratiani* (*c.* 1139) and in the decretals of Alexander III, would be the law of the English ecclesiastical tribunals. The great quarrel between Henry II and Thomas of Canterbury brought this system into collision with the temporal law of England, and the king's ministers must have seen that they had much to learn from the methodic enemy. Some of them were able men who became the justices of Henry's court, and bishops to boot. The luminous *Dialogue of the Exchequer* (*c.* 1179), which expounds the English fiscal system, came from the treasurer, Richard Fitz Nigel, who became Bishop of London; and the treatise on the laws of England came perhaps from Glanvill, perhaps from Hubert Walter, who was to be both primate and chief justiciar. There was healthy emulation of the work that was being done by Italian jurists, but no meek acceptance of foreign results.

Bracton

A great constructive era had opened, and its outcome was a large and noble book. The author was Henry of Bratton (his name has been corrupted into Bracton), who died in 1268 after having been for many years one of Henry III's justices. The model for its form was the treatise of Azo of Bologna ("master of all the masters of the laws," an Englishman called him), and thence were taken many of the generalities of jurisprudence: maxims that might be regarded as of universal and natural validity. But the true core of the work was the practice of an English court which had yearly been extending its operations in many directions. For half a century past diligent record had been kept on parchment of all that this court had done, and from its rolls Bracton cited numerous decisions. He cited them as precedents, paying special heed to the judgments of two judges who were already dead, Martin Pateshull and William Raleigh. For this purpose he compiled a large Note Book, which was discovered by Professor Vinogradoff in the British Museum in 1884. Thus at a very early time English "common law" shows a tendency to become what it afterwards definitely became, namely, "case law." The term "common law" was being taken over from the canonists by English lawyers, who used it to distinguish the general law of the land from local customs, royal prerogatives, and in short from all that was exceptional or special. Since statutes and ordinances were still rarities, all expressly enacted laws were also excluded from the English lawyers' notion of "the common law." The Great Charter (1215) had taken the form of a grant of "liberties and privileges," comparable to the grants that the king made to individual men and favoured towns. None the less, it was in that age no small body of enacted law, and, owing to its importance and solemnity, it was in after ages regarded as the first article of a statute book. There it was followed by the "provisions" issued at Merton in 1236, and by those issued at Marlborough after the end of the Barons' War. But during Henry III's long reign the swift development of English law was due chiefly to new "original writs" and new "forms of action" devised by the chancery and sanctioned by the court. Bracton knew many writs that were unknown to Glanvill, and men were already perceiving that limits must be set to the inventive power of the chancery unless the king was to be an uncontrollable law-maker. Thus the common law was losing the power of rapid growth when Bracton summed the attained results in a book, the success of which is attested by a crowd of manuscript copies. Bracton had introduced just enough of Roman law and Bolognese method to save the law of England from the fate that awaited German law in Germany. His book was printed in 1569, and Coke owed much to Bracton.

The comparison that is suggested when Edward I is called the English Justinian cannot be pressed very far. Nevertheless, as is well known, it is in his reign (1272–1307) that English institutions finally take the forms that they are to keep through coming centuries. We already see the parliament of the three estates, the convocations of the clergy, the king's council, the chancery or secretarial department, the exchequer or financial department, the king's bench, the common bench, the commissioners of assize and gaol delivery, the small group of professionally learned judges, and a small group of professionally learned lawyers, whose skill is at the service of those who will employ them. Moreover, the statutes that were passed in the first eighteen years of the reign, though their bulk seems slight to us nowadays, bore so fundamental a character that in subsequent ages they appeared as the substructure of huge masses of superincumbent law. Coke commented upon them sentence by sentence, and even now the merest smatterer in English law must profess some knowledge of *Quia emptores* and *De donis conditionalibus.* If some American states have, while others have not, accepted these statutes, that is a difference which is not unimportant to citizens of the United States in the twentieth century. Then from the early years of Edward's reign come the first "law reports" that have descended to us: the oldest of them have not yet been printed; the oldest that has been printed belongs to 1292. These are the precursors of the long series of Year Books (Edw.

II–Hen. VIII) which runs through the residue of the Middle Ages. Lawyers, we perceive, are already making and preserving notes of the discussions that take place in court: French notes that will be more useful to them than the formal Latin records inscribed upon the plea rolls. From these reports we learn that there are already, as we should say, a few "leading counsel," some of whom will be retained in almost every important cause. Papal decretals had been endeavouring to withdraw the clergy from secular employment. The clerical element had been strong among the judges of Henry III's reign: Bracton was an archdeacon, Pateshull a dean, Raleigh died a bishop. Their places begin to be filled by men who are not in orders, but who have pleaded the king's causes for him —his serjeants or servants at law—and beside them there are young men who are "apprentices at law," and are learning to plead. Also we begin to see men who, as "attorneys at law," are making it their business to appear on behalf of litigants. The history of the legal profession and its monopoly of legal aid is intricate, and at some points still obscure; but the influence of the canonical system is evident: the English attorney corresponds to the canonical proctor, and the English barrister to the canonical advocate. The main outlines were being drawn in Edward I's day; the legal profession became organic, and professional opinion became one of the main forces that moulded the law.

The study of English law fell apart from all other studies, and the impulse that had flowed from Italian jurisprudence was ebbing. We have two comprehensive text-books from Edward's reign: the one known to us as *Fleta,* the other as *Britton;* both of them, however, quarry their materials from Bracton's treatise. Also we have two little books on procedure which are attributed to Chief-Justice Hengham, and a few other small tracts of an intensely practical kind. Under the cover of fables about King Alfred, the author of the *Mirror of Justices* made a bitter attack upon King Edward's judges, some of whom had fallen into deep disgrace. English legal history has hardly yet been purged of the leaven of falsehood that was introduced by this fantastic and unscrupulous pamphleteer. His enigmatical book ends that literate age which begins with Glanvill's treatise and the treasurer's dialogue. Between Edward I's day and Edward IV's hardly anything that deserves the name of book was written by an English lawyer.

Fourteenth and Fifteenth Centuries

During that time the body of statute law was growing, but not very rapidly. Acts of parliament intervened at a sufficient number of important points to generate and maintain a persuasion that no limit, or no ascertainable limit, can be set to the legislative power of king and parliament.

Very few are the signs that the judges ever permitted the validity of a statute to be drawn into debate. Thus the way was being prepared for the definite assertion of parliamentary "omnicompetence" which we obtain from the Elizabethan statesman Sir Thomas Smith, and for those theories of sovereignty which we couple with the names of Hobbes and Austin. Nevertheless, English law was being developed rather by debates in court than by open legislation. The most distinctively English of English institutions in the later middle ages are the Year Books and the Inns of Court. Year by year, term by term, lawyers were reporting cases in order that they and their fellows might know how cases had been decided. The allegation of specific precedents was indeed much rarer than it afterwards became, and no calculus of authority so definite as that which now obtains had been established in Coke's day, far less in Littleton's. Still it was by a perusal of reported cases that a man would learn the law of England. A skeleton for the law was provided, not by the Roman rubrics (such as public and private, real and personal, possessory and proprietary, contract and delict), but by the cycle of original writs that were inscribed in the chancery's *Registrum Brevium*. A new form of action could not be introduced without the authority of parliament, and the growth of the law took the shape of an explication of the true intent of ancient formulas. Times of inventive liberality alternated with times of cautious and captious conservatism. Coke could look back to Edward III's day as to a golden age of good pleading. The otherwise miserable time which saw the Wars of the Roses produced some famous lawyers, and some bold doctrines which broke new ground. It produced also Sir Thomas Littleton's (d. 1481) treatise on Tenures, which (though it be not, as Coke thought it, the most perfect work that ever was written in any human science) is an excellent statement of law in exquisitely simple language.

Legal Education

Meanwhile English law was being scholastically taught. This, if we look at the fate of native and national law in Germany, or France, or Scotland, appears as a fact of primary importance. From beginnings, so small and formless that they still elude research, the Inns of Court had grown. The lawyers, like other men, had grouped themselves in gilds, or gild-like "fellowships." The fellowship acquired property; it was not technically incorporate, but made use of the thoroughly English machinery of a trust. Behind a hedge of trustees it lived an autonomous life, unhampered by charters or statutes. There was a hall in which its members dined in common; there was the nucleus of a library; there were also dormitories or chambers in which during term-time lawyers lived celibately, leaving their wives in the country. Something of the college thus enters the constitution of these fellowships; and then something academical. The craft gild regulated apprenticeship; it would protect the public against incompetent artificers, and its own members against unfair competition. So the fellowship of lawyers. In course of time a lengthy and laborious course of education of the medieval sort had been devised. He who had pursued it to its end received a call to the bar of his inn. This call was in effect a degree. Like the doctor or master of a university, the full-blown barrister was competent to teach others, and was expected to read lectures to students. But further, in a manner that is still very dark, these societies had succeeded in making their degrees the only steps that led to practice in the king's courts. At the end of the Middle Ages (*c.* 1470) Sir John Fortescue rehearsed the praises of the laws of England in a book which is one of the earliest efforts of comparative politics. Contrasting England with France, he rightly connects limited monarchy, public and oral debate in the law courts, trial by jury, and the teaching of national law in schools that are thronged by wealthy and well-born youths. But nearly a century earlier, the assertion that English law affords as subtle and civilising a discipline as any that is to be had from Roman law was made by a man no less famous than John Wycliff. The heresiarch naturally loathed the Canon law; but he also spoke with reprobation of the "paynims' law," the "heathen men's law," the study of which in the two universities was being fostered by some of the bishops. That study, after inspiring Bracton, had come to little in England, though the canonist was compelled to learn something of Justinian, and there was a small demand for learned civilians in the court of admiralty, and in what we might call the king's diplomatic service. No medieval Englishman did anything considerable for Roman law. Even the canonists were content to read the books of French and Italian masters, though John Acton (*c.* 1340) and William Lyndwood (1430) wrote meritorious glosses. The Angevin kings, by appropriating to the temporal forum the whole province of ecclesiastical patronage, had robbed the decretists of an inexhaustible source of learning and of lucre. The work that was done by the legal faculties at Oxford and Cambridge is slight when compared with the inestimable services rendered to the cause of national continuity by the schools of English law which grew within the Inns of Court.

Chancery

A danger threatened: the danger that a prematurely osseous system of common law would be overwhelmed by summary justice and royal equity. Even when courts for all ordinary causes had been established, a reserve of residuary justice remained with the king. Whatever lawyers and even parliaments might say, it was seen to be desirable that the king in council should with little regard for form punish offenders who could break through the meshes of a tardy procedure, and should redress wrongs which corrupt and timid juries would leave unrighted. Papal edicts against heretics had made familiar to all men the notion that a judge should at times proceed *summarie et de plano et sine strepitu et figura justitiae.* And so extraordinary justice of a penal kind was done by the king's council upon misdemeanants, and extraordinary justice of a civil kind was ministered by the king's chancellor (who was the specially learned member of the council) to those who, "for the love of God and in the way of charity," craved his powerful assistance. It is now well established that the chancellors started upon this course, not with any desire to introduce rules of "equity" which should supplement, or perhaps supplant, the rules of law, but for the purpose of driving the law through those accidental impediments which sometimes unfortunately beset its due course. The wrongs that the chancellor redressed were often wrongs of the simplest and most brutal kind: assaults, batteries and forcible dispossessions. However, he was warned off this field of activity by parliament; the danger to law, to lawyers, to trial by jury, was evident. But just when this was happening, a new field was being opened for him by the growing practice of conveying land to trustees. The English trust of land had ancient Germanic roots, and of late we have been learning how in far-off centuries our Lombard cousins were in effect giving themselves a power of testation by putting their lands in trust. In England, when the forms of action were crystallising, this practice had not been common enough to obtain the protection of a writ; but many causes conspired to make it common in the fourteenth century; and so, with the general approval of lawyers and laity, the chancellors began to enforce by summary process against the trustee the duty that lay upon his conscience. In the next century it was clear that England had come by a new civil tribunal. Negatively, its competence was defined by the rule that when the common law offered a remedy, the chancellor was not to intervene. Positively, his power was conceived as that of doing what "good conscience" required, more especially in cases of "fraud, accident or breach of confidence." His procedure was the summary, the heresy-suppressing (not the ordinary and solemn) procedure of an ecclesiastical court; but there are few signs that he borrowed any substantive rules from legist or decretist, and many proofs that within the new field of trust he pursued the ideas of the common law. It was long, however, before lawyers made a habit of reporting his decisions. He was not supposed to be tightly bound by precedent. Adaptability was of the essence of the justice that he did.

The Tudor Age

A time of strain and trial came with the Tudor kings. It was questionable whether the strong "governance" for which the weary nation yearned could work within the limits of a parliamentary system, or would be compatible with the preservation of the common law. We see new courts appropriating large fields of justice and proceeding *summarie et de plano;* the star chamber, the chancery, the courts of requests, of wards, of augmentations, the councils of the North and Wales; a little later we see the high commission. We see also that judicial torture which Fortescue had called the road to hell. The stream of law reports became intermittent under Henry VIII; few judges of his or his son's reign left names that are to be remembered. In an age of humanism, alphabetically arranged "abridgments" of medieval cases were the best work of English lawyers: one comes to us from Anthony Fitzherbert (d. 1538), and another from Robert Broke (d. 1558). This was the time when Roman law swept like a flood over Germany. The modern historian of Germany will speak of "the Reception" (that is, the reception of Roman law) as no less important than the Renaissance and Reformation with which it is intimately connected. Very probably he will bestow hard words on a movement which disintegrated the nation and consolidated the tyranny of the princelings. Now a project that Roman law should be "received" in England occurred to Reginald Pole (d. 1558), a humanist, and at one time a reformer, who with good fortune might have been either king of England or pope of Rome. English law, said the future cardinal and archbishop, was barbarous; Roman law was the very voice of nature pleading for "civility" and good princely governance. Pole's words were brought to the ears of his majestic cousin, and, had the course of events been somewhat other than it was, King Henry might well have decreed a reception. The role of English Justinian would have perfectly suited him, and there are distinct traces of the civilian's Byzantinism in the doings of the Church of England's supreme head. The academic study of the Canon law was prohibited; regius professorships of the civil law were founded; civilians were to sit as judges in the ecclesiastical courts. A little later, the Protector Somerset was deeply interested in the establishment of a great school for civilians at Cambridge. Scottish law was the own sister of English law, and yet in Scotland we may see a reception of Roman jurisprudence which might have been more whole-hearted than it was, but for the drift of two British and Protestant kingdoms towards union. As it fell out, however, Henry could get what he wanted in church and state without any decisive supersession of English by foreign law. The omnicompetence of an act of parliament stands out the more clearly if it settles the succession to the throne, annuls royal marriages, forgives royal debts, defines religious creeds, attaints guilty or innocent nobles, or prospectively lends the force of statute to the king's proclamations. The courts of common law were suffered to work in obscurity, for jurors feared fines, and matter of state was reserved for council or star chamber. The Inns of Court were spared; their moots and readings did no perceptible harm, if little perceptible good.

Coke

Yet it is no reception of alien jurisprudence that must be chronicled, but a marvellous resuscitation of English medieval law. We may see it already in the Commentaries of Edward Plowden (d. 1585) who reported cases at length and lovingly. Bracton's great book was put in print, and was a key to much that had been forgotten or misunderstood. Under Parker's patronage, even the Anglo-Saxon dooms were brought to light; they seemed to tell of a Church of England that had not yet been enslaved by Rome. The new national pride that animated Elizabethan England issued in boasts touching the antiquity, humanity, enlightenment of English law. Resuming the strain of Fortescue, Sir Thomas Smith, himself a civilian, wrote concerning the Commonwealth of England a book that claimed the attention of foreigners for her law and her polity. There was dignified rebuke for the French jurist who had dared to speak lightly of Littleton. And then the common law took flesh in the person of Edward Coke (1552–1634). With an enthusiastic love of English tradition, for the sake of which many offences may be forgiven him, he ranged over nearly the whole field of law, commenting, reporting, arguing, deciding,—disorderly, pedantic, masterful, an incarnate national dogmatism tenacious of continuous life. Imbued with this new spirit, the lawyers fought the battle of the constitution against James and Charles, and historical research appeared as the guardian of national liberties. That the Stuarts united against themselves three such men as Edward Coke, John Selden and William Prynne, is the measure of their folly and their failure. Words that, rightly or wrongly, were ascribed to Bracton rang in Charles's ears when he was sent to the scaffold. For the modern student of medieval law many of the reported cases of the Stuart time are storehouses of valuable material, since the lawyers of the seventeenth century were mighty hunters after records. Prynne (d. 1669), the fanatical Puritan, published ancient documents with fervid zeal, and made possible a history of parliament. Selden (d. 1654) was in all Europe among the very first to write legal history as it should be written. His book about tithes is to this day a model and a masterpiece. When this accomplished scholar had declared that he had laboured to make himself worthy to be called a common lawyer, it could no longer be said that the common lawyers were *indoctissimum genus doctissimorum hominum.* Even pliant judges, whose tenure of office depended on the king's will, were compelled to cite and discuss old precedents before they could give judgment for their master; and even at their worst moments they would not openly break with medieval tradition, or declare in favour of that "modern police-state" which has too often become the ideal of foreign publicists trained in Byzantine law.

Hale

The current of legal doctrine was by this time so strong and voluminous that such events as the Civil War, the Restoration and the Revolution hardly deflected the course of the stream. In retrospect, Charles II reigns so soon as life has left his father's body, and James II ends a lawless career by a considerate and convenient abdication. The statute book of the restored king was enriched by leaves excerpted from the acts of a lord protector; and Matthew Hale (d. 1676), who was, perhaps, the last of the great record-searching judges, sketched a map of English law which Blackstone was to colour. Then a time of self-complacency came for the law, which knew itself to be the perfection of wisdom, and any proposal for drastic legislation would have worn the garb discredited by the tyranny of the Puritan Caesar. The need for the yearly renewal of the Mutiny Act secured an annual session of parliament. The mass of the statute law made in the eighteenth century is enormous; but, even when we have excluded from view such acts as are technically called "private," the residuary matter bears a wonderfully empirical, partial and minutely particularising character. In this "age of reason," as we are wont to think it, the British parliament seems rarely to rise to the dignity of a general proposition, and in our own day the legal practitioner is likely to know less about the statutes of the eighteenth century than he knows about the statutes of Edward I, Henry VIII and Elizabeth. Parliament, it should be remembered, was endeavouring directly to govern the nation. There was little that resembled the permanent civil service of today. The choice lay between direct parliamentary government and royal "prerogative"; and lengthy statues did much of that work of detail which would now be done by virtue of the powers that are delegated to ministers and governmental boards. Moreover, extreme and verbose particularity was required in statutes, for judges were loth to admit that the common law was capable of amendment. A vague doctrine, inherited from Coke, taught that statutes might be so unreasonable as to be null, and any political theory that seemed to derive from Hobbes would have been regarded with not unjust suspicion. But the doctrine in question never took tangible shape, and enough could be done to protect the common law by a niggardly exposition of every legislating word. It is to be remembered that some main features of English public law were attracting the admiration of enlightened Europe. When Voltaire and Montesquieu applauded, the English lawyer had cause for complacency.

The common law was by no means stagnant. Many rules which come to the front in the eighteenth century are hardly to be traced farther. Especially is this the case in the province of mercantile law, where the Earl of Mansfield's (d. 1793) long presidency over the king's bench marked an epoch. It is too often forgotten that, until Elizabeth's reign, England was a thoroughly rustic kingdom, and that trade with England was mainly in the hands of foreigners. Also in medieval fairs, the assembled merchants declared their own "law merchant," which was considered to have a supernational validity. In the reports of the common law courts it is late in the day before we read of some mercantile usages which can be traced far back in the statutes of Italian cities. Even on the basis of the excessively elaborated land law—a basis which Coke's Commentary on Littleton seemed to have settled for ever—a lofty and ingenious superstructure could be reared. One after another delicate devices were invented for the accommodation of new wants within the law; but only by the assurance that the old law could not be frankly abolished can we be induced to admire the subtlety that was thus displayed. As to procedure, it had become a maze of evasive fictions, to which only a few learned men held the historical clue. By fiction the courts had stolen business from each other, and by fiction a few comparatively speedy forms of action were set to tasks for which they were not originally framed. Two fictitious persons, John Doe and Richard Roe, reigned supreme. On the other hand, that healthy and vigorous institution, the Commission of the Peace, with a long history behind it, was giving an important share in the administration of justice to numerous country gentlemen who were thus compelled to learn some law. A like beneficial work was being done among jurors, who, having ceased to be regarded as witnesses, had become "judges of fact." No one doubted that trial by jury was the "palladium" of English liberties, and popularity awaited those who would exalt the office of the jurors and narrowly limit the powers of the judge.

Equity

But during this age the chief addition to English jurisprudence was made by the crystallisation of the chancellor's equity. In the seventeenth century the Chancery had a narrow escape of sharing the fate that befell its twin sister the Star Chamber. Its younger sister, the Court of Requests, perished under the persistent attacks of the common lawyers. Having outlived troubles, the Chancery took to orderly habits, and administered under the name of "equity" a growing group of rules, which in fact were supplemental law. Stages in this process are marked by the chancellorships of Nottingham (1673–82) and Hardwicke (1737–56). Slowly a continuous series of Equity Reports began to flow, and still more slowly an "equity bar" began to form itself. The principal outlines of equity were drawn by men who were steeped in the common law. By way of ornament a Roman maxim might be borrowed from a French or Dutch expositor, or a phrase which smacked of that "nature-rightly" school which was dominating continental Europe; but the influence exercised by Roman law upon English equity has been the subject of gross exaggeration. Parliament and the old courts being what they were, perhaps it was only in a new court that the requisite new law could be evolved. The result was not altogether satisfactory. Freed from contact with the plain man in the jury-box, the Chancellors were tempted to forget how plain and rough good law should be, and to screw up the legal standard of reasonable conduct to a height hardly attainable except by those whose purses could command the constant advice of a family solicitor. A court which started with the idea of doing summary justice for the poor became a court which did a highly refined, but tardy justice, suitable only to the rich.

Blackstone

About the middle of the century William Blackstone, then a disappointed barrister, began to give lectures on English law at Oxford (1758), and soon afterwards he began to publish (1765) his *Commentaries.* Accurate enough in its history and doctrine to be an invaluable guide to professional students and a useful aid to practitioners, his book set before the unprofessional public an artistic picture of the laws of England such as had never been drawn of any similar system. No nation but the English had so eminently readable a law-book, and it must be doubtful whether any other lawyer ever did more important work than was done by the first professor of English law. Over and over again the *Commentaries* were edited, sometimes by distinguished men, and it is hardly too much to say that for nearly a century the English lawyer's main ideas of the organisation and articulation of the body of English law were controlled by Blackstone. This was far from all. The Tory lawyer little thought that he was giving law to colonies that were on the eve of a great and successful rebellion. Yet so it was. Out in America, where books were few and lawyers had a mighty task to perform, Blackstone's facile presentment of the law of the mother country was of inestimable value. It has been said that among American lawyers the *Commentaries* "stood for the law of England," and this at a time when the American daughter of English law was rapidly growing in stature, and was preparing herself for her destined march from the Atlantic to the Pacific Ocean. Excising only what seemed to savour of oligarchy, those who had defied King George retained with marvellous tenacity the law of their forefathers. Profound discussions of English medieval law have been heard in American courts; admirable researches into the recesses of the Year Books have been made in American law schools; the names of the great American judges are familiar in an England which knows little indeed of foreign jurists; and the debt due for the loan of Blackstone's *Commentaries* is being fast repaid. Lectures on the common law delivered by Mr. Justice Holmes of the Supreme Court of the United States may even have begun to turn the scale against the old country. No chapter in Blackstone's book nowadays seems more antiquated than that which describes the modest territorial limits of that English law which was soon to spread throughout Australia and New Zealand and to follow the dominant race in India.

Bentham

Long wars, vast economic changes and the conservatism generated by the French Revolution piled up a monstrous arrear of work for the English legislature. Meanwhile, Jeremy Bentham (d. 1832) had laboured for the overthrow of much that Blackstone had lauded. Bentham's largest projects of destruction and reconstruction took but little effect. Profoundly convinced of the fungibility and pliability of mankind, he was but too ready to draw a code for England or Spain or Russia at the shortest notice; and, scornful as he was of the past and its historic deposit, a code drawn by Bentham would have been a sorry failure. On the other hand, as a critic and derider of the system which Blackstone had complacently expounded he did excellent service. Reform, and radical reform, was indeed sadly needed throughout a system which was encumbered by noxious rubbish, the useless leavings of the Middle Ages: trial by battle and compurgation, deodands and benefit of clergy, John Doe and Richard Roe. It is perhaps the main fault of "judge-made law" (to use Bentham's phrase) that its destructive work can never be cleanly done. Of all vitality, and therefore of all patent harmfulness, the old rule can be deprived, but the moribund husk must remain in the system doing latent mischief. English law was full of decaying husks when Bentham attacked it, and his persistent demand for reasons could not be answered. At length a general interest in "law reform" was excited; Romilly and Brougham were inspired by Bentham, and the great changes in constitutional law which cluster round the Reform Act of 1832 were accompanied by many measures which purged the private, procedural and criminal law of much, though hardly enough, of the medieval dross. Some credit for rousing an interest in law, in definitions of legal terms, and in schemes of codification, is due to John Austin (d. 1859) who was regarded as the jurist of the reforming and utilitarian group. But, though he was at times an acute dissector of confused thought, he was too ignorant of the English, the Roman and every other system of law to make any considerable addition to the sum of knowledge; and when Savigny, the herald of evolution, was already in the field, the day for a "Nature-Right"—and Austin's projected "general jurisprudence" would have been a Nature-Right—was past beyond recall. The obsolescence of the map of law which Blackstone had inherited from Hale, and in which many outlines were drawn by medieval formulas, left intelligent English lawyers without a guide, and they were willing to listen for a while to what in their insularity they thought to be the voice of cosmopolitan science. Little came of it all. The revived study of Germanic law in Germany, which was just beginning in Austin's day, seems to be showing that the scheme of Roman jurisprudence is not the scheme into which English law will run without distortion.

Recent Changes

In the latter half of the nineteenth century some great and wise changes were made by the legislature. Notably in 1875 the old courts were merged in a new Supreme Court of Judicature, and a concurrent administration of law and equity was introduced. Successful endeavours have been made also to reduce the bulk of old statute law, and to improve the form of acts of parliament; but the emergence of new forces whose nature may be suggested by some such names as "socialism" and "imperialism" has distracted the attention of the British parliament from the commonplace law of the land, and the development of obstructive tactics has caused the issue of too many statutes whose brevity was purchased by disgraceful obscurity. By way of "partial codification" some branches of the common law (bills of exchange, sale of goods, partnership) have been skilfully stated in statutes; but a draft criminal code, upon which much expert labour was expended, lies pigeon-holed and almost forgotten. British India has been the scene of some large legislative exploits, and in America a few big experiments have been made in the way of code-making, but have given little satisfaction to the bulk of those who are competent to appreciate their results. In England there are large portions of the law which, in their present condition, no one would think of codifying: notably the law of real property, in which may still be found numerous hurtful relics of bygone centuries. So omnipresent are statutes throughout the whole field of jurisprudence that the opportunity of doing any great feat in the development of law can come but seldom to a modern court. More and more, therefore, the fate of English law depends on the will of parliament, or rather of the ministry. The quality of legal textbooks has steadily improved; some of them are models of clear statement and good arrangement; but no one has with any success aspired to be the Blackstone of a new age.

Law Reporting

The Council of Law Reporting was formed in the year 1863. The council now consists of three *ex-officio* members—the attorney-general, the solicitor-general and the president of the Incorporated Law Society, and ten members appointed by the three Inns of the Court, the Incorporated Law Society and the council itself on the nomination of the general council of the bar. The practitioner and the student now get for a subscription of four guineas a year the reports in all the superior courts and the House of Lords and the judicial committee of the privy council, issued in monthly parts, a king's printer's copy of the statutes, and weekly notes, containing short notes of current decisions and announcements of all new rules made under the Judicature Acts and other acts of parliament, and other legal information. In addition the subscriber receives the chronological index of the statutes published from time to time by the Stationery Office, and last, but not least, the Digests of decided cases published by the council from time to time. In 1892 a Digest was published containing the cases and statutes for twenty-five years, from 1865 to 1890, and this was supplemented by one for the succeeding ten years, from 1891 to 1900. The digesting is now carried on continuously by means of "Current Indexes," which are published monthly and annually, and consolidated into a digest at stated intervals (say) of five years. The Indian appeals series, which is not required by the general practitioner, is supplied separately at one guinea a year.

Legal Education

In the sixteenth and seventeenth centuries the corporate life of the Inns of Court in London became less and less active. The general decay of the organisation of crafts and gilds showed itself among lawyers as among other craftsmen. Successful barristers, sharing in the general prosperity of the country, became less and less able and willing to devote their time to the welfare of their profession as a whole. The Inns of Chancery, though some of their buildings still remain—picturesque survivals in their "suburbs"—ceased to be used as places for the education of students. The benchers of the Inns of Court, until the revival towards the middle of the nineteenth century, had wholly ceased to concern themselves with the systematic teaching of law. The modern system of legal education may be said to date from the establishment, in 1852, of the council of legal education, a body of twenty judges and barristers appointed by the four Inns of Court to control the legal education of students preparing to be called to the bar. The most important feature is the examination which a student must pass before he can be called. The examination (which by degrees has been made "stiffer") serves the double purpose of fixing the compulsory standard which all must reach, and of guiding the reading of students who may desire, sooner or later, to carry their studies beyond this standard. The subjects in which the examination is held are divided into Roman law; Constitutional law and legal history; Evidence, Procedure and Criminal law; Real and Personal Property; Equity; and Common law. The council of legal education also appoint a body of readers and assistant readers, practising barristers, who deliver lectures and hold classes.

Meanwhile the custom remains by which a student reads for a year or more as a pupil in the chambers of some practising barrister. In the eighteenth century it first became usual for students to read with a solicitor or attorney, and after a short time the modern practice grew up of reading in the chambers of a conveyancer, equity draftsman or special pleader, or, in more recent times, in the chambers of a junior barrister. Before the modern examination system, a student required to have a certificate from the barrister in whose chambers he had been a pupil before he could be "called," but the only relic of the old system now is the necessity of "eating dinners," six (three for university men) in each of the four terms for three years, at one of the Inns of Court.

The education of solicitors suffered from the absence of any professional organisation until the Incorporated Law Society was established in 1825 and the following years. So far as any professional education is provided for solicitors or required from them, this is due to the efforts of the Law Society. As early as 1729 it was required by statute that any person applying for admission as attorney or solicitor should submit to examination by one of the judges, who was to test his fitness and capacity in consideration of a fee of one shilling. At the same time regular preliminary service under articles was required, that is to say, under a contract by which the clerk was bound to serve for five years. The examination soon became, perhaps always was, an empty form. The Law Society, however, soon showed zeal for the education of future solicitors. In 1833 lectures were instituted. In 1836 the first regular examinations were established, and in 1860 the present system of examinations—preliminary, intermediate and final—came into effect. Of these only the last two are devoted to law, and both are of a strictly professional character. The final examination is a fairly severe test of practical acquaintance with all branches of modern English law. The Law Society makes some provision for the teaching of students, but this teaching is designed solely to assist in preparation for the examinations.